D1519746

see
p. 210

Agricultural fluctuations
in Europe

Agricultural fluctuations in Europe

From the thirteenth to the twentieth centuries

WILHELM ABEL

translated by
OLIVE ORDISH

with a foreword and bibliography by
JOAN THIRSK

ST. MARTIN'S PRESS
New York

First published as Agrarkrisen und Agrarkonjunktur *by*
Verlag Paul Parey, Hamburg and Berlin (third edition 1978)

© 1966, 1978 *Verlag Paul Parey*

This English translation first published in 1980 in the
United Kingdom by Methuen & Co. Ltd and in the United States
of America by St. Martin's Press Inc.

© 1980 Methuen & Co. Ltd

Contents

Foreword

Wilhelm Abel's work always opens up wide views of the European scene. This study of economic cycles and crises was, and remains, the pathfinder through the tangled territory of agrarian developments from the thirteenth to the twentieth centuries. It identifies the major landmarks in the movement of agricultural prices, wages, rents, population and agricultural production. It also investigates in a preliminary way the specialities of regions, whereby new vistas open out. It reveals similarities in the expedients used in widely separated areas to meet changing circumstances; and it indicates also how increasing specialization could lead adjoining regions along divergent paths, and yet tie them firmly in a network of complementary functions. In this experience, moreover, England was never an island unto itself, but always a part of the main.

The study of English agriculture has made great strides in the last thirty years. But England is still considered something of a special case differing from other European countries because it dismantled its feudal structure early, enclosed land before others, and advanced towards an agricultural revolution before all the rest. In some respects, England deserves to hold this unique place, but in others it also needs to be drawn back into the mainstream of European development. This translation of Professor Abel's work, by making a panoramic European survey more readily available to English readers, should promote this end.

Originally published in 1935, this widely praised and influential book has been twice revised, in 1966 and in 1978, but it still does not do full justice to the work of English agrarian historians. They, in their turn, have not yet fully explored at what points English agricultural advance was the same as, or different from, the rest of Europe. At times England owed everything to continental stimuli. In the sixteenth and seventeenth centuries, for example, many new agricultural crops and a whole new system of horticulture were introduced from the Continent. At this time England lagged well behind Italy, France, Germany, and Holland in interesting itself in these matters. Yet, when Englishmen started to write books of advice on agricultural practice, they were among the leaders in publishing in the vernacular rather than in Latin, in homely language, and cheaply. When all countries of Europe suffered in the seventeenth century from the depressing effects of low grain prices, England's recourse to brewing and distilling as a way of using up corn was exactly the same as that used in countries as distant as Poland and Bohemia. English experience here blended harmoniously into the general European scene. In its social organization of the agricultural community making and selling the alcohol, however, England revealed important differences; the financial gain from such activities was far more widely dispersed among the rural farming classes, a fact that was to be of crucial importance in stimulating further increases in agricultural productivity. In the later eighteenth century, when the Norfolk four-course rotation made English farming the cynosure of foreign eyes, its basic principle of alternating grain with fodder crops (turnips and clover) was nothing new. The elements in the system had been known in the Netherlands and England since at least the fifteenth century. Its success in the later eighteenth century was due to a variety of other circumstances, notably the rise in grain prices that made intensive tillage systems unwontedly profitable. But this affected the Continent of Europe too; what gave the English their peculiar advantage was their system of land tenure.

In bringing before English readers the major themes of agricultural change in Europe, then, Professor Abel's book will help to refine explanations how, when, and why Englishmen took their singular path, and in the later eighteenth century forged ahead so that their farming became the model throughout northern Europe. The appearance of this translation is long overdue, and yet, coming at this moment, is timely. Western Europe has yet to find a common agricultural policy that deals fairly with its eccentric English member; Englishmen, for their part, need a better understanding of Europe's interlocking, and interdependent systems of agricultural production in the past. Here is a wide-ranging, scholarly survey and much food for thought.

JOAN THIRSK
Oxford, October 1979

From the preface to the second edition

It is more than thirty years since the first edition of this book appeared. Its aim was to explore a field hitherto almost entirely neglected by historians. Prices, wages, rents, agricultural production, population movements, the living standards of broad strata of the people would all have to be investigated in order to get nearer to answering the key question: to what extent (and not so much in what ways) has the rural economy of western and central Europe solved the problem of satisfying demand? Admirable works on the spirit, technology, laws and organization were ready to hand, but what lay within that framework was still largely unknown. That was the starting point of my research.

I can venture to say that the attempt was not entirely unsuccessful. *Die Spatmittelalterliche Agrarkrisis* (The agrarian crisis of the late Middle Ages) became part of the German and international literature. The sixteenth-century 'price revolution' is now more often seen as a peculiarly agrarian phenomenon, and recently there has been a spate of works dealing with the downward trend and depression in certain sectors of the western and central European economy at the end of the seventeenth and beginning of the eighteenth centuries. But to me it seems far more significant that, quite apart from those themes, the main line of research used in the book found supporters. The dispute about method, which in the early 1930s had split economic historians and economic theorists into two warring camps, died down. In France there were efforts to construct a science of 'quantitative economic history'; in the United States they are already speaking of 'cliometrics'. Perhaps the term is too pretentious, but beneath it lies the conviction that history and economic theory have entered a new and fruitful union.

So it might have been said that this book had already fulfilled its purpose and could henceforward be left to the antiquarians. But it was, in fact, only a trial balloon. The intention from the first had been to expand the work. Originally the material of the one book was to have been divided into several volumes, the first to be called 'The lost villages of the late Middle Ages'. Other matters, however, intervened and the programme could not be carried out as originally planned. A new edition was suggested so that fresh material could be incorporated.

The framework remained the same but much else was changed, including the old title. The investigation does not stop at the nineteenth century as it did in the first edition. It continues up to the present day and does not pass so cursorily over the shorter-term effects. The depressions of the fourteenth-fifteenth and sixteenth-seventeenth centuries are seen as periods of stagnation and, where possible, analysed. The harvest cycle is considered and its fluctuations as well as its secular trends traced through an evolution that ceased only on the brink of the industrial age.

WILHELM ABEL
Göttingen, December 1965

Preface to the third edition

Interest in the questions explored in this book has not lessened during the last decade. Regional and local studies (on prices, wages, rents, etc.) have appeared in growing numbers and, in not a few cases, carry considerable weight. Where I have been able to verify these works they have been quoted in the text. Also, the bibliography of works on the history of farm prices and wages, to be found in the appendix, has been brought up to date. Some critics have suggested that I should widen the scope of this book, but that I feel disinclined to do. Undoubtedly there are connections between the economic facts considered and their 'superstructure', here merely sketched in as a framework. Where such connections are clearly in evidence they are mentioned (e.g. in regard to the establishment and expansion of landed estates in the sixteenth century), but the building of airy bridges between 'being' and 'consciousness' is not in my line. My concern is simply to bring neglected facts to light, examine them, arrange them and present them in as readable a form as possible. If in addition, as Ruggiero Romano kindly suggested in his preface to the Italian edition of this work, my exposition has become a 'model' – a model for a general design, a certain way of marshalling the facts and their intrinsic content, development and related ideas – that is a bonus. Should this book inspire similar complementary studies it will have fulfilled its purpose.

WILHELM ABEL
Göttingen, May 1978

Introduction

Secular trends in the movements of grain prices in western and central Europe since the thirteenth century

The argument

Research into the history of prices has provided a basis from which we can follow the long-term movements of cereal prices in England, France, northern Italy, Germany and Austria from the thirteenth or fourteenth century up to the present day, and compare them with each other. If the figures are converted to a common system of weights and coinage and plotted as trinomial ten-year moving averages, as in figure 1, they reveal the following three secular trends:

1. an upward movement during the thirteenth and, to some extent, the early fourteenth century is followed by a downward curve in the late Middle Ages,
2. another upsurge in the sixteenth century comes to a halt in the seventeenth century,
3. a third upward trend during the eighteenth century breaks up during the nineteenth century into short-term and sometimes contrasting movements that converge only at the end of the nineteenth century and in the twentieth century.[1]

What do these trends mean?

The problem

Ever since the time of Jean Bodin – the sixteenth century – there have been attempts to connect long-term price movements with the hypothesis that price levels depend on the quantity of money obtained from the exchange of goods. Bodin (1568) was the first to trace the price revolution of his time back to the enormous import of silver from America. Two centuries later Adam Smith (1776)

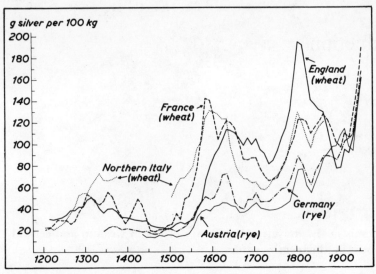

Fig. 1   Grain prices in western and central Europe from the thirteenth to the twentieth centuries.

sought to explain the low level of English cereal prices during the last part of the seventeenth and first half of the eighteenth century by a scarcity of money reserves and hence a 'rise in the real value of silver'. Again, a few decades later, at the turn of the eighteenth century, many people believed that the true, indeed the only, explanation of the new, sustained rise in the price of grain lay in the increased amount of precious metal available.

However, it was at this time, the end of the eighteenth century, that the advocates of such theories first came up against a number of writers who claimed that it was not the money situation but changes in the internal economy that caused long-term price movements. The increase of money was not by itself an adequate explanation of price variations, especially in the case of rising prices for cereals and other foodstuffs; a more fundamental reason for the growing cost of food was the rapid increase in population, or so argued Sir Edward West, Arthur Young and many of their lesser-known contemporaries. This view, though seldom expressed in so many words, was the basis of the quantity theory; that, other things being equal, an increase in money leads to a general rise in prices. A sustained increase in the quantity of money, as John Stuart Mill later pointed out, engenders, after a certain interval, an increased demand for goods of all kinds, with the consequence that these goods go up in price though perhaps not all at the same rate. This increased value 'would do no good to anyone; would make no difference except that of having to reckon pounds, shillings and pence in higher numbers ... would not enable anyone to buy more [goods] than before. Prices would have risen in a certain ratio, and the value of money would have fallen in the same ratio' (Mill, 1852:299).

Indeed during the second half of the eighteenth century by no means all prices, or income derived from prices, rose to the same extent. While the prices of land and rents as well as of cereals had soared to a level many times higher than they had been in mid-century, the prices of numerous industrial products stood hardly higher than fifty years earlier. These shifts in relative prices and incomes turned the attention of contemporaries to questions which, in the writings of West, Malthus and Ricardo, were expressed in the theories of 'diminishing returns from the land' and 'declining food resources', 'rising purchasing power of agricultural produce' and 'diverging movements of wages and rents'.

'Population has a constant tendency to increase beyond the means of subsistence', Malthus announced to an attentive world (1958:6). For after a certain and not very advanced stage in the development of agriculture, production from long-cultivated land can no longer keep pace with the rise in consumption. If cultivation is extended to land that was not considered worth tilling in the earlier years of settlement, the increased yield is obtained only at the cost of greater effort and expense. Thus the needs of a growing population must be paid for by rising costs and higher prices. As a consequence of the higher prices the owner of fertile and favourably-situated land could obtain a rent, whereas the labourer's wage, determined by the natural yield of the latest soil brought into cultivation in order to satisfy consumption, inevitably lagged behind the increasing cost of life's necessities.

> As population increases, these necessaries will be constantly rising in price, because more labour will be necessary to produce them ... money wages ... would rise; but they would not rise sufficiently to enable the labourer to purchase as many comforts and necessaries as he did before the rise in the price of those commodities ... the condition of the labourer will generally decline, and that of the landlord will always be improved. (Ricardo)[2]

Half a century later these prophecies were proved false. The population did indeed continue to grow but for the broad masses living standards improved; real wages began to rise. The demand for foodstuffs certainly increased, but agricultural depressions occurred, in the course of which many farmers and landowners lost their houses and land. As the supply of foodstuffs grew even faster than demand, grain prices fell and rents declined. Since then, technical advances have pushed back with mounting speed the threshold at which agricultural production begins to diminish, and it was soon being expounded that this development, too, followed regular laws. 'As in the past, so in the foreseeable future will mankind's food supply tend to expand' (Oppenheimer, 1924:905, 1073).

Since the refutation of Malthus's theories, prophecies regarding food resources are rightly suspect, but to trace past development with greater accuracy is surely not impossible. It is to the eternal credit of Malthus and Ricardo that their speculations led the way in this historical research. For however much the theories of 'diminishing returns from the land', 'rising purchasing power of agricultural produce' and 'diverging movements of wages and rents' were based on assumptions that have since shown themselves to be of a shifting nature, yet they opened up a rich new source of economic and historical information: the history of prices and wages. For Bodin, Adam Smith and many later price historians the evidence for historical price movements was limited to the question of how far, in a given society, the supply of money changed in relation to the demand for money and hence its value. Until quite recently much time and trouble was expended in ascertaining these money values at different periods of European history, but without much success. That the task of tracing the fluctuations of the 'value of money' and 'purchasing power of money' through long periods of time must, for methodological and practical reasons, inevitably fail has been repeatedly stressed ever since J. B. Say described this project as 'squaring the circle of national economy'. As Sombart said, 'we must finally free ourselves from the illusion that we can determine the purchasing power of money for any particular period, or even describe its fluctuations during the course of centuries, in a single figure'. According to Harms: 'It is high time we stopped speaking of purchasing power being doubled, trebled, quadrupled or quintupled in any particular period. In view of the lack of any firm basis of information, generalisations of this kind are positively ridiculous.'[3] It is not so much the scarcity of money that is significant as the shortage of goods and production; it is not the varying price levels but individual price movements, price groups and wages that are the key to the history of prices. For a comparison and succession of commodity prices in elastic or non-elastic demand, in limited or unlimited supply, the ratios between wages and foodstuff prices, and between wages and rents, tell us something of how men in past times managed to overcome the obstacles set in their path by an unfriendly Nature.

What is the real meaning of the long-term fluctuations in grain prices shown at the beginning of this introduction? Are they simply the consequence of variations in the money resources of central and western Europe, or may they also be a symptom of the changing relations between population and food supply? Did the population of these parts of Europe grow at a fluctuating rate, or did agricultural and commercial improvements sometimes catch up with population for a while? Was the rise in the purchasing power of cereals continuous in relation to industrial products? Did the purchasing power of wages, that is to say real wages, invariably diminish at a steady rate? How did wages develop in comparison with rents?

The characteristics of economic development dealt with in the present volume can be traced back to the high Middle Ages. Thus, for the purpose of this book, the whole period from the thirteenth to the twentieth century can be treated as a unity.

The economic system and the distribution of income

The evolution of a money economy and the division of labour between the eleventh and thirteenth centuries

Around the first millennium A.D. trade in central and western Europe still consisted almost entirely in the exchange of a few, usually inessential commodities within a very limited area.[4]

In inland districts and in places off the main highways and trade routes the economy of the manors and farms was almost exclusively of the subsistence type. Home-produced goods supplied almost all the needs of the farmer's family; produce from the estate and the services of its artisans came near to supplying everything that was required in the manor house.

Without doubt the economy of villein farms, especially the larger and more territorially continuous ones, already included division of labour to an advanced degree, but it was the lord's decision and not contract that controlled the production and distribution of commodities. As yet prices and wages had little importance. Such prices and wages as have come down to us often leave us uncertain as to whether they were still the symbols of a fixed system of values, rooted in law and tradition, or whether they had already become values of exchange, determined by the scarcity of goods.

Since the eleventh and twelfth centuries there had been growing up in inland northern Italy as in France, Germany and England numerous towns whose demand for foodstuffs and raw materials could no longer be satisfied by produce from their own farmland so that they were driven towards trade and division of labour. It must be remembered that, owing to the meagre yields of medieval husbandry, a town with no more than 3,000 inhabitants needed about ten fields, each measuring 8.5 square kilometres, to supply them with their bread grain alone.[5] Thus the bonds were loosened between labour and land, as between production and consumption. Numerous individual enterprises began to spring from occupations that had once been an integral part of the organization of farm or lord's estate. In the towns occupations multiplied; there arose a growing number of landless people ready to hire themselves out to work wherever they were needed. The town now depended on the country for its food supplies and its labour force.

In rural areas the form and content of land-owning and peasant economy was changing. The old ties between lord and peasant slackened, degenerated or evolved into new patterns that interwove urban with rural economy. In parts of Europe the old type of manorial estate developed into privately-owned commercial properties adjusted to the marketing of agricultural produce. In other regions, where manors had degenerated into mere renting businesses, the farms of the estate both large and small, formed close ties with the urban market. In this way the agrarian economy acquired a new character: as early as the thirteenth

and fourteenth centuries the farms and manorial estates of western and central
Europe were already, to some extent, adjusted to market turnover and production
for profit.

Knapp's description of the medieval lord's estate as still in a condition of
subsistence economy, and the lord himself as 'having, so to speak, nothing to
do with markets ... only allowing people dependent on him to plant on land
reserved for his own use crops destined to be eaten by himself and his
family' (1891:47) was no longer true when it came to the high Middle Ages.
In challenging Knapp's view, Aubin stated that in east Prussia the landlords did
indeed have connections with the market (1911:63). Dopsch drew our attention
to the satires of the so-called Little Lucidarius who, at the close of the thirteenth
century, made fun of the Teutonic knights and pictured them at court discussing
the price of wheat, cheese, eggs and sucking pigs, the milk yield of their cows
or the falling-off of their harvests (1928:329). English historians refer to the
numerous accounts kept since the thirteenth century by the stewards of feudal
estates. One example of these, taken from the account books of the bishopric of
Winchester in southern England, is reproduced in table 1 (from Gras, 1915:
appendix A, 261f.). From the farms of that estate in the years shown, up to
70 per cent of the wheat crop and up to 40 per cent of the barley as well as a
third of the oats were sold.

Table 1   Grain yields and sales on thirteenth-century English farms

Kind of Grain	Yield in quarters per acre		Proportion of yield sold	
	1208–9	*1299–1300*	*1208–9*	*1299–1300*
Wheat	0.54	1.35	48.5%	70.0%
Barley	0.92	1.56	27.9%	39.6%
Oats	1.02	1.14	17.0%	34.3%

As the surpluses regularly sent to market increased, the landlord and farmer
began to feel the need of more money. By the middle of the fourteenth century
wages, especially in England, were already taking up a considerable proportion
of the lord's expenses. Among farmers the gradual change from payment of
rent in goods and services to rents paid in cash resulted in a steady and often
quite high demand for money. There were also maintenance and running costs
requiring money, which was sometimes scarce. In a document relating to an
early sixteenth-century lawsuit an English farmer complained of the low prices
he received for his wheat and other crops while having to buy iron for the
plough, harrows and carts, tar for the sheep, shoes, caps, linen and woollen
cloth; 'for', he says, 'if all husbandmen and gentlemen ... should be compelled
to sell their thinges good cheape, and yet buy all thinges deere ... I cannot see
how they should longe prosper' (Stafford, 1876:38).

It remains an open question whether integration into a market economy was indeed so strange and unwelcome to the 'true' peasantry. The nature of the 'true' peasant is a debatable matter and not everyone would agree with Werner Sombart when he says: 'The work of the true peasant, like that of the true craftsman, is a solitary and creative activity: silent and absorbed, he devotes himself to it. He lives in his work as does an artist, and shrinks from assigning it a market price' (1928:36). Sombart undoubtedly idealized his subject but, be that as it may, when the countryside became dotted with towns that could no longer obtain their own food and raw materials from their own soil, the peasant economy throughout western and central Europe became dependent on markets. In Germany alone there were at the end of the Middle Ages about 4,000 market towns or villages. They were scattered over the land at some four to eight hours' travelling distance from each other. Trade and traffic grew with them. Urban wares spread into country households; the services of town and village craftsmen supplanted the skills once practised in the rural home; farming itself became more intensive and covered wider areas till it outgrew the confines of home consumption. While surplus production had once been used only for luxury which could be dispensed with easily enough, the proceeds from the market were spent on essential maintenance and supplies. Thenceforward production for trade became a necessity.

Feudal incomes and rents

With the growth of trade in the west, source material for the history of prices and wages became more readily available. Papers on prices and wages from the ninth to the tenth century have been published by some historians, but the documentary evidence is still too meagre to allow more than a vague estimate of relative price levels and fluctuations.[6] From the thirteenth and fourteenth centuries onwards the evidence is more abundant and from that time on we can perceive the long-term movements already mentioned.

At first sight it might appear that in the last years of the Middle Ages rents were hardly affected by the changes in prices and wages. Rogers showed that English farm rents had remained unaltered from the high Middle Ages right into the sixteenth century. He maintained, however, that this was because medieval rents were something quite different from the new rents, 'No one who knows anything about early economic-history, can doubt that rent was originally, and for centuries, a tax imposed by the strong on the weak in consideration of a real or pretended protection of the tenant' (1894:167).

Rogers followed up this argument with a fierce attack on Ricardo's theory of rents, which he claimed to have unmasked as the purest 'speculation'. He proceeded from the concept of rents as formulated by Ricardo: rent is 'that portion of the produce of the land which is paid to the landlord for the use of the original and indestructible powers of the soil'. It is true that this definition takes no account of the dues, socage and other services paid by the peasant farmer to his landlord – to say nothing of other lords – during the late Middle Ages and even after. Not only in England but also on the continent such payments survived, often – though not invariably – for centuries, adhering to the rules of a social order whose considerable influence was preserved not by power alone, but by tradition, custom and law.

This is particularly clear in the case of the payments designated as taxes, such as the jurisdiction tax (*vogtsteuer*). Because it was at first considered to be a subjective right, it was often called jurisdiction right (*vogtrecht*) in the documents. Its essential immutability depended on its legal status. And law was what was sanctified by tradition. To be classed as a 'law' a tax had to remain at the same level year in, year out. This concept is reflected in many utterances of the time, e.g. 'Jura ... ab antiquo ordinata et statuta, servata et servanda' (from the Cologne vassal laws *c.*1154). It was this desire to preserve the ancient laws that produced the first of the many legal codes (Krause, 1964).

Nevertheless, the evidence that many of the villein farmers' payments were in the nature of taxes did not, as Rogers supposed, exhaust the problem of rents during the middle and late Middle Ages. For, besides the charges that Diehl (1932:28) so aptly called 'feudal rents', there was at that time a market rent as well, conditioned by the shortage of land, the convenience or inconvenience of its situation and the varying quality of the soil. It amounted to the proportion of the gross agricultural yield represented by the soil as a specific source of production. Although not usually easy to separate from the expenditure of labour and materials, there is no doubt about its development as soon as the old arable no longer sufficed, and when there arose market towns whose massive requirements of agricultural produce could be regularly supplied by purchase or barter. These 'differential rents' are already evident in twelfth- and thirteenth-century valuations of properties lying near towns. Thus, for example, one farm in 1332 fetched a higher price than another 'because it lay nearer to the town of Soest' (Anton).

Feudal rents, on the other hand, rooted as they were in might, right and custom, present a very different problem: the distribution of the agricultural yield.

The effects of harvest fluctuations on the circulation of money and goods in pre-industrial economy

So far we have considered only the long-term trends of the agricultural market. Now we shall examine these short-run fluctuations and, where necessary, add a few words of explanation.

The Labrousse theory of depressions

At roughly the same time as the first edition of this book appeared Labrousse produced a theory that any decline in prosperity during the pre-industrial era was determined by harvest losses. Good harvests caused an upswing and poor harvests a recession in the overall boom period. The old type of depression was a matter of shortages caused by a crop failures.

Specifically Labrousse saw the sequence of events as follows:

1 A harvest failure drove prices up.
2 For the majority of farmers a bad harvest meant a loss of income inasmuch as the higher price per unit did not make up for the drop in marketable produce. To that loss must be added the loss to the labourers of employment and income because less corn had to be gathered and processed.
3 Owing to the bad harvest the townspeople were forced to spend more on provisions. To buy essential foodstuffs they had to do without other commodities. Demand for the services and products of industry fell off.
4 Owing to this, and because the peasants could not buy so much, markets and trade stagnated. There was less demand for labourers; wages were low or sank still lower; men sought work and could not find it.
5 As soon as better harvests were brought in, distress began to recede. Farm prices went down, the farmers' income increased, the townsfolk could afford to buy more goods. An upward swing developed and continued until poor harvests plunged town and country into yet another crisis. (See Labrousse 1933, 1944; this summary follows Landes, 1950:195f.)

This theory of depressions being due to scarcity was widely accepted. It 'entered the creed of French historiography practically unopposed', as Landes put it. Nor can it be disputed that it described and interpreted some of the connecting circumstances correctly. On the other hand it omitted others that were perhaps no less important. If empirical research is not to be too narrowly confined from the start, Labrousse's ideas must be supplemented.

An attempt to widen the scope of the inquiry

Before going any further it must be observed that the effect of harvest fluctuations depended on the extent to which the crop varied from the norm. According to the amount of the deficit (or surplus) grain prices rose (or fell) to a greater or lesser degree and this, as King emphasized, in magnified ratio to the extent of the crop variation. King estimated that with a harvest 10 per cent below the normal or average level, grain prices rose by 30 per cent. If the deficit was 20 per cent they rose by 80 per cent; if it was 50 per cent the increase was 450 per cent. King's calculations, made in the seventeenth century, can no longer be verifed, but plain figures from a much later period (from the Report of the Committee on Stabilization of Agricultural Prices, 1925:21) demonstrate that scant harvests had a higher market value than plentiful ones. That does not, of course, mean that this 'strangest anomaly of the agricultural market', as the committee on stabilization described it, was promptly converted into hard cash for the farmer. The extent to which variations in harvest affected the financial proceeds of farming also depended on the gross amount of marketable production. The larger the product's share in the market the more agricultural yield and prices tended to move in opposing directions; the smaller the share, the more likely were yield and prices to move in the same direction.

A national example illustrates this rule:[7] suppose that for a normal crop of grain, with the price standing at 20 per 100 kilograms, three farms of different sizes, A, B and C had the quantities to sell as shown in table 2.

Table 2   Normal harvest (price of grain 20 per dz)

	A	B	C
Harvest	250 dz	500 dz	1,000 dz
For home consumption	200 dz	300 dz	400 dz
For sale	50 dz	200 dz	600 dz
Money proceeds	1,000	4,000	12,000

dz = double zentner = 100 kg

Now let us suppose that the crop failed and the yield of grain dropped by 20 per cent while the price of grain rose by 80 per cent (as King estimated). If the amount for home consumption remains unaltered we get the figures shown in table 3. In the case of the big farm C the reduction in quantity for sale is more than compensated by the greater scale of the rise in price; the middle-sized farm B gets less money than with a normal crop, while the small farm A can spare no grain for sale at all.

Table 3   Failed harvest (deficit 20%, price of grain 26 per dz)

	A	B	C
Yield	200 dz	400 dz	800 dz
For home consumption	200 dz	300 dz	400 dz
For sale	—	100 dz	400 dz
Money proceeds	—	3,600	14,400

The three types of farm featured in the above example existed during the entire period under consideration. They remind one of the manorial farms belonging to the bishopric of Winchester towards the end of the thirteenth century, which sold 70 per cent of their grain harvest (as shown in table 1). More evidence pointing in the same direction will be found below. Here it will suffice to quote a German writer of the eighteenth century who described the effects of the devastating crop failures and sharp rise in prices during 1771–2 as follows: 'Who can forget the terrible years of soaring prices in the early seventies [1770s] that so harshly oppressed almost the whole of Europe?' The writer, who was also a practising farmer, went on: 'Yet, believe it or not, it was this very rise in prices that brought prosperity back to farming.' The cost of a bushel of oats rose from 12 groschen in the beginning of 1771 to 5 thalers at the end of the year. 'A man who normally sold 24 bushels but through the bad harvest had only 12 to sell nevertheless received 60 thalers for his goods in place of the 12 thalers he had made in the spring. And, since the farm bread was made from his own corn, he spent neither more nor less than in other years although he made much more profit' (von Engel, 1798:124).

It may be that this German author did not mean to include middle-sized farms in his generalization; it certainly does not apply to the smaller farms. These either had nothing to sell or actually became consumers themselves for, as another farmer said of the lean years around 1816, 'instead of having goods to sell, they were forced to buy some of their household necessities to save their farms from ruin' (Stelzner, 1826:61).

In hard times like these the price of grain always rose far higher than that of farm products in more elastic demand, or of industrial goods; nor did wages keep pace with prices. The standard of living went down so that the townspeople could afford only the necessities of life. Consequently the turnover of goods stagnated, which could well have led to further pressure on wages. A slump was under way, exactly as expounded by Labrousse.

All the same, it cannot be said that this view covers the whole subject of slumps in the pre-industrial era. The question of agricultural depressions, those characterized by falling prices at any rate, has not been touched upon. Yet, during the 1730s there was a lawsuit in the Halle district between a parson and his ecclesiastical patron because the former refused to include in his church service a prayer that the price of corn might not sink too low. The case finally came before a higher authority, which decided that 'it shall be permitted during church services to pray that grain shall not become so cheap as to bring it into contempt' (Abel, 1976:114). This sort of thing could happen in the eighteenth century. In the late Middle Ages and just afterwards the court might have arrived at a different verdict, but it must also be borne in mind that the contemporary writers and lawyers whose words colour our picture of their times were almost all townsmen. If we turn our eyes to the country we may well see the reverse side of the 'cheap years'. Thus we find here and there in records and registers of the period remarks such as the following (from the chronicle of Spangenberg in Mansfeld in 1507) 'this year it cost certain farmers more to till their land than they gained from their plentiful harvests'.

It must not be forgotten, however, that the effect of a good harvest on the farmer's financial profit depended on the level of his marketable production. To illustrate the point we will return to our notional example: supposing that the yield exceeded the norm by 20 per cent, and the price, as King postulated, sank by 40 per cent, we get the results shown in table 4. The smallest cash revenue relating to a normal harvest occurs at farm C, which has the highest marketable production. The middle-sized farm's revenue has dropped by 400, or 10 per cent, while an equally plentiful yield at the small farm increases its revenue by 200, or 20 per cent.

Table 4   Good harvest (increased production 20%, price of grain 12 per dz)

	A	B	C
Yield	300 dz	600 dz	1,200 dz
For home consumption	200 dz	300 dz	400 dz
For sale	100 dz	300 dz	800 dz
Money proceeds	1,200	3,600	9,600

A passage in Shakespeare that tends to puzzle literary scholars is that in which the porter in *Macbeth* (Act 2, Scene 3) asks 'Who goes there i' the name of Beelzebub?' only to answer himself, 'Here's a farmer that hanged himself on the expectation of plenty.' Shakespeare (not the imaginary courtier or scholar but the actor and, as we are told, cornchandler) wrote *Macbeth* in 1603, when grain prices in England had been driven downwards by a series of good harvests. An anonymous author must have had a similar situation in mind in 1767 when he wrote, 'The farmers are always more afraid of a good year than a bad one … They prefer half a crop … to a full harvest' (Ashton, 1959:41).

Some contemporary authors went still further; they developed the theory that a crisis was the result of prices falling too low. It was a mistake, wrote Boisguillebert in France at the end of the seventeenth century, to suppose that industry and the towns could reap only advantage from cheap grain prices. If the price of corn became too low, the tenant farmer tended to leave his fields untilled. The farm labourer then had no employment and the landlord no profit, so that there was no turnover for industry. A crisis arose and soon spread to the towns simply because corn was sold too cheaply: 'the lower the price of grain, the more even the poor suffered'.

In many of his writings, some of which have now become rarities owing to having been suppressed in his native France, Boisguillebert put forward these ideas. He also, fortunately for historians, illustrated them with examples such as this: in Paris in 1706, when the price of wheat had fallen to half its 1699 level, there were three times as many bankruptcies as in the earlier year.

Here we will leave Boisguillebert and his theories, since it is not general depression in the pre-industrial age that is the subject of this book. They are mentioned here because they show that the fluctuations in price and quantity resulting from the harvest cycle cannot be considered apart from long-term price movements. Boisguillebert lived and wrote at a time when the price of cereals in France – and in other lands – was gradually falling.

There remains, however, the income level of the poorer classes to be considered. When wages were so low that the labourers could scarcely make a living from a normal harvest, how much worse were crop failures for these people, who had no savings in reserve to spend on the necessities of life. But now the wages and wage-like incomes of pre-industrial society underwent a long series of changes, not only nominal but real, that is to say in their purchasing power in relation to grain.

Part One

Changes in the agrarian economy of western and central Europe from the thirteenth century to the end of the fifteenth century

1 Rising agrarian prosperity during the high Middle Ages

Price movements

Price fluctuations and the long-term trend

By far the richest material for the history of thirteenth- to fifteenth-century prices is to be found in England. It was first investigated by Rogers; Gras and Beveridge contributed further reports and ideas; still later Farmer made a study of thirteenth-century prices (1957–8:207f.); and more recently Farmer's work has been supplemented by Titow (1959–60; 1970:312ff.).

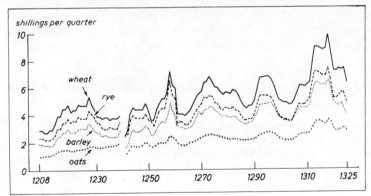

Fig. 2   English grain prices 1208–1325 (seven-term annual moving averages, after D. L. Farmer).

As Farmer's research shows prices fluctuated considerably (see figure 2). Although the annual fluctuations are smoothed out by the seven-year moving averages, the peak figures are still two or three times higher than the lowest points. While Beveridge thought these fluctuations were largely due to changes in coinage and measures, Farmer rejected this view as an explanation of most of the price movements, but admitted the possibility of the higher prices in the early thirteenth century being caused by the depreciation of currency. Judging by contemporary records even that is doubtful. Halfway through the 1220s there were harvest failures in England and on the continent. The chronicles report famines in Germany, the Low Countries and eastern France, in Lorraine, Bavaria and the middle Rhine region (see Curshmann, 1900; Hanauer, 1878; Schmitz, 1968:87). The famine reached as far as Russia (Widera, 1963).

If one continues to follow English prices, comparing them with continental records, it becomes clear that price movements depended on variations in the harvest. When prices next declined in England the Alsatian chroniclers reported good harvests and low prices in their country; a measure of wine was worth no more than one pfennig in 1236. In 1257, when the highest prices of the century were being paid in England, similar famine prices reigned in France, Swabia and the Rhineland; when the English prices went down again, the 'corn and vines' of the west German river valleys were flourishing. The chroniclers report that in 1260, in spite of Strasbourg being under siege, a quarter of wine could be bought there for only 4 pfennigs and rye cost only 4 schillings. During 1261 and 1262, as the good harvests continued, it was said that in the Rhineland towns wine barrels cost more than the wine. Then again, in Germany around the year 1288 grain was so cheap that the chroniclers were still recalling its low price more than a hundred years later (Hanauer, 1878). From all this it can be established that the rise and fall of prices were determined by the abundance of the harvest, which varied according to a cycle of some twenty to thirty years.

It is not without significance to our subject that during the thirteenth century, as Curschmann observed, the word *fames* (famine) used in documents was gradually replaced by *caristia* (high cost of living). The change of wording did not mean that poverty had grown less but rather that a new economic concept had arisen, corresponding with an increasing dependence on markets and price movements during medieval times.

*

Over and above these fluctuations in grain prices a long-term upward trend is discernible. If we group Farmer's wheat prices into 25-year averages we see that they rise from 100 in the first quarter of the thirteenth century to 110, 136 and 147 in the ensuing quarters till in the first quarter of the fourteenth century they reach 181.[1] Rogers' series develops in much the same way. In this, if the years 1201–25 are taken as 100, the 25-year average wheat prices go up to 111, 140, 149 and 188. The two series deviate only slightly, the difference between the two final 25-year averages (181 as against 188) amounting to no more than 2.6 per cent.

No such firmly-based and mutually-confirming series are available on the continent. However, the few prices shown in figure 3 indicate the direction in which the economic historians' conjectures – they cannot be called more than that – are leading. The figures of France were drawn from d'Avenel's findings, though these were admittedly from many different and widely separated localities. Usher investigated the information more closely and extracted from it a series

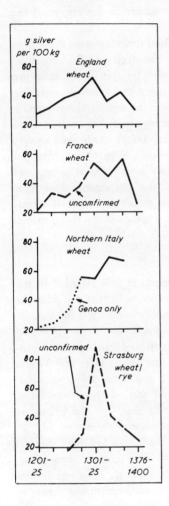

Fig. 3 European grain prices 1201–1400 (25-year averages).

referring exclusively to Albi (in the department of Tarn) but for that reason marred by considerable gaps. The series begins with 34 grams of silver for one setier of wheat in 1202, rising to 64 grams during the years 1301–25 (Usher, 1930:159f.). Guy Bois, to whose work we shall return later, based his estimates on the prices collected by Fourquin from the Paris area. According to these the price per setier of grain in Parisian sous doubled between 1284 and 1303 and rose still higher between 1320 and 1342 (Bois, 1976:243).

For Germany only the Strasbourg prices have been used, and even these must be labelled 'unconfirmed'. However, when these and the few existing single items of evidence are all taken into account (see especially Lamprecht, 1885:613f. and Mone, 1859:43f., 189), we can venture to state that cereals in Germany – and in northern Italy – were gradually becoming dearer in the course of the twelfth and thirteenth centuries.

It is surprising to learn that in such an early period this long-term movement of grain prices prevailed not only in England but also deep into the continent. The trade in cereals may have been partly responsible for this, for its influence already spread over a wide territory. The Flemish towns and Friesland were importing grain from the western Baltic region before the end of the thirteenth century,[2] while some English counties were exporting their surplus harvest to Flanders, Brabant, Holland and France. Moreover, a corn trade had already established itself in the river valleys of western Germany, in parts of France and in Flanders itself, though it can have affected only inter-regional prices, not their long-term rise. It is far more likely, indeed, that the extension of trade routes and the widening of the trading area helped to keep the cost of cereals down. So we must look elsewhere for the underlying causes of the rising prices.

The circulation of money

First place among the influences on price movements is still awarded to the amount and the velocity of money circulation. It cannot be denied that from the beginning of the twelfth century the supply of precious metals and the circulation of money increased rapidly throughout western and central Europe. Gold and silver had been discovered in Bohemia, Moravia and further into south-eastern Europe. There were mines in Switzerland and in the Harz and Vosges Mountains. The rivers Isar, Inn, Danube, Rhine and Elbe deposited gold-bearing sand. Gold was mined at Heidelberg; gold and silver in Pomerania. In addition, precious metals were imported from the East, and the Crusaders brought a certain amount of gold and silver back home with them.

Some of this metal may have been hoarded or made into jewellery, but no small part of it was minted, which, under otherwise static economic conditions, would be bound to lead to inflation. The economic conditions, however, did not remain static. For as the circulation of money increased during these centuries of budding rural and urban prosperity, so also did trade begin to expand. We do not know whether prices in general, i.e. the total cost of living, rose at the same rate as the price of grain. Cattle and other agricultural products were certainly dearer, but whether and by how much industrial products rose in price we cannot say, because comprehensive tables of prices for this period are lacking.

Such information as we have does not give the impression that there was a general increase in the cost of living. A memorandum dealing with rising prices, written in 1367, mentions only that grain was growing more expensive (d'Avenel, 1894–1926:I, 14). In Old Germany one of the effects of the price movement was that certain dues fixed as cash payments, but actually payable in farm produce, were reduced,[3] which hardly suggests a general increase in the cost of living. Moreover, the complaint that it was the merchants who were responsible for the rising cost of corn and wine – a complaint repeated when prices went up in the sixteenth and eighteenth centuries – was already to be heard during the mid-fourteenth century (Rulman Merswin in Lamprecht, n.d. 102).

So there is good reason to examine the conditions of demand and supply then reigning.

Population growth and expanding agriculture

Population growth 1100–1350

Accurate data on population trends are hard to come by till quite late in the modern era, but there are certain indications that help us indirectly to trace the course of population growth. The rising number of settlements, the spread of agricultural techniques and organization are signs that allow the historian to draw cautious conclusions.

From the multiplication of villages between 1000 and 1237 Lamprecht reckons (1885–6:I, 163) that the number of inhabitants in the Moselle area must have more than trebled, which corresponds to an annual increase of 0.48 per cent.[4] And this is always supposing that the size of the settlements remained constant at 220 inhabitants each, which, with such a rapidly growing population, is unlikely. From information of this kind German historians have long held the opinion that population growth in medieval Germany, a very slow process at the turn of the millennium, gained speed rapidly during the twelfth century, reached its peak in the thirteenth century and came to a stop at the time of the Black Death, 1347–50 (Schmoller, 1919:173; Inama-Sternegg, n.d. (*a*):882; Inama-Sternegg and Häpke, 1924:671; Kötzschke, 1908:87).

Brodnitz (1918:61) estimates that England's population, roughly assessable from entries in the Domesday Book and tax-rolls, was 1.5 millions at the time of the Norman Conquest and rose to 4 or 5 millions just before the Black Death. Russell (1958:95f.) puts it at 1.3 millions (without Wales) in 1086 and at 3.7 millions in 1346.

Even these figures may be too conservative. According to accounts of poll-tax received in the farming district of Taunton, belonging to the bishopric of Winchester, the taxable male population over twelve years old increased from 612 individuals in 1209 to 1448 individuals in 1311, that is to say at a cumulative annual rate of 0.85 per cent, almost double the rate of population growth in England during the eighteenth century (0.44 per cent). And Taunton was one of the oldest farming districts belonging to Winchester; in more recently-settled places, with the likelihood of earlier marriages, the rate of growth may well have been higher (Titow, 1961–2:218f.). Some years ago Postan estimated that the rural population of England at the end of the thirteenth century was as dense, possibly even more dense, than at the beginning of the eighteenth century. It was Hallam's opinion (1961–2:71f.) that population in some parts of the Fen district in eastern England reached a level at the end of the thirteenth century that was not regained until the first half of the nineteenth century, in about 1830.

Levasseur (1889: *passim*) calculated that the population of France must have trebled between the second half of the eleventh century and the middle of the fourteenth. According to Russell the number of inhabitants within the 1794 frontiers of France must have been about 6.2 millions in 1100 and about 17.6 millions in 1346 (1958:95f.). It is to be noted that Marc Bloch made the population growth of this period one of the central points in his important studies. More recent research relating to particular regions in France confirms in principle this long-term growth and its abrupt end in the fourteenth century (see Bartadier, 1961; Fierro, 1971:941ff.).[5]

It was Cipolla's opinion (1963:417) that the population of Italy rose from 5 millions in the mid-tenth century to 7–8 millions at the end of the thirteenth century. The lively building activity in the towns and the great expansion of cultivation on the land suggest that the last may be a minimum figure. It was stated in Venice (in a resolution passed by the Senate, dated 17 August 1326) that there were far more lawyers and lawsuits than formerly, 'quia terra crevit et Deo gratias multiplicatur continue'. In the district of Pistoia in Tuscany in 1244 some 34,000 people inhabited an area of 900 square kilometres, which amounts to 38 per square kilometre, or, if we include the roughly 10,000 inhabitants of the town of Pistoia, 49 per square kilometre (Herlihy, 1965:32). Nor was that unusually many. According to Fiumi's careful calculations (1962; see also 1961:101), the population density of San Gimignano (Tuscany) in 1332, taking town and rural district together, was 85 per square kilometre while Herlihy considers that in the later thirteenth century Tuscany as a whole contained about 1,800,000 inhabitants a density of population greater than at any time before the nineteenth century.

In the Scandinavian countries the population also increased rapidly during the twelfth and thirteenth centuries. Danish historians estimate the population of Denmark in the late eighth century to have been approximately 550,000, rising to about 850,000 in the year 1000. This was followed by a decline and then, in the twelfth century, by a new and still steeper ascent. In the years preceding the Black Death (1347–50) Denmark's population, excluding the towns, was said to be nearly 1.5 millions or, within the boundaries of today's Denmark, about 930,000 inhabitants, a density of rural population not overtaken till 1800. In Norway (and Sweden) too 'people reclaimed land and built a great deal, not only in Telemarken but all over the eastern part of the country, especially in the highlands' and remote mountain valleys' (Skappel, 1937–40:191; see also Inama-Sternegg, n.d. (*a*):882f.).[6]

If the total populations of the different countries (for example France, with double the population of Italy) are considered together with those of the regions newly or almost newly settled during the twelfth to fourteenth centuries (eastern Germany and the north of the Scandinavian pensinula) it can be fairly confidently stated that the population of western and central Europe approximately trebled between the end of the eleventh century and the middle of the fourteenth.

Changes in systems of land tenure and progress in farming practice

That this growing multitude of people could be fed only if agricultural activity were increased goes without saying. While the agrarian advances of the age were a pre-condition for the growth of population, it could also be said that the population growth was a cause of the expansion and intensification of agriculture. Marxist economic historians support the hypothesis that existing resources determine economic conditions and hence the increase in population (see Ljublinskaya, 1959:95f.).[7] But this is as hard to prove as the opposite view that population growth was the 'prime cause', the 'only begetter', of the developing economy of the time (see examples in Mombert, 1929:12f.). The relationship between economic, social and demographic phenomena is more complicated than either of these theories would imply. Progress in agriculture is connected with changes in the methods, economy and organization of farming that cannot be attributed automatically to the growing pressure of population or to an increase in the price of agricultural produce. Its roots go deeper. They reach into the political and social tensions of the age. They are involved with the spirit of mankind, which is determined only to a very limited extent by economic aspirations.

Therefore it must remain an open question as to what extent the spread of new agrarian systems – described below in barest outline – was the cause or the result of population growth. It will suffice if we can establish a connection and for that there is evidence enough. The old manorial system, which had begun to break up both north and south of the Alps after the twelfth century, was based upon numerous services by the villeins as well as their obligatory attachment to their farms – conditions that blocked the way to improvement in land organization. The decline of the economic system of territorial lordship and the transformation of manorial obligations into rent opened the way to a more free and intensive agrarian economy. Changes in tenancy and ownership of land became easier, new forms of hereditary ownership established themselves, personal services became attached to the farm and land, and while the total of services and fees may not have been greatly reduced, at least some of the more burdensome duties were abandoned, such as the services at harvest time when the farmer and his family had more than enough to do in their own fields. The final elimination of the old territorial and manorial lordships during the eighteenth and nineteenth centuries resulted in a considerable improvement in agricultural production. It may well be that this first loosening of the bonds of lordship had a similarly favourable result. It had the effect of an 'artificial expansion of the area of cultivation' (Sombart).

Changes in land management led in the same direction. From the eighth century onwards in western and central Europe, side by side with the old one- and two-course rotations, the burn-and-fell method and convertible husbandry, there appeared the new system of three-course rotation. In the twelfth and thirteenth centuries this system began to expand. Already, in the region of the lower Rhine, fodder crops, peas and lentils were being sown in the fallow. That was the start of the 'improved' three-course rotation that was to make such great advances later on in the sixteenth and eighteenth centuries. Around the larger towns the growing of vegetables and fruit began to develop and the first beginnings of dairy farming became evident. Cultivation of the vine increased in the Rhineland, Moselle and parts of France. In Germany the vineyards climbed up the hillsides, which are still the best growing areas today; they spread northwards to Schleswig-Holstein and as far east as the lands of the Teutonic Order of Knights in East Prussia. Although in the big open fields only the main crops might be grown, the many smaller fields were planted with table vegetables, hops, flax and dye plants.

Not only soil and plants but water too was better managed. We hear sometimes of irrigated meadows, but more often of fish ponds and fish breeding. Still more important was the use of water to work the mills. There were, indeed, water-mills in Europe as early as the sixth century and even in Roman times (third century A.D.), but they must have been rare. It is probable that by the year 1000 the greater part of the corn harvest in western Europe was still ground by hand. From the eighth and ninth centuries onwards we begin to find water-mills in France, Germany and England. They reached Ireland in the tenth century and Scandinavia in the twelfth century, spreading with surprising rapidity. By 1300 there were districts, such as Mittelstormarn in Holstein, where nearly every village had its own mill.

Mention of the water-mill brings us to the equipment needed at an earlier stage of grain production – ploughs, harrows, hand implements, carts, and harnesses for horses and oxen. It is not certain when the use of the big-wheeled plough with coulter and share, known in Roman times, first became widespread, but it is not unreasonable to suppose that it occurred about the time the open-field system became established inland, while along the coasts and in low-lying areas the heavier soil was coming under attack. On the other hand, the harrow, which had displaced the brushwood or hand-rake in very early times, long kept its first simple form, with wooden teeth and a plain framework of beams. The small sickle, too, was much more usual than the big and costly scythe right up to the end of the Middle Ages and until well into the modern era. The threshing-flail gained popularity far sooner because it beat the grain so much more vigorously than a plain stick. Since the two-piece flail also required no metal, it is no wonder that it spread through Europe so rapidly in the early and high Middle Ages.

The method of harnessing horses requires some clarification. It has been said that the older kind of harness consisted of straps that were slung round the animal's neck so that when it pulled a heavy load its breathing was constricted. Whether this applies to the post and freight wagons of the ancient Romans is uncertain. What we do know is that a much more functional type of harness is shown in a very early illustration, from about A.D. 800, in the so-called *Trèves Apocalypse* (reproduced in Abel, 1962:11). It consists of a head-collar which allows the beast to exert its full strength, augmented by its own weight, to pull the burden. At about the same time horseshoes became more widely known. It is possible that they were used by the Gauls in the fourth century (Heichelheim) but, if so, they were subsequently forgotten. From that time there is no further record of horseshoes until the ninth century, after which they spread rapidly. The 'ringing of iron-clad hoofs' was heard by the poet of the Waltharilied, composed in about 930. A 'nailed horse' was seen and handled by St Ulrich, whose *Life* was written towards the end of the tenth century. In the course of the twelfth and thirteenth centuries the horseshoe came into general use.

Perhaps Georges Duby's description 'the agrarian revolution of the Middle Ages' is something of an overstatement when applied to the changes outlined above (1954:316f. and 1962:131f.).[8] But we have every right to speak of 'great progress' if, indeed, the technical and organizational changes during the high Middle Ages must be expressed in a phrase. The question of what these developments meant economically, however, still remains to be answered. To give an adequate answer to this much more complicated question we must turn our attention for a moment to the expansion of the cultivated area and the changes in income that accompanied both the expansion and the intensification of agriculture.

Reclamation and settlement

The high Middle Ages were the period when land reclamation was at its peak. Marc Bloch, who repeatedly stressed the great importance of this reclamation even for us, the distant descendants of the early settlers, set its beginning in the middle of the eleventh century and its end in the mid-fourteenth century (1956:7). This may hold good for the peak period of reclamation, but, in fact, the clearances started earlier and never entirely stopped. Nevertheless it is true enough that it was only after A.D. 1000 that the appearance of western and central Europe began to change, and then at a rate surpassed only during the industrial revolution.

In Germany land was cleared here and there (in the Munich district, for instance) as early as the seventh century but large-scale, continuous reclamation did not begin until after A.D. 1000. From the west and south towards the east and north, land was progressively cleared for cultivation in the Vosges, the Black Forest, the forests of the Palatinate, Bohemia, Franconia and Thuringia, in the Harz and Sudeten mountains, the Erzgebirge and the Spessart hills. By the time the great period of reclamation was over the new arable, carved out of scrub and forest, was many times larger than it had been before. One example will illustrate how much the landscape changed. In 1073 the Emperor Henry IV was beleaguered by the Saxons at Harzburg on the northern edge of the Harz Mountains. He was forced to save himself by a three-day journey of immense difficulty through virgin forest, following a narrow path discovered by a huntsman. On the fourth day he arrived at Eschwege, 'utterly exhausted' (Lampert von Hersfeld, n.d.:189). Two hundred years later Eschwege, 90 kilometres distant from Harzburg as the crow flies, lay amid a landscape of fields and villages.

As to France, d'Avenel tells us that 'day by day new land was being put under cultivation'. Marc Bloch devotes one of the most impressive chapters of his seminal work to these reclamations; in his *Économie Rurale* (1962) Duby gives a summary of the subject. It would be superfluous to add to this testimony, which covers many different parts of the country.

In England, as we learn from the Domesday Book compiled towards the end of the eleventh century, the forests were still huge and dense. The clearances must have begun at just about that time. Thus, for instance, Ramsey Abbey, north of Cambridge, described in the Domesday Book as situated among dense woods, became the owner of numerous farms as early as the second half of the twelfth century. In the middle of the twelfth century the deforestation started, but at first it did not mean much more than that the king claimed the sole right to grant land for reclamation in the proscribed forests. Later most of the land clearance was in woodlands that did not lie under the king's forest jurisdiction, and it was here that the activity continued so energetically during the twelfth and thirteenth centuries (Raftis, 1957:72, 175).[9]

Then came the cultivation of swamps and marshes. Ramsey Abbey was founded in the tenth century by the Bishop of Worcester on a wooded island surrounded by marshland. In 1301 the River Nene, which flows through that region, was provided with dams to protect the newly-reclaimed land from floods. The Fen country of Lincolnshire and (English) Holland were sufficiently well cultivated by 1300 to support a quite dense population (Hallam, 1961–2).

The first great dykes in the Netherlands were probably constructed about A.D. 1000. They were no longer mere protection against flooding, but 'dykes on the offensive', built to win land from the sea. Assisted by the digging of canals that carried away the superfluous water, they enclosed wide new areas of arable and pasture (Slicher van Bath, 1964:13f.; Verhulst, 1964a:447f., 1965).

The most important document relating to the German marshes was an agreement drawn up between an ecclesiastical lord and some Dutch settlers in the year 1106. These people, the contract stated, had 'earnestly requested us to allow them to farm on land in our bishopric that was hitherto remained untilled, marshy and of no use to our vassals'. The agreement concerned land in the Weser marshlands. A charter of 1158 bears witness to the state of the marshes along the river Elbe. In this charter Emperor Frederick I confirmed the rights of the archbishopric of Hamburg over 'the lands near and beside the Elbe, whether cultivated or uncultivated'. Without the protection of a dyke cultivation in that low-lying region threatened by storms and high water would have been impossible. As to the west coast of Schleswig-Holstein (Ditmarsch, Eiderstedt, North Friesland) and a part of the Wattenlake, which now separates the Halligen sands from the mainland, excavations and aerial photography reveal that the land there was colonized during the high Middle Ages and must have been protected by dykes not later than the twelfth century.

*

To cultivate the land there had to be people living in rural settlements. The little hamlets and single farmhouses which, after the great period of migration was over, grew from the centre outwards, set the pattern – at least in Germany – for all subsequent settlements. The single farms developed into hamlets, the hamlets into villages, the villages, in special circumstances, into small towns. In Italy, at the height of the Middle Ages, there were hill towns that numbered their inhabitants in thousands. It has been suggested that these places were the result of the residents' desire for protection, as is often attested by the names *castello* and *borgo*. Others may have offered greater safety only against the diseases, such as malaria, that ravaged the lowlands.

North of the Alps there were no such overgrown villages, although the wish for safety cannot have been absent. Habit, too, and neighbourliness and the advantages of neighbourly co-operation must have worked to keep the rising generation of a farming community at home. But as the population of a community increased, so did the farming area and, with that, the length of the journey that people and animals had to make to their places of work and pasture. From this arose the tendency to emigrate, first to the immediate neighbourhood and later to more distant parts.

Such movements, once started, seemed to become catching, so that even the settled farmers were affected. In north-west Germany from the twelfth century onwards, villages were reverting to single farms, so much so that often only the church and a few craftsmen's cottages were left in the old place. The farmers moved their homes outside the village, though that was chiefly so that their beasts could be kept under closer supervision in the protected enclosures.

At first the names of new settlements in the Middle Ages tended to describe their topographical situation, but after A.D. 1000 they were more often derived from literary sources.

The new communities often grew out of a nearby nucleus (and ancient hamlet, a single farm or perhaps a castle) and extended from it in one of several patterns such as a strip, a circle or a network. That was only the beginning.

When this extension became overcrowded in its turn, some of the inhabitants took a long jump, as it were, and settled further into the forest, higher up the mountain or deeper into the valleys. In a surprisingly short time whole areas that had scarcely been trodden by human feet were covered with hamlets and villages.

Here is one example from Germany: in the year 500 the country round the Diemel, west of Reinhardswald and lying today mostly in the Hessian district of Hofgeismar, contained hardly more than seventeen settlements. They lay along the edges of the wooded and swampy valleys. There was little arable and the population was scanty. Indeed, the average settlement consisted of no more than four to ten farmhouses. Cultivation commenced along the flood boundaries in the valleys, beside the old highways and in pockets scattered over the countryside; then it began to spread. By the end of the period of expansion a dense network of more than a hundred communities covered the area. Only the heart of the Rheinhartswald remained untouched (Jäger, 1951).

Neighbourhood settlement turns into colonization of more distant land once the nearby country is opened up. Near and far are relative terms, but the great migration of the Germans towards the east, and of the Scandinavians northward, must surely count as distant colonization. They are to be understood as the result of pressure and of drawing power: the closing-in of home country and the attraction of far-off lands. Which force was the more potent we cannot tell. More importantly, although the economic, social and political effects of these migrations can hardly be overestimated, it is easy to exaggerate their extent (Kuhn, 1964:131f.). Kuhn considers that in the twelfth century only some 200,000 people, and not many more during the next century, emigrated from Old Germany, though once in their new homelands they multiplied rapidly. If that is true, east Germany can have drawn no more than 4 per cent of its population from Old Germany.

Movements of rents and wages

Rising rents

If we consider the effects of the relationship between population growth and agrarian development outlined in the preceding pages, one thing seems certain: by the time the great increase of population between the eleventh century and the first half of the fourth century had reached its peak, land was in relatively short supply. That is the basic fact behind the forces which, on the 'commodities' side of the money situation, determined contemporary price movements. The increase in money at that time only loosened the surface from beneath which the rising prices would grow. The economic explanation of the increasing cost of farm produce was its relative scarcity; it became dearer, as Ricardo propounded, as a result of the increasing difficulty of feeding a growing population. That being the case, rents, in so far as they expressed the value of those products whose sole source was the soil, would also rise.

It is not easy to disentangle rents from the confused strands that enshrouded them in the Middle Ages. Villeinage, feudal tenure and inviolable church property were the three major influences on the movement of land ownership and thus of the land prices handed down to us in the lords' registers. These prices were not, as a rule, the sums farmers paid for using the land, but rather reflect the value of the farms and land profits to the landlord. They represent, if often in a rudimentary way, capitalized profit in the form of rents, interest or services (sometimes involving social and political motives) exacted from the peasants by the landowners (or those in power).

Nevertheless Lamprecht in the Moselle area (1886:11, 614) and d'Avenel in France (1894–1926:11, 508) have been able to find some of these land prices, which, expressed in a common measure and coinage, are shown in table 5. The series of prices shown in the table have been compiled from various sites, with all irrelevant values due to buildings or other such objects on the land eliminated. However, naturally there are reservations regarding average land prices for so wide an area as France or the Moselle region. The price of real estate varied greatly according to its quality and situation. But the agreement in the course of the prices in both series until the mid-thirteenth century is clear enough for the general tendency of land prices up to that point to be stated with confidence. During the second half of the century French prices fell while in the Moselle region they continued to rise. Here d'Avenel's averages may be at fault for, in the first quarter of the fourteenth century at least, there was no sign of any slackening in the demand for land in France, a circumstance to which Levasseur drew attention in a review of d'Avenel's works (Levasseur, 1892:363). A declining demand for land seems unlikely in view of Bois' (1976) evidence for Normandy.

Table 5   Price per hectare of arable land in France and the Moselle
area from 1100–1350 in grams of silver

Period	France	Moselle area
1100–1200	–	520
1201–1250	806	734
1251–1300	1,050	737
1301–1350	745	928

According to Lamprecht the price of arable land in Germany continued to rise right up to the fourteenth century. Mone (1859:30) came to the same conclusion, calculating, though on rather sparse information, that the price of arable per morgen in south-west Germany went up by 100 per cent from 1200 to 1300. A number of land prices from the north-west of Lower Saxony are available, 110 from the twelfth century and 179 from the thirteenth. Prices rose from an average of 9.4 Cologne marks between 1150 and 1200 to 15 marks between 1200 and 1250 and 28.3 marks between 1250 and 1291 – threefold in approximately one hundred years, if one reckons from the middle years of the period averaged (Teute, 1910).[10] However, it must be stressed that these land prices do not refer to the financial means of the peasant but to his payments and services expressed as a capital sum in the landowner's register.

The rising price of land was undoubtedly a reflection of the higher price of farm produce, which benefited the recipient of agricultural payments in kind. There were, however, varying factors in farm dues. Postan calls our attention to the entry fines on customary holdings levied on long leases. He reports that these sometimes amounted to as much as fifteen to twenty-five times the value of the annual harvest (1959–60:80).[11] On the estates owned by Ramsey Abbey in the eastern counties of England the sum that a son had to pay when he succeeded his father was about £1 in the year 1250, but after 1300 it often amounted to as much as £3 (Raftis, 1957:238). Obviously the purpose of fines was to give the recipient a share in the profits of the soil which could not be recovered entirely from the ordinary rent.

Similar fees were paid by the tenant farmers of the Heiliggeistspitales (Hospital of the Holy Ghost) at Biberach on the Riss in the sixteenth century (see p. 127). There is not yet any parallel information relating to the high Middle Ages, but there can be no doubt that comparable taxes, such as payments on change of tenancy, already existed under a wide variety of names in different parts of the country. Hermann Wiessner mentions finding 'investitures' and analogous expressions used in the documents (1934:179ff.). It may be that at first these charges, payable in either kind or money, had a merely symbolic value. In German-speaking lands the exact period in which they rose to the level of subsidiary rents, as they had done in Biberach by the sixteenth century, remains uncertain.

Where the leasehold system was already established rents could be raised after still shorter periods. Indeed, in England leasehold was known as early as the end of the eleventh century, as can be seen from Raftis' studies of the Ramsey Abbey estates (1957:10, 17, 35, 36, 41, 43, 83, 99, etc.) By the mid-thirteenth century at latest the great religious houses of France, especially that of Saint-Denis, rented out land, rights and even whole economic complexes for leases of three, six or nine years (Fourquin, 1966:7ff.; also Duby, 1962:11, 584). In Cologne leasehold was increasingly used by all the religious institutions during the thirteenth century. Farms were let for periods of five, nine, twelve or fifteen years. This arrangement, as Edith Ennen (1976) rightly remarked, enabled the landowners to adjust their revenues from time to time to suit changing circumstances, and also to exercise some control over farm management. That was, in fact, what happened, as we learn from England (Halcrow, 1954–5:345ff.; Hatcher, 1969:214; and Postan, 1959–60:80), France (d'Avenel, 1894–1926:11, 508) and the Moselle region (Lamprecht, 1885–6:11, 614), where increased rents were demanded for temporary use of the land.

Yet, in spite of these variable rents (which Halcrow has described as 'competitive leasehold rents' because they were the result of bargaining between owner and tenant) rents in general remained unchanged. Rogers' extensive researches show that, in spite of rising prices, ordinary rents in England remained at a level of 6d. to 8d. per acre of arable (1894:167). In Germany there were fixed rents supposed to stay the same 'for all time', and in France 'rentes qui ne croissent ni decroissent' (Kulischer, 1965:1, 119f.).

D'Avenel tried to define the difference between fixed and changeable payments coming under the system of feudal rights (*droits féodaux*) and rents and leasehold payments (*locations* and *fermages*). In his opinion the real worth of the former had greatly diminished through the years, whereas the latter were related to the productive value of the land. Ideas of this sort are interesting and have their uses, but unfortunately they tell us nothing about the degree to which landowner and tenant repectively profited from the increased returns from the land.

The farmer's standard of living

Lamprecht and von Below (p. 440, supplement) felt that the study of rent in medieval Germany fell into two separate periods. The first period, lasting from the ninth to the twelfth century, they characterized by rising income accompanied by fixed dues, with the result that 'the territorial lords were, economically speaking, disinherited, while the landowning peasants benefited from the full value of their land'. The second period saw the change from villein farms to leasehold farms. 'Thus, through leasehold rents, and even to some extent from feudal and hereditary rents, the landlord could once more enjoy the full revenue from his property.' However, Lamprecht himself cited exceptions and even said: 'One would not go very far wrong in supposing that from the twelfth century onwards at least four-fifths of the income from land went to the farming classes, only one-fifth to the territorial lords' (1886:111, 622).

The poetry, chronicles and records of the time reinforce the impression summarized at the end of this section, but they too are not free of contradictions. This applies even to Seifried Helbling, so often quoted as evidence for the peasants' prosperity. Admittedly he shows us (in *Meier Helmbrecht*) a farmer who spends money lavishly on his clothes and finery. His embroidery alone, the poet tells us, cost the price of a fat cow. And then there is the father who sets before his homecoming son a rich meal of meat with herbs, a ripe, creamy cheese, a goose baked with lard, a roast chicken and a stewed hen. On the other hand we have Helbling's story of the peasant (1, 942ff.) who told his wife to be very sparing with the ham and fat bacon. Thereupon, for his next day's dinner, his wife gave him only vegetables in which she had hung a piece of meat on a threat. As soon as the herbs were cooked she pulled out the meat and used it to flavour several more herb-stews. The same peasant, owner though he was of a farm with farmhands – or one servant maid at least – supped off barley-bread and porridge.

No one who has made any study of the realities of life in the high Middle Ages, with their motley collection of leasehold, sub-let, hereditary and owner-occupied farms, would venture to give a general verdict as to how much of the steadily increasing income from land went to the landlord and how much to the farmer. One must consider all the tasks and dues included in the various services together with the payments in kind and cash payments received by the landlords, charitable foundations, monasteries, towns, nobles and even farmers (when they sub-let their land). The size and location of the farms should also be taken into account.

During the high Middle Ages there were farms and smallholdings that barely provided the peasant with a poor subsistence. Postan examined them at some length. His view was that 'so small were the holdings of the great majority of medieval serfs, so low was the yield of their lands and so great were the various compulsory payments weighing upon customary tenancies, that the net produce of an average medieval smallholding was only just sufficient to maintain a family on the margins of the barest subsistence' (1967:576ff.). My rough estimates strongly suggest that the vast majority of medieval customary holders occupying subsistence holdings (those comprising up to half a virgate of arable land of average quality) had to part with at least half of the gross yield of their land in favour of the landlord, the church and the tax-collector. What this meant for the budget of an average servile holding a simple computation will show. At best, under a three-field system an average semi-virgate of fifteen acres would have ten acres under crop in any year (and the average semi-virgate frequently contained fewer than fifteen acres and was worked under a two-field system). If at least one half of the output had to be set aside for rent, taxes and similar outgoings, what would be left is 30 bushels or some 1,800 pounds of mixed grain. This would provide a family of five with the equivalent of about one pound of cereals per head per day – 'less than the minimum that the FAO now postulates as required to keep an agriculturalist in regions of moderate climate alive and at work'.

Thus it seems established that the rising rents also benefited the peasants as long as their farms were not too small and their dues and services were converted into fixed cash payments. When that was not the case, the landlords, as Lamprecht and von Below surmised, took a very considerable share. Even though precise statements accompanied by figures are not quoted here, the separate pieces of evidence presented leave little doubt that by far the greater part of the rents, as Ricardo suggested, was absorbed by the *Feudalrent*, which, under various names, weighed on the peasants and their farms.

Evidence relating to wages

As more towns sprang up, more people became dependent on wages. Rogers and Beveridge have compiled quite comprehensive wage tables for England, d'Avenel less extensive ones for France. In both countries the money wages of the various groups of craftsmen and labourers, whether expressed in grams of silver or not, went up noticeably. However, movements of money wages do not necessarily indicate the level of real wages. The 'purchasing power of wages' – for that is the true meaning of the term 'real wages' – is hard to trace over a long period. Here it must suffice to calculate the real value of wages, using Rogers' figures (1886–1902:1, 303f.), by the classic method of reckoning how much corn a labourer could buy with money earned at that place and time. Table 6 shows the movements of the 'corn wages' paid to some of the chief groups of workers in England.[12] It shows clearly that in England the wages of artisans and farm hands after the middle of the thirteenth century went up even faster than cereal prices.

Table 6   Day and piece workers' wages in England from 1251–1350 measured in kilograms of wheat

Period	kg wheat per day		Thresher 1 kg wheat to each quarter threshed
	Mason	Carpenter	
1251–1275	9.6	11.9	7.7
1276–1300	11.3	11.9	7.7
1301–1325	10.0	12.3	7.0
1326–1350	12.7	15.4	9.3

We have Beveridge's research to thank for English wage and price series, which can be further sub-divided. Broken up into ten-year averages the fluctuations become more noticeable, but still leave the impression that even before the mid-thirteenth century the English labourer's wages were, in the long run, rising faster than the price of grain. After the Black Death, of course, wages rose much more rapidly than prices, as figure 4 illustrates (Beveridge, 1936–7; 38f.).

In Germany at the end of the twelfth century wages seem to have been very low. In the book *Iwein* by Hartmann of Aue, written in 1205, the goldsmiths and silk weavers complain that they have to expend great trouble and labour before they can earn enough 'even to keep ourselves from dying of hunger ... the wages are too low to furnish us with food and clothing'. Karl Lamprecht concluded from the few wage entries he was able to examine that wages began to go up in the thirteenth century. He traced this increase back to the colonization of the east having reduced the number of workers in the western labour market,

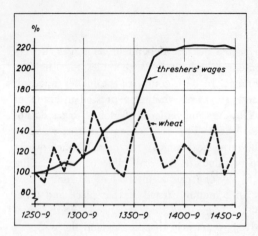

Fig. 4   Threshers' wages and wheat prices in England 1250–1459 (money of the period 1250–9 = 100).

but according to his own statements the population of Old Germany was still increasing rapidly even after the migrations (1885–6:11, 617).

A better explanation of the German wage rises, and one that includes France and England as well, lies in the contemporary development of industry. The thirteenth and fourteenth centuries were the period of the 'first industrial revolution'[13] of Germany and central Europe. The towns, with all their industrial and commercial activities, were growing at a great pace. Perhaps the purely technical progress was less important than the increasing division of labour (to which Adam Smith first drew attention). This meant that people produced more, with the result that not only was the 'difficulty of providing a growing population with sufficient food' overcome but that the growing population could be better fed than before. Not until the nineteenth century, in the time of the 'second industrial revolution' – admittedly on a far greater scale – was such a state of affairs to occur again.

2   The fourteenth-century recession

The agrarian decline and its underlying causes

The downward trend in the agricultural market

Intensified interest in the late medieval slump aroused by the first edition of
this book has called forth not only sundry corroborations and supplements but
also some objections concerning the causes and extent of the long-lasting depression (of which more later) and the date of its beginning (see Graus, 1969).[1]
Three or four starting-points quite far apart in time have been suggested: the
end of the thirteenth century, the second decade of the fourteenth century, and
the middle or the last quarter of the fourteenth century. Although these estimates
may sound incompatible, the events they are based on were probably inter-
connected in at least two, perhaps even three, of the cases. During the last
quarter of the fourteenth century there was a long-term decline in prices. In mid-
century the Black Death, which was a distant if not the immediate cause of the
decline, swept over Europe. In the second decade of the fourteenth century the
west European lands were stricken by severe and persistent famine, leading to the
fall in population that lay behind the agricultural decline of the fourteenth and
fifteenth centuries.

On the other hand, certain events that took place in the thirteenth century
were not related to the long-term slump either as cause or effect. Of these,
particularly, were the difficulties that occurred in territorial lordship in both
Germany and England. Two examples will clarify my drift.

From Germany we have an inquiry (Sattler, 1962) into the financial position of
a group of sixteen knights of Ortenau, between the Rhine and the Black
Forest. It is based on an inventory of sales and mortgages of the knights' estates.
In the decade 1280–9 the value of the sales was 59 German pounds. Between
1310 and 1319 it rose to 4,500 German pounds and then dropped again, but

still remained far above the 1280–9 level during all the rest of the period under review (up to 1390–1400). Sattler concluded from these figures that there was an economic 'crisis' among landowners that began quite early and finally flowed into the general agrarian depression of the fourteenth century. He considered – and rightly – that in the late thirteenth and early fourteenth centuries the debasing of currency played a decisive part. One result of the repeated reduction of silver content in the coinage was that the purchasing power of the knights' cash revenue declined, for probably a large part of it was in fixed amounts.

Raftis (1957:218f., 232f.) has published reports of difficulties in England towards the end of the thirteenth century. From Ramsey Abbey, the possessor of numerous estates and rights in the area north-west of Cambridge, came complaints that the abbey's revenue no longer covered its expenses. That may, however, have been chiefly due to the royal taxes which began to grow heavier in the middle of the thirteenth century. In accordance with the findings of price history, Raftis emphasizes that agricultural prices were still relatively high; the decline in the cultivated area, which is also reported, may have had causes outside the field of market economy.

The Ghent historian, Verhulst, who has written on the events and significance of the late medieval depression, is also of the opinion that the roots of the trouble can be traced back to the end, perhaps even to the middle, of the thirteenth century (Verhulst, 1964*b*:232f., 1964*c*). Among the causes he names, the shortage of land takes first place. While that factor undoubtedly exercised an influence on the price of agricultural products and on rents (in the Ricardian sense), these did not benefit the stock-farmer of enclosed land who, again according to Ricardo, depended only on the returns from labour and capital. For the smallholders whose production was for home consumption alone, a shrinking acreage meant a lower standard of living; it might even drive them below the biological mimimum necessary for life.

The crisis of feudalism

The latest and most penetrating study of the 'crisis of feudalism' to date is by Guy Bois (1976). His field of research was the eastern part of Normandy, an area developed early, densely settled and by the middle of the thirteenth century cultivated up to the limits of tillable land. Production faltered, lordly incomes stagnated or even fell. Confused coinage, financial difficulties and military disaster added to the trouble. The 'system' was stretched as far as it would go.

From that point Bois follows the developing stress, which in the course of time resulted in a triangular lord-peasant-land situation. Bois's work is carefully thought out and thoroughly verified, and while largely agreeing with his thesis, and in no way denigrating its value, I consider some questions and remarks on the origins of the feudal crisis still remain to be put.

Firstly: Bois's observations on a region of Normandy can be extended to the most densely settled areas of western Europe where land was becoming short, for example in parts of England, Flanders and western Germany. (In central Germany, and still more east of the Elbe and Saale, clearances continued well into the fourteenth century.) As the land shortage grew, rents tended to rise. Even though the general trend did not produce the same results in all regions or among all groups or even individual receivers of rent, it cannot well be doubted that in most of western Europe feudal rents rose in accord with farm rents. Various data concerning land prices and tenants' payments are to hand to confirm the point.

For the rest: the land shortage (here and there) of the later thirteenth century merged into an abundant availability of land in the fourteenth and fifteenth centuries. The feudal crisis followed the agrarian crisis, and it is difficult to unite the two under one roof. If one takes production, or, more exactly, farm production, as the backbone of the economy, it must be observed that at the end of the thirteenth century the (natural) yield of labour sank owing to the ever wider exploitation of land, while during the fourteenth and fifteenth centuries it rose again because of the general retreat of cultivation to more fertile ground. If we turn to the institutional and structural situation, it is beyond doubt that feudal pressure intensified the crisis resulting from the changed man/land ratio in the fourteenth and fifteenth centuries, but it is not clear how that crisis could have arisen from the feudal system.

Jurgen Kuczynski was of another opinion (1963:284f.). He rejected the hypothesis that population decline had finally caused the change in production, prices and incomes. He thought that where the feudal system was fully developed an agricultural crisis could arise only as a crisis of feudal production processes, and not as the result of natural phenomena such as a high death rate brought about by epidemics. He thus evades the question of timing by setting the feudal crisis in the fifteenth century; the fourteenth century he sees as a period when feudalism was still in 'full flower'. In this view, therefore, the agrarian crisis cannot be attributed to the fourteenth century but must have dated from the fifteenth. In so far as deserted villages are concerned his position has been challenged (Rubner, 1964:433f.). It is difficult to see how the population factor can be discounted when deserted villages and similar signs of crisis are under discussion. Kuczynski has not as yet replied to that question.

My book has been criticized for a certain narrowness of conception. True, it presents a 'pattern' of economic development, but does not relate it to the social and institutional side of events.[2] No historian, however, can be blamed for putting in the foreground aspects of his subject that interest him most; others may build further. Here it is the phenomena surrounding agrarian booms and slumps that will be described and interpreted.

These phenomena include prices. The extent of their influence depends, of course, on the strength of the bonds that unite prices to the other economic and social forces. Caution, but also perception, are essential for not only near-contemporary events affect prices but also those far removed in time. That will become clear when we examine circumstances that arose many years before the long-term movement of prices, but which in my opinion were related to the price movements.

The famine of 1315–17

Its extent and severity

A long, hard winter, a wet summer, hail and floods brought on the famine in the second decade of the fourteenth century, a famine that in its duration, severity and extent far surpassed all (recorded) earlier dearths – and there had been many. It began in the years 1309–11 in south, central and west Germany and to some degree in England, was interrupted by a few better harvests, and then broke out once more and spread. In the years 1315–17 the afflicted area included England, France and the Scandinavian countries, Belgium, Holland, the Rhineland, Westphalia, south Germany, Brandenburg and the Baltic coast deep into Russia (Carpentier, 1962:1062f.).[3]

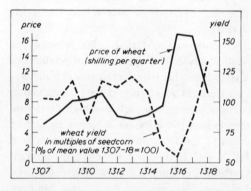

Fig. 5   Wheat prices and yields in Winchester 1307–18.

In England there are documents that enable us to calculate the degree of harvest failure during the critical years. The records of the bishopric of Winchester, quoted earlier (see figure 2), can be used to reconstruct the grain prices of the thirteenth century. Titow (1959–60:36of.) arranged the wheat yield figures (entered in the episcopal account books as multiples of the seed wheat used) and the wheat prices into the series from which figure 5 has been compiled. As the graph shows, the harvest of 1310 was already noticeably (about 16 per cent) below the average of the years 1307–18. There followed a few good years and then the years of hunger began: in 1315 the wheat yields on the bishop's estates dropped below the 1307–18 average by 36 per cent, in the next year the figure was 45 per cent and in 1317 the deficit was still 13 per cent.

In Winchester between 1313 and the middle of 1317 the price of wheat increased threefold or, from the lowest price in 1313 to highest recorded price in 1317 (24 shillings) nearly fivefold (Titow, 1970:345). From Strasbourg Hanauer (1878:91) reports a trebling of rye prices during the same years; in France, according to d'Avenel's somewhat sparsely-based estimate, the average price of wheat increased ninefold. The dearth even reached Norway, as we can see from King Haakon's edict of 30 July 1316 (see Naudé, 1896:210), by which the export of stockfish and butter from Norway was permitted only to those who imported malt, flour and similar commodities in their place.

'The date of this famine', wrote Spangenberg in the *Mansfeld Chronicles* (1585:1, 206) 'lies in the last word of this line of verse

Ut lateat nullum tempus famis ecce
CVCVLLUM.'

By transposing the letters of that word we get MCCLLVVV, so that the poem gives the year 1315. According to other evidence the shortage grew even worse in the years that followed. The chronicler of the Cistercian monastery at Camp in the region of the lower Rhine recorded that in 1317 men were eating animals found dead. This caused so much disease that in many places the graveyards had to be enlarged and whole villages died out. In 1318 or 1319, perhaps as a consequence of harvest failures, England suffered from a cattle epidemic that brought serious losses. On one of the Ramsey Abbey farms in 1319 forty-five out of forty-seven beasts perished (Raftis, 1957:319). In a letter to the king (dated September 1319) the Abbot of Ramsey complained of the abbey's poverty, adding that a pestilence had attacked the cattle so severely that their many corpses poisoned the very air and human beings were becoming infected by the disease.

From accounts of the death duties (heriots) paid by the Winchester estates Postan and Titow (1958–9:392f.) deduced that the 1317 death-rate was more than double the average for 1310. In some Flemish towns there are old account-books giving details of the expenses incurred by the town council for the burial of what were probably only the poorer inhabitants. In the town of Ypres between 1 May and 1 November 1316 these funerals numbered 2,794, yet the total population in 1310 had been only about 20,000 to 25,000 inhabitants. That brings the death-rate to 10 per cent of the population, and it was probably even higher (van Werveke, 1950b:11).

Of Germany, Spangenberg's *Mansfeld Chronicles* report that in Thuringia, and especially around Erfurt, many fields were left untilled for seven years.

Because nothing but weeds grew in the fields, and provisions in the town were all consumed, many people sickened and died of starvation. They lay in the streets surrounded by so many dead that in Erfurt the carts were halted so that the cadavers could be loaded on to them and conveyed to Schmiedistedt where sundry graves had been prepared, and here the survivors buried them.

According to the Thuringian-Hessian *Chronicles of Gerstenberg* some people, many of them house-owners, left all their goods standing and went into foreign lands. Where they went we do not know, for better conditions were hard to find anywhere. The Prussian chronicler, Kaspar-Schutz, tells of many deaths from pestilence, perhaps from famine-typhus or dysentery. Many thousands died in the towns, he says, but more still among the peasants in the countryside, 'so that almost all the land lay waste and there was no one left to till the fields' (see documentary evidence in Abel, 1976:86ff.).

The population decline, which became even more pronounced in the middle of the fourteenth century, may have been started by the famine of the earlier years, even if the next generation soon filled the gaps left by the great hunger (Watts, 1967:54f.). Watts pointed out that after the 'temporary check of the great famine' land was once more tilled, sometimes more intensively than before; yet on the continent many fields and villages remained deserted (Abel, 1967:88). The long-term population movement, which extended far into the fifteenth century, was determined by the short-term fluctuations in the death-rate early in the fourteenth century. The next of these fluctuations, which will be reported after a brief digression, rose still higher and influenced the long-term population trend to a still greater extent.

Were western and central Europe over-populated?

The effects of the great famine of 1315 must be distinguished from its causes. In Postan's opinion western and central Europe were over-populated in the early fourteenth century (1959–60:77f.). The population of England during the twelfth and thirteenth centuries increased by at least 0.4 per cent annually. Farms were split up and smallholdings grew in number to such an extent that very few concerns could pay their way. Entry fines and uncontrolled rents went up and new settlements were often made on marginal land capable only of production well below the average. Postan considers that, at the low level of yield obtained even on the better soils, it would have been hard in Europe to maintain above the hunger line even half the population of western Europe estimated by Beloch at (a grossly over-estimated) 100 million. And yet there can be little doubt that production on the peasant farms was lower than that used in Postan's estimates.

Postan's over-population theory, partly based on the late thirteenth century 'feudal crisis', is supported by evidence from other countries (see page 37). Genicot deduced that already in 1289 there were three villages in the county of Namur in which respectively 38 per cent, 54 per cent and 73 per cent of the peasants owned less than 4 hectares apiece. The division of farms was particularly marked near the towns, but also, according to Genicot, reached danger point in many of the villages (1962:5f.).

The question is whether these reports amount to a proof that there was general over-population. It seems unlikely when we look at the towns, which were still capable of absorbing more people, as the rising, or at worst constant, real wages bear witness. We must remember the description of the 'first industrial revolution': industrial labour and commerce produced more goods. That may have compensated, even over-compensated, for the increasing agricultural difficulties, as it did during the later industrial revolution. Students of the symptoms of over-population in the history of western and central Europe will find a much fuller range of symptoms, falling real wages included, in the years around 1600 and 1800.

However, a certain population limit may have been reached. Population and over-population can only be judged in the light of contemporary technical, economic and social conditions. A simple calculation may be of use here. Assume that in the year 1300 the area contained within the 1930 boundaries of Germany had 13 million inhabitants, that is 24 to the square kilometre. (And this may well be a minimal figure. The estimated population density of France at that time was 35 to the square kilometre, that of Flanders at least 60 per square kilometre.) Assuming further that the annual consumption of bread grain was 150–200 kilograms per head of the population and that the yield per hectare was 750 kilograms, then an area of about 4.3 million hectares for growing bread grain, and further arable area three to four times as large, some 15 million hectares, would be needed to feed the population. That would be roughly a third of the whole country, nearly the same proportion as was cultivated in Germany in about 1800 (33 per cent). This is perfectly possible, for there was considerably less grassland in 1800 than in 1300 – in 1300 the plough had bitten far more deeply into the woodland, as we can still see from the 'fossil' fields in present-day woods and scrubland.

Thus the arable area was very big in proportion to the whole country; but the yield was low. That is important, because the smaller the seed/yield ratio, the more damaging is a crop failure. When with a seed/yield ratio of 1:3 a third of the harvest is lost, the available food supply is already halved, since half the remaining corn must be kept for seed. This ratio was the deciding factor in the famines of the pre-industrial age. It can already be observed, among other things, in the hardly less severe dearth of 1437–8, when the population of western Europe, compared with that of 1300, had shrunk by little less than a third.

With the proposition that crop failures, famine and the consequent epidemics account for the population decline of the fourteenth and fifteenth centuries,[4] we fall back, consciously or otherwise, on Malthus' theory of the endogenous population cycle. (The population, according to Malthus, has a constant tendency to increase beyond the means of subsistence, and can be kept down to that level only by the constant operation of the strong law of necessity.) Malthus' theory of the control of population by food supply does not stand up to the facts of history. The plague, which claimed far more victims than the famine of 1315, came from the East. It was an exogenous factor in the movement of European population.

This theory certainly promotes chance to a higher place than the mind seeking an unbroken chain of cause and effect is willing to afford it. It is also obvious that the rate of population growth in the high Middle Ages could not have continued, for, had it done so, the population of modern Germany would have been nearly 250 millions by 1930. In spite of that, the endogenous population cycle of Malthusian theory is unacceptable. Nor can the Hundred Years War in France, or the Thirty Years War in Germany, be blamed for the shortage of food. It can only be said that the history of population in western Europe presents problems which have not yet been solved and perhaps never will be, at least not along the simple, naturalistic lines of Malthus.

The Black Death of the mid-fourteenth century

The decline of population in Europe during the plague years

The Black Death – a bubonic plague characterized by black boils and abscesses – was brought into Europe from the East towards the end of 1347. From the

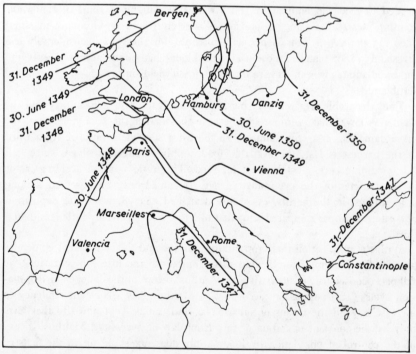

Fig. 6   The Plague in Europe 1347–50 (after E. Carpentier).

Mediterranean coast it spread out in waves over France, Spain, England, west Germany and the northern and Baltic countries, as shown in figure 6. Few regions were spared. Among those that escaped were parts of the Netherlands and Belgium, a few districts at the foot of the Pyrenees in France, and large sections of Poland and Bohemia. However, in Bohemia, until recently considered to have been free of plague, Graus has established that there was an outbreak in 1350. Even where the records are silent one cannot be sure, as Carpentier stresses, that a place was necessarily immune.

Documentary evidence is especially meagre in rural areas. A document from Languedoc mentions that the death rate was particularly high among the peasants (*potissime cultoram et agricolarum*) but that is unlikely. Equally unreliable is the assertion of the German author, Hecker, that, according to contemporary evidence, 200,000 hamlets and villages had lost all their inhabitants. However, reports such as that of Heinrich von Hervord that in Westphalia there were no herdsmen left to look after the cattle and no reapers to cut the corn, are confirmed by many contemporary documents. We also have a few relevant figures from France: in three parishes south of the lake of Geneva the number of households (*feux*) sank from 411 in the year 1347 to 197 in the year 1349, thus to fewer than half (Duparc, quoting Carpentier, 1962:1065).[5]

One would imagine that there were fewer deaths in the country than in the towns, with their narrow streets and stream of traffic, but there is no proof of it. The chronicles and the few available figures suggest a decline in rural population on much the same scale as among the townspeople. At least these figures render invalid a theory put forward by Kelter (1953:175). He sets the urban death-rate (though without giving his sources of information) at 35 per cent but the rural rate at only 20 per cent. From this he concludes that there was an 'overspill' of rural population which explained the continuous influx of countryfolk into the towns. It is true that many people moved into the towns, but that an 'overspill' of rural population existed is out of the question as the lost villages, among other things, bear witness. The migrations had other causes (see p. 53).

The older generation of historians (Rogers, Cunningham, Denton, etc.) estimated that deaths in England during the years of the Black Death amounted to one-third to half of the population. A later assessment (Russell) puts the decline at 20 per cent during the first wave of the epidemic at the end of the 1340s and at 40 per cent during the subsequent plague years between 1360 and 1375. Bean's more recent research establishes that, although the death-rate varied widely from place to place, the mortality over the whole of England during the years 1348–9 was probably about one-third (Bean, 1963:423f., Russell, 1958).

Levasseur thinks that France's population just before the Black Death was 20–22 million, a figure not reached again until the early eighteenth century. Paris numbered 80,000 inhabitants (Dollinger, 1956:35f.).[6] In some parts the rural population was as dense as it is today, in others even more dense. In the past it was thought that within a few years the population of France was halved. Later, more careful investigation of individual town, rural districts and social groups gives a quite different picture. The loss varied between one-eighth and two-thirds of the inhabitants. For the whole of France a mortality in excess of one-third of the population in the worst year of the plague (1348) is still considered probable.

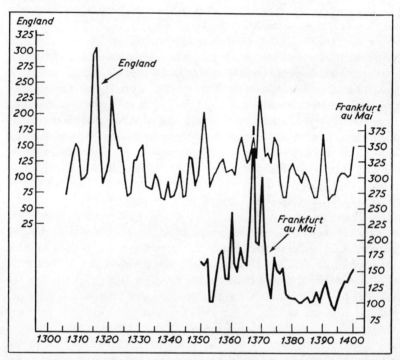

Fig. 7   Prices of English wheat and Frankfurt rye in the fourteenth century (contemporary money).

Northern historians have reached similar conclusions. In Sweden and Denmark it is conjectured that one-third to half the population died during the years 1349–50. In Norway a household tax known as Peter's Pence gives a clue. After the Black Death the tax yield dropped by one-third or slightly more. Since the loss of individuals must have been higher than the loss of 'households' the conjecture that Norway's population as a whole declined by one-third seems justified.

For Germany there are some statistics from the Hanseatic towns. Reincke's researches (1951:9f.; 1954:88f.) show that 18 out of 40 butchers died (45 per cent), 12 out of 34 master bakers (35 per cent), 27 out of 50 civil servants (54 per cent) and 16 out of 21 town councillors (76 per cent), thus, from 145 men whose fates are known to us, 73, or more than half, perished during the plague years. In Luneburg 36 per cent of the town councillors died in the years

1349–51; the same group in Wismar lost 42 per cent of its members and in Reval the figure was 27 per cent. In Bremen there was a census of roughly 7,000 plague victims, to which must be added the 60–70 per cent unidentified inhabitants who perished. These figures, supported by numerous reports in the chronicles, make it safe to say that the death-rate in Germany was no lower than in other lands.[7]

The economic consequences of the Black Death

At first sight it seems incomprehensible that the epidemic in the middle years of the century had no immediate effect on the movement of grain prices. As Malthus said 'one should naturally have expected that after the great pestilence of 1348–50 the quantity of good land being abundant compared with the population, corn would have been very cheap. It was, however, on the contrary, dear' (Matthus, 1798). Corn prices rose. In England, according to Rogers, the price of wheat in 1351 was double the 1348 price (see figure 7).

Table 7 Profit and loss account from Cuxham Manor during the years 1332–3 and 1350–1 (in pounds and shillings)

Credit					Debit				
	1332–3		*1350–1*			*1332–3*		*1350–1*	
	£	s	£	s		£	s	£	s
Rents	5	8	1	18	Buildings and				
From cereal sales	33	10	20	2	inventory	5	11	3	17
Cattle	6	5	3	9	Wages	7	0	14	14
Animal products	2	7		17	Cattle	4	15	1	10
Sundries	3	0		13	Seedcorn	1	18	4	15
Unsold goods	7	3	6	7	Sundries	8	3	4	9
TOTAL	57	13	33	6	TOTAL	27	7	29	5

   That situation was also related to the depopulation of rural areas. There were not enough men to till the soil; moreover, they demanded higher wages from the people who had been spared by the plague. 'Many of those who survived', wrote Abbot Li Muisis after the great epidemic in France, 'grew arrogant and demanded high pay for their work. In many parts vineyards and fields were left untilled for lack of labour. Farmhands and servants presumed to ask for higher wages than usual.' Because of the shortage of labour, complained the Abbot of the diocese of Clermont in France, farmland was going to waste 'and farmhands and servants were demanding payment above the customary level' (Denifle, 1889:60; Vivier, 1920:206f.; Levasseur, 1900:500). It was much the same in Germany. The plaint in the German-language *Vienna Chronicle* (Pez,

1721:971), that 'servants and maid-servants now earn so much, they are hard to come by' was echoed in many other towns. Some citizens of Metz replied to a government inquiry that they would not accept land as a gift because the cost of cultivating it, wages in particular, was too high (Hertzog, 1911:34f.).

How the reciprocal relation between the wages and other costs of production on one side and the selling price of farm produce on the other affected the profits of farms is shown, for instance, by the profit and loss accounts of a southern English estate in a year before the Black Death and a year after it. Table 7 is a contracted version of Rogers' table (1866–1920:1, 68of.); the original prices have not been converted.

While the outgoings for 1350–1 exceeded those of 1332–3 by a bare £2, the income for the year after the plague was more than £24 lower. The drop in rents and the diminished proceeds from cereal sales are particularly marked, although cereals fetched higher prices in 1350–1 than in 1332–3, and there is nothing to indicate bad weather or crop failures. The cause lies in the decline of the arable area. There were just not enough people, either farmers or labourers.

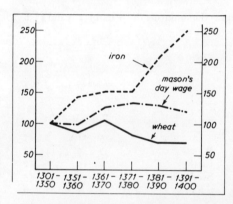

Fig. 8   Prices of wheat, iron and wages in England in the second half of the fourteenth century (silver content of coinage 1301–50 = 100).

This also answers Malthus' query as to why grain prices did not fall after the Black Death of 1348–50. As the arable shrank the supply of grain dwindled but, on the other hand, although there were also fewer consumers their purchasing power had increased. The many legacies they had inherited, together with the higher wages and prices, had given them a margin bigger than ever before. Francesco Berni (1469–1536), a poet of Rome, even composed a song in praise of the plague, because that 'golden time of pestilence' knew neither boredom, exertion nor poverty. Many contemporary writers described how the throng of newly-rich spent their overnight fortunes on riotous living. Another consequence of the Black Death was that food became enormously expensive in the years immediately after the plague.

Most English historians agree that the sharp decline of revenue from seigneurial rights did not continue; on the contrary, the value of the rights revived. This Levett was able to establish for the estates of the Bishop of Winchester and

St Albans Abbey. Holmes (1957:114f.) contributed evidence from a later time which suggested that, on the whole, the income of the English territorial lords up to about 1380 was not substantially – only some 10 per cent – lower than it had been in the 1340s. Some activities, such as sheep farming, were hardly affected by the pestilence, while the revenue of the territorial lords actually increased here and there through the lively commerce in rights consequent on the high death-rate.

In Germany too there were signs of nascent recovery not long after the plague. The land inventory of Emperor Charles IV is a reliable source of information about the villages of the Brandenburg Marches. Although it shows that even in the 1370s numerous places were still deserted or nearly so, there is also evidence of fields being reoccupied (for example, 195 hides in Uckermark). As these fields were entered in the inventory only when they were still tax-free, and the tax-free period was very short – two to three years at most – we may take it that in reality many more farms were reoccupied after the Black Death.

Perhaps the term 'counter-currents', coined by northern historians, best describes the developments of that time. In Denmark, as in Sweden and to some degree in Norway, there were already quite a number of deserted farms as early as the middle of the century, but some villages entered in the Bishop of Roskilde's land register of about 1370 had the same area, or even more, of arable as in earlier accounts; indeed, a few were new settlements. It was only *after* 1370 that the decline became serious in Denmark. Hardly a document relating to land purchase or inheritance of any importance is without its mention of *Ødegarder* (deserted fields). In the account books of the Skov monastery the 1467–81 incomes of 400 farms can be traced. They demonstrate the landowner's 'losing battle against the dereliction of the farms'. When we add this to the other evidence it is clear that 'it amounted to an economic depression' (A. E. Christensen, 1938:55f.; see, further, Abel, 1976:24f.).

The Great Death, as it is called in Norwegian documents, does not always take its rightful place in the considerations of some, and especially German, historians. However, it would be wrong to assign secular consequences to a single event; the regenerative powers of the late medieval population were too great for that. Birth-rates as high as 40 per 1000 have been recorded at still later dates. Furthermore, as Russell pointed out, it was pre-eminently the old, the weak and the very young who succumbed to the plague; fewer died among those in the prime of life. Moreover young people married earlier. Russell's opinion is confirmed by contemporary comment: 'After the plague, there were more weddings. The women were very fecund and brought two to three living children into the world at one birth' (Jean de Bel). Although we may feel slightly sceptical as to the frequency of multiple births, the age was indeed blessed with many children. The age structure of the population was changing, reflecting the economic and psychological consequences of the Black Death, such as the increase of wealth from the many legacies, the rise of industrial profits and wages, the love of living and the greed for life. Thus we cannot but share in Russell's conclusion that after the Black Death the birth-rate rose even higher – for a short time – than before. The population would soon have regained its original level if the first outbreak of plague had not been followed by others.

More will be said of this in the next chapter, for the effects of epidemics, and not of the Black Death alone, were the main cause of the agrarian depression of the late Middle Ages. Before we can discuss the causes of the trouble, however, its symptoms must be described.

3 The late medieval agrarian depression

Price and wage movements

Price movements in the late Middle Ages

It appears that a series of good harvests heralded the long-lasting slump of prices in the fifteenth century. The summer of 1375 was hot and dry, 'and in that year was an abundance of corn and fruit the like of which had not been seen for fourteen years' (*Limburg Chronicle*). In Alsace the harvest of 1375 produced more corn than could be used, and so many fruitful years ensued that people 'grew tired of them' (Hanauer). The silver value of rye in Nuremberg dropped from 74 grams of silver per 100 kilograms in April 1375 to 33 grams per 100 kilograms in 1376 (Hegel, 1862:256).[1] A few years later (winter 1382–3) it was recorded in the *Augsburg Chronicles* that 'corn was cheap in the German lands'. In 1395 the bakers began to make farthing loaves because 'a pennyworth of bread is too much for one man to eat'. 'Nothing like it has been seen before' reported the Alsatian chroniclers (see extracts in Hanauer, 1878:81).

At about the same time prices started to fall in England. In 1375 the expectation of a plentiful harvest kept the price of grain somewhat below that of the previous year. Next year it was considerably less and by 1377 it had reached its lowest point for thirty years (Rogers, 1866–1902:I, 214). The level dropped still further during the next few years. In 1381 the English parliament announced that 'the commodities growing in the realm are now of smaller price than they ever used to be, and the merchandises which come from abroad are of greater price than they used to be' (Holmes, 1957:116).

The arrival of the new century did not halt the fall in cereal prices, though it was interrupted by short-term fluctuations. Divided into 25-year averages in which these ephemeral movements are hardly perceptible, the price of grain in western and central Europe reached its nadir in the second half of the fifteenth century. This can be seen in figure 9, compiled from the same price data as table 1 on p. 304 of the appendix. The few divergencies between the price movements are probably due to political circumstances such as the Hundred Years War in France, to inadequate documentary evidence or to other reasons that will not be discussed at this point. They did not affect the overall downwards direction of prices, which is revealed in the available information.

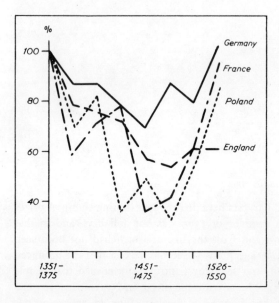

Fig. 9   Grain prices in western and central Europe 1351–1550 (twenty-five year averages).

Apart from the prices shown in figure 9 and repeated as 10-year averages in the appendix, we have some further information that unfortunately does not lend itself to statistical or diagrammatic treatment. From Königsberg in Prussia there is a price series assembled by an unknown author from the account books of the Order of Teutonic Knights and converted into Königsberg measures (scheffels) and silver[2] (*Deutsche Vierteljahresschrift*, 1850:159; see Naudé, 1901:619). The information, apparently collated with great care, has one fault: the author of this 'fairly complete series', which is assembled into 40-year periods has 'for the sake of brevity indicated only the value prevailing in the most significant years'. The converted series is shown in table 8, from which we can see that the price of rye in Königsberg fell between 1399 and 1508, and then slowly began to climb again, thus coinciding exactly with the price movements in England, France and western Germany.

In lower Austria, too, where consecutive price series earlier than the mid-fifteenth century are not to be found, it is quite likely that prices also fell during the first decades of the century. On the basis of some isolated data from which the years of abnormal inflation and cheapness have been eliminated Grund

Table 8   Rye prices in Königsberg (in grams of silver per 100 kilograms)

Date	Price	Date	Price
1399	18.2	1494	9.0
1405	16.2	1508	8.5
1432	15.5	1536	14.7
1448	14.5	1556	22.1

(1901:213) estimates that the price of grain in lower Austria fell by about 35 per cent during the fourteenth century.

There are no grain price series from northern Italy in this period. Some flour prices from Venice (Magaldi Fabris, 1878:47f.) suggest that cereals were cheap there between 1436 and 1477, but no certain conclusion can be drawn from so few and such varied prices.

When we speak of a downward trend in grain prices it is in relation to the precious metal content of the currency, the *bonitas intrinseca*. Owing to the continual debasement of coinage during the late fourteenth and early fifteenth centuries, the *nominal* value of grain mostly went up or at least remained constant. From there it is not a far cry to the notion that this debasement was the cause of the fall in prices when reckoned in precious metal, especially as nominal prices did not, in fact, always react to the reduction of silver in the coinage with a proportional rise. This explanation, setting the reason for the falling prices in the realm of money, becomes more convincing when it is remembered that the reduction of gold and silver content in the coins accompanied a decrease in the overall amount of precious metal in circulation. D'Avenel (1894–1926:I, 23f.) refers to the growing use of gold and silver for jewellery, furnishings and other domestic uses, as well as the hoarding that was so frequent during the war-stricken times between 1360 and 1450, and the general decline of mining. Sombart, who followed the fluctuations of the production and circulation of precious metal even more exactly, concluded for a number of reasons that 'during the fourteenth and part of the fifteenth century the production of precious metals, particularly silver, was greatly reduced' (1919:I, 2, p. 522). Undoubtedly such a decrease in money, when not accompanied by a corresponding decrease in trading turnover, must have exercised pressure on the level of prices. But it does not account for the fluctuations of prices during the late fourteenth and the fifteenth centuries.

It was repeatedly stressed in the old literature that industrial goods were very expensive in Germany during the fifteenth century. In Saxony, according to Falke (1869:380, 386) two ells of the cheapest blue velvet cost more than a fat ox. Cuno (1929:50f.) says that the price 'of foreign goods increased while that of farm produce and land went down.... For instance, in the big towns of Wurtemberg in the early sixteenth century a lady's dress of moderately good quality cost 9–10 guilders whereas a morgen of good land could be bought with 2–3 guilders' (see also Janssen, p. 304).

Instructive though such isolated examples may be, they cannot take the place of consecutive price series. What is more, they may be no more than exceptions peculiar to one region. Therefore we shall try to construct and compare a few reasonably consecutive series from the many series contained in the works of Rogers, d'Avenel, Elsas and Pelc. For this purpose each price series and each wage series from the different countries has been converted to the intrinsic silver value of the coinage and arranged in 50-year periods. Then each series is compared with the base value (1351–75 = 100) and from the relative value of each group of commodities and wages the arithmetical mean is formed. The result of this calculation can be found in figure 10[3].

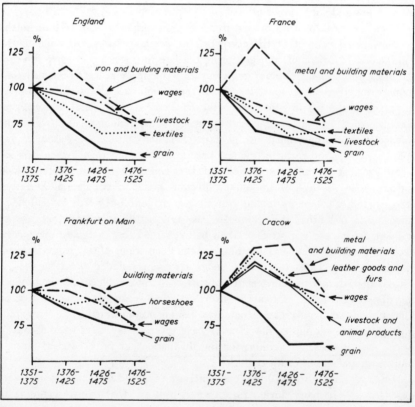

Fig. 10   Price and wage movements in western and central Europe 1351–1525 (50-year averages, silver content of coinage, 1351–75 = 100).

As the graph shows, the price of cereals sank rapidly after 1351–75 in all four countries and cities. Only gradually and after an initial counter-movement did the prices of livestock and livestock products, textiles, building materials and metals follow its downward course. Thus, contrary to Ricardo's rule for long-term price movements, the mid-fourteenth to mid-fifteenth century saw the purchasing power of grain decline in relation to livestock products in elastic demand and to industrial products.

An exception to that rule was to be found in some areas of north-western Europe. Genicot and colleagues established that in the county of Namur prices and wages pursued an almost parallel course (upwards in the currency of the time, downwards in the precious metal content of the coinage). The authors considered that demographic and political factors in Namur led directly – that is to say without the connecting link of prime cost/sale price ratios – to the agricultural depression, which was also apparent in their field of inquiry in the form of lower interest rates, overdue interest payments and temporarily deserted farms (Genicot, 1970: passim).

The golden age of the craftsmen

The purchasing power of grain also sank in relation to wages. It was a complex process. Sometimes wages stayed nominally constant but decreased in silver value, while the price of corn fell even more steeply; sometimes the wages nominally rose with silver remaining constant or falling only slightly; sometimes the silver value of the wage increased as well (as in Cracow between 1351–75 and 1376–1425). In each of these cases, which lie concealed behind the series shown in figure 10, the purchasing power of wages outstripped that of grain when compared with the years 1351–75.

Perhaps the ascent of real wages had started even before the Black Death in the 1340s, but after that time its pace accelerated. In many territories and estates wage ordinances were imposed, seeking to enforce maximum wage-rates that should be adhered to by both workers and employers. In Tirol (1352), Saxony (1466 and 1482) and the estates of the Teutonic Order of Knights (from 1406) the landlords established regulations to that end. Sometimes they referred to the rural depopulation brought about by the plague (as in the Tyrolean land ordinance of 1352), at other times blame for the high wages was laid on other employers who unscrupulously lured away servants and labourers with the promise of unduly high pay. Without doubt the wage ceiling itself went up, sometimes repeatedly, but even so the regulations were quite often broken. Thus in 1452 a farm labourer on the Prussian estates was supposed by regulation to get no more than $3\frac{1}{2}$ marks a year; the Knight Commander of Schönsee, however, is shown by the account rolls to have paid him 5 marks. It was the same in England. There a statute of Henry IV stipulated that a bailiff's pay should be 23 shillings, 4 pence, 'but at Hornchurch the bailiff receives double these wages,

and other servants also in certain years what is greatly in excess of these rates'
(Rogers, 1866–1902:IV; 118; and Abel, 1976:108).

Some of the most authentic wage series in Europe are shown in figure 10.
However, a few additions and comments may not be out of place. Here we
will return to the methods of the classic writers on peasant economy, who used
to express wages in measures of grain (corn wages). Cereals were the staple
food of the time, and food took up the major part of a labourer's or artisan's
wages. In this Albrecht Thaer and Johann von Thünen, the founders of modern
agrarian studies in Germany, followed the lead of the English political economists,
for not only the true value of the wage-earner's income but also its true cost
to the employer was best expressed in kilograms of grain. Cereals were – right up
to 1800 – agriculture's most important market product, and so the old method
of reckoning still remains the most suitable for the period.

According to Rogers' lists of prices and wages, an English mason in the
years 1301–50 earned the equivalent of 11.3 kilograms of wheat; in the 1451–75
period he earned 20.4 kilograms, almost double. Rogers' material was supplemented by information from Beveridge's study. From this material it is clear
that wages in southern England, again reckoned in corn, though over rather
different lengths of time, increased almost two and a half times (see table 9).[4]

Table 9   The wheat equivalents of wages in southern England

Period	Artisan	Labourer
1300–09	100	100
1440–59	241	236

In France it would appear from d'Avenel's figures that the wage of an unskilled labourer rose from about 7.6 kilograms wheat in the 1301–50 period to
14.3 kilograms in 1451–75. The accuracy of d'Avenel's data has been questioned.
Nevertheless, Perroy (1955–6:232f.), who had cast most doubt on d'Avenel's
estimates, himself quoted the example of the St Omer textile worker who had
managed to get three wage increases, one after the other, in the year following
the Great Death of the mid-fourteenth century, on the plea that the cost of
living had risen so steeply. He also reported a sharp rise in wages between the
years 1410 and 1430 on the estate of the Archbishop of Bordeaux and mentions
how well the villeins ate on the seigneurial estates. In spite of the doubts raised
about some of his evidence, d'Avenel's industriously-collected data from many
different places show the longer-term movements of prices and wages correctly.
That much has been confirmed by more recent research: in Saint-Denis the price
of grain between 1320–36 and 1467–74 sank by about 24 per cent, while the
nominal wages of masons and manual labourers in Rouen during the same period
increased two and a half times, so that in one hundred years their purchasing

power expressed in grain was trebled (Bois, 1976:76, 98, citing Fourquin and other data).

There were great differences in wage levels. It is difficult to grasp them accurately since coinage and quantities were so varied and can only with strict reservations be united on a common denominator. Let us do our best, however, starting with the single year 1379. For that year bread and grain prices and mason's wages are available from the south of England, from Antwerp and from Rostock. If the coinage is reduced to its precious metal content (grams of silver), the quantity of grain converted to units of weight (kilograms) and the masons' wages based on their purchasing power in grain, we get the figures shown in table 10.[5]

Table 10   Bread grain prices and masons' wages in 1379

	Rye or wheat per 100 kg in grams silver	Mason's day-wage in grams silver	Bread grain equivalent of wages in kg rye or wheat
England	41.3 (wheat)	7.8	19 (wheat)
Antwerp	21.0 (rye)	10.1	42 (rye)
Rostock	15.2 (rye)	5.6	37 (rye)

The table shows, as was to be expected, wide differences in both prices and wages. They may be partly due to the particular origins of the evidence and to errors in conversion, but they do reflect the various economic conditions in the districts in southern England and towns from which data were drawn. The downward slope of grain prices from west to east may already indicate the influence of greater consumption needs in the more-densely-settled west, although in the late fourteenth century the corn trade seldom took advantage of such opportunities. Wages, reckoned in silver, were less divergent, yet Antwerp stands out. In the purchasing power of wages expressed in bread grain, however, the building labourer in Rostock was not much worse off than his counterpart in Antwerp.

For Germany there is some supplementary information. In the municipal accounts of the city of Nuremberg Hegel (1862:1, 258) found mention of some wages during the last quarter of the fourteenth century. Two labourers, working for three days on the castle in 1377 earned 13 heller schillings; two builders who worked in the wood for two days received 11 heller schillings. Converted to the silver content of the coins, that comes to about 5 grams of silver a day. Hegel remarks that according to that figure wages were little different to those of the present day (then 1860!). In fact, he adds, 'it even came to more, because bread grain was only half as dear'. Unfortunately that cannot be confirmed. If, for the missing Nuremberg price of corn, we substitute the average rye prices for 1317–80 in the towns of Xanten, Frankfurt am Main and Brunswick, 100 kilograms of rye cost 21.6 grams of silver (according to table 2 in the appendix, part B), which would bring a day's wage for ordinary, unskilled labour in Nuremberg to about 23 kilograms of rye, compared with little more than 10 kilograms in 1860.

According to the *Runtinger Book* (quoted here from Eikenberg, 1976:286f.), a labourer in Regensburg between 1397 and 1403 received 3 Regensburg pfennigs per working day for carrying earth or loading it on a cart; the master plasterer and master mason earned 10 Regensburg pfennigs per day, while their journeymen probably got about 5–7 pfennigs. A zentner of rye in 1399 cost 9 Regensburg pfennigs. Given that the Regensburg zentner then equalled about 51 kilograms, the above wages would correspond to 17 kilograms of rye for an unskilled labourer, 28–40 kilograms of rye for a journeyman, mason or carpenter, and 57 kilograms of rye for a master plasterer or mason.

Franz Irsigler obtained some figures from Cologne (1975:303f.). He based the builders' day-wages available for the year 1374 on the retail prices in the Cologne market recorded in the household accounts of Hermann von Goch (1392–94). According to those, a day's wage for a carpenter, stonemason or tiler could buy 8 pounds of beef, half a lamb, 9 pounds of mutton, 3 chickens, 2 partridges, 1 hare, 37 herrings, 36 place, a medium-sized pike or carp, 3 pounds of honey, 4 pounds of rice or 87 eggs. Converted to rye, a better yardstick when comparing diverse times and places, a manual worker's daily earnings in 1390 amounted to some 24 kilograms.

The lowest wages yet discovered were paid during these years to navvies working in Frankfurt am Main (Elas, 1940: *passim*). In the 1380s, during the winter months, they earned only about 14 pfennigs or 2.3 grams of silver. In 1379 in Frankfurt rye cost 110 pfennigs an *achtel*. If an *achtel* in Frankfurt measures equalled 115 litres, or in my reckoning, 84 kilograms, and 1 pfennig was worth 1 heller in 1368 currency, then 1 pfennig contained 0.167 grams of silver and 84 kilograms of rye cost approximately 22 grams of silver. Accordingly, this labourer's daily wage, without food, came to about 10.6 kilograms of rye – always supposing the uncertain Frankfurt measure/currency ratio to have been interpreted correctly. Even this wage, considered very low for the fourteenth century, was considerably higher than those recorded in the wage and price registers several centuries later, in the age of pauperism (see below, page 000f., and Abel, 1974).

During the fifteenth century records of wages become more frequent. One of the earliest to bring a clear picture is a series of wages and rye prices from Göttingen between 1401 and 1640 (see figure 11). The wages were for chopping a load of wood, an unskilled labourer's work. The wage, calculated in rye equivalents, reached its highest point in the decade 1461–70, then declined until the second half of the sixteenth century, when it had fallen to about one-third of its maximum (Kullak-Ublick, 1953, using material from Göttingen archives). Figure 11 shows the curve of real (corn) wages. There were violent fluctuations.

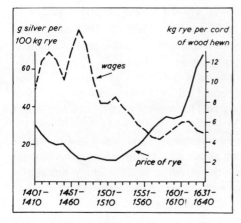

Fig. 11 Wages and price of rye in Göttingen 1401–1640 (trinomial 10-year moving averages).

While longer-term trends overrule these movements, the latter are far from useless, since they give a bird's-eye view of wages in the fifteenth century.

To that end we add a few more examples to indicate the average level of wages in the fifteenth century. We have van der Wee to thank for the extensive collection from Antwerp. After a conversion sum necessary for purposes of comparison, it appears that between 1437 and 1500 the average day-wage of a mason and his labourers was in the neighbourhood of 26 kilograms of rye (van der Wee, 1963a:1, 540f.).[6] For Rostock, too, there is quite a long series of wage entries (Hauschild, 1973:201). Taking an average from 54 years during the fifteenth century (between 1412 and 1498), for the 300 working days per year covered by Hauschild, a mason in Rostock earned an annual wage of some 229 scheffels of rye, or, if a Rostock scheffel then equalled about 40 kilograms, 9,160 kilograms, which comes to 30.5 kilograms a day.[7]

Table 11 Day-wages in Germany in the fifteenth century in kilograms of rye

District	Unskilled labourer		Mason	Carpenter
	without board	*with board*		
Alsace	29.7	18.1	37.6	25.3
Coblenz Valley area	20.5	10.1	27.5	27.5
Saxony	–	14.3	28.7	26.0
East Prussia	30.0	–	–	–
Holstein	–	14.5	25.0	20.0

Just to supplement these statistics, a few less-well-authenticated day-wages from various parts of Germany are shown in table 11.[8] These too, as far as possible, are calculated as averages for the whole fifteenth century. Of table 11 it need be said only that even the lowest wages seem quite high when compared with thirteenth-century or even sixteenth-century wages. Thus, for example, the wages with board of unskilled labourers in the Coblenz Valley (about 10 kilograms of rye a day) were twice as high as those paid to the corresponding group of workers in upper Alsace during the second half of the sixteenth century (about 5 kilograms of rye per day, according to Hanauer's list of prices and wages (1878)).

This is not the place to weigh the significance of these wages to a history of handicrafts. However, we might spare a glance for a group of craftsmen brought together for a special reason, namely the building of St Victor's Church at Xanten on the lower Rhine. Connected with this enterprise there are memoranda and accounts referring to the building administration, dating from 1356 to well after 1600, which supply us nearly year by year with information about expenditure, revenue, wages, prices and many other matters (Beissel, 1883, 1885).

First the men employed on this building: there were the master builder and his journeymen, stone masons, carpenters, joiners, tilers, smiths, paviours, glaziers, painters and bell-founders, to say nothing of the bargemen, carters, carriers and clerks, in all a motley crew, some of whom had come from far and wide – from Westphalia, Cologne, the Netherlands and southern Germany. Everyone was grouped according to his craft: a master craftsman with one or two journeymen, maybe an apprentice and a few assistants, joined together to work at a special task; but often a master carried out the work alone. There is little sign of social distinctions. Certainly a master craftsman valued his title (*magister* as it is called in the documents) but he was not too proud to work under another master on occasion, and sometimes individual tasks were entrusted to journeymen. In the same way there was generally no differentiation in the method of payment. Masters, journeymen and apprentices were all paid by the day. Only the master builder, who was responsible for the whole undertaking, received a bonus in addition to his day-wages, to remunerate him for his services as architect and overseer. Nor were the wages paid to the various ranks so very different. One example will do for many: Gisbert von Kranenburg, a master stonemason, who 'cut the stone for the church', but also was employed to build a bakehouse and a gateway, received in the summers between 1415 and 1424 a daily wage of 53 denari; each of his two or three journeymen were paid 40 denari. The apprentice received 15 denari, but he may have had to give some of it up to the master.

Finally we turn to the wages themselves. In Xanten, between the years 1340 and 1450, a master stone mason was paid the equivalent of 34 kilograms of rye, a master joiner 29 kilograms and a master tiler 30 kilograms. In addition there were occasional supplements and bonuses, such as danger money for the tiler working on the church tower, or extra payment to the stone mason for unusually careful work. In the same period a journeyman mason received money wages for which he could have bought about 28 kilograms of rye in Xanten. Of course he did not buy that quantity, for 2 or 3 kilograms a day in the form of bread were quite enough for him, and he could spend the rest on other things or save it up for feast days, of which there was no lack.

For it must be owned that the artisans did not overwork. Even in the high Middle Ages in Xanten, and no doubt elsewhere, there was a kind of five-day week, as can be seen from some day-wage payments in the randomly-selected years 1356 and 1495. In the first year, during the 49 weeks covered by the accounts, work was done on 250 days; in the second year there were 270 working days out of 53 weeks: thus an average of five working days a week. The remaining days were Sundays or the numerous holidays such as the feasts of saints Peter and Paul, Mary Magdelen, James and John, Laurence, Bartholomew, Matthew, Michael, Victor, the feast of St Peter's chains, the Assumption of the Virgin Mary, the feast of the 11,000 virgins, etc. – in fact a feast day as well as a Sunday in every week.

There is further evidence to support the view that the late Middle Ages were the great days of craftsmanship. One calls to mind the considerable number of craftsmen living in the cities (in Frankfurt am Main at the end of the fourteenth century 50–60 per cent of the inhabitants were of the artisan class (K. Bücher, 1886:148)) and their attitudes to their work, social life, guilds and to political power. The craftsman's income, moreover, matched his importance. When it was not spent on display it could become the foundation of a fortune. Indeed the late Middle Ages were not only the great but the golden days of the artisan.

Famine and slump

When historians are looking for the pervading, the continuous currents of history, they are forced to take a bird's-eye view. Setbacks in trade, harvest failures, cattle diseases disappear; even a war may escape their attention. The main trends stand out, not necessarily the situation in one particular place and time.

That applies particularly to the years of inflation, and there were plenty of those in the fifteenth century. Without enumerating them or wishing to describe them,[9] it must be said that in the very first years of the century the summers proved wet and hailstorms damaged the crops. 'It was a troublous time, especially among the poor, who suffered hunger and poverty', the *Mansfeld Chronicles* of 1401 and 1402 tell us (Spangenberg, 1585). During 1408, 1416 and 1426 there were further, if less disastrous, crop failures, and 1438 was a year of renewed and still more terrible poverty. 'In the 1438th year', we learn from Adami Ursini's *Thuringian Chronicle*,

> prices went up so high in Thuringia and other places that people were dying of hunger. They fell dead in the streets and villages and lay long

unburied. A morsel of bread no bigger than a nut cost a pfennig, which is why once a year in Erfurt they bake loaves of this size known as 'thrift-bread' in perpetual memory of that time. Furthermore, the corpses lay so long above ground that they infected the air and, over and above the high cost of food, brought a swift pestilence that killed yet more people than had died of starvation ... and at last there were villages, even small towns, left empty with no person anywhere to be seen.

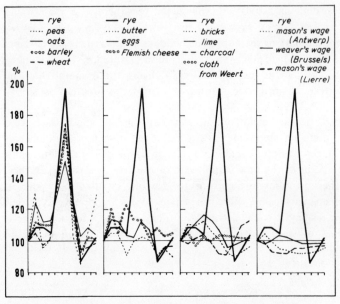

Fig. 12   Price and wage movements in the Netherlands in periods of poor harvest during the fifteenth century (after van der Wee).

It was inflation of this kind that inspired Labrousse's theory (described in the introduction) and also a study by van der Wee that goes back to the fifteenth century (1936*b*:209f.). From Netherlands sources van der Wee has worked out price-series for five years before and five years after each year of serious inflation. A series thus comprises eleven years. This produced eight cycles in all (centred on the years 1408–9, 1416–17, 1426–7, 1437–8, 1446–7, 1456–7, 1468–9, 1481–2), which he converted to a single cycle by taking the arithmetical mean. The impressive graphs that emerged are reproduced in figure 12. Reading the graphs from left to right reveals that during the bad harvest years:

1 The price of the staple bread-cereal (rye in the case of the Netherlands) rose more steeply than that of fodder crops and wheat.
2 The price of cereals rose more than that of livestock products in elastic demand.

3 The price of industrial products lagged still further behind.

4 In some cases wages dropped below their initial level.

The correlations are so clear that comment is almost superfluous. As grain prices increased people had to lower their standard of living. The poor had to exist on grain or grain substitutes. Trade stagnated. Hunger, even death from starvation, was the final stage in this sad sequence, and may have exerted an additional pressure on wages. When starvation stares one in the face one accepts employment, if only to keep body and soul together.

But it is open to question whether the shrinkage of agricultural yield during the inflationary years postulated by Labrousse and van der Wee was really as widespread and extreme as they maintain, and whether these depressions due to dearth, apparent only in this theory, were separate phenomena or merely part of the general late-medieval depression.

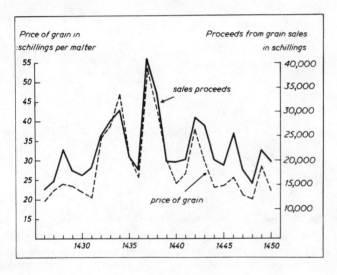

Fig. 13 The price of grain and the sales proceeds on the Hohenberg estate (Wurtemberg) 1426–50.

By luck we have some figures of cereal prices and sale proceeds from an estate in central Germany during the lean years around 1437, among the worst of the fifteenth century (K. O. Müller, 1959:11ff.). Figure 13 shows, that, although the price of corn soared, receipts from sales rose just as steeply. The reduction in the quantity sold (from over 900 measures in the early 1430s to about 770 in 1437) was more than made up by the increase in price, so that in the estate accounts the famine year stood out as the year of highest profit.

However, the importance of these isolated instances must not be exaggerated. If a piece of bread no bigger than a walnut cost a penny, money was flowing in such restricted channels that in the short run its redistribution was not possible. The few amassed wealth, the great majority grew poorer.

But how were things in the 'years of plenty'?

*

To distinguish the good harvests from the bad, and the low prices from the high, we must study all the years of the late Middle Ages. The mean annual price of grain could be used for the purpose, but then a good deal of extraneous material would intervene. Annual moving averages are more suitable, though with them we must accept that the periods into which the series are divided may vary somewhat according to circumstances. To avoid these variations becoming too big, it is best to use short divisions of time, but then again, the shorter the period the more frequent are the peaks and valleys. A middle way must be found. Seven years is the length of time that brings the harvest cycle most clearly into prominence.

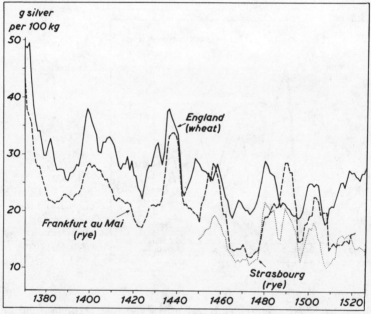

Fig. 14   Grain prices in England and Germany 1370–1526 (seven-term annual moving averages).

Figure 14[10] shows prices from England (Rogers, 1886–1902), Frankfurt am Main (Elsas, 1936, 1940) and Strasbourg (Hanauer, 1876, 1878). The agreement between the movements in England and Germany may seem surprising at first. The European countries were more involved with one another at that time than is always realized even today. However, the close agreement between the series was also determined by the fact that the climates of southern England (whence the

English prices came) and central Germany are affected by roughly the same weather conditions and therefore have more-or-less the same harvest fluctuations. The years of high prices established by van der Wee for the Netherlands, such as 1408, 1416 and especially 1438, are still very apparent.

Yet more striking, however, are the steep descents that follow such years. There are five in all and, as they are to be discussed further on, it will be best to date them.

1 After 1370, the prices in England being lowest in 1387, and in Frankfurt am Main lowest in 1383 and 1393.
2 After 1400, with lowest English prices in 1426, lowest Frankfurt prices in 1423.
3 After 1438, with lowest prices during the 1440s.
4 During the 1450s, with lowest English prices in 1473 and lowest German prices in 1464–5.
5 After 1480 with lowest prices (in Strasbourg) in 1484, 1495 and 1509.

The question is whether these years of agrarian slump were boom years for the late medieval economy. The answer could be lost in speculation, but there are some data that throw light on the subject, especially on agricultural income, which Labrousse also took as the basis of his argument.

Re 1: From England we have Rogers' report (1866–1902:I, 677; II, 608) of the two farm tenants of 1387 who had to be granted a reduction of rent 'propter vilitatem predii bladorum'. Maitland, Davenport, Postan and other English historians have added further evidence of rent reduction. For example, in 1384 a tenant of the Wilburton estate gave notice to quit the farm allotted to him because he could not afford the rent, upon which the land was made over to another peasant for 3 shillings instead of the 5 shillings that had been charged hitherto (Maitland, 1894:423f.).

In the Antwerp district between 1379 and 1385 rents for polders which were let to the highest bidder in free competition dropped by 25 per cent (van der Wee, 1963a:I, Appendix 40–1, 478).

A similar process was taking place in Denmark. There the rent which the inhabitants of Hedlinge were obliged to pay to the officiating bishop was reduced by a third of the amount their fathers had paid before them (C. A. Christensen, 1930–1: 461; 1964:257ff.; and Petersen in A. E. Christensen, 1966:219ff.).

In Germany the same sort of thing was happening. In the 1380s there were a number of entries made in the books of Diesdorf monastery in Altmark to record that the monastery *propter paupertatem* remitted this or that peasant's dues. Wentz (n.d.: 53, 55), who made a study of these accounts, remarks of one of these years (1386) 'in nearly every village there was a number of farms where the prior had reduced the sitting tenant's rent by several shillings'.

In Prussia and Poland the *Mehlmann Chronicle* announces that the Grand

Master of the Teutonic Order 'took the rents in grain and stored it in the castles by the water', at the very low price of 5 marks for a load (quoted by Naudé, 1896:258 from a manuscript he found in the Danzig Town Library).

Re 2: During the next downward movement of prices, lasting for the first twenty years of the fifteenth century, the English peasants' rents were reduced again, and sometimes more than once, by a third to a half as far as we can tell. Many farms were left vacant. For example, in Wilburton Manor five out of the total fifteen and a half farms, and from time to time ten out of the ten to twelve smallholdings. When the price reached its lowest level the export of corn was permitted – a rare occurrence in late medieval England, as Rogers assures us. The distress of the landed interests must have been great indeed if it forced them to allow grain to be released for export.

The steady, irresistible progress of the fall in prices is attested by some information from Constance. A council was held there between 1414 and 1418. At the request of the papal legate and the other spiritual and secular lords assembled in Constance, the town council had fixed and proclaimed carefully-considered ceiling prices for all food and feed-stuffs, for beds ('whereon two could lie with their blankets') and for wages. Further, a court of arbitration was set up to settle arguments on the matter. However, reported Ulrich von Richtental (1882:38f.), 'there came never a dispute before that court as long as the council lasted'. The controlled prices were adhered to and often undercut, although thousands of visitors with well-lined purses thronged the city. White bread cost one pfennig, and 'you could get as much as you wanted'. Meat was there in plenty of any kind desired; venison, fowl, pork, lamb or beef. Beef cost 3 pfennigs a pound and pork 4 pfennigs. There was some grumbling that hares, at 8 plapharts[11] apiece, were too expensive, but the chronicler, who heard it only at second hand, had his doubts: 'I have bought them for four', he writes. Wages were the only grievance. They went up and remained high even after the crowd of visitors – estimated to be 50,000 strong – had left Constance.[12]

Ulrich von Richtental attributed the low prices to the town's favourable trading situation, which had also played some part in the choice of Constance as a meeting place. Eberhard Gothein (1892:486f.) thought they were due to the activity of the many shopkeepers, bakers, etc. assembled in the city. The chief reason, however, was that prices stood low at that time outside Constance as well as in.

The chronicles do not tell us how the peasants reacted to the low prices. Peasants are sparing of words and make few appearances on the stage of history until they resort to arms. In the neighbourhood of Worms it came to a rising in 1431. The peasants marched to the gates of the city to demand the cancellation or abatement of their debts. There seems to have been no mention of prices, but it may be supposed that their debts grew heavier as less was paid for the goods whose sale was the peasants' only means of settling those debts. A glance at figure 14 shows that only a few years before the revolt the price of corn, reckoned in silver, was at its lowest point since the century had begun.

Re 3: After the great famine of 1437–8 bread grain prices dropped rapidly and (in Frankfurt am Main) continued to do so at a slower rate up to the end of the 1440s. In 1441 the Knight Commander of the bailiwick of Coblenz, once among the richest of the Teutonic Knights' possessions, asked the Grand Master to be relieved of his post, for, he said, 'the debts and annuities have grown too great and I cannot find the means with which to pay them, since corn and wine are not worth as much as in former years and yet I must sell much more cheaply than usual in order to buy bare necessities and to pay debts' (Abel, 1976:150f.). In Prussia the states' assembly in 1448 complained of the imports from Poland and the low Danzig prices: 'Thus when the knights and their men bring corn to Danzig, they must sell it at the Danzigers' price' (Toeppen, n.d.: III, no. 44).

More significant still is a letter of 11 November 1444 from the administrator of Dirschau to the Grand Master of the Teutonic Order, [14] in which we read:

> Knights and tenants declare that they suffer great loss when buying and selling in that they and their poor peasants have to sell their corn and goods very cheaply, but for the wares they want to buy in return, such as beer, salt, shoes and iron, they have to pay the highest prices ... then the servants, farmhands and serving-maids demand too high wages, and the more time goes by, the more they ask. The knights and tenants own it is because so many are deserting the land for the town ... but on that count they also complain of people coming into the country from Pomerania and Poland to flood the market in all our towns with the same goods that you and your poor subjects produce at home and must therefore sell more cheaply than ever.... They complain too that the charges are too highly assessed, as are also the rent of a morgen of land and the tithes.... Moreover they desire that the law should be changed so that no peasant may move away from his lord or landowner unless he has a letter freely given from the said lord or landowner, and that no other lord or landowner shall accept the peasant without such a letter from his former lord.

In this letter we have an account – indeed the first account – indeed the first account given in this form – of the basis upon which the Prussian peasant's bond to the soil was founded. The state ordinances of 1427, 1441, 1444 and 1445 had laid it down that if a tenant farmer turned his inheritance over to dependable hands in a satisfactory condition and at the right time, and paid his lord all he owed him, 'he could move to wherever he wanted'. It is true that already a letter of reference could be asked for, but if it was arbitrarily withheld the peasant was free to sue. Now the protective barriers were gone. By the time the letter in its new form became law – though that had to wait for the state ordinance of 1526 – the male half of the German rural population was, as Aubin pointed out, already tied to the soil, in practice if not in law.

But this, too, is only on the margin of our subject. The first part of the Dirschau document, dealing with prices and wages, is more important. In it the knights and lords grumble about the low price of their farm produce, while everything they have to buy is very dear. They complain about wages being out of proportion to the price of the agricultural goods they produce, and when it is added that not only the farmhands but the farmers too were leaving the countryside for the town, we have all the main symptoms of what was later to be called an 'agricultural depression'.

The expression dates from the nineteenth century, but in 1821 a British parliamentary committee appointed to look into the distress of British farmers stated with truth that: 'However much this revulsion is to be lamented, both as it affects the common interest and the interests and immediate prospects of a most meritorious class of the community, it is a revulsion of the same nature (whatever may be its degree) as many which have occurred in different periods of our history' (Select Committee on the depressed state of agriculture, 18 June 1821:4).

Re 4: However, prices in the 1440s were not the lowest of the fifteenth century. Between 1450 and 1469 they dropped still further till they reached a level where resentment grew louder or at least – to the historian – clearer both in Germany and abroad. In Saxony in 1474 the knights and administrators replied to an inquiry from the Prince Palatine with a detailed account of their revenue and expenses, their possessions and their debts (see long extracts in Schulze, 1896:378ff.). Some of the lords disposed of extensive seigneurial rights; dominion over ten villages or more was no rarity. Apart from these they nearly always had farms of their own. Yet neither of these sources brought in much revenue. The administrator of Beltitz stated that among all the men of good repute there was none could earn his living from his farm alone; they all agreed that they had to supplement it with their rents. Balthasar von Lipczk said he would be satisfied if he could lay aside enough to pay the interest on 300 guilders. Seiffard von Lüttichau in Grosskmehlen wrote, 'I needed some 100 guilders to buy new Sunday clothes, if the farms would yield that much, but they did not yield it'.

On the estates of the Diesbach monastery in Altmark during those years the peasants' dues had to be remitted, as they had been during the earlier depression in the 1440s, *propter paupertatem* (Wentz n.d.: 55). From the village of Franken in Upper Alsace it is recorded that in 1462 the tithes were no longer to be auctioned locally but in Altkirche, because the Franken farmers would not bid, seeing no advantage in such payments when the price of corn was so low (Mone, 1859:113).

That corresponded with the decline of interest and rent on leased land. In the years 1468–76 the polder near Antwerp fetched the lowest rents of the century per unit of area, 15 per cent less than in 1465 (van der Wee, 1963a:1, appendix 40/1, 478f.). Of the manor of Forncett in Norfolk, England, it was recorded that the yearly rent per acre sank from just 11 pence in the years

1376–8 to 9 pence in the first decade of the fifteenth century, then to $6\frac{1}{4}$ pence during the period 1451–60. In France, at the monastery of St Germain des Prés, rents went down from 84 denari per arpent in the middle years of 1360–1400 to 56 denari in 1422–61 and to 31 denari in 1461–83, although the silver content of the denari was debased during that time.

In places where the amount of silver in the coinage decreased even further, prices and rents might have remained nominally the same or even have risen slightly. That meant little as long as the price ratios were not altered, but, when they were altered the blame for the low prices was laid on the poor quality of the currency. In Prussia, for instance, where, during the Thirteen Year War with Poland, the silver content of the mark sank to one quarter of its former value, the assemblies complained continually of 'the inferior coins that ruin our country'.[15] The lords were thinking of the money dues that came to them in the devalued currency and the prices they received in Danzig. The prices were certainly low, if the silver content of the coins is considered, but it was not the fault of the coinage. Even reckoned in pure silver, grain was very cheap in many countries at that time. In Frankfurt am Main and Strasbourg between 1465 and 1473 it reached its lowest price level of the century.

Re 5: The last of the long-term price slumps of the fifteenth century, with its three successive downward curves most clearly evident in the Strasbourg prices, as figure 14 shows, extended into the first decade of the sixteenth century. But by 1484–5 the price of rye in Strasbourg was already nearly 75 per cent less than it was in 1481. This drop in prices, which was not confined to Alsace, formed the background of a suit decided in the Breslau law courts in 1485 (Franz, 1967:584f.). It concerned a peasant who wanted to leave his farm, and his landlord who did not want him to go. The farmer pleaded that he was too poor to run the farm and, in any case, had no children. He asked to be freed from his obligation. The landlord replied: 'If I allowed all my tenants to leave their land like that, my village would be deserted. In good times, when corn fetched a decent price he enjoyed the advantages of the situation. Now that corn is not worth so much he wants to leave the farm. I hope he will get a capable man to look after it as the law and good usage requires.' The court decided against the tenant: he had to obtain a substitute to run the farm if he did not stay there to work it himself.

After a short upward swing in 1489–92 the price of corn dropped again. The Archbishop of Magdeburg sent 300 wispels (a wispel being about 24 bushels) of his 'home-grown corn' to Hamburg, where part of it was sold for 15 marks, while the rest had to be stored and was not accepted by the Hamburgers as 'an ordinary purchase'. The archbishop complained and demanded its return, which the Hamburg authorities refused (Helbig, 1953:81f.). This happened in 1495 when, as the graph shows, corn was hard to sell, even at the lowest price.

*

Here we will leave our review of price series. There are two conclusions to be drawn from them. Firstly, that the historians of late medieval price movements and their effects on agriculture were right. The (relative) identity of the shorter- and longer-term phenomena is supported by the rather primitive method of sampling by periods which they have used to trace the economic trend of the late Middle Ages. The method is almost forced on them by the scantiness of the sources, but that alone would be a poor excuse if it were not justified by results. The short-term 'sample' reflects the long-term trend, in miniature perhaps, but clearly enough.

It must also be remembered that the agrarian depression was far more acute in some years than in others, when it might almost, if not quite, disappear. Farming was caught up in a cycle whose revolution brought years of plenty and superfluity interspersed with years of inflation and dearth. It is on the latter that Labrousse and van der Wee rightly laid stress. These years saw industrial crises as well, but it is hunger that hurts. It hurts more than the emptiness of money-chests drained by the low prices so much lamented by the lords, knights, and farmers in town and country.

But feelings cannot be our criterion, and the sources give us little else with which to measure the extent and severity of the late medieval depression. It remains only to say that the phenomena described above refer to two sorts of depression, the crisis of supply and the crisis of turnover. The latter was the dominant force by the last years of the late medieval depression.

Land utilization, rents and agricultural wages

The decline of grain cultivation in western and central Europe

In a Constance land register of 1383 stands the sentence 'Curia et agri in toto vacabant et fuit pascua pecorum' (farms and fields were left empty and used for pasture). That sentence is the earmark of an epoch which belongs among the darkest in the history of German and west European agriculture.

For England we have the verdicts of Postan and Beresford. From the study of almost 500 property registers it is clear that the law passed by Henry VII in 1489 was justified: 'where once 200 persons worked and lived by their honest labour, now only one or two herdsmen are employed. Farming is in decay, churches are demolished, the rites of the Church unobserved, the dead neither buried nor consecrated.'

Besides Postan's work and the results of Beresford's wide-ranging research in his book *The lost villages of England* (1954) we have the research results of the Deserted Medieval Village Research Group (mimeographed since 1953) and a number of occasional papers edited by Finberg. How depopulation and the dispersal of tenant farmers combined when arable was converted to pasture is shown by Thorpe (1965) through the example of Wormleighton village in Warwickshire.

It seems probable that in France, north of the Loire, where the war with England was raging, almost half the cultivated area had returned to waste after the middle of the fourteenth century. Even in 1484, thirty years after the English had left, the deputies of the États-Généraux reported that from Dieppe to Rouen they saw neither man nor farm. In southern France, too, practically unaffected by the war, there was rural depopulation, though to a lesser extent (d'Avenel, 1894–1926 II:275, 508; Levasseur, 1889:189; see also, among others, Bois, 1976 and Le Roy Ladurie, 1966). However, the same did not apply altogether to livestock and cattle rearing (which will be enlarged upon in the next section). Scholars interested in the history of woodland and forest found that in the Forest of Chaux (Department of Jura) between 1370 and 1450 the number of pigs, as well as of cattle, had increased enormously and that the woodland was overpopulated ('surpeupléee de porcs') (Rey, 1967:78).

In Denmark in 1500 there were vast tracts of land which two hundred years earlier had stood under waving corn but now lay empty and desolate (Nielsen, 1933:125; also particularly A. E. Christensen, 1938). Some property lists that have been preserved in Norway reveal that in one part of the country (Oslo district) two-thirds of the arable area existing in the first half of the fourteenth century had by the fifteenth century been converted to pasture (Holmsen, 1941; see, further, Schreiner, 1948). The tenants' payment in kind was now often in the form of dairy products in place of grain. Some units of property and debt in western Norway were entered under the heading of *laupsbol* instead of the older *mamatabol*, indicating that the rent was no longer payable in corn or butter, but in butter only (Hasund, 1933:193). In Iceland the cornfields disappeared completely.

For a long time Scandinavian scholars believed that the decline of the arable in northern Europe was due to a change of climate. But the climatic theory, which was also taken up by some German historians, is not convincing. Beyond vague conjectures it was not until quite recently possible to trace the past course of climate. No change of climate could be found to correspond with the period of rural depopulation, nor was it possible to explain why a deterioration in the weather – with lost villages and reduced production – should drive farming prices down and wages up. For these reasons we shall not discuss this theory further, except to add that Le Roy Ladurie, who made an extensive study of climatic fluctuations in Europe, believed he had established a slight improvement in the weather between 1350 and 1550 when compared with the period of land reclamation (1200–1350). However, he too rejected the theory that the changes in late medieval agriculture were due to climatic variation.[16]

In Germany evidence of the decline of the cultivated area comes not only from the abandoned fields (*Wüstungen*), of which more later, and from original documents, but also, during the last few years, from botanical research. By analysing the fossilized pollen grains found in peat layers formed in the late Middle Ages (for example in the moors of the Rhön, Solling and the Upper Harz mountains) it has been established that the proportion of cereal pollen in the total pollen count was much smaller there than in earlier layers (see pollen diagrams of Roten marsh in Abel, 1967:118, and in more detail in Abel, 1976:56).

Animal husbandry, special crops and the consumption of farm produce in income-elastic demand

'Et fuit pascua pecorum.' The unploughed fields could still provide enough food for cattle. In England sheep grazing expanded, as did cattle farming in Norway. England exported wool, Norway butter, and Hungary great quantities of livestock. Hungarian economic historians have estimated that in about 1480 livestock formed 55–66 per cent of the country's total exports to the west. The oxen, far the most valuable part of the trade, came mostly from the great pastures between the Danube and Theiss, where the citizens of the market towns possessed extensive grazing rights. The Debrecen pastureland stretched as far as 40 or 50 kilometres from the town in some parts. There the 'wealthy cattle breeders and traders of these towns ... kept vast herds, which they drove to market in Debrecen, Keoskemet, Szeged or elsewhere – indeed at times drove even further, either by themselves or by means of merchants in the town, to markets abroad' (Pach, 1960). In Vienna they often met German merchants who took over the transport of their beasts. The Hungarian cattle were driven on to Cologne or deep into south-west Germany. At a meeting on 24 October 1492, at which the town council of Cologne were trying to regulate the confused monetary system, it was said, 'Also let it be known to the gentlemen of the council, that all kinds of oxen are brought to market here, from Hungary, Poland, Russia, Denmark and Eiderstedt'.

At this time stock farming had increased enormously in Germany too, especially in relation to arable farming, and to population. Records of many village fields left untilled and used for grazing bear witness to that. I will give a few examples. From Swabia it was recorded in the Zimmern family archives of 1550 'that our descendants may not forget' ... 'many years ago' the villages of Engelswies, Grub-stetten, Reinstetten, Oberstetten, and Haldenstetten (all near Messkirch in the Baden area) became so neglected and derelict that no more than the walls of the church were left standing. The barons von Zimmern acquired these deserted places and, continues the chronicler, 'only because they were used neither for ploughing nor grazing, the old lord [Werner von Zimmern] put the land to no use himself but mortgaged it all for interest and a thousand guilders capital sum. Thus the citizens of Moskirch came to pasture all their cattle there and used it just as they liked.' In Altmark in 1444 the vacant fields of the hamlet of Mildenhöft were used for grazing by the neighbouring village of Zienau, as can be seen from a document of 1487 in which the Archbishop of Magdeburg granted Neuendorf monastery Lubeck '5 punths of the abandoned village of Mildehouedh, that the parish of Synou uses for pasture'. Research into the lost villages of Germany has brought hundreds of similar cases to light. Indeed, in a study of the Westerwald area it was asserted that the chief cause (!) of the villages' decay was 'the conversion of arable to pasture' (Becker, 1912:64).

That is true only inasmuch as the production of meat and wool was greatly encouraged by the growing purchasing power of the townsfolk. The demand for cereals is relatively inelastic. It changes with the size of population and, as we shall show, when population declined during the late Middle Ages so also did the demand for grain. The demand for meat, on the contrary, is elastic. It changes according to the income of the consumers, and since, at the end of the fourteenth and beginning of the fifteenth centuries, purchasing power became more widely distributed among the people, the growth of income could to some extent make up for the declining number of consumers by increasing the consumption of animal products.

Unfortunately it is not possible to gauge meat consumption during the twelfth and thirteenth centuries. It can only be established that by the late Middle Ages it was very high. Certainly in Germany it amounted to more than 100 kilograms per head per year. To justify this statement it is not even necessary to quote the meat consumption of the wealthier classes, a quantity that passes the imagination, to say nothing of the physical capacity, of twentieth-century people. The less-well-endowed sections of the population ate an enormous amount as well. From another source we learn that in Berlin, at that time a town of some 8,000 inhabitants, the consumption of meat in 1397 came to a daily 3 pounds a head. A Berlin regulation of 1515 stipulates that the bakers' assistants who were sent to the mill were entitled to a daily ration of 4 pounds of meat, 8 quarts of beer and plenty of bread. According to a bill of fare drawn up by Erasmus zu Erback of Odenwald in 1483, even the villeins got 'meat, bread and half a jug of wine twice daily, except on fast-days, when they may have fish or some other nourishing food' (see, further, Abel, 1967:122ff.).

Like livestock farming, the fish industry was 'relatively profitable'. Leingärtner, who has gone into the question of why so many fields in the Amberg district of Bavaria were turned into fish ponds during the fifteenth century, pointed out that in the Amberg tax-rolls of 1438 a pound of carp was stated to be worth 12 denari whereas a hundredweight of rye cost no more than 18.5 denari: thus a pound of carp was worth 66 pounds of rye. On this evidence he considered that fish had driven out grain (1956:87). It would be truer to say that fish had taken over as grain retreated. The Amberg evaluations, which have not been checked, seem to vouch for exceptionally high fish prices. With the help of other known fish prices it has been estimated that in the late Middle Ages herrings fetched ten times the price of rye, common table fish five times, per unit of weight (Abel, 1976*b*:24, 35).

Fruit, too, found a profitable market in the late Middle Ages. Johannes Butzbach, who knew the Rhineland well in the years around 1496, tells of a farmer who made a profit of 30 guilders in a single year at the Mainz market – and 30 guilders could buy about 7,000 kilograms of rye. In the big Rhineland towns there were people appointed to supervise the wholesale trade; *obsthocker* (fruit vendors) carried on the retail trade. There were market regulations for fruit, for example, no selling of fruit before the market was open, special fruit markets, market charges, and so forth. Attempts were made to encourage people to eat more fruit, not for its own sake, of course, but to discourage the excessive consumption of other foods. In 1476, for instance, the Würzburg senate ordered that christening-party refreshments should be limited to raw fruit, cakes, cheese, bread and Franconian wine.

Fruit brings us to the vine. Wine-growing in Germany was never so extensive as in the time of corn's deepest decline. Along the lower Rhine valley vineyards spread as far as Xanten. Wine-growing reached Munster, Göttingen, Brunswick and even Itzehoe and Preetz in Schleswig-Holstein. There were vineyards along the Oder and Vistula, around Torun, Tapian, Rastenburg and Königsberg in East Prussia. Winrich von Kniprode, Grand Master of the Teutonic Order (who died in 1382), allowed vinegrowers to come from south Germany and Italy to lay out the East Prussian vineyards in the southern manner.[17]

Industrial crops became more important. The flax of the Moselle region was famous; in Thuringia, especially around Erfurt, the growing of woad, saffron, aniseed and all sorts of vegetables spread apace. The cultivation of madder, the plant from which the highly esteemed Turkish red dye was obtained, undoubtedly expanded during the second half of the fourteenth century in the Speyer district, while in various parts of Germany hop-growing flourished. As early as the end of the thirteenth century the town of Lubeck let out farmland on the understanding that every year a certain proportion of it was to be planted with hops. There were at least forty hop gardens round Kiel in 1430. The town of Brunswick even prohibited the planting of hops on more than one-third of the town's arable, because it was feared that not enough cereals would be grown (Saalfeld, 1960:13).

Agriculture in northern Italy

The same sort of activities were still more prevalent in northern Italy. The rulers were the pacemakers; private entrepreneurs followed in their footsteps. A profit of 15–20 per cent on capital invested was quite usual. There was even talk of an 'agrarian revolution' (Cipolla, 1959:15f.; 1950:182; Dowd, 1961:143).

Underlying the improvements was an extensive irrigation system connected with the rivers and canals. The canals were built in the first place to serve the interests of trade (and the efforts of the dukes of Milan to create a regional state), but they benefited agriculture as well. The system formed a network of drainage and irrigation channels over the Lombardy plain and made it possible to run dairy farms on which the grass could be cut six to eight times a year. There arose a live-stock industry whose products, such as parmesan cheese, might be found in markets far from their homeland.

Then there was the cultivation of the mulberry to obtain the raw material for north Italy's flourishing silk industry. It is said that in Milan during the 1460s some 15,000 workers were employed in the textile industry. That industry required the dyestuffs supplied by agriculture. The richer citizens spent freely on fruit, table vegetables and the costlier dairy products.

Cipolla reproached his northern colleagues for not paying enough attention to these developments in Lombard farming. They do not fit in with the talk of 'late medieval agrarian depression'. So Cipolla, Dowd and other historians postulated a sort of antithesis: north of the Alps, stagnation and decline; south of the Alps, a dazzling growth of agriculture (Dowd) or as Cipolla expressed it 'with the beginning of the fifteenth century, rural investment developed with ever-growing intensity'. Cipolla compared it to the conquest of the West in nineteenth-century North America. 'Wide territories were won for agriculture,' he wrote, 'for houses, canals, dairy farms and pastures. It was this extraordinary growth of agricultural investment that maintained the upward trend of the whole economy characteristic of the century.'

This interpretation of events did not go unchallenged (see Miani, 1964:569f.; Romano, 1966:588ff.; Werner, 1969:223ff.).[18] It cannot be denied that similar developments, if not quite so marked, could be found in other parts of Europe such as the north German towns, the Rhineland and the north-western corner of Europe, in Flanders and Brabant. That suggests a continuum rather than an antithesis. From the livestock industry on the deserted village pastures of central Germany, through the sheep farms of southern England and the intensive cultivation of the Netherlands and Rhineland, to the irrigated fields and meadows of the Lombard plain runs a continuous strand connecting all these phenomena with one another and with *towns*:

1 The upward trend was not a matter of cereal-growing alone. The increase of agrarian activity included the more specialized products of farming, among which we must count rice – its cultivation was gaining popularity in Lombardy – and also in Lombardy as elsewhere in Europe, livestock products. Cipolla himself remarks that animal husbandry in northern Italy was expanding at the expense of grain-growing. The Duke of Milan, who wanted to see his land 'rich with wheat', ordered that on no estate might pasture take up more than a certain proportion of the farmland (Cipolla, 1963a:402).
2 The driving impulse of the development came from the towns or, more precisely, from their purchasing power. Agricultural products in income-elastic demand achieved the most profitable turnover. It seems that in Lombardy it was the urban entrepreneurs who carried out the farming innovations. This certainly has its significance but, seen in a wider context, means only that capital and enterprise followed the market's initial stimulus more quickly, and perhaps more energetically, in Lombardy than elsewhere.
3 Agricultural progress in Italy was limited to the more urban part of the north. Even in Tuscany there was no advance, as we can see from the shrinking area of cultivation associated with the population decline and falling rents in that area (see below).

These are merely notes on a subject whose more intensive study must be left to the Italian economic historians, so we shall turn our eyes to the lands north of the Alps to trace the course of agrarian income as best we may.

The decline of agrarian income in western, northern and central Europe

By agrarian income we mean the sum of all the revenue obtained directly or indirectly from farming. The indirect or derived income went partly to territorial, juridicial or manorial lords, partly to the church and also in part to burgesses and big farmers. It is not easy to grasp the whole system even for one small district, let alone a larger area. That, however, will not be attempted here. It will be enough to study its evolution and to present the available evidence.

In the Scandinavian countries a farmer's chief burden was the 'land debt' or similarly-named sum charged as interest on the land. In Norway, Sweden and Denmark receipts from the charges began to fall after the last quarter, middle, or even first half of the fourteenth century (the charges varied). In Norway, for example, it happened between the middle of the fourteenth and end of the fifteenth century: in the western regions rents dropped by up to 25 or 30 per cent, in Romerike by 30 per cent and in the Sogn district by a little over 14 per cent. In Sweden the decline was less marked, but there is no doubt that there, too, the larger estates yielded considerably less interest. The long series of the Domkirche land registers at Uppsala has much to tell on the subject (Schreiner). By 1376 farm labour was already becoming scarce; rents sank by 25 per cent compared with those of the first half of the century. The registers of 1447, 1450 and 1470 show that the decline continued, though at a more leisurely pace. Even in the second half of the fifteenth century Vadstena Monastery, one of the greatest landowners in Sweden with over a thousand farms, suffered severe loss through the falling-off of rents, which was barely compensated by the acquisition of many new estates (Norborg, 1958: *passim*). In Denmark the decline began in the mid-fourteenth century or even sooner. A farm that in 1292 had paid 16 units of corn, in 1450 paid only 2 units (Abel, 1976:138ff.).[19]

Scandinavian research has also provided some land prices. It is a matter of the renting value of the land, comparable with modern land values. According to Schreiner's compilation, the price of land in Denmark dropped from 100 in 1334–9 down to 77.1 in the decade 1391–1400; in Sweden from 100 in 1318–49 down to 47 between 1410 and 1419; in Norway from 100 before the Black Death to half or less at the end of the fifteenth century. These prices relate to such very different estates that the average values may appear rather suspect. However, the general movement is clear enough for such objections to carry little weight. We can safely say that the price of land diminished (which was only to be expected with the drop in rents), and with it declined the wealth of the landlords.

The available evidence suggests that in England rents were already going down in the late fourteenth and early fifteenth century (see above, page 62f.; also Halcrow, 1954–5:345ff.) and continued to do so during the whole long-term decline in the price of cereals. On the Forncett estates in Norfolk the annual rents, expressed in pence per acre, were almost halved between 1376–8 and 1451–60. In the estate books there are a few notes that throw considerable light on the cause of the trouble.

One of the Forncett farmers explained that he wished to give up his tenancy 'because he wanted to make more profit during the harvest season'. On that remark Schreiner rightly comments that it reveals the basic problem of the time. Wages stood too high in relation to the price of farm produce. It made the farmer dissatisfied with the conditions of his leasehold and forced the landlord, when all else failed, to reduce the rent.

From the county of Namur in Belgium Genicot (1943:289; 1970) quotes prices on estates containing eleven properties in all. With a single exception, prices sank after 1350 by between a quarter and a half of their original level. Rents charged on seigneurial lands almost all went down by one-third to one-half (with considerable scattering: out of a total of 22 cases investigated, the decline from 1368 to 1468 ranged from 10–15 per cent in two of them, by 25 per cent in two others, by 33 per cent in three and by 50 per cent in the remaining cases). In spite of this, there were accumulating arrears of rent between the years 1368–70 to 1374 and 1392–5 to 1412–13: *une baisse de long durée* is evident in the material from this north-western corner of our continent.

Table 12   Average rents in rural Pistoia 1201–25 to 1401–25

Period	Staia per storio of land	Kg per hectare	1201–25 = 100
1201–1225	1.50	238	100
1226–1250	2.30	364	153
1251–1275	2.67	423	178
1276–1300	2.50	396	167
1301–1325	2.50	396	167
1326–1350	2.50	396	167
1351–1375	1.60	253	107
1376–1400	1.50	238	100
1401–1425	1.40	222	93

The conversion was based on: 1 staia = 25.92 litres; 1 storio of land = 0.1265 hectare; 1 litre wheat = 0.733 kilograms.

In Italy as a whole, landowning was not always as profitable as it was in parts of Lombardy. We hear from Tuscany of farm rents in the district of Pistoia between 1251–75 and 1401–25 being reduced by more than a third (Herlihy, 1965). Evidence on rents goes back far enough for us to detect their rise during the thirteenth century, the era of land reorganization and reclamation which, in Pistoia, dated back to the last quarter of that century. However, rents remained at the same level, considerably higher than at the beginning of the period, until the mid-fourteenth century. Only then did the sharp decline set in, forcing the average payments down to below their value at the start of the fourteenth century (see table 12, from Herlihy, 1965:240f.).

In parts of France, too, the landowners were obliged to grant considerable reductions in rent. Thus, between 1350 and 1460 Norman seigneurial incomes dropped by 70–75 per cent (Bois, 1976:201). Moreover, in France, certain legal concessions were introduced, for example, a relaxation of the farmer's liability to pay charges on abandoned farms (d'Avenel, 1894–1926:111, 193). All this, in addition to the burdens and difficulties imposed by the long war with England, resulted in the French nobility, with a few exceptions, becoming greatly impoverished. Bertrand de Preignan, the last of his line, petitioned to be counted as a commoner so that he might gather wood from the common woodland with the other villagers. The widow of another debt-encumbered lord ran an ale-house for her living. The 'beggar lords' became a byword and their houses were called *châteaux de la misère*. In 1530, when things were beginning to improve, there were 121 *seigneurs* in one region of northern France who had a combined income of 21,400 livres. The wealthiest among them received 5,000 livres, the second wealthiest, 200 livres, and the rest an average of 138. In the towns there were merchants with incomes of up to 65,000 livres (Nabholz, 1941:557f.).

It was in fifteenth-century Germany that the robber barons won their ill repute. Rolewinck, the son of a rich farmer, gave the following colourful description of the landowners of his native Westphalia in 1425:

Their wretched poverty drives them to many misdeeds. So barren is their land that it would be waste did they not dwell on it themselves.... Methinks no one can see without tears how day by day the fine lords strive, by hook or by crook, to gain their miserable dole of bread and clothing, only to keep hunger and poverty at bay.... The struggle for land and wealth, the desire for tournaments and courtly show, are not for them. They have no higher ambition than to get their daily bread.

In plain figures the financial position of a group of 139 members of the Swabian nobility was as follows: in roughly two-thirds of all cases the individual income around the year 1490 was under 200 guilders a year, in one-third of the cases between 200 and 800 guilders, and in only 2.1 per cent of the cases over 800 guilders (Sattler, 1962). For comparison it may be noted that in 1518 the wedding of an Augsburg merchant, who was well off, but not one of the richest citizens of the town, cost 991 guilders. That sum exceeds the 650 guilders paid by the Swabian knight Werner von Zimmern in 1453 for a whole village and all that went with it. 'So worthless had empty farms become in those days', added a later chronicler of Zimmern (about 1550).

Consistent series of German land prices and rents for this period are, alas, few and full of obscurities. In Silesia, Meitzen (1871:411f.) tells us, 38 demesne and peasant holdings of roughly the same soil quality were sold in the fourteenth century for the average price of 14.5 Polish marks apiece. In the fifteenth century, in spite of a sharp devaluation of the Polish mark, they were still worth only 15 marks each. It was not till the end of that century, and more notably during the next, that these Silesian farms went up in value once more. Unfortunately, Meitzen does not tell us to what extent the currency depreciated. In the case of some farms belonging to the municipality of Göttingen, the rents of the period 1501–50, reckoned in bullion content, were only one-tenth of what they had been in 1431–50. It appears, however, that in this instance, some unusual circumstances were involved.

Loss of income and fortune is often easier to pinpoint in the case of ecclesiastical lordships. The Teutonic Order, for example, possessed some estates which were used as bases for supplying the Order's headquarters in Prussia with men and materials. As Prussia grew poorer and this help was more urgently needed, the sources of supply dried up. A statement written in 1450 from the Teutonic Master, the representative of the Grand Master of the Teutonic Order in Old Germany, gives us to understand that the total indebtedness of the German bailiwicks, which in 1361 stood at about 79,000 guilders had risen to 106,000 guilders at the time of the statement, although a loan of 60,000 guilders made to them in 1394 had been almost entirely remitted. The Grand Master commented that the gap between income and expenditure, far from diminishing, grew wider day by day. He had taken counsel with the local governors, seeking for ways and means of improving the situation. He had even 'offered several times to sell or mortgage all our Order's possessions in that territory', but the princes and lords had flatly refused to buy. Conditions in Germany at that time were such that neither by selling nor mortgaging farms and estates could an adequate sum of money be raised (Abel, 1976:142f.; Maschke, 1963).[20]

A second example comes from Bavaria. The archives of the Tegernsee Monastery

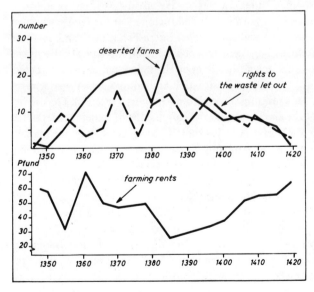

Fig. 15 Lost villages and declining rents in the Tegernsee district of Gevild 1346–1420 (after H. Rubner).

are a rich source of material for economic historians. They contain, among other things, information on wasteland, land leased out as waste and normally-occupied farms, as well as on the monastery's revenue from farming rents. From Rubner's research (1964:433f.) we learn that in 1355 in the jurisdiction of Gevild on the Bavarian plateau, out of 155 of the monastery's properties 4 were deserted and 9 were let out as rough pasture, that is to say let for a reduced payment to a farmer willing to improve the land. In the following year the proportion of estates abandoned had risen to a fluctuating 18–20 per cent of the total, while at the same time and from the same causes the total value of the farm rents dropped to less than half of what it had been in 1350. The nadir was reached in 1385. Unfortunately, the series breaks off in 1420 (see figure 15).

North Germany supplies a third example. In 1437 the treasurer of the Schleswig Cathedral chapter compared the chapter's revenue in his time with that of 1352. The comparison showed that the total received in 1352, including both cash and goods in kind, amounted to 7,600 tons of wheat, but that by 1437 it had dwindled to about 2,400 tons. The procurator thought that war and flooding were responsible for the deficit. The Danish historian, C. A. Christensen (1960), however, who checked the calculation and assessed the difference to be even greater (6,000 tons), was of the opinion that the great flood which overran Friesland in 1362 was to blame for only 730 tons of the total loss. War, he considered, had had no important effects on the domain of the cathedral chapter in Schleswig. Most of the decline in income was due to the depopulation and the many lost villages which we know existed at that time. It was a part of the general agrarian slump in Europe. It is far harder to arrive at a universally-valid assessment of the *farmer's economic situation* in the late Middle Ages. This is because the peasant's income came from several quite different sources, though it was always possible that one or another might dry up: wages for the peasant himself and members of his family working with him, rent for his share of the cultivated land, interest on capital, and possibly some gain as an entrepreneur. Now when, as happened in the late Middle Ages, wages went up and rents went down, the effect on the individual peasant's income could vary greatly according to the size, situation and equipment of his farm.

A yeoman farmer, such as might be found in north-western Germany, approached the status of the smaller landlords and, like them, sometimes let out a part of his land, but it brought in very little profit. Those dependent on the market and employing a large number of farmhands felt at a disadvantage when farming prices were so low in relation to farming costs, especially wages. Here and there one of them might turn to the production of wool, meat or butter, which fetched better prices, but not many had the opportunity.

There are no account-books extant from this type of farm. The next best thing is the account of some Saxon knights in 1474 (which was discussed above, page 66). From the knights' figures it seems fairly certain that their proceeds from tilling the soil barely covered the expenses of farm and household. Seiffard von Lüttichall tells us that they did not make enough money to buy Sunday clothes. When this report was written the time had long gone by when the lady was content to dress in homespun wool, and a suit of armour was enough for her husband. In the account-book of the knight Hans von Honsperg of Cloden in Saxony, the sum allotted for the family's clothing in 1474 was equivalent in value to 41,700 kilograms of rye (which in West Germany in 1976 was worth Dm20,000). Half of this amount was taken up by the knight's clothes, a little over a third went to his wife, and the rest was divided among the daughters. Though this expenditure sounds high when compared with today's standards, it did not seem excessive at the time. Thus a sumptuary law imposed in Regensburg, which differed little from other towns in this respect, set the upper limit of what might be spent on dress for a lady or young girl at a sum worth about 100,000 kilograms of rye. Whether the women kept within the law is not known; but the husband had to buy clothes as well. This bears witness to a tremendous expenditure in the towns that leaves the Saxon knight far behind.

Matters stood very differently for the smallholders, who existed in great numbers in the villages and hamlets of central Europe after the great migrations were over. If the taxes were too high, the soil too poor or the plot too small, they simply left. Their labour was in demand: they could earn high wages in the cities and in the country they were needed to run the many vacant farms and also to perform the industrial tasks which since the high Middle Ages had expanded in the villages and hamlets, in particular in the textile industry.[21] All over northern and central Europe there were offers of free years, reduced rents and other inducements to lure them back to the land. Nor were friendly words and actions lacking. According to a West German source (Gondenbret, n.d.) if a yeoman chanced to meet a man in search of land, he should put him up behind him on his horse and carry him into the country. If the stranger saw a plot that pleased him, sprang off the horse and decided to cultivate it, the yeoman should at once grant him 15 morgen. There was plenty of land. It was men that were scarce.

Neither the yeoman nor the smallholder, however, was the typical figure in western and central European agriculture during the late Middle Ages. The centre-post of that agriculture – and the social structure it supported – was another sort of farmer, the tenant of a middle-sized holding. He was not independent of hired labour, but wages were less burdensome to him than to the big yeoman farmer. Prices were of concern to him, but his essential needs were supplied from his own land, or from work done for his neighbours or landlord. The biggest items in his budget were the services and payments due to his feudal, territorial, juridical and manorial lords. If these taxes as in Germany, but which we know was also the case in other countries,[22] took a quarter to a third of his farm income, there was very little left for him after he had deducted the next year's seed-corn. To maintain his farm and his standard of living was like 'walking on a tightrope'.[23] It needed only one bad harvest, a cattle plague or a war, with its looting and arson, for the wretched peasant to give up his calling and leave; the farm would be deserted.

The lost villages of the late Middle Ages

The significance, extent and distribution of the lost villages

The word *Wüstung* (lost village) in German indicates a village that has disappeared from the face of the earth (Beschorner, 1904:1). That definition is a modern agricultural concept too limiting for an historical study of the phenomenon. For this there are three reasons.

Firstly, it leaves out of consideration the fate of the fields and meadows that belonged to the village. It is to the land, but also to its economic use, that the term *Wüstung* (from *wüst*: deserted, empty, desolate) is most often applied in the documents and registers of the late Middle Ages and of the dawning new age. It meant that the fields were no longer cultivated; they were neglected and becoming waste. Sometimes the sources make this clear, at other times not, but at least we must try to distinguish between deserted *villages* and deserted *fields*.

Secondly, not all the lost villages and fields remained deserted. Geographers may be more interested in the permanently-abandoned sites, but that is not necessarily true of historians. To understand this 'wasting' process in depth we must not leave the *temporarily*-lost villages and fields out of consideration.

Thirdly, not all lost villages and fields were *completely* abandoned. Beside those that were totally lost were others that were but partially so, where only part of the settlement or cultivated area went to waste. Research into lost villages has produced many errors and false conclusions which could have been avoided if these partially-deserted places had been taken into consideration.

Since these complications have rendered the definition 'lost villages' inadequate, it will be best to follow the lead of Scharlau (1933: enclosure; 1954–5:72f.) who has replaced the concept of lost villages with a schematic arrangement. Scharlau distinguishes between lost villages and lost arable and divides each of these types into the partially lost, when any of the inhabitants or cultivation remained, and the totally lost, when settlement and fields were quite given up. If temporary desertions are brought into the picture we get the scheme shown in figure 16. It must be

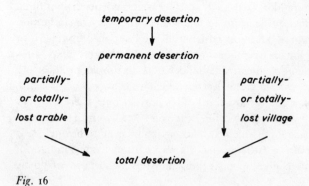

Fig. 16

emphasized that this diagram represents only a concept, not an inevitable process, although partial desertions often became total and, in Germany at least, temporary desertions tended to become permanent.

Research into lost villages began with settlements that had 'vanished off the face of the earth'. Their occurrence was being recorded in Germany as early as the sixteenth century. Several treatises on the subject were written during the eighteenth century, and since the middle of the nineteenth century the literature of lost villages has grown apace. Today it comprises many hundreds of works whose aims and stature vary considerably. Often they merely list and locate the lost villages; seldom is there any attempt to date them or to find the cause of their downfall; still more rarely is the result of individual research checked with local information. Nevertheless it might be possible, though not without its hazards, to assemble these bits of jigsaw puzzle into one picture that could help us to answer some of the more important questions.

The first of these would be the question of *when* the settlements were abandoned. The tendency in Germany today is to study the lost villages in two periods: the medieval era of land improvement, and the later Middle Ages. The lost villages of the first period were the result of war, of the growth of towns, the establishment of monastic estates or the combination of several individual settlements into one large one. Although in particular cases the cause may be debatable, there is no doubt that at that time more new settlements were begun than land and villages were lost; moreover, losses of land and villages were far greater in the late Middle Ages.

To get some idea of the *number* of late medieval lost villages we must turn to the above-mentioned studies, even if they are not all that could be desired and distinguish none-too-clearly between settlements abandoned in the early, the high or the late Middle Ages. Let us divide the total number of known medieval settlements in a particular district by the number of proven, probable or merely possible lost villages of the late Middle Ages: the resulting relationship can be called the lost-village quotient. If we further compare this quotient with the present density of settlements in the district, we have a basis from which to calculate the loss of villages in larger areas and ultimately in the whole country. For Germany as a whole (with boundaries as in 1933) the lost-village quotient comes to about 26 per cent, that is to say, every fourth settlement known to exist at the end of the high medieval agricultural boom had disappeared by the end of the Middle Ages.

There were wide regional differences, however. In some areas as many as 40 per cent and more of twelfth- to fourteenth-century villages were lost. The highest figures of all occur in high-lying country such as the Rhön, Solling and Hessian mountains. There were other parts where the losses did not exceed 10 per cent. This was especially true of the north-western coastal region and the plain of the lower Rhine. The area of medium quotients, approaching the German average, included the arable country inland from the Baltic coasts of Schleswig-Holstein, Mecklenburg and Pomerania up to East Prussia, as shown in figure 17.[24]

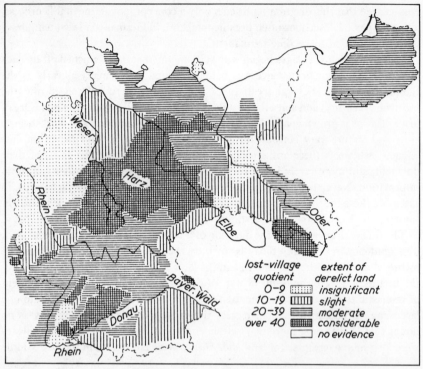

Fig. 17   The lost villages of Germany in the late Middle Ages (after H. Pohlendt).

In England, too, many villages were deserted during the later Middle Ages.[25] In some counties their number reaches 20 per cent of all the settlements listed in the 1334 tax rolls; the toll was 22 per cent on the Isle of Wight. There were other counties where the losses were no higher than 5–10 per cent, and a few districts in which, as far as is known at present, no villages were abandoned at all.

In England, as in Germany, the grasslands were the least affected. The majority of lost villages occurred in the arable area, and there principally where conversion to pasture was feasible, or where the soil was too poor to be worth tilling. John Saltmarsh reported that on a single afternoon on the barren lands of south Norfolk he encountered five ruined churches that must have succumbed to the sands during the era of deserted villages. Postan points out the vulnerability of the smallholdings. On 130 estates extending over sixteen different counties during the fourteenth and fifteenth centuries, he writes, the number of smallholdings under five acres diminished by nearly 35 per cent, as against only about 10 per cent of the larger properties.

Information on the era of lost villages can be found in a list compiled by Beresford (1954), based on the researches of Hoskins and Parker in Leicestershire. From the total number of traceable lost villages in that county, the list tells us, 7 per cent were deserted in the twelfth and thirteenth centuries, 5 per cent at the end of the fourteenth century, 38 per cent between 1400 and 1509, and 12 per cent from 1510 to 1548. (The remainder amounted to 5 per cent during the years 1549 to 1603, going up to 13 per cent after 1604, and leaving 21 per cent deserted at an undetermined date.) The process of farm evacuation lasted longer in England than on the continent, probably because the expanding textile industry continued to pay high prices for wool. However, the 'losing' of farms in the sense of their purchase and/or driving out of the tenants, had been going on for a long time. Hilton gives a number of examples from which he concludes that 'far from driving out the tenants', the landlords (Compton, Verney, Kingston, Chesterton, the bishops of Worcester and others) did their best before 1410 to let the deserted farms 'at a low price' (1968:107).

Research into lost villages in the Netherlands and Belgium did not start till quite late. Documentary evidence is certainly scarce, but *argumentum e silentio* is, as Jansma truly remarked (1960:135), a doubtful basis for the assertion that there were none. Careful research in various parts of the two countries has shown that the number of permanently and totally lost villages was small. In the county of Namur up to 1430 only about 6 per cent of the rented properties were lost (Genicot, 1970:18). More often it was a case of temporary desertion. For instance, in a steward's day-book found by chance in Twenthe, many of the entries are marked *vacat, quia non colitur, vacat similiter* or *quasi vacat*. A document from Utrecht states that 'many farms in the Utrecht region have become vacant through death'. Slicher van Bath (1964:69) has established that in the Veluwe, the northern part of Gelderland, where until the mid-fourteenth century land reclamation was extensive, the revenue from the cultivated area (*Novalzehnt*) sank rapidly between 1369 and 1393, and reports of deserted farms, land gone to waste and sand-drifts became frequent.

However, it seems to be true that permanently-lost villages and fields in the Netherlands, as in most of France, were very rare, certainly much rarer than in Germany. A study of the subject by Pesez and Le Roy Ladurie (1965:257f.) assures us that since the earliest inventories of rural settlements in northern, western and central France were made, extremely few villages had perished; in Artois, for example, hardly a dozen, although this district was in the battle zone during the Hundred Years War and many of its settlements were deserted in the fifteenth century (52 in 1414 and a further 31 in 1475). In eastern and southern France permanently-lost villages were more usual. Straub (1887:3f.) had previously arrived at an average for Alsace of 17 per cent of villages lost out of all those known; in parts of Provence badly hit by the slump the quotient rose to 37 per cent.

But though the very uneven distribution of permanently-lost villages in France – and elsewhere in Europe – stands much in need of clarification (see Abel, 1961:1f., Pesez and Le Roy Ladurie, 1965:270) we must not forget the temporary desertions which, while deserted, seemed little different from the others. Such temporarily-abandoned villages were quite frequent in France. Rather than cite numerous individual examples, let me quote from a contemporary witness, Basin, who wrote:

> From the Loire to the Seine, from the Seine to the Somme the peasants are
> dead or fled, the fields unploughed, the ploughman gone.... With my own
> eyes have I seen how the great plains of Champagne, Brie and Beuce ... lie
> deserted, waste, uninhabited, with brambles and scrub their only crop.... Tilled
> fields are found only close to towns, fortified houses or castles, within sight of
> a watcher from a tower or some other high place.

Basin's contemporaries thought all this to be the effect of the long war with
England. French historians did not question this view until d'Avenel pointed out
that had the war been the sole cause of the general misery, prices, especially
food prices, would have risen, which they did not, and wages would have fallen,
whereas in fact they went up, though not perhaps to the degree d'Avenel supposed.
Moreover, more recent research has revealed that lost villages were also to be found
far from the scene of war. Thus at Oisans, an Alpine district south of Grenoble,
the number of dwelling houses dropped by 46 per cent between 1339 and 1428,
and in the years that followed they decreased even more rapidly. Dopsch observed
exactly the same picture in the Austrian Alps. Permanent settlements, which by
1300 had climbed further up the mountain slopes than ever before, were afterwards abandoned. The upward limit of settlement became lower. This is hardly
compatible with the war theory (Dopsch, 1930:133f.; Allex, 1933:141f.).

The Vienna woods and basin were investigated by Alfred Grund to whose earlier
work (1901) students of lost villages are indebted not only for the first general
survey of the widely-scattered results of local historical research but also for his
elucidation of the central problem. He showed that between the fourteenth and
sixteenth centuries over 40 per cent of the villages disappeared, especially among
the arable farming communities, though less often where vines were the chief crop.
From this he deduced a slump in arable farming. Considerable extra information
has been supplied by Pongratz for the woodland area which adjoins the Wienerwald
on its northern boundary (1955–6:131). In this under-populated, mostly rather
barren part of lower Austria he traced some 11 per cent of partial desertions in the
Weitra farmlands (1499) and 15 per cent partial desertions in the Zwetter land
register of 1457. These are apart from the figure of approximately 20 per cent for
totally-lost villages. Such evidence of partial desertions has hitherto been too little
regarded by German and Austrian researchers in favour of the more striking total
losses.

In other parts of Austria too (as we see, for instance, in the Salzburg region,
Styria and northern Burgenland) there were a large number of lost villages. Czech
research has already discovered 3,000 deserted medieval settlements in Bohemia
and nearly 1,400 in Moravia. By 1400 in many Hungarian villages 20–40 per cent
of the farms were unoccupied. In Poland, even before the expansion of the seigneurial estates, a process that did not reach its full strength till the sixteenth century,
up to a third of all the farmsteads were deserted. Most of the villages lost in the

Moscow area – some 50 per cent or more of the settlements – were abandoned in the second half of the fourteenth century or the first half of the fifteenth.

The late medieval loss of villages also seems to have been very serious in some Mediterranean lands. In Greece the first period of mass desertion of the land occurred in the fourteenth century (the second was in the nineteenth century). In the Spanish province of Navarre about 60 per cent of all the authenticated cases occurred between 1348 and 1500. In Italy, during the fourteenth and fifteenth centuries, some 10 per cent of the Tuscan farmsteads settled in the high Middle Ages disappeared, as did 25 per cent in the neighbourhood of Rome, and as many as half in Sardinia. As in other lands, there were wide regional differences in the number of villages deserted. Moreover, the mere number gives very little idea of the true extent of the decline. In some accurately-investigated districts of Tuscany the percentage of villages lost in the fourteenth and fifteenth centuries was about 20 per cent, but the loss of homesteads stood at 70 per cent (Third Congress of Economic Historians, 1965: collective report; Abel, 1976*a*).

In northern Europe, where research into lost villages has, up to now, advanced further than elsewhere, the phenomenon is clearly related to the great pestilence of 1349–50. The people did not forget it and regarded it as a second Deluge. Whole villages had perished, they said, 'to the last man' or 'the last woman', from whom the later inhabitants – and even some names of villages – were supposed to be descended. (There are in Norway two big villages, Mandal (mandale) and Kvinnedal (womandale), which the inhabitants believe were named after one single man and one single woman who survived the Black Death.) Other epidemics followed which, added to the unfavourable prices and wages of agriculture, drove people to abandon their farms. A law of 1437 ordered all peasants who had taken refuge in the towns not to settle there but to come back to their farms and services. A few years later, in 1442, Christoffer's Land Law decreed that if a tenant left his farm before the lease had run out, he might be fetched back 'by force'. In an act passed in 1437, and in further acts of 1442, 1459 and 1483, there was a clause intended to prevent the accumulation of farming land, stipulating that no peasant might take on more land than he could cultivate efficiently. And, indeed, much good land went untilled. Recent research shows that out of the thousand farms owned by the Vadstena monastery in 1502, when signs of improvement were already perceptible, 158 were vacant. In 1447 the number had been even higher (Norborg, 1958:172 and 1959–60:19f.).

The district of Eidsvoll, north of Oslo, is the part of Norway that has been most carefully studied up to the present. According to the episcopal land registers, 38 per cent of the farms in that region in 1400 were deserted. Later and more comprehensive sources produce far higher figures. A tax roll of 1514 lists two-thirds of the farms as derelict. In other parts of Norway there do not seem to have been so many lost villages. The 1440 land register of Archbishop Aslak Bolt describes only 15 per cent of the 2870 estates as waste (*Ødegårder*). The same percentage of deserted farms appears in the register of Munkelev monastery in

1463. Compared with Eidsvoll the proportion may seem low, but it is almost certain that to arrive at the true figure for 'lost farms' the numerous holdings described in these books as vacant must be added to those specifically marked 'deserted' (*Ødhofe*).

In Norway most of these farms came under cultivation again. In Denmark, in one case (Falster) out of the 108 settlements mentioned in King Waldemar's land register, 25 per cent vanished for ever, while in another case (Frederiksborger Amt) the proportion was 30 per cent of the newer foundations only. C. A. Christensen, to whom great credit is due for the light he has thrown on the late medieval agricultural slump, established (1964:346) that 11 per cent of the episcopal farms in Roskilde lay abandoned during the years 1361–80. The number rose to 26 per cent between 1401 and 1420 but sank again to only 8 per cent in 1441–60 (see table 13). Thus the worst years of the depression in Denmark would seem to have occurred during the early decades of the fifteenth century.[26]

Table 13   Deserted farms among the possessions of the Bishops of Roskilde

Period	Occupied farms	Deserted farms	Proportion of deserted farms (%)
1361–1380	277	33	10.6
1381–1400	553	103	15.7
1401–1420	750	264	26.0
1421–1440	436	92	17.4
1441–1461	499	43	8.0

As this cursory survey demonstrates, there were a considerable number of abandoned farms and villages in many European countries. What stands out and needs further investigation is the uneven distribution of the lost villages within the countries and in relation to one another. There is also the fact that in Scandinavia, the Netherlands, Belgium and western France the great majority of lost villages came into cultivation once more, whereas in Germany and, to a lesser extent, in England they have remained lost to this day. The answer to the question of what proportion of the losses was only temporary must be sought in the period of agrarian recovery, especially in the sixteenth century. During the late Middle Ages it was not possible to distinguish between permanently- and temporarily-lost villages, for both classes of village, farm or field were abandoned, or at best only fractionally cultivated, and therefore appeared 'lost'.

The evolution of lost villages

Many thousands of villages were destroyed in the later fourteenth century and during the fifteenth century by wars and feuds, declared or undeclared, 'illegal' predatory raids. In France the Hundred Years War with England raged. England was in the throes of the civil war between the houses of York and Lancaster, Denmark was harassed by the feuds of the nobles, and Germany by countless wars, large and small. Twelve hundred villages were demolished in the wars between the towns of south-west Germany alone. The towns sent out flying columns, led by a 'fire master', to set fire to the houses, drive away the cattle and destroy the fields. Branches were tied to the horses' saddles the better to spoil the growing corn, and mustard was strewn over the ground to make its future cultivation more difficult. All this was done to break down the enemy's reserves in the form of their villages, peasants, cattle and land. When these raids were associated with national hatred and religious fanaticism the devastation became magnified to chaos. In Bohemia alone, the march of the Hussites left at least 1,500 ruined hamlets in its train. More villages went up in flames when they reached Germany proper.

Other villages dwindled slowly away. Farms and fields became vacant, sometimes to be half-heartedly tilled by their neighbours for a while. Rents were still entered in the landlord's register but they were lower than before. Now and again an empty farm was reoccupied, but more usually the wasteland spread. It advanced and embraced other parts of the arable and village. Its name was no longer written in the estate books, and finally it vanished from the landscape altogether.

Since the sources of information seldom divulge details of this process, the seeker after the causes of lost villages is given a wide scope. Some investigators, no doubt wishing to be on the safe side, compiled long lists of possible causes: plagues, fires, raids and looting, earthquakes, floods, poor soil, bad weather, fragmented fields, pressure to co-operate in a three-course rotation or pressure not to, or leaving a small farm to join up with a larger concern. But lists of this kind mean very little. It is left to the reader to select from the many possible, even probable, causes those that are truly significant and decisive.

We can simplify and so clarify the matter by turning our attention to the *people* who lived in these places. If they vanished from the scene at a particular time there can be, on the purely human – demographic – level, only two explanations: either deaths exceeded births, or emigration exceeded immigration (or possibly both). Thus the search for the causes of a village's demise narrows down to discovering the reasons for the surplus of deaths or emigration.

In 1356, the writer of the *Limburg Chronicle* tells us, there arose once again 'great lamentation, for the second terrible pestilence had broken out and people in Germany were dying in great numbers of the same plague that had killed so many in the first Great Death. Those who had not been carried off in the earlier year died now, and so everyone perished.' The epidemic reached Pomerania, the Prussian territories, Silesia and Bohemia. The Archbishop of Prague ordered masses and processions in 1359 'because of the plague's return'. In England 22.7 per cent of the population died in the epidemic of 1360, little fewer than the 25 per cent claimed by the Black Death (according to Russell).

The plague broke out again in Germany in 1362, reached Italy in 1363 and appeared sporadically during the next few years until, in 1369, the epidemic again grew to European proportions. In England in that year, according to Russell, it claimed 13.1 per cent of the population as its victims. On the continent, Vienna, Bohemia and, in the ensuing years, the towns and countryside of central Germany were sorely afflicted. There came a few years' respite – which coincided with the beginning of the long-term slump in prices – then in 1380 'all Germany' was, as the *Spangenberg Chronicles* inform us, overwhelmed by pestilence. It raged particularly fiercely in Augsburg, along the Rhine, in Vienna and in Bohemia. It is said that, in 1381, 15,000 of the Viennese victims were buried in St Stephan's graveyard alone. The single recorded contemporary witness in the Czech territories declared that the plague of 1379–80 was the most terrible of all the plagues of the fourteenth century (Graus). The Master of the Teutonic Order in Livonia informed the pope in a letter that there were so many deaths from plague in 1379 that barely one person out of ten was left alive (Ahvenainen, 1963:70, note 23).

As the fourteenth century turns into the fifteenth it becomes more and more difficult to pin down outbreaks of plague. It appears that the great epidemics characteristic of the Black Death's early phase petered out into local outbreaks of illness that struck here and there over the whole former area of attack, but with ever less interconnection. Perhaps further research will enable us to discover connecting links but, even in their absence, there is no doubt that bubonic plague (and other epidemics) maintained a persistent influence on the natural balance of western and central European population during the whole of the later Middle Ages.

However, Norwegian researchers were the first to point out that a surplus of deaths could not be the sole reason for the diminishing number of settlements. From comparing the prices of farms before and after the Black Death, Hasund concluded that the desertion of fields and villages occurred most often in the narrow valleys of Valdes, Gudbrandsdal and the interior, and less frequently in the lower-lying and more populous districts round Oslo, in Romerike, Østfold and Trøndelag. Skappel was able to supplement these observations from some tax-rolls, which showed that the yield of Peter's Pence (a tax paid to the papal court at the rate of 1 pfennig per household) sank in proportion to the then present-day (1937–40) amount of mountain pasture in any particular district. Thus, for instance, the drop in tax yield in the Oslo district, where in 1937–40 hill pastures took up only 1.5 per cent of the farmland, was only 14.5 per cent in the years from 1325–32 to 1553–7, whereas, during the same period in the Stavanger district, with its 38.2 per cent of mountain pasture to farmland, the yield from Peter's Pence fell by 68.7 per cent. As it cannot be assumed that the plague was at its most severe in the more remote regions, it would seem that migration must have contributed to the depopulation. Skappel learnt from his sources that there was indeed such a migration 'from the pastures to the arable, from the highlands to the lowlands, from the narrow mountain valleys to the broad plains and from the interior to the coast'.

Much the same situation was found to have existed in the Austrian Alps. Among the papers left by the Benedictine monastery in Salzburg, Herbert Klein discovered a hitherto-unnoticed collection of minutes taken down at the annual meetings of various departments of the institution, as well as from visitations in 1350, the year of the Great Death. The results of his extensive calculations can be summarized as follows: between 1348 and 1352, in the Pongau district, south of Salzburg, deep in the mountains, about 66 per cent of the farms lost their tenants (24 per cent were vacant, 16 per cent were joined to neighbouring farms and 26 per cent changed hands). In two other mountain districts, Pinzgau and Ennstal, changes of occupier after the 1348–9 catastrophe were equally frequent; many new names crop up in the coastal plain and the valleys too, after 1349, but here there was no combining of properties and, above all, no vacancies. The obvious explanation is that after the Black Death people began to move away from their old homes to the valleys, to richer soil, to areas of lower taxation or maybe just to an easier life (Klein, 1960:91f.; see also Abel, 1976:29f., 98ff.).[27]

Migration of this sort was manifestly not confined to Norway and Austria. In the Magdeburg Börde, the less well-watered parts were the first to be abandoned; in Middlemark and Altmark it was the villages built on sandy soil. In Würtemberg most of the lost villages are situated in woodland bordered by open and long-settled country, for example on the northern slopes of the Keuper Highlands towards the Franconian Plateau, and on the border of Schönbuchs by the Neckar Valley. In the Harz and Thuringian forests the exodus was most marked from newer settlements, recognizable by the name-endings *-rode*, *-hagen*, *-hain* and *-feld*. The same applies to the Göttingen area. Out of the 67 lost villages 21 have place-names ending in *-rode* or *-hagen* and are situated mostly on the wooded hills and hardly at all in the areas of old cultivation. In the Hildesheim region practically no farms were abandoned in the long-settled parts with ancient names, but many that were situated on mountain slopes, on poor soil, or far from the valley roads were left empty. The list could be prolonged, but these examples should be enough to show that geographical factors played an important part in the development of lost villages.

*

Something should be said about the *motives* for emigration. Poor soil, a hard climate and remoteness from trading centres were conditions very unfavourable to farming. The demand for land during the period of colonization had probably driven the settlers into areas where the soil was not suitable for permanent cultivation. The disadvantages were then borne for generations because there seemed no alternative. After the great plague had broken out more-favourably-situated properties became free. Nothing was more natural than that the occupiers of property constantly threatened by floods and landslides or eroded by over-cultivation should leave their old farms to start afresh under better natural conditions. 'A sort of natural selection of villages', Alfred Grund commented (1901:139). The better-situated holdings survived the crisis, the less-favourably-situated succumbed and disappeared.

Legal and social factors were often associated with the geographical ones. The Magdeburg town records (*Schöppenchronik*) reported that the peasants were so severely oppressed by Archbishop Albert III of Magdeburg during the three years he was in office (1368–71), that more than 3,000 farmers abandoned their holdings. In contemporary registers and documents we often find comments like these on the villages near Bremervörde in 1500: 'the village was deserted because of the heavy farm services demanded', on another, *propter servitia multa*, or on a third, *propter multiplicia servicia quibus quotidie gravantur coloni.*

Finally we must consider the economic situation of the time. Many bear witness that agriculture had grown unprofitable in England (Beresford, 1954ff.). Farm labour was expensive and in short supply. The prices of farm and household articles such as iron for ploughs, harrows and carts, tar for the sheep, shoes, caps, linen and woollen materials had not gone down nearly as much as had the price of corn (Stafford, 1876:34).[28] Corn-growing was, however, the life-blood of the farming community. If a peasant involved in the open-field system found it impossible to make his living, he left the way open – voluntarily or by constraint – to others, who turned his fields into meadows. 'I take the principall cause thereof', explained a 'doctor' (Stafford, 1876:84) in one of those dialogues so popular in the succeeding centuries,

> [to be that] grasing requires small charge and small labor, which in tillage consumes much of the mens gaines; ... another great cause is that whatsoever thing is reared upon grasing hath free vents ... to be sold at the highest penny. It is contrary of all thinges reared by tillage, for it requires both great charge of servaunts and of labor. And also if any good cheape be of corne, it paieth scant for the charge of the tillage ... which maketh every man forsake tillage and fall to grasing, which bringeth in all these Inclosures.

Because the price of grain stood at a low level, while animal products brought in good money, and labour, moreover, was scarce, intensive agriculture was giving way to extensive stock farming. In England the economic results of this extensification during the fifteenth century are plain to see. It used to be said that the 'greed' and 'covetousness' of the landlords was to blame for the arable being converted to pasture, but today we must grant these lords that they were only following the movements of the market.

> DOCTOR: What maketh men to multiply pastures and Inclosures thus gladly?
> KNIGHT: Marry, the profit that groweth therebye.
> DOCTOR: It is very true and none other thing.   (Stafford, 1876:55)

Neither the state of the market nor the cost-and-price motivations evident in England and other parts of western and central Europe applied in the wide circle of countries surrounding those regions. Even in northern Norway, in the Trøndelag district, the last island of agriculture in the country, the economic climate of the times made itself felt: the proportion of inland farms waned while that of fishing villages increased. 'There can be no doubt that sea fishing was the deciding factor' (Sandnes, 1970:199). Agriculture no longer paid; fishing offered better opportunities. It is difficult to know where in Europe to draw the borderline beyond which the immediate effects of the population decline merged with other indirect effects through movements in money, prices and wages. In this 'grey area', the main/primary/first/? causes of the population decline (the decisive causes, after all) have been pushed into the background.

In Germany, too, there were farms working in conditions of pure natural economy, but that was no longer the rule in the later Middle Ages. As a rule the farmer needed cash for paying money rents and wages as well as for buying household necessities and equipment for the farm. That money could come only from the farmer's own production and labour. Squeezed between falling income and comparatively static expenses, the source from which his needs were supplied dried up. Furthermore, the peasant could now compare his lot with that of the townsman. He saw that a small artisan could live in a better style than his lord, let alone himself. He knew that in the city a simple workman received, in addition to board and lodging he would have considered lavish, a money wage that was the equivalent of 15 or more kilograms of rye. He knew too that in towns the legal position was clearer, the work easier and life more secure than on the land.

So he moved into the city, as the lists of urban newcomers in many of the towns bear witness. They also show that towns needed this steady flow of men and women from the country, if they were not to share the demographic fate of the villages.

The causes of the late medieval agricultural slump

Economic theories of money and land

If one holds fast to the fact that falling agricultural prices alone were not responsible for the severe agrarian slump in the fifteenth century, but that the wide range of prices for industrial goods and the counter-movement of wages and rents shared in the responsibility, one will not fall into the trap of supposing that currency debasement and shortage of bullion were the ultimate reasons for the depression. Why should a decrease in money circulation have had such widely-varied effects on farming prices and wages? A decrease in money supply only means that in the long run – and we are discussing long-term trends – all prices and all income derived from the price structure must necessarily go down unless the conditions of land economy have altered. Even less sophisticated are the theories of a general levelling-out of trade upon which some historians build far too much. They signify only that, if in Period B prices and/or the trade turnover are lower than in Period A, the amount of money in the economy and/or the speed of its circulation must be lower than in Period A. That is, of course, a simple tautology. The key questions of history remain unanswered. The solutions must be looked for in the economic output and productivity of the time.

The theories that money was the root of the evil are obviously still in circulation. Some time ago d'Avenel and Grund believed they had explained late medieval price movements by relating them to the depreciation of the coinage. Now new monetary explanations have cropped up. Robinson (1959:63f.) and Hamilton (1960:144f.) have been converted to these ideas. Postan (1959–60) has already replied to Robinson's somewhat hypothetical formulation (in the style of 'it may also have been . . .'). Hamilton's lecture at the Eleventh International Historian's Congress on 'the history of prices before 1750' was more debatable in that once again the history of prices was based more-or-less solely on the movements of all prices together, that is to say the price level, and from this inappropriate platform he attacked the arguments of Postan and other historians regarding the disparity of prices and incomes. No one denies that there is a relation between money and prices, but the money aspect does not supply an answer to the crucial questions of economic history.

Karl Lamprecht, the only German scholar apart from the geographer Grund to study and seek to interpret the fifteenth century agrarian slump (1885–6:1, 1, 623) in the days before the first edition of this book appeared, came nearer to understanding the forces that shaped the period than did Grund, d'Avenel and others who overstressed the role of the bullion shortage. Lamprecht named two 'important direct causes': over-production of grain and the distributive interference of trade. But in view of the decrease in arable land during the fifteenth century, can we really speak of 'over-production'? What makes the idea still less acceptable is that there was no sign of technical improvements in late medieval farming.

Guy Bois considers that the possibility of a drop in the cost of production has not been sufficiently stressed in my thesis (1976:86, quoting Abel, 1973:130). I can only repeat: in the greater part of Europe during the late Middle Ages the agricultural progress on which Bois bases his argument will be sought for in vain. Admittedly the neglect of marginal land may have raised farming productivity and reduced costs, but that occurred as a result of population decline and the flight from the land, so cannot be antedated and cited as one of the causes of the relative fall in the price of agricultural products.

The influence of trade may well have led to a more even supply of and demand for goods over different times and places, but the long-term depression cannot have been affected by a merely distributive activity. The causes must be sought in a dis-proportion between production and demand, and since the cause could not have lain in the sphere of production, it is to demand that we have to look. The demand for grain being inelastic, it is the natural movement of population that must be examined. All the signs of the time, the decrease in arable area, its conversion to extensive grazing, the falling cereal prices and high wages all point to the conclusion that Europe's population growth came to a halt in the late Middle Ages.

The late medieval decline in population

There was a high death-rate during the later Middle Ages. That is common knowledge to historians of many countries.[29] Recent research in France has confirmed that Levasseur's earlier estimate of the decline in population there was but little exaggerated: it is possible that the number of inhabitants went down by one-third between the last third of the fourteenth century and the last third of the fifteenth. That is of course a very rough estimate. Newer and much better-testified figures, albeit referring to a smaller area, suggest that the population of Languedoc, numbering some 1.5 millions in 1328, had dwindled to 1 million by 1450, a loss of one-third of the inhabitants (Le Roy Ladurie, 1966:144). Between 1339 and 1474–6 in the Dauphiné and some neighbouring districts the loss was from 38 to 75 per cent, and in some cases even higher (Fierro, 1971:941ff.).

In Belgium and the Netherlands there were contrasting developments in the populations of different towns (for example, in Antwerp and Ypres), but on the whole it was more a matter of a standstill or slight reduction than a long-term decline in population (see van der Wee, 1963*a*:536; and, further, Helleiner, 1967:15ff.).

In Italy, too, it is impossible to give an overall estimate: in all too many parts of the country there has been practically no research done. However, there is recent work which is of the greatest interest. It relates to the territories of Volterra and San Gimignano in Tuscany, which together comprise a district of some 40,000 hectares, about 1.7 per cent of the area of Tuscany (Fiumi, 1962:249f.). Fiumi ascertained that in the year 1326–7 the town and surrounding countryside of Volterra contained 3,142 dwelling-houses. By 1426 only a third, 966, were left. The number of homes in the San Gimignano territory diminished on much the same scale. But that does not exhaust the information. It begins in the thirteenth century and continues into the modern era: a rise of population in the thirteenth century was followed by a decline after 1350, then it increased until the seventeenth century,

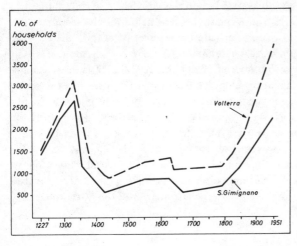

Fig. 18   The population of the Volterra and San Gimignano districts of Tuscany 1227–1951 (after E. Fiumi).

when there was another setback, and after the last quarter of the eighteenth century came the final and steepest ascent, as is shown in figure 18. That is a truly amazing example which graphically represents – as, indeed, the author has shown – an equally amazing parallel. It mirrors on a tiny scale (only 400 square kilometres) the great movements of population that traversed all Europe and decisively affected the prices, the cultivated area and farming incomes of the whole continent.

For England we now have Russell's calculations based on post-mortem inquiries by royal officials, and some other data. Russell estimates that the population of England sank from 3.8 million in 1348 to 2.7 million in 1360, then to 2.25 million in 1374 and about 2.1 million in 1430. Russell's calculations were supplemented and in principle confirmed by Postan, who was working from quite different points of departure such as prices, wages, rents and the number of occupied farms. Postan considered that the population probably began to decline during the first half of the fourteenth century, then fell much more rapidly after 1350, and finally, throughout most of the fifteenth century underwent violent fluctuations, but in the long term neither rose nor fell. Postan named 1470 as the turning point at which the population began to increase again.

Norway did not regain its pre-Black Death level of population until 1600. The late fourteenth century and the fifteenth century brought Norway a deep and long-lasting decline that may have stood out against that of the rest of Europe in its intensity but not in its timing. In Sweden and Denmark the occasionally ascertainable number of taxpayers, supplemented by lists of occupied farms, allow one to conclude that the population curve began to fall in about 1330, or perhaps even 1320, and did not rise again till much later. Even at the time of the Reformation the number of occupied farms in Falster, for example, was 25 per cent less than in the thirteenth and fourteenth centuries; in the northern part of Funem Island it was 40 per cent less (see also Bolin, 1942:471f.).

It has been accepted for some time that the rural population of Germany sank during the later Middle Ages, but a verdict on the population of the country as a whole is more difficult to arrive at owing to the view held by many historians that the urban population increased. A more careful examination of these urban populations, however, casts doubt on that assumption. In 29 towns where there are two or more sets of figures on the number of inhabitants (or, as a basis for reckoning, the number of burgesses, taxpayers, householders or houses) during the fourteenth and fifteenth centuries, the population declined by 19 per cent between the first and last year covered by each set of figures (see Abel, 1976:48). Admittedly this calculation, deduced from widely-varying periods of years, is open to serious objections. Nevertheless it proves that, on the whole, the German towns lost inhabitants. If we add to this the undoubted decline in the rural population, we can safely conclude that the whole population went down by a quarter or more from the first half of the fourteenth century to the last quarter of the fifteenth century.

*

It is quite possible that a sinking birth-rate also had its share in the population decline. Aeneas Silvio Piccolomini, who visited Vienna in 1440, observed that the burghers of that town did not have large families. He accounted for this phenomenon, which had also been noticed in other places, by the fact that the young men chose as their first wives rich elderly women from whom they had no children. As soon as they were widowers they married again, usually young women, but by this time they were too old to beget a long line of children. It is also known that prostitution increased during the late Middle Ages, and that there were considerably more females in the population than males. To every 1,000 men there were 1,100 women in Frankfurt in 1385; 1,207 women in Nuremberg in 1449; 1,080 women in Basle in 1454; and 1,410 women in Zurich in 1487 (Keyser, 1943:300).

While it is true that the above observations on the birth-rate cannot be confirmed by statistics, we might nevertheless consider the following proposition: assuming that before the agrarian slump began the annual average surplus of births was 6 per thousand, but that during the depression deaths exceeded births by 2 per thousand per year (which would correspond with the surmised population movement), the shift between birth- and death-rates would be something like that shown in table 14.

Table 14   Theoretical shifts between birth-rates and death-rates

Period I *Period of reclamation,* *eleventh–thirteenth century*		*Period II* *Agrarian depression,* *fourteenth– fifteenth century*	
	Per 1000		Per 1000
Birth-rate	42	Birth-rate	39
Death-rate	36	Death-rate	41
SURPLUS DEATHS	6	SURPLUS DEATHS	2

The figures in the table do not come out of thin air. Birth-rates, fluctuating around 40 per thousand, are often confirmed by those of later centuries, while the death-rates can be reconstructed more-or-less. However, the purpose of the table is merely to point out that the high mortality of the earlier centuries necessitated an equally high proportion of births. If deaths rose above the norm, it needed only a very slight drop in the birth-rate – in the above example, from 42 per thousand to 39 per thousand – for excess births to turn into excess deaths. That such shifts in the basic population figures of the late Middle Ages did occur is likely, although not provable. Yet the possibly-diminished birth-rate in the late medieval period was still far above the level found in industrial countries today (the 1975 birth-rate in West Germany, Great Britain, France and the United States being under 15 per thousand, whereas in Egypt, Tunisia and Ecuador it is over 35, and in Guatemala over 40 per thousand inhabitants).

Part Two

Changes in the agrarian economy of western and central Europe from the sixteenth century to the mid-eighteenth century

4 Farming and the standard of living in the sixteenth century

The upward trend in agriculture

Population growth in western and central Europe

It is probable that in most European lands the number of inhabitants began to increase once more as the fifteenth century came to an end, despite von Below's view (1909:169) that such opinions are based on 'rather uncertain ground'. It cannot be denied that evidence regarding population movements has remained very scanty until quite recent times. Contemporary records and observations are the most valuable sources of evidence, but unfortunately first-hand testimony of this kind is rare.

Speaking of the German population, Schmoller (1919:173; 1871:343f.) maintained that the causes behind its stagnation, indeed decline, during the fourteenth and early fifteenth centuries had ceased to take effect by the second half of the fifteenth century. Inama-Sternegg (n.d.(*b*):660) was of the same opinion, and Mombert (1929:79) believed that 'there is much to be said for the idea that the population increased considerably during the sixteenth century'. Certainly, the political circumstances of that period favoured growth of population in Germany. Internal peace had been restored, the nobles had given up their feuds, and after the first half of the century a long period of peace set in. The Peasants War had cost many lives. However, the Baltic and North Sea coastal areas and the border states of Silesia and Bavaria had been spared, while even in the directly-affected regions the losses seem to have been made good very quickly. In the preface to his *Deutschen Chronik* (1538) Sebastian Franck declares that although a hundred thousand men must have died in the Peasants War 'there are so many people everywhere, no one can move'. An anonymous writer from Saxony (see Lotz, 1893:6, 110) reported in 1530 that the population had increased noticeably; the next year the same author wrote 'this country is more crowded than it ever was in the time of our forefathers'. Sebastian Müller wrote of Alsace in 1550 that there were 'plenty of people' there, and the Zimmer family chronicler, also in 1550, remarked 'in our day the people in Swabia, as indeed in other lands, have greatly increased and multiplied'. In eastern Friesland the number of newly-erected mills, markets and fairs was so great it can only be assumed that there must have been an 'extraordinary growth' of population to match (Hagedorn, 1912:2f.) while the land registers of Schleswig-Holstein (R. Hansen, 1897:239) indicate that many of the farming villages there had more inhabitants then than at the end of the nineteenth century. This evidence alone leaves little doubt that Germany's population increased very rapidly between the last quarter of the fifteenth century and the end of the sixteenth.

It does not, however, give us any idea of the extent of the increase. At this point we could cite a long series of numerical examples of farms, houses, citizens, etc. from various towns, villages and rural districts, but it is not necessary. There exists Körner's compilation (1958, 1959) which may well be representative for the whole of Germany. It covers an area of about 100,000 square kilometres containing 676 towns and 14,193 villages. The population rose by about 0.71 per cent per annum between the years 1520 and 1530; in the mid-sixteenth century the increase was about 0.62 per cent and at the end of the century it was about 0.33 per cent. The growth rate for the whole period, 1520–1600, was 0.55 per cent annually (calculated as an arithmetical mean of Körner's ten-year sub-divisions).

Many people living in England during the sixteenth century received the impression that the population was increasing by leaps and bounds. William Harrison (cited in Steffen, 1901:1, 462), in his report of the discussion on the Poor Laws, declared that some complained of the great increase in population at that time (1580) and thought a good herd of cattle would be more use than so many extra people. Between 1570 and 1600 (according to Rickman) the population of England was increasing by 0.56 per cent annually. Helleiner, who accepted that figure, estimated that in two or three generations the country's population rose from the low level it had reached in the first half of the fifteenth century to regain, or nearly so, the level at which it stood before the Black Death (Helleiner, 1967:29ff.).

In the Netherlands and Belgium the first half of the sixteenth century brought 'no small increase' (see Mols, 1954, 1959; Slicher van Bath *et al.*, 1965). After the religious wars there was a quick recovery that led up to a population peak between 1650 and 1670. Slicher van Bath and his colleagues estimate that between 1500 and 1650 the population of the Netherlands doubled. A large part of this increase was taken up by the towns. The urban population of this early-industrialized north-west corner of the continent had long been the densest north of the Alps. Its share of the country's inhabitants was (according to Mols) 35 per cent in Brabant, 29 per cent in Hennegan, 40–45 per cent in Flanders and 52 per cent in Holland.

That there was also a great growth of population in France between the end of the Hundred Years War and the beginning of the religious wars cannot be doubted. In 1561 the Venetian ambassador wrote: *La France est très peuplée ... tout lieu y est habité autant qu'il peut l'être* (Levasseur, 1889:189). This was, of course, the customary contemporary exaggeration, but it reflected ascertainable fact. In the region south of Paris, where rural depopulation in the mid-sixteenth century had been almost total, we can base our estimate of the total population curve on the number of births, which increased three- to sixfold between 1470 and 1564. In 1560 the rural population in the vicinity of Paris was greater than at any time in the seventeenth century. It was the same in Normandy and the south of France, while in Languedoc the population grew *au galop* (Deveze, 1961:11, 16, citing Bezard, Tulippe and others; see also Braudel (1949:353); Jacquart's figures for the Paris region (1974), here quoted from Le Roy Ladurie (1975:1397ff.); for Languedoc, Le Roy Ladurie (1966:225)). The French religious wars may have checked the increase, but then, as the evidence clearly shows, a strong, new upsurge set in, leaving no doubt that the number of inhabitants in France increased rapidly between 1475 and 1600.

Conditions were much the same in Scandinavia. Documents and registers bear witness to the increase of farms and the growing yield of taxes. Sars has produced an estimate of Norway's total population (n.d.:281f.) which puts the number of inhabitants at 246,000 in 1520 and 359,000 in 1590, representing a rise of 46 per cent in seventy years, or an annual average of 0.56 per cent over the entire period. That was almost the same rate of growth as in Germany during the same period (0.55 per cent between 1520 and 1600).[1]

Expanding agriculture

The growing population began to cultivate the land that had returned to waste during the late Middle Ages. The chronicler of the Zimmer family commented unequivocally on the subject in 1550. After recording that the population of Swabia and other provinces had greatly increased, he added 'so they started to plough the fields and stock the meadows once more, and the place where a village had stood years before began to look like a village again'. The same thing was happening in so many places that 'never in the memory of man has the land been so much opened up. No corner, even in the densest forest or highest hills, but is ploughed and inhabited.' These new settlements on formerly-deserted territory and in the woods were called 'new islands' after those islands Christopher Columbus had discovered across the ocean a few decades earlier (Herrmann, 1932:209).

It can be assumed that by 1560 the population of Germany had at last regained its density of before the Black Death in 1349. That can be gauged from its growth rate during the sixteenth century and the probable extent of its decline during the late Middle Ages. To this it can be added that contemporary witnesses received the impression that the land was becoming more densely populated, even over-populated. 'It seems to me', wrote Sebastian Franck in his *Deutschen Chronik* (1538), 'if God does not inflict a war in which many die, we shall be forced – chosen by lot or some such way – to travel like the gypsies in search of a new land. If some hundred thousand men, as I reckon, with their wives and children and dependents left, with God's help, to occupy all Hungary with German people, it would make little difference to Germany.' Ulrich von Hutten thought a new war with Turkey might solve the problem. In another work it was suggested that plagues and epidemics were needed because the country was too full of people (Jolles n.d.:197; see also Janssen n.d.:304).

Since, however, neither emigration, nor war, nor epidemics inhibited the population growth of the sixteenth century to any significant degree, land that had hitherto been almost or quite neglected had to be brought into cultivation to provide food. Great stretches of moor and wasteland were ploughed up, marshes were drained, pastures were converted to arable and woodlands were cleared. Deforestation reached such a pitch that rulers of more than one German state found themselves compelled to forbid further reclamation. 'It is manifest', proclaimed a Wurtemberg decree of 1536, 'that the woods and timber are becoming seriously depleted due to the multitude of people, increasing daily in number, who chop the woods down everywhere to make fields. The careless felling of trees and driving of cattle are also much to blame.' Burning and reclamation were thus prohibited and cattle droving reduced, but how obediently these rules were kept we do not know. The peasants were under pressure to provide food for themselves and their families. Need forced them to till land little suited to permanent cultivation. We hear from the small town of Frankenberg in Hessen that between 1530 and 1570 some 137 morgens of only fairly good arable land and 26 morgens of 'the worst and poorest soil' had been put under the plough (Probst, 1963), and in 1601 from the little Swabian town of Balingen: 'during the recent weary years of rising prices many rough and stony soils have been torn up and ploughed that they may bear fruit for a few years and then lie fallow for twelve, fifteen or twenty more' (König, 1958).

Along the coast of the North Sea, drainage and dyke-building were making rapid progress. In the Netherlands 8,046 hectares were won from the sea between 1565 and 1590; between 1590 and 1615 the figure rose to 36,213 hectares, so that altogether 44,000 hectares of new land had been gained in fifty years. It was 200 years before as much was reclaimed again (Baasch, 1927:29f.). Men were working with equal energy on the German North Sea coast to win back the great stretches of land that had been engulfed during the fourteenth and fifteenth centuries. Fields and villages had sunk beneath the waves. Considerably more than 1,000 square kilometres of land must have been lost from Eiderstedt and Ditmarsch and the Coasts of North Friesland and Lower Saxony.

To illustrate this, my colleagues Dr Saalfeld and Dr Wiese have prepared a map, figure 19, which shows how much dry land was lost and won along the German North Sea coast during the late Middle Ages. During the high Middle

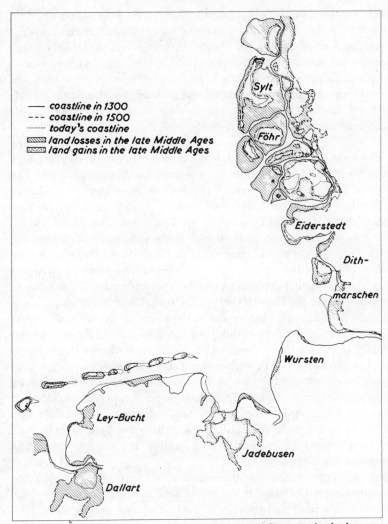

Fig. 19   Land gains and losses on the German north Sea coast in the late Middle Ages.

Ages the land between the mainland of Schleswig-Holstein and the present-day islands was continuous. The settlers, traces of whose occupation can still be seen below the water in aerial photographs, had built dykes, dug canals and planted fields. In this way the organic formation of the top soil layers may have been disintegrated. It is possible, as archaeologists now believe, that owing to turf-cutting, salt-pans, canals and cultivation, the protected lands sank beneath the then average high tide level. When the dykes broke under the force of the flood tides the water no longer flowed back into the sea. This must be the explanation of how such wide expanses of land, especially between the little islands of North Friesland and the mainland, literally 'went under'. But it must also be remembered that the greatest flood tide of the late Middle Ages, known as the 'Man-drinker', which probably engulfed the town of Rungholt, occurred in 1362, and that as early as 1352 an entry in the Schleswig cathedral chapter register recorded that the episcopal revenue was diminishing 'because so many died during the terrible plague of 1350'. It would thus appear that there was already a shortage of people to repair the dykes even before the great flood. Perhaps the destruction of Nygenstad on the lower Elbe, a town with charter and seal, fits into the same picture. The town was lost at the end of the fourteenth century; its ruins were long discernible beside the banks of the present-day Elbe (Meyn, 1966:93ff.). The lament of a priest living near Jever in 1423 gives us some idea of the state of affairs along the German North Sea coast of those days: 'The presbyteries are vacant, the glebelands untilled or spoilt by brackish water. The churches stand empty, their bells, communion plate, prayer books and reliquaries stolen, the villages deserted.' That is all too reminiscent of the derelict villages of the late Middle Ages. (But we will not pursue that train of thought at present.) It remains only to add that, on similar evidence, Verhulst (1965:57f.) calls our attention to the lost territory along the Flemish coast in the late Middle Ages.

At the end of the fifteenth century and in the course of the sixteenth a great programme of drainage and dyke-building was set in motion. In the Harlebucht, the Leybucht and along the outlying coast of the Jever district about 40,000 hectares were reclaimed during the sixteenth and early seventeenth centuries. That is more than two-thirds of all the known new territory gained in Lower Saxony between the thirteenth century and the middle of the nineteenth century. Although in neighbouring Schleswig-Holstein the great land losses of the late Middle Ages were not by any means made good, it is thought that some 8,000 hectares were reclaimed from the sea during the sixteenth century and the first half of the seventeenth (see Abel, 1967:152ff.).

The sixteenth century also saw the second great wave of reclamation and colonization in eastern Germany. It was remarkable, as Kuhn has shown (1957), for the many and various movements that made it up (see also Schulz, 1938). Limited in extent though they were, and independent of each other, they were nevertheless all directed by the same forces. Lithuanians migrated to East Prussia, Dutch Mennonites settled round the mouth of the Vistula. German peasants from eastern Pomerania penetrated the ridges and sandy areas in the south of the country that had been left untouched by the first invasion; from Neumark and Lower Silesia peasant settlers moved into the wide forest belt that still lies between Germany and Poland. Offshoots of the general drift, freed by the dissolution of the manorial system and impelled by the explosion of population, travelled via western Prussia and Posen to central Poland and Wolin. The extent of this movement can be gauged by the fact that on the Filehne estate in the course of two generations, between *c.* 1590 and 1650, the area of arable land increased eight-fold.

French farming, too, had suffered severe setbacks during the fifteenth century. Both in the north and south of the country great expanses of territory were quite depopulated. Yet, if we can take the word of an early sixteenth-century writer, the cultivated area had already increased by one-third at the beginning of the sixteenth century (Seissel, quoted in Araskhaniatz, 1882:32). Again, a few decades later, the Venetian ambassador wrote that France was inhabited to the limits of possibility (quoted in Levasseur, 1889:189).

Some isolated instances follow to confirm these general impressions. In 1545, at an inquiry held in the parish of d'Auzon (Yonne), it was stated that 'in the last forty years we have ploughed up land that had lain waste as long as any man can remember'. The forest of Orléans, once covering 60,000 hectares, had by 1533 dwindled to 20,000 hectares. In 1507–9 the forest of Laigne (Oise) contained 1,063 farms entitled to use the woodlands; by 1547–9 the number had grown to 1,336, an increase of 25 per cent in forty years. An historian of French forests in the sixteenth century headed one of his chapters 'The woodland crisis of the first half of the century' (Deveze, 1961, part 3), a true description from his point of view, for arable farming and animal husbandry were pushing back the boundaries of woods and scrub.

Table 15   Cultivated areas of Lattes, near Montpellier, in the years 1547 and 1607 in hectares

	1547	*1607*
Vineyards	61	42
Meadows	245	250
Grain	814	1287
	1120	1579

From the 1560s onwards the expansion of the arable area was interrupted by the religious wars, but by the end of the century reclamation had started again with renewed vigour. There are figures relating to a district in the south (Lattes near Montpellier) which roughly cover the war years (see table 15). These records, discovered by a fortunate chance, reveal that the farming area increased by over 400 hectares. The increase was nearly all taken up by cereal-growing, which expanded by more than half during the period. The meadow area remained much as before while vineyards even decreased a little (Le Roy Ladurie, 1957:223f.;[2] 1966:196ff.; see also d'Avenel, 1894–1926:I, 277, 346, 376).

In England the conversion of waste and poor meadowland to arable culture was held back for a time by the sheep farming inherited from the late Middle Ages. This will be referred to later in connection with the enclosures.

The agricultural situation in Scandinavia was little different from that of the rest of the continent. There, too, as the population grew, arable farming took up more space.

Intensification and regional differences in farming production

In Italy, England, France and Germany a stream of books on agriculture poured from the presses. Besides advice on household matters, medicine, child care, hunting and forestry, there were, of course, chapters dealing with farming and livestock, and the organization, calculations, book-keeping and taxation that went with them. I will name only a few of the better-known works. In Germany there were Martin Grosser's *Kurze Anleitung zu der Landwirtschaft* (1590); Johann Coler's *Landwirtschaftliche Kalendar* and several editions of *Rei Rusticae Libri Quattuor*, by Conrad Heresbach, the first of which appeared in 1570 and was translated into English in 1577. In France the doctor and printer Cardus Stephanus, together with his son-in-law, Jean Libault, wrote a highly-regarded book on farming in the Latin and French lanuages, which was published in Strasbourg in a German translation in 1579; Olivier de Serres produced *Le Théatre d'Agriculture*, whose third edition, published in 1605, bore the description *là est répresenté tout ce qui est requis et nécessaire pour bien dresser, gouverner, enrichir et embellir la maison rustique*. From England there was Anthony Fitzherbert's *Book of Husbandry* (1523) and Thomas Tusser's *Hundred Good Pointes of Husbandry* (1557). That Tusser's work went through no fewer than thirteen editions before the end of the century, and that the few surviving copies are dog-eared and incomplete, indicates the enthusiastic readership enjoyed by agronomical writers in the sixteenth century.

And here and there were, it seems, a considerable number of practical disciples. The repeated admonitions to plough more deeply, manure more richly and pay more attention to the very different requirements of the various crops appear to have taken effect. In the densely-populated and early-industrialized Netherlands, especially, a truly intensive agriculture developed. Belgian and Dutch leasehold farmers grew cabbages, beans, clover and flax in the fallow, as well as a quantity of catch crops and forage plants. They also used plenty of manure. The notes written by a farmer in Hitsum, four kilometres south-west of Franeker, suggest that the proportion of grain to pulse-growing was 7 : 1. On this farm in the 1570s the fallow had been practically abolished. The farmer bought 200 cartloads of dung to which he added 40 more produced from his own farm. The seed yield ratio of wheat was 1 : 10, of barley 1 : 9. One cow yielded 43 kilograms of butter and 28 kilograms of cheese, that is to say at least 1,350 litres of milk for the market alone.

Slicher van Bath, who (with Loder and Hemmema, 1958) has described the astonishing development of Dutch agriculture in the sixteenth century more thoroughly and perceptively than anyone, distinquished three forms into which during that century the traditional three-course rotation (derived itself from still earlier roots) in the Netherlands had evolved:

1 Rotations of several courses with the fallow relegated to the fourth, fifth or sixth year.
2 Regulated convertible husbandry with two years of grain cultivation followed by one fallow year and three to six years of grazing.
3 A crop rotation with fodder crops grown in the fallow year or as a catch crop, which foreshadows the crop rotation system popularized by the English enthusiasts during the eighteenth century (see particularly van der Woude, 1972; also Faber, 1960, 1972).

In spite of the high intensity of farming achieved in the Netherlands during the sixteenth century, output was not enough to satisfy the rapidly-growing demand in the Dutch towns. The influence of this demand, concentrated though it was in such a narrow area, reached far beyond the Netherlands. Johann Heinrich von Thünen, the German economist and founder of the theory of agricultural location, demonstrated with a diagram how a site might be affected economically by its distance from the market, a situation that first became a reality on a continental scale in Europe during the sixteenth century.

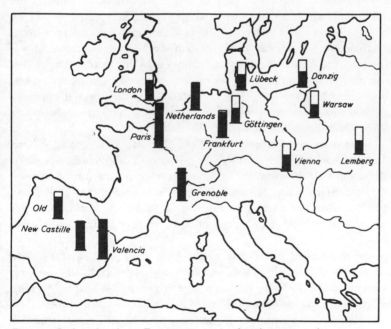

Fig. 20   Grain prices in 14 European towns and regions 1551–1600.

Since Thünen based his arguments on cereal prices, we will do the same, using Achilles' figures (1957, 1969). Price averages have been calculated for different towns and regions during the second half of the sixteenth century. The Netherlands price is set at 100, to make the decline towards the east more easily discernible (see figure 20).

The French price, which will not be discussed further at this point, was higher than the Dutch. It appears that grain was occasionally exported from the Netherlands to France, but the market in France, and especially in Paris, was determined by forces of its own. It should, however, be noted that there were marked price gradients within France itself, in two directions: one from Paris, the other from the Mediterranean coast. If the price of wheat in Paris for the years 1601–10 is taken as 100, it was 76 in Beauvais, 70 in Amiens, 65 in Noyon, 59 in Peronne, 86 in Rozoy, 70 in Châteaudun, 54 in Langres and 136 in Aix-en-Provence. Thus the price sank in proportion to the distance from Paris until it reached Provence, where the price level was exceptionally high (Goubert, 1960:224).

This picture of European grain prices in the early modern era can give us only a rough impression of the trend of trade. Among other obstacles, such as wars, tariffs and trade restrictions, were problems of transport, which were formidable when the routes lay overland. Thünen reckoned that even in his day, the early nineteenth century, the cost of land transport equalled the value of the rye it carried by the time it had travelled 375 kilometres. Carrying grain for long distances overland was worthwhile only in winter on sledges, or when villein labour and cartage, which cost the owner nothing, could be used.

Transport by water was a different matter. When, in the period 1551–1600, the price of corn in Danzig was 53 per cent of the Netherlands figure, it was worth exporting it to Amsterdam in great quantities. Indeed in 1600, 80 per cent of the grain brought to Amsterdam by sea came from Danzig. Danzig rye exports rose to over 100,000 tons a year. The city extended its harbour and improved its organization and credit arrangements to cope with the ever-growing maritime trade. While Danzig was the centre of the Baltic grain trade, there were a number of other ports in the same business, including Riga, Königsberg, Elbing, Stettin, Lübeck, Kiel and other smaller cities. Kantzow, the Pomeranian writer, between 1532 and 1541 described the lively export trade in grain carried on along the whole Pomeranian coast. Heinrich Rantzau, a big landowner of Holstein recorded that in 1600 the wheat grown on the isle of Fehmarn in Lübeck Bay was so famous that it could fetch a good price as far away as France, Italy and Spain.

Against this background, cereal-growing along the whole Baltic coast from Kiel to Lübeck, Stettin, Danzig, up to Riga and far inland, developed and prospered. On the west coast of Schleswig-Holstein a type of convertible husbandry called the enclosure system (*Koppelwirtschaft*) gained ground. It consisted of about three years of cereals alternating with four of pasture. That was, as Thünen remarked, a very intensive form of grain-growing since the droppings of the grazing animals benefited the ensuing agriculture and were not wasted as in the three-course rotation. The beginnings of a multi-course rotation were taking hold on Fehmarn and inland of Lübeck, then advancing eastwards. With this system, as in the Netherlands, the fallow was becoming increasingly more uncommon.

Beyond this region, as Thünen noted, was the area of three-course rotation, with a fallow period every third year (winter corn – summer corn – fallow) and large expanses of permanent pasture. Although this was a very extensive form of agriculture, it was perfectly suited to the economic conditions of its time and place. Let us take another look at figure 20. How could the peasant of the Danzig countryside compete with the Dutch farmer who lived at the gates of a 'world city'? The prices he received were too low and his expenses too high, in spite of underpaid – or even unpaid – labour.

The spread of three-course rotation in eastern Germany and Poland was related to the advance of the farming industry and a manorial system based on the compulsory services of the peasant and his family. Some writers, particularly Marxist economic historians, see the 'exploitation of the peasantry' as the one foundation of the great grain export trade from eastern Europe, though they, of all people, should not need reminding that while social structure is determined by economic conditions, there is a reciprocal action between society and the economy. It is more satisfactory to see the growth of the farming industry as a result of the favourable export prospects offered to east German and Polish agriculture in the sixteenth century, and the rise of the manorial system there as a symptom of the improved opportunities for trade, but not as a *conditio sine qua non* of export. Farmers working under freer conditions were also capable of producing surpluses from a three-course rotation and selling them with profit on the world market as it then was. That happened occasionally even in the sixteenth century and became common in the eighteenth century, when not a few east German landowners voluntarily supplemented, or even replaced, their serf labour with wage labourers.

The rise and growth of east European trade was the main topic at the First International Conference of Economic Historians in Stockholm in 1960. Since then there has been a clarification of the very divergent opinions expressed in Poland. Maczak summed up ten years of discussion in the following words: 'Polish agriculture responded to a market challenge' (1972:676). Wyczanski (1963:81ff.) developed an interesting idea as to how the numerous noblemen owning medium-sized estates were able to find a way between the opportunities offered by the market and the constraint forced on them by the shortage of servile labour to take some small share in the agricultural boom of the sixteenth century.[3]

*

Beyond the corn belt lay the pastureland that supplied central and western Germany with the produce of its animal husbandry, chiefly cattle and sheep farming and, to a lesser extent, pig-breeding. It stretched over parts of Russia, Poland, the plains of Hungary and as far as the Black Sea coast when the way was not blocked by the Turks. The cattle trade started in the Middle Ages (see above, page 70). During the sixteenth century it developed considerably, becoming largely a trade in oxen. The principal trading centres for the cattle from south-east Europe were Vienna, Breslau and Brieg; for the Russo-Polish cattle, Posen, Frankfurt on the Oder and Buttstädt, a little town north of Weimar to which often 15,000, 16,000, even 20,000 oxen were driven, according to a letter dated 1551 from the duke Johann Friedrich of Saxony to his steward regarding the customs duties and convoy expenses paid by the cattle merchants (Helbig, 1973:73f.). In the larger towns of south Germany there were efficient market organizations, that of Nuremberg, for instance, even being divided into three sections, one for the butchers and their guild, another for the livestock wholesalers, and the third a city 'ox board' that supplied the traders with credit. It is recorded that traders sometimes dealt in lots of 1,000 oxen and more, for example in 1596 a merchant from Prague offered the Nurembergers 1,500 Siebenburg oxen.

This remarkable cattle trade has already been the subject of some discussion. A certain amount has come to light about the routes and intermediate stopping places of the long drives (well over 1,000 kilometres), how long they took, the dangers that lay in wait for them, the commercial risks and the potential profits (see Bog, 1971; Pickl, 1971:1).[4] We also know that the demand for beef in several German towns and at the courts of a number of princes was supplied largely by the oxen from eastern Europe. Thus, for example, of the 4,652 cattle consumed at the court of the Count of Marburg and Kassel in twenty-five years between 1528 and 1618, about two-thirds came from Russia, Poland, Hungary and other easterly regions (see further details in Abel, 1967).

However, some notes written by the Count of Hesse's clerk of the kitchen, and some other pieces of evidence, show us that during the sixteenth century the east European trade in oxen was faced with a formidable rival in what were already known as 'Friesian cattle'. The cattle of the North Sea marshlands had long been renowned, but it was not until the sixteenth century that a really big trade in cattle developed along the route from north to south-west. The tax registers of Rendsburg in northern Schleswig tell us that around 1565 some 45,000 cattle passed through the customs every year and that in 1612, the peak year recorded, the number was 49,519. In the spring of that year 43,724 head of cattle – 88 per cent of the year's total – were dealt with. A small proportion of the cattle went to Lübeck, Hamburg and further south towards central Germany. The majority, as we can see from the ferry-boat accounts of those shipped in the vicinity of Hamburg (Wedel, Blankensee and Zollenspieker), were driven on to the pastures of Friesland, Oldenburg and Holland where, as an old document reports, 'in a single summer the rich pastures make them as fat as bacon, so that they are ripe for slaughter by the autumn'.

We are better informed about the no less remarkable north-south and north-west trade (Wiese, 1963, 1966). Not only are the ox trails, stopping-places and

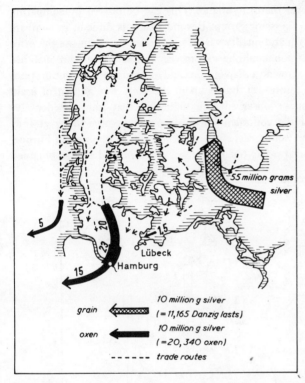

Fig. 21 Export values. from the Baltic area.

the risks and dangers of the trade known to us, but also the profits and the prices at the point of export from Denmark and at the markets in Germany and Holland. The values can be calculated, then converted and compared with those of other commodities in this inter-regional commerce, for example with the value of the grain that passed through the Sound tolls. We get some relatively high figures. Between 1601 and 1620 the average annual value, expressed in the silver content of the currency used, of the Baltic grain despatched from the Sound (by far the most important customs office for this commodity) amounted to 55,000 kilograms of silver. On the other hand, the oxen from Schleswig-Holstein and the Danish islands were exported to the value of approximately 5,000 kilograms of silver by water along the North Sea coast to Friesland and Holland, 23,000 kilograms of silver by road to Hamburg, 15,000 kilograms of silver over the Elbe, and 1,500 kilograms of silver by water to Lübeck, thus altogether (allowing for double-counting) a value of about 30,000 kilograms of silver (see figure 21). That was over half the value of all the grain entered in the customs book.[5]

As it was with grain, so it was with oxen: the further they had to go, the higher became their price. In Antwerp oxen were dearer than in Hamburg, and in

Hamburg they were dearer than in Jutland. This can be proved by comparing the cost of animals from the same group. Beyond that it is difficult to compare prices, since point of origin and quality varied so much. One might use the price of meat instead, but meat, too, could be sold in very different ways and qualities. Nevertheless, it is worth showing a map of meat and ox prices in various European towns and regions (see figure 22) drawn up in the same way as that of grain prices (figure 20). It can be observed from figure 22 that from the densely-populated north-west of the continent outwards prices became lower as they receded towards the north, south, east and, except for France, the west of Europe. Unfortunately the Antwerp price, once more set at 100, could not be obtained

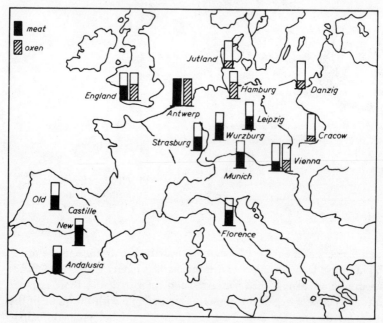

Fig. 22   Prices of meat and oxen in 15 European towns and regions 1551–1600.

from the average prices of the whole period as the original compilers (Verlinden and Scholliers) calculated it from the highest and lowest prices of one particular year. If the distortion due to this and to the inadequacy of the available material is taken into account, the following picture emerges:

1 Meat price percentages in relation to the price at Antwerp: England 51, Strasbourg 47, New Castile 75, Andalusia 72, Old Castile 51, Florence 56, Vienna 34, Munich 56, Augsburg 46, Würzburg 59, Leipzig 45.
2 Ox price percentages in relation to the Antwerp price: England 59, Vienna 37, Hamburg 59, Jutland 26, Danzig 27, Cracow 15.[6]

Side by side with the export of fat oxen and other livestock, including horses, an intensive dairy-farming industry was developing in the marshlands of the North Sea coast and on the grassy farmland round the bay of Kiel. Butter and cheese were sent from there in great quantities to Amsterdam and Groningen, the trading centres for those products, as well as to Hamburg, Bremen and further into Germany. The little region of Eiderstedt in the duchy of Holstein alone exported 2–3 million pounds of cheese a year between 1583 and 1600 (Matthiessen, n.d.:264f.; see also Jürgens, n.d.:27f.). There are no export figures for Friesland, but the numerous references to the cost of these products that have come down to us show how important the dairy trade was to that province. It was the main cash product of the region: the Friesian deputies even declared in 1586 that butter was the region's only source of income (Swart, 1910:206; see also Hagedorn, 1910:9, 31, *passim*). Still further to the west, between the Zuider Zee and the North Sea and close to Amsterdam, Haarlem and Utrecht, dairying appears to some extent to have taken the place of fat-cattle breeding (Kuske, 1956:202).

The production of cattle and animal products was based on the permanent pastures provided by the marshlands bordering the North Sea coast and the western shores of the Baltic. It is often overlooked, however, that it was also the result of intensive farming methods. In the Netherlands an early form of crop rotation was to be found (see above page 107), and there was regulated convertible husbandry on the Schleswig-Holstein enclosures. The origins of this system, whose chief characteristic is a temporary conversion of arable to pasture, is lost in the mists of time. It may have arisen here and there from a primitive type of convertible husbandry or from three-course rotation, but it was not till the sixteenth century that it became at all general. It enabled the farmers, as Thünen observed, to grow more corn to the acre because the dung from the grazing beasts was not wasted, while at the same time it improved and intensified stock raising. Thus there was already a division of labour between the agriculture of the Baltic coast and that on the maritime plains by the North Sea. Not only their favourable soil and climate but their location determined their roles in the economy of the industrial and trading centres of the north-west. The dense swathe of Dutch and Flemish towns from Bruges and Ghent to Amsterdam and Groningen, with their huge demand for farm produce, was the decisive factor in the direction taken by agriculture in northern Germany and beyond. The immediately-neighbouring regions specialized in dairy products and fat-cattle grazing, those situated further off reared cattle and grew cereals.

Seen from this angle, from the point of view of the market, the differences in farming systems reveal their economic causes. The 'Thünen circles' were evolving in the sixteenth century. To a great extent, distance from the market determined the system. This confirms the hypothesis that the Dutch multi-course rotation, the convertible husbandry of the Holsteiners and the three-course rotation of the east German, Baltic and Polish estates were the 'relatively best agrarian systems' (Thünen) for their particular regions, not only because of soil and climate but also in relation to the market.

*

And what was happening in England while these developments were under way? Land was being enclosed there during the sixteenth century, and even in the modern literature of economic history we quite often meet with the opinion that this was necessarily associated with a transition from arable farming to extensive grazing. This can only be maintained unconditionally of the fifteenth century and perhaps of the very early sixteenth. It was then that the demand, together with the relatively rising cost of agricultural overheads and the falling grain prices, made a transition to extensive livestock farming inevitable. It was then that the contemporary laments over 'man-eating sheep' (Thomas More) were justified. But later in the century, when agriculture in the neighbouring countries was expanding and intensifying under the pressure of a growing population, the English landlords ceased turning cornfields into meadows. 'The heyday of sheep depopulation was over by 1550, checked by popular hostility, government action and the recovery in the relative profit of corn as against wool' (Beresford and St Joseph, 1958:120).

An important, perhaps decisive, factor in the structural changes that occurred in English farming was the relation of the price of corn to that of wool. Until the 1540s the ratio changed very little. Only from that time did corn prices begin to rise more rapidly (see below, figure 27). Bowden (1967:593ff.), in his penetrating research on English agricultural prices, farming profits and incomes in the sixteenth century, does not confine himself to telling us of long-term developments. He also examines the shorter price fluctuations and comes to the conclusion that the sheep farmer's chance of profit rose or fell in inverse proportion to the price of corn. That chimes in with my own theory, based on wider material, of the harvest cycle in the sixteenth century and after (Abel, 1974: especially 167ff.). When harvests failed, the limited elasticity of the demand for grain attracted the available purchasing power to the sector of essential foodstuffs, whereas when the harvest was plentiful and the price of corn low, goods in income-elastic demand, among them the raw materials of the textile industry, found a good turnover. The only questionable points are the time-spans Bowden uses for purposes of comparison in his table 23: the periods are too long and not definite enough. Bowden himself notes that during the sixteenth century poor harvests occurred at 'fairly regular intervals' of eleven years (as Jevons had already suggested). His time-spans overlap these eleven-year cycles without, however, entirely suppressing them.

Here it would be as well to summarize the results of recent research. Firstly, Bowden's investigations convincingly demonstrate, in spite of the unsuitable time-spans mentioned above, that the change from wool boom to corn boom did not occur overnight and once and for all. It developed in cyclic waves determined by the fluctuations of corn harvests and prices. Nevertheless, in the long term, 1550 can be considered as the turning-point. Secondly, it must not be forgotten that any such date is subject to variations dependent on the geographical situation, both natural and in relation to trade, of the estate in question. Thirdly – as pointed out by Thirsk in her penetrating study of enclosures (1967:200ff.) – there is the circumstance that methods of farming, whether by choice or by necessity, could delay matters, for corn-growing, especially on poor soil, could hardly prosper without the dung that sheep provided.

That brings us to the farming systems that took over from pure pasturage in England. German historians (Roscher, Hanssen and others) have long pointed out that in England, until 1550 at least, the prevailing system was not, as is so often supposed, unadulterated livestock farming, but an evolved convertible husbandry which, besides being favoured by soil and climate, produced a much higher yield on the enlarged enclosed farms (G. Hanssen, 1880:508f.; Roscher, 1885:980f.). Ashley (1896:11, 278) was of the same opinion: 'What happened in England was the change from the cultivation of open fields to a meadow economy – but not to continuous sheep-grazing – whereby the pasture-land had to be ploughed every two years for one or two harvests.' One is reminded of the Holstein rotation system, and still more of the Mecklenburg variant, which resembled English convertible husbandry even more closely in that it was based on extensive sheep farming. A contemporary described it as a four-year rotation of pasture and arable land, including a fallow period at the beginning and another in the middle. In this way the Mecklenburg farmer 'did not only get useful grazing for his flocks, but also had occasion to set up sheep pens and folds. . . . Now he could fold the sheep on the first fallow and manure the intermediate fallow with dung from the pens, which brought the corn on amazingly and also improved the grass' (Able, 1967:311). Such fallow years may have been used in England, too, but that is only conjecture. There is more evidence to support the statement that in England corn-growing increased, whether by the old methods or the new. Harrison (quoted in Steffen, 1901:1, 460) wrote in his description of England (1577) that the cornfields were bigger than ever before, and Gras (1915:220) concluded that the corn-growing areas of England yielded an ever-increasing surplus of grain throughout the century.

The gradual advance of corn-growing can be deduced from the fact that after the mid-sixteenth century arable rents rose more rapidly than rents for meadows and pasture (Bowden, 1967:593ff.; see also Kerridge, 1953–4).

Sheep and cattle farming found other, more suitable locations. To some degree cattle breeding shifted from England to Ireland. In 1663 some 61,000 lean cattle were shipped over the Irish Sea to be fattened in East Anglia (Trow-Smith, 1957:229). Shortly afterwards parliament passed a bill, which the East Anglian graziers were unable to stop, prohibiting the import of Irish cattle to England. This occurred in 1666, when the first of a long series of farming crises marked the end of the long-term boom during the sixteenth century and first half of the seventeenth century.

*

Sheep farming moved into Spain. In spring and autumn vast flocks were driven across the peninsula from north to south and back again. New discoveries in the archives show that in Castile alone, without Aragon, there were 3 million nomadic sheep in addition to flocks that remained in one locality. Three-quarters of the sheep farmers, as later reports indicate, owned flocks of between 50 and 5,000 animals; the remaining quarter consisted of about sixty members of the high nobility and rich monasteries. The greatest part of the wool was exported. When, on one occasion, Charles V tried to limit the export to half the amount shorn he met with fierce resistance from the Mesta, the celebrated organization whose function it was to protect the rights of the sheep farmers against towns, villages and the Crown itself.[7]

*

To sum up, it can be said that during the sixteenth century the production of foodstuffs in Europe greatly increased. European agriculture expanded enormously. This was done by ploughing up wastes, moors, and marshes, pastures and woodlands, as well as by reclaiming land from the sea. In addition to this great expansion of the arable area, farming became more intensive and there was better communication between regions. Agriculture grew more specialized to suit the conditions of its location and trade formed the bridges, thus facilitating a greater division of labour to make the best use of the relative advantages of each area. The structure of society and state became more flexible, more interwoven. In spite of all the territorial differences, a great part of Europe, from Spain far into the Russo-Polish east, could henceforth be regarded as a unity grouped round the centres of industry and trade.

Though this statement is broadly true, it is not enough for the economic historian. The reality beneath the surface has not been penetrated; the essential economic problem lies deeper. The purpose of the economy is to satisfy demand, and so we must inquire further whether, in fact, the progress of agriculture was sufficient to cover the growing demand, whether it sometimes even exceeded it or whether it lagged behind.

The 'price revolution' of the sixteenth century

The movement of grain prices

The sixteenth century was the age of the 'price revolution'. The term should be written in inverted commas because it is easily misinterpreted (see Cipolla, 1955:513f.). If we take the price of grain – which increased more than most prices – as a yardstick, it will be seen that between the first and last decades of the century the price in England rose by 424 per cent, in Belgium by 379 per cent, in France by 651 per cent, in the Netherlands by 318 per cent, in Germany by 255 per cent, in Austria by 272 per cent, and in Poland (Cracow) by 401 per cent (see appendix). The simple arithmetical mean for the seven countries during these nine decades comes to an increase of 386 per cent or an annual average of 4.3 per cent equivalent to a compound interest of 1.52 per cent. When it is taken into consideration that years of steep inflation alternated with others in which prices rose only slightly or even diminished, it is clear that the name 'price revolution' is a gross exaggeration. Prices went up less than in our own day when no one talks of a price revolution, and even much milder expressions annoy the politicians.

Another widely-disseminated error is that inflation spread out in waves from Spain towards the east. The idea is based upon the import of silver from America but, in fact, prices began to rise in western and central Europe long before the first silver fleet landed on the coast of Spain. Quite apart from that, figure 23 shows that grain prices in England, Belgium, Germany, the Netherlands, Austria, France and Poland kept very much in step with one another, while in France and Poland there were great differences in the timing of the price changes. The wave theory cannot be maintained in the face of this evidence, although it is possible that improved methods of research will one day reveal that the idea contains a modicum of truth.

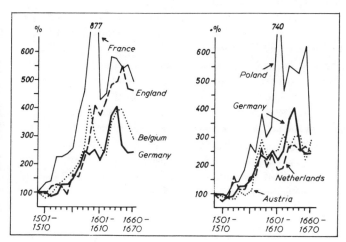

Fig. 23   Grain prices in western and central Europe 1500–1670 (decennial averages, grams silver per 100 kilograms).

The above figures are too general to show us the similarities and differences in place and time that would help us to follow the way in which the price movements spread through Europe. Since prices were influenced by trade, we must study the course of trade. It appears that where trade was lively the 'price waves' were short-term affairs. So, at least, a comparison of the mean annual prices in the Vistula area and between that area and the Netherlands corn-importing region would seem to prove. The co-efficients of variation of the annual price movements are checked by calculating the correlation (Achilles, 1959:32f.). In the Vistula area we get the following result:

Danzig to Warsaw   1551–1600 r = 0.787 ± 0.076
Danzig to Cracow   1551–1600 r = 0.773 ± 0.061
Danzig to Lemburg 1551–1600 r = 0.719 ± 0.073

The east-west overseas trade produces the following high co-efficients:

Danzig to Utrecht   1551–1600 r = 0.950 ± 0.017
Danzig to Amsterdam 1551–1600 r = 0.881 ± 0.033

A correlation co-efficient of 0.9 or over, such as could be established for the mean annual prices between Danzig and Utrecht during the sixteenth century, and between Danzig and Amsterdam in the first half of the seventeenth century, means that the series moved in a parallel direction. This does not exclude the possibility of short-term fluctuations in price level that might be due to a reduction of transport costs or an improvement in trading facilities, but these would be more likely to narrow than to widen the price gap. Decreases in the cost of transport may also explain a phenomenon seen in figure 23: grain prices went up earlier and higher in Poland than in the Netherlands.[8]

Contemporaries did their best to trace the cause of the inflated prices. Some saw them as a punishment from God, others as the result of usury, greed, avarice, speculation and market-cornering. Others assigned the blame to poor harvests. It is true that there was quite a series of harvest failures during the sixteenth century, but it is unlikely that these bad seasons were any worse or more numerous than in previous and subsequent centuries. This opinion was shared by Bodin (1568) who thought that 'the chief and almost the only cause' of the price inflation of his time was the excess of precious metal. Undoubtedly, from as early as the mid-fifteenth century, a considerable quantity of silver had been mined in the Tyrol. In 1471 the rich mines of Schneeberg were opened and in 1496 those of Anneberg. The mines of the Joachim Valley in Bohemia were first exploited in 1516. There must have been a great increase in the amount of silver in circulation even before the American mines began to send bullion to Europe. According to Hamilton (194:42f.) the quantity of silver reaching Europe from there by legal means between 1521 and 1530 was 149 kilograms, between 1611 and 1620 the amount was 2,192,256 kilograms and during the entire 1521–1620 period it was about 12 million kilograms. It is possible that during those years some 'sharp customers' used as a means of exchange a certain amount of bullion that formerly had been hoarded. Furthermore, inflation, once set in motion, may have increased the velocity of the circulation of money and reduced the tendency to hoard it. There is no doubt that credit greatly expanded. All this led to a drop in the value of money and a rise in prices.

Sebastian Franck (1538:759f.) depicts very graphically how the cost of living gradually went up, a rise in the price of one kind of goods leading inevitably to other commodities becoming dearer. It did people no good in the end, he said, when they raised the cost of their products:

> Suppose a farmer sells his farm for a thousand guilders after buying it for less than half as much, and sells a cartload of hay for four or five guilders, a cow for ten guilders, a horn for one, the tail for two and the hide for three, neither he nor the rest of the world will profit by it, for then the butcher will have to charge seven or eight pence for a pound of meat, the tanner will charge four or five guilders for a hide and the cobbler asks half a guilder for a pair of shoes. With such expenses to bear, the potter, the tailor and the smith will put up their prices too, so that a penny pot will cost a kreuzer, a horseshoe three kreutzers and a wheelwright will charge three times as much for a wheel as he used to. Thus things are just the same as when they were cheap, except that they have to be paid for with coins of a higher denomination and the kreutzer has taken the penny's place.

But gradually, and unnoticed by contemporary eyes, changes in the price structure begain to creep in. While some commodities and groups of commodities rose steeply and continuously in price during the sixteenth century, other goods and services (measured by the silver content of the coinage) went up only slowly, and with some reverses, above the level of the mid-fifteenth century. More will be written on this subject in the ensuing pages.

Wages and the price of industrial commodities

It would add little to the purpose of this work to present series of isolated prices for all the countries dealt with here. Their enumeration, moreover, would overflow our pages and exhaust the reader's patience, for many hundreds of such series have already been compiled by international research. We must select and summarize. The material, as well as the author's view of the problem, has determined the method. Grain, industrial commodities and wages have been selected, each of these groups including several products or occupations, especially the industrial commodity group, which contains quite a large and varied collection of products. All the price and wage series were based on the silver content of the coinage and divided into 25-year sections. These sectional values were then compared individually with the base period, and finally the relative values thus obtained were converted by simple arithmetical averaging to the group values for grain, etc. The result of these calculations is shown in figure 24.[9]

In all the countries shown in figure 24 industrial commodities (a group that admittedly includes some industrial raw materials) lagged behind grain in price. The gap varied, doubtless because of the very different structure of the indices and probably, among other factors, because of the relative wage movements. The

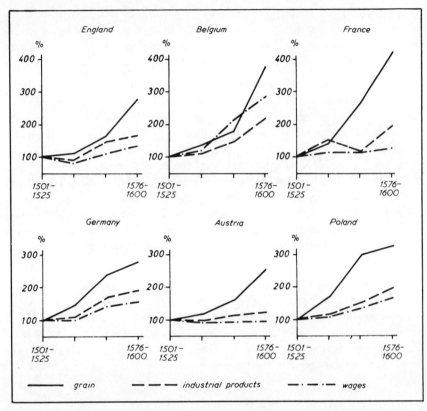

Fig. 24   Price and wage movements in western and central Europe during the sixteenth century (25-year averages, silver content of coinage, 1501–25 = 100).

gap itself is manifest and undisputed, however. It is also true of other lands not included in the graphs, for example Sweden (see Hammarström, 1957:145), and of other 25-year price averages besides those shown here.

From the material assembled by Rogers and Beveridge, Doughty worked out a still-more-broadly-based index of southern English industrial prices, which he compared with the agricultural price index (1975:177ff.). Since his study does not start till 1401 it cannot be referred to for price movements during the late medieval depression, which began earlier. However, being based on annual prices and ten-year averages, it does give a more accurate idea of sixteenth-century developments than the above-mentioned 25-year price averages. According to Doughty, the industrial price index rose between 1491–1500 and 1631–40 from 101 to 349, thus about three and a half times, whereas the price index of agricultural products rose from 99 to 689, almost sevenfold.

In England, France, Germany, Austria and Poland wages lagged behind the price level of industrial goods. In Austria the wage level of the last twenty-five years of the sixteenth century, reckoned in silver, was actually lower than that of the first quarter (95 per cent). The increase in England was 131 per cent, in France 126 per cent, in Germany 157 per cent and in Poland 165 per cent – increases ranging from a quarter to two-thirds. This was less than the rise in industrial prices, which came to 165 per cent in England, 194 per cent in France, 187 per cent in Germany, 123 per cent in Austria and 197 per cent in Poland. Only in Belgium did wages rise faster than the prices of industrial goods (by 282 per cent as against 218 per cent) and sometimes even more steeply than the price of grain. (In 1551–75 wages stood at 215 per cent, grain prices at 181 per cent and industrial commodities at 147 per cent of their level during the 1501–25 period.)

These calculations are, of course, very rough. Isolated commodities and wages, associated only by the chance of their discovery, are bundled together, and only a handful of towns in each country is included in the picture. Supplementary data will be useful at this point (see figure 25).[10] Hamburg has been chosen as

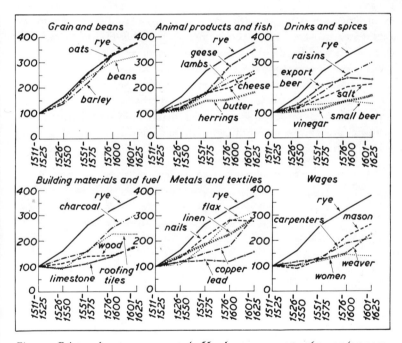

Fig. 25   Price and wage movements in Hamburg 1511–25 to 1601–25 (25-year averages in silver content of coinage, 1511–25 = 100).

the sample city because it was the meeting point of so many trade routes, and its archives, before they were partly destroyed during the war, contained a rich store of material for the history of prices. The price groups in figure 25 are made up partly from the point of view of demand and partly from the production angle. The top left graph contains not only grain prices but also a price curve for beans. Like cereals, beans are rich in calories and, in terms of food value units, cheap even when the price seems high. In fact the price of beans followed that of cereals very closely. On the other hand, with a few exceptions, the price of livestock products, fish, liquor and spices lagged behind. The same is true of building materials, fuel, metals and textiles. The price of these commodities rose more steeply in only a few cases (charcoal and flax). Mostly the increase was very slight, for example 83 per cent for lime, 53 per cent for lead. Wages, too, remained far behind the price of rye. Compared with the starting date, as the bottom right graph shows, a mason's wage went up by 265 per cent, a carpenter's by 20 per cent, a weaver's by 225 per cent and women's wages by 138 per cent, whereas, in the same length of time, the price of rye increased by 375 per cent.

The prices of some farm products in income-elastic demand

Just as the curve of meat and butter prices in Hamburg stayed lower than that of rye, so in other towns too the price of animal products did not rise to the same extent as that of cereals. The reason for this probably lies in the different elasticity of the demand for the two types of product in relation to income. The quantitative demand for meat and butter is relatively income-elastic. If the income sinks (or if the contents of the shopping basket grows too expensive) the purchaser can turn to other, cheaper articles of food. One of these is (and was) cereals. Although their cost went up relatively more than that of animal products in most European towns during the sixteenth century, they were still, judged by food value, cheaper than the animal products.

Table 16   The purchasing power of journeymen masons' or carpenter's wages in the period 1575–1600

Commodity	Kilogram	Calories
Peas	6.8	23,868
Rye	8.9	22,250
Butter	0.95	7,144
Pork	2.4	6,456
Beef	3.0	5,820

The second column of table 16 shows each commodity a journeyman mason or carpenter could buy with a day's wage.[11] The third column gives the number of calories obtained for the money spent. Peas would provide the most calories, and sure enough, in the case of Göttingen where sixteenth-century prices have been mapped accurately, the price of peas soared even more steeply than that of rye (Kullack-Ublick, 1953). Rye grain (bread was somewhat dearer) came next on the list. Butter, pork and beef followed at a considerable distance.

But wages and similar incomes formed only part of the pattern of demand. Other sorts of income were growing more rapidly and, when local differences are also taken into account, it is no wonder that there were many exceptions to the rule that grain prices always rose more steeply than others. Perhaps the outstanding exception was the increase in the price of oxen and rye in the rearing and grazing areas of north-west Germany. As figure 26 shows, during the sixteenth century in Schleswig-Holstein the price of oxen, of which a very thorough study has been made (Wiese, 1963), rose further than the price of rye (Waschinski, 11, 1959). This was due to the proximity of the big markets of the lower Rhine and the Netherlands.

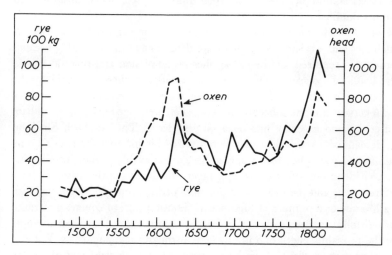

Fig. 26   Prices of oxen and rye in Schleswig-Holstein, 1470–1820 (decennial averages, grams of silver).

Several other products of arable farming, animal husbandry horticulture and the cultivation of special crops (wine for instance) could be brought into the picture, and would certainly repay study, but that would be to stray beyond the boundaries set for this book. So, in conclusion, it remains only to say that the sixteenth-century 'price revolution' encompasses many and varied processes to which relative prices are the key. It is on this, and not on the much-discussed changes in price level, that research should be concentrated.

Rising rents

Rents with conditions

Commercial rents must be distinguished from the rents paid in earlier centuries. Rogers considered that the old rents were in the nature of a tax and remained constant for long periods. As to that we cannot be sure, but it is incontestable that in England these rents rose abruptly in the sixteenth century. In his sermons before Edward VI between 1547 and 1553 Bishop Latimer stormed about the 'greed of the landlords' who, by raising rents, had caused bread and other products of the soil to become dearer. His father had owned a farm for which he had paid three or four pounds a year in rent; now that rent was sixteen pounds and more (Kerridge, 1953–4:16f.).[12] Already twenty years earlier William Roy had complained of landlords raising the rents by half as much again and demanding excessive entry fines. During the last quarter of the sixteenth century rents seem to have gone up even more rapidly. According to Kerridge the rent of farmland increased sixfold between 1590–1600 and 1640–50, while meadow and pasture rents doubled or trebled.

Rents were not the only payment landlords asked for and obtained. Besides a few small fees and services which the owner dared not assess too highly because some return was required for them, the fines on admission and renewal helped to fill the landlord's pockets. These entry or admission fines were paid by the tenant on taking over a lease for a lifetime or longer – sometimes two or three lifetimes. A certain amount of bargaining was usual. Kerridge tells us how William Poton offered £300 as entry fine on a 99-year lease. The landlord, Sir John Thynne, demanded £450, whereupon Poton raised his bid to £360 and Thynne countered with £400. They finally agreed on £370, payable in four instalments.

Three considerations affected these payments: the length of the lease, the level of the current rent and the production potential of the property. When the lease was for a lifetime or a number of lifetimes its duration was, of course, uncertain, but Kerridge tells us that as early as the sixteenth century there had been attempts to gauge the probable length of a life by certain rough pragmatic rules. Without some such estimate it would have been impossible to calculate how the entry fine was to be apportioned over the years that the lease might last. Tables to help in this matter came in at the beginning of the seventeenth century. They showed how much payments at different levels and for different numbers of years were worth in ready money. In this way the landlord could reckon up his effective rents and it only remained to adjust this income according to the property's potential yield. The tenant who concerned with the same question and by a process of haggling the price for the use of the land was settled.

Under the general heading of rents, Kerridge has calculated prices of properties belonging to some estates in the south of England. The result of his work is shown in figure 27. It shows that between the second decade of the sixteenth century and the years 1570–9 rents (that is to say rents plus instalments of the entry fine) went up fourfold, and after that, with a short interruption in the 1580s, to nearly twice as much again. As the accompanying wheat and wool curves indicate, the rise in rents easily overtook the increased price of the English farmer's main products.

This fact may first have been brought to light by later historians, but it was obvious enough to contemporaries that rents were going up, and many, if not most of them, sought a plain answer to the question of who was 'guilty' (much more rarely did they seek the cause). Some blamed the landlord for asking too much, others the tenant for offering too much. Norden, a contemporary writer, who had himself seen how leaseholds were bid for as in an auction, described his amazement at the 'sadness' and jealousy of the would-be tenants. 'Shall the lord then seek to hinder such hot spirits from climbing to the lord's advantage as high as their will, or perhaps their capability, will allow? I think it would be a great folly for a lord to refuse what is so willingly proffered.'

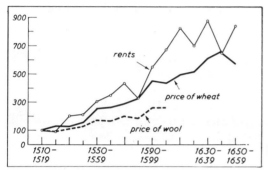

Fig. 27 English rents and prices 1510–19–1650–9.

The question of blame, which arose in Germany as well as England, can be left open. It is mentioned only because it throws light on the situation and not because it requires an answer from the historian. A different matter was a contemporary observation that the increased rents were the cause of farm products becoming more expensive. In one of Hale's discourses of 1549 (Stafford, 1581) we read: 'I think it is longe of you, Gentlemen, that this dearth groweth, by reason yee enhaunce your lands to such a height, as men that live thereon must needes sell deare again; or els they were never able to make their rente.' Perhaps this remark need only have been quoted purely as an illustration of contemporary thinking if the historian to whom rent research owes so much had not attached a great deal of weight to it. Kerridge (from whom the material above has largely been drawn) commented that the contemporary view was not so far off the mark because rent is, after all, a factor in production costs and therefore has a determining influence on prices. So a steep rise in rents in the early sixteenth century could have been 'one of the causes or even the main cause of inflation.'

Ricardo met a similar argument in a very similar situation two hundred years late. He rejected it on the grounds that agricultural yield was determined by the amount of work spent on the poorest soil even if no rent were paid for it. 'Corn is not high because a rent is paid, but a rent is paid because corn is high'; he wrote in the chapter on rents in his classic work, *The Principles of Political*

Economy and Taxation. 'It has been justly observed', he continued, 'that no reduction would take place in the price of corn although landlords should forgo the whole of their rent. Such a measure would only enable some farmers to live like gentlemen, but would not diminish the quantity of labour necessary to raise raw produce on the least productive land in cultivation.' To this day there is nothing essential to be added to that.

An interesting variant of the distribution of agricultural profit is described by Le Roy Ladurie (1966:1, 297ff.) in reference to Languedoc in 1590. He reconstructed the costs and profits of a large farm, 140 hectares under the plough, with a rotation of wheat-oats/rye (the crop being changed every second year), a yield of 10 hectolitres per hectare from the wheat (or, by my method of calculation, 770 kilograms per hectare) and about 60 per cent of the wheat value from the other crops, a total of 560 hectolitre wheat equivalents (hlWE) from the arable land. In addition, there were the yields from other crops (wine, oil, etc.) amounting to about 140 hlWE plus the livestock yield of about 140 hlWE, so that the gross yield of the whole farm represented some 840 hlWE. From this must be deducted the outgoings for seed, rent and tithe, roughly 440 hlWE, and a sum of 155 hlWE for wages, leaving 245 hlWE for the farmer. Le Roy Ladurie compares this net farming income for the year in question, 1590, with the income from a similar farm in 1480. Then the same investment yielded less than half the income (115 hlWE). The notable difference was caused by wages and (!) rents remaining so low while the price of corn was rising rapidly. In this connection Le Roy Ladurie observed that the low rents and wages of the sixteenth century encouraged the rise of a *bourgeoisie rurale de fermiers capitalistes.*

But the *rentes immobiles* (without goods or services) were still an exception in sixteenth-century Europe. In Germany, among many other types of tenure there was the *pacht* or leasehold, which, until far into the modern era, had a double aspect. One looked towards the market economy, the other was still based on feudal custom that cared little what names were given to peasant payments and services. In Rügen and in parts of Mecklenburg the word 'rent' meant the payment that a serf had to make to his lord in addition to other burdens imposed on him. In other places, especially along the North Sea coasts and on municipal estates, 'rent' signified a contract freely entered into, settled by free discussion. It was under such conditions that the rents recorded at Eiderstedt in Schleswig-Holstein were fixed. Between 1526–50 and 1576–1600 they rose from 60 grams of silver per hectare to 173 grams, thus nearly threefold or, expressed in the equivalent rye value, from 292 kilograms to 513, that is to say by about 175 per cent.[13]

The same free competition took place between would-be tenants when the polders near Antwerp were leased out. These rents, found by van der Wee, rose from 26 per cent in 1470 to 100 in the base year, 1569, and (except for the years 1584–97) to 129 by the end of the century, thus fourfold in little more than 125 years.

In other places rents were less easily altered, but in Germany too the land-lords, bound by tradition and custom though they were, knew how to protect their interests by increasing the payments made when property changed hands. This can be seen, for instance, in the dealings, illustrated in figure 28, between the Hospital of the Holy Ghost (Heiliggeistapitales) at Biberach on the Riss and its tenant farmers (Heimpel, 1966:19ff.). The hospital's peasants nearly all held their land on so-called *fallehen* (life tenure) by which the land went back to the landlord on the death of the tenant. They were charged corn rents, tithes and

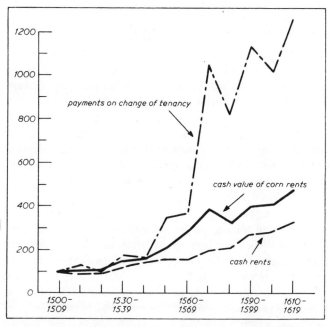

Fig. 28 Rents paid by peasants to the Heiliggeistspitals at Biberach on the Riss 1500-9 to 1610-19.

other payments in kind which stayed fairly constant in quantity throughout the sixteenth century, while in real value they went up more or less with the price of corn. There was also a certain sum to be paid in cash, and this amount dropped below the corn price in value. To make up for this deficit the hospital took advantage of the life tenure. The entry fine was increased greatly: between 1500-9 and 1610-19 it went up twelvefold. Thus, in spite of the falling value of the cash rents, the hospital kept the real value of its income from the land at approximately the old level of 180 kilograms of rye per hectare.

But of course the chroniclers did not indulge in these rather difficult calculations. They judged by what they could observe, such as rents, interest, tithes and per-haps the changeable nature of the entry fines. They compared these with the price of farm produce and concluded that most of the advantage lay on the farmer's side. 'When you think of all the butter, cheese and other produce the tenant farmer has to sell', remarks an east Friesian landlord in one of the dialogues so popular at that time (in Beningas, 1910:201f.), 'and remember what a high price they fetch, more than twice as much as twenty years ago, you will not consider that interest and rents have gone up so much.' When a year has passed one will 'find the money with the tenant and the empty purse with the landlord'. Circumstances varied from district to district, indeed from village to village and farm to farm. No pronouncement on the distribution of agricultural income is universally valid.

Farming revenue, the price of land and speculation in real estate

The anonymous author of the Saxon Ernestine polemical pamphlet on the coinage, written in 1530, headed a section of his treatise 'The rising cost of land' (Lotz, 1893:48). In this section he argued that in Saxony and other German provinces the price of landed property had risen considerably during the last decades. 'Do but look at Franconia, Swabia, Bavaria and Brandenburg', he urges. Unfortunately he has provided us with no examples of these rising prices. Later on, German interest in this matter dwindled, so that trustworthy evidence on the course of land prices at that time is rare indeed. One example we do have is of the estate of Carthause in Altenburg, which was bought for 4,100 guilders in 1578 and sold again in 1615 for 8,950 guilders (Löbe, 1845:45).

Research in France, however, has produced a whole series of prices which bring into relief the great increase in the cost of landed estates during the sixteenth century. A few examples must be cited from the voluminous material published by d'Avenel (1894–1926:I, 356f.) and Raveau (1924a:382). In 1531 the *métairie* of Petit Guignefol near Poitiers was bought for 2,700 pre-war frances (equivalent to 4.5 grams of silver); seventy years later, in 1599, the same small farm was sold for 13,500 frances: the price had increased five-fold. The baronial estate of Chateauneuf-en-Thimerais, which was sold for 10,140 francs in 1370, fetched 200,400 francs in 1600. The sale price of the domain of Maillebois (Eure-et-Loire), which was 6,200 francs in 1383, had risen to 372,800 francs by 1611. An estate in Jarnac was sold three times: in 1441 for 11,300 francs in 1587 for 54,400 francs and in 1593 for 70,000 francs.

In weighing up these prices, however, there are three circumstances to bear in mind. Firstly, between the middle of the fifteenth century and the beginning of the seventeenth century the rate of interest on long-term capital investment appears to have dropped from about 8–10 per cent to 5–7 per cent. Secondly, it is doubtful to what extent these prices may have been influenced by improvement of the soil and farm buildings and equipment, or by alterations in the feudal rights and charges. Thirdly, the price of French estates sank particularly low during and after the Hundred Years War, when much of the land was practically worthless.

Belgian land prices, which were less affected by abnormal conditions, are shown in figure 29 (after Ruwet, 1943:103).

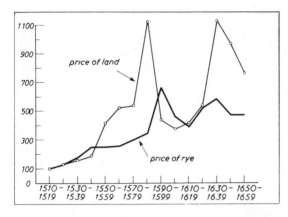

Fig. 29 Prices of land and rye in Belgium 1510–19 to 1650–9.

Land prices continued to rise much more notably than the price of rye during the 1580s. A sharp reverse followed, due to the wars raging at that time, and then a new upswing occurred, bringing land prices once again high above the rye level.

Some further prices for plots of fragmented farmland in Germany may be compared with French prices. It will not be necessary to use d'Avenel's regional averages (1894–1926:II, 508f.), which are more the result of studying a wide range of material and arranging it in an intelligible form than the product of systematic calculations.[14] Accurate data exist for a more limited area: the immediate and more distant surroundings of Poitiers and Montmorillon in Poitou (Raveau, 1924a:383f.).[15] The figures are shown in table 17, from which it can be seen that in France the price of land trebled between the first half and the last quarter of the sixteenth century. Because these series represent averages over long periods,

Table 17 Prices of 1 ha of farmland in Eiderstedt (Germany) and France in silver g.

Period	Poitiers, town precincts	Poitiers, rural	Montmorillon rural	Eiderstedt (Holstein)
1501–25	} 495	222	} 234	350
1526–50				784
1551–75	828	322	373	2135
1576–1600	1585	912	795	5193

the accelerated rise during the closing years of the century is not realistically reflected. At that time prices as high as 200 to 213 Tournois livres (equivalent to 2,340–2,500 grams of silver) per hectare were not unusual. Indeed, plots of meadowland around Charroux were sold for 1,200 to 1,600 livres, that is over 6,660 grams of silver (Raveau, 1924a:364, 368). In Eiderstedt, Holstein, the prices shown in the last column increased fifteenfold from the first quarter-century to the last. This enormous increase can be accounted for partly on statistical grounds. Whereas the figures for France and the two middle periods in Eiderstedt are averages covering long periods, the first and last 25-year periods in Eiderstedt are derived from only two entries, although those can fairly be claimed as representative of the whole region. The data in question are as follows: the chronicler, Ivar Peters, tells us that in 1515 the Duke of Koldenbüttlern was prepared to pay 600 Lübeck marks for 100 demats of land, but the people of Geest offered 400 marks more, so that the final price amounted to 10 marks, or 350 grams of silver, per hectare. Towards the end of the same century, according to Peters, one demat of land cost 300 Lübeck marks, roughtly 5,190 grams of silver, per hectare. The two entries represent the first and last values of a century-long price inflation that is underemphasized in the long-term averages.

But there was another, very real reason for the huge increase in the Eiderstedt land prices. The coastal strips from Holland to Schleswig drew more profit than most from the sixteenth-century agrarian boom. It was in these areas, favoured by soil and climate, that the intensive arable and pastoral farming already described grew up. Their produce, especially butter and cheese, found a lucrative market in the ports and industrial centres of north-western Europe. In this region, so favourably situated for trade with the big cities of the era, arose the regulated convertible husbandry that fetched much higher rents than the more distant three-course rotation areas. The wood carvings in the churches of Ditmarsch, the splendid reception rooms of the farmers and the great brick country houses they built themselves, all still bear witness to the rich profits that were to be won at that time. It is said that towards the end of the sixteenth century some of the farmers covered their roofs with copper and set up cannon in front of their houses. The old saying that in the countryside of Eiderstedt gold and silver were more common than iron and brass is still current.

*

That brings us back to farming incomes. Another reason why these revenues were high in Ditmarsch was that the peasants were almost complete masters of their own land and labour. For Ditmarsch was a free peasant state where the old Germanic freedom of the people and political independence had lasted into the sixteenth century. And although in 1559 the peasants were defeated by the king of Denmark and the dukes of Holstein after bitter fighting, they were able to preserve their personal freedom and a large number of their old privileges. They were allowed to keep their 'own and inherited estates' and contrived to limit their payments and services 'according to the customs of Friesland, Strande, Eiderstedt,

Krempe and Wilstermarsch'. This was written in the peace treaty and it appears that the lords kept to it.

Equally-secure rights of ownership linked to low payments were also to be found in other parts of Germany, especially in the Alpine and near-Alpine regions, in German-speaking east Switzerland, in upper Bavaria and in Swabia. Where these rights appertained to property of a reasonable size, the peasants in those places were prosperous, as can be gathered, among other things, from their houses which since the late fifteenth century had been divided into kitchen, parlour and bed-rooms. In the sixteenth century the parlours were decorated more richly, and in the second half of the century they acquired the all-over panelling that we still admire in museums.[16]

In eastern Germany these property rights were uncommon, but they were not entirely absent. The Pomeranian chronicler, Thomas Kantzow, reported in the 1530s that there were farmers in his country with heritable rights in the properties on which they lived. 'The farmer pays a modest fee for his farm and is obliged to perform certain services. If neither he nor his children want to continue living there, he may sell it, with his lord's permission, and give the lord a tenth of the price' (1817 edn:11, 406, 416). Peasants like this were as prosperous as the city burghers. They wore 'English and other fine cloth just as good as the nobility and townsfolk used to have, and indeed get so much above themselves that it can bring them to harm. That is why everything is taxed so highly and goods have all become more expensive. The good times are passing.' Kantzow, who acted as secretary to the dukes of Pomerania, shared the opinion that the farmers' extravagance had led to rising agricultural prices (!). The opposite con-clusion would have been more correct.

But there were other peasants in Pomerania and parts of east Germany whose lot was very different:

They have no rights in their farms and must render their lords as much service as he demands. Sometimes these labours leave them no time for their own work, and so they grow poor and flee away. These same peasants have a saying that they 'serve only six days a week; on the seventh they carry letters'. Such farmers are no better than bondsmen, for their lords can send them away at will, but if the farmer or his children want to move elsewhere against their lord's wishes, he can fetch them back as his own bondsmen.

It is worth quoting the passage to its end, for it tells us how the pressure could be applied:

And the children of this same peasant, whether sons or daughters, may not move away from the estate farms. It is not enough that their father's farm is occupied, but they must accept and cultivate some deserted holding of the lord's choice. So many flee or move secretly away that many a farm is left empty, and the owner must arrange for it to be occupied by another peasant.

If the fugitive has left nothing behind to stock the farm, the landlord has to provide the new occupant with horses, cows, pigs, carts, plough, seed and other things, and perhaps forego his interest for a few years, until the place is in working order again. Then the new man and his children become as much his bondsmen as the other peasants. If he or his family move away, even with the lord's permission, they must leave behind them everything that was supplied at the beginning or its equivalent. And they may be sent away on the lightest pretext, or may flee away of their own accord.

Unlike the west German landowner, the aristocratic landowners east of the Elbe had always been farmers. When, during the sixteenth-century price revolution, the value of rents began to decline and farming grew more profitable, these knights, now freed from military service by the use of mercenaries, devoted themselves more than ever to cultivating their own land. The estates were enlarged at the expense of the peasants' land, and the peasants with their families were made to give more of their labour. In those days there were serfs in east Germany, and while the peasant farmers often, although not everywhere,[17] fell into great distress, the power and wealth of the landlords increased.

*

It is not easy to understand the distribution of agricultural income with any accuracy. Some of the French nobles grew poor because they were not allowed to raise the rents; some of the German nobility were limited to their traditional farm rents because their sovereigns were eager to skim off the growing agrarian profits by imposing taxes. Rich monasteries ran into debt because the demands of their rulers and bishops increased even more rapidly than their revenue. There were many, from farmer to king and pope, who wanted their share of the soaring profits of agriculture.

The city burghers were not last in the queue. All over western Europe urban capital was being invested in landed estate. The Fugger and Welser families led the way in Germany; in Saxony the mine-owners, merchants, cloth manufacturers, even university professors and upper civil servants were buying farms or sometimes knight's estates. Melichor von Ossa (1506–57), a Saxon statesman, put forward a regulation against 'townspeople, other than the nobility, holding knights' estates. For they earn money quickly in their trades and crafts and can acquire estates more easily than the nobles by paying bigger prices, and thus prevent others from buying.' If such an order ever was passed it seems to have been ineffective (Blaschke, 1958:135). In north Germany it seems that minor tradesmen and artisans too were eager to invest every spare schilling in land. The east Friesian register from which Swart (1910:205f.) has made extracts, contains a long series of records of land purchase by sixteenth-century burghers, sometimes of very small plots down to half a hectare. In 1527 the mayor of Emden announced that he was investing his whole fortune in land. R. Hansen also points out (1897:230f.) how eagerly the citizens of Ditmarsch took part in this land rush.

From England we hear of a petition in the reign of Henry VIII complaining of enterprising merchants, clothmakers, goldsmiths, butchers, tanners and other 'foolish and greedy men' who 'daily buy more land than they can sow with corn'. In 1535 there was talk of a law to limit the amount of land a tradesman could buy. A little later the people of Rheims were protesting 'if only the tradesmen would stick to trade and leave the land to those who make their living by it' (Brentano, 1927:79; R. Faber, 1888:22f.). In Franche-Comte (Febvre, 1911:242f.) and Poitou (Raveau, 1924*b*:341f.) it is established that during the sixteenth century citizens bought up a great deal of land either to let it or to manage it themselves. In some parts of France competition between would-be buyers gave rise to 'veritable battles for the soil' (Raveau). In France, as elsewhere in western Europe, citizens purchased land from very varied motives. Some hoped to rise in the social scale, other desired security, others again, perhaps, wanted only rest after the hard struggle for gain in trade or industry. But all over Europe an important incentive must have been the increasing profits to be won from the soil in the sixteenth century.

The decline in real wages

Real wages and corn wages

In most of western and central Europe wages lagged far behind rents and the price of food. The subject has already been discussed (above, p. 119), but not exhausted, for up to this point labour has been treated as a factor of production and wages as business expenditure. But now that we are discussing wages in the light of income it will be as well to cast our net wider to deal with certain phenomena connected with the decline in real wages.

First comes the increase in the number of beggars. Wars and natural disasters have always thrown people out of work. The Hundred Years War between England and France during the latter half of the fourteenth century and the first half of the fifteenth century gave rise to huge bands of beggars in the ravaged areas of France. Yet everywhere there was work to be had and wages were high. It was d'Avenel's opinion (1894–1926:III, 38) that 'never had the farm worker's real wages stood so high in medieval France, and never would they stand as high in all the ensuing centuries as they did in the last quarter of the fifteenth century'. This judgement may be open to criticism, but in principle it cannot be gainsaid. The sixteenth century, however, brought a sudden wave of unemployment in west and central Europe.

It is a long time since Levasseur (1889:188f.) and Sombart (1919:I, 2:788f.) assembled the evidence that testifies to the prevalence of beggary. For instance, in about 1578 a report from the Amiens law courts stated that there were some five to six thousand labourers 'living on the charity of prosperous citizens'. In the last years of the century l'Estoile commented on 'processions of the poor filling the whole street so that one can scarcely get by'. In England there had been practically no beggars before 1500; by 1600 they had become a chronic plague. According to Thomas Harman, as early as 1521 a growing multitude of tramps was making the streets unsafe. In 1580 William Harrison was complaining of the 'many unemployed beggars' who 'within the last sixty years or less have grown so numerous, and have recently become a real pest of the countryside' (see especially Leonard, 1900:11f.). From Denmark in 1600 came indignant remarks about 'the swarms of vagrants' who troubled and despoiled the land (C. A. Christensen, 1930–1:464). A book appeared in Germany as early as 1514 complaining of the increasing vagabondage (*liber vagatorum*), and Martin Luther often referred to the nuisance caused by beggars. Ulrich von Hutten and some of his contemporaries sought ways to improve the situation. The landowners closed ranks. They issued orders, edicts and mandates against the 'masterless mob of pests and beggars' (10 April 1595) and the 'unemployed vagrants, impostors and idlers' (20 October 1599). These two quotations come from the Mylius collection of Brandenburg and Prussian edicts between 1565 and 1735, which includes over fifty regulations regarding beggars and the poor, between which groups very little distinction was made at that time (see Abel, 1974:28f.; Hinze, 1927:13f.).

The rise of unemployment was not entirely unconnected with a certain ossification of the trade guilds. Conditions in Germany point in that direction. During the sixteenth century protests about the misuse of the guilds were continuous.

> The entry fees were high, excessive payments were exacted for apprenticeship and the title of master; it was quite usual for the guilds to insist on expensive 'master works' that were so old-fashioned as to be unsaleable. The feasts that the apprentices were called upon to provide on gaining their independence often involved them in debt from which they never emerged for the rest of their lives.

That is Hinze's description (1927), and it confirms the earlier conclusions of Schmoller and other historians as to the degeneracy of the city guilds. Hinze continues:

> Other regulations sought to limit the number entitled to join guilds by excluding certain social groups: apprentices should be of gentle birth; the sons of some types of workers, such as grooms, court ushers, gamekeepers, herdsmen, watchmen, gravediggers, street sweepers and barbers were for ever excluded because of their low birth, and might never change to another calling. To crown it all the guilds often closed for definite or indefinte periods, masterships became closed shops, and hence arose the expression 'eternal apprentice'.

This situation was related to the decline in real wages. The English historians Brown and Hopkins (1956) have attempted to measure the purchasing power of wages by comparing a builder's wages with a collection of commodities including, in addition to essential foodstuffs, some cloth, leather goods and other articles of daily use. The price of this collection of commodities increased fivefold between 1450 and 1610–19. Measured by these commodities, a builder's wage in southern England sank to less than half (40 per cent) of its original value, as figure 30 illustrates.

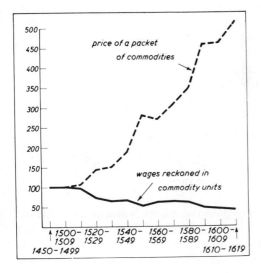

Fig. 30   Purchasing power of a builder's wage in southern England.

Although for France and Germany there are some price series which would make it possible to assess the value of the wage of a working man or woman by equating it with the contents of a 'shopping basket' in this way, it has never been done. The disproportion between prices and wages would obviously have led to shifts in consumption which could be calculated only if we knew how much the demand for the different consumables fluctuated, and for that we have no quantitative standards at all.[18] It can only be assumed (and where possible verified) that the proportion of goods in income-elastic demand would sink in relation to those for which demand is comparatively independent of income. So we come back to the classical method of expressing the worth of real wages by their 'corn value'.

Figure 31 depicts wages in various German cities represented in this way (Abel, 1967:187). The diagram shows the wages paid to navvies and farmhands such as mowers in Munich, reapers in Augsburg, harvest workers in Würzburg, Frankfurt am Main and Göttingen, as well as labourers occupied in extending town fortifications. The wage series have been assembled into indices which are not directly comparable from town to town. Their movement is nevertheless more significant than the relative wage level because the latter may be affected by the shortcomings of the data. As the graph makes clear, the corn wages sank by more than a third in all five towns. In Augsburg, Würzburg and Frankfurt am Main,

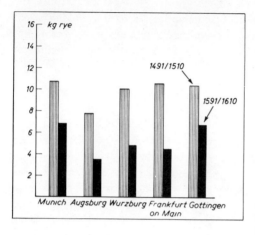

Fig. 31   Rye equivalents of money wages in Germany 1491–1510 and 1591–1610.

indeed, they dropped to below half the value they had had at the beginning of the sixteenth century.

D'Avenel considered it established that the money wages of an unskilled labourer in France sank in value from 14.3 kilograms of wheat in the period 1451–75 to 3.0 kilograms in 1576–1600 (D'Avenel, 1894–1926:111, 39f.; wheat prices 11, 517f.). As in some other instances, d'Avenel's averages are slightly unsatisfactory. They probably exaggerate the extent of the fall in wages, but nevertheless the general trends of price and wage movements are correct. That much is substantiated over and over again, for example by Boissonade (1927), who estimated that in the course of 75 years in France wages had risen by no more than 20 to 30 per cent whereas the cost of living had gone up fourfold. In the sixteenth century, according to Raveau (1926: introduction), 'real wages' in Poitou sank by a third. For Languedoc, Le Roy Ladurie (1968:759ff.) reckons that with his cash wages a day labourer could buy 15 kilograms of bread in 1480–1500, 9 kilograms in 1530–50, and by 1600 only 6–7 kilograms. Richet (1968:759ff.), who quotes Le Roy Ladurie, spoke of a 'workers' Waterloo'.

For Italy, there is an admittedly doubtful calculation (based on few and vague accounts) that the cash wage of an unskilled labourer dropped from about 10.5 kilograms of wheat in 1476–1500 to 6.7 kilograms in 1576–1600 (Bartolini, 1878:196).

It must be stressed again that the above wage values reflect but one aspect of sixteenth-century wages. Only their worth in corn sank to that extent. Their silver value increased almost everywhere, and the money wages grew faster still. To clarify this complex situation an example will be arbitrarily selected from the above data. In the Portogruaro neighbourhood in northern Italy at the end of the fifteenth century a farmhand was paid 17 solidi a day, while at the end of the sixteenth century he earned 40 solidi daily. Since, however, the silver content of a solidus had diminished greatly during the hundred years, the silver value of this day-labourer's wage had risen only from 6.8 grams to 9.9 grams of silver. Thus its nominal value had increased by 235 per cent, but its silver value by only 145 per cent. Meanwhile the price of grain in the district had risen far more steeply, so that, in fact, the farmhand's corn wages had gone down.

How much did wages actually fall?

On the subject of the decline of real wages there are some reservations which refer less to the statistics – which can be accurately calculated, as far as they go – than to the relevance of these figures discussed above. It is said that the sixteenth-century labourer, craftsman or other wage-earner often received payment in kind over and above his cash wages and that, when the former remained constant, to reckon the real value of the wage by the money payment alone obviously gives a false picture. That is undeniable and brings us to the further question of the degree to which these conditions prevailed. Certainly servants always counted as members of the employer's household. In the country there were some types of worker for whom the money wage was only a modest supplement to the bed and board, clothes, shoes and other personal necessities they received. Among the craftsmen and tradesmen of the town, at least the apprentices were given free board and lodging. But that does not answer the question as to the proportion of workers receiving payment in kind compared with the total number of wage- and salary-earners, or what proportion of the whole wage was represented by these payments in kind. An exact answer is hardly possible, but the sources do sometimes distinguish board wages from wages without board. If the latter are used in the calculation the difficulty of the wage being only a partial testimony is removed. However, this more accurate assessment refers only to the workers who were paid purely cash wages.

Le Roy Ladurie went to the trouble of calculating the 'mixed wages' of a bailiff in Languedoc (1966:1, 269ff.). In 1480 the man received wages in cash and kind amounting to about 41 livres in all; by 1590 that sum had increased to 138 livres, thus by more than three times. Meanwhile the price of corn had risen eightfold. At the same time the proportion of the monetary value of the payment in kind to that of the cash wages shifted from 24 (cash) and 17 (goods) in 1480 to 36 (cash) and 101 (goods) in 1590. It is noteworthy that a reaper's pay in the form of a share fell from one sheaf in ten during the 1480 harvest to one in sixteen in the years 1600–30. Thus between 1500 and 1600 Le Roy Ladurie concluded from his extensive calculations, all wages reckoned in corn value, whether of men, women, farm labourers or artisans, and whether in cash, goods or a mixture of both, sank in the following proportions: the reaper's share in kind from 10 per cent to 6 per cent, the labourer's cash wage from 100 to 54, and the mixed wage of a farm bailiff from 31 hectolitres of wheat to 17: *baisses comparables, tendances commune.*

Moreover, the labourers, craftsmen and even the major and minor officials of the town or landed estates often had other sources of income in addition to their wages or salary. Among the lower groups it could be a little house or a plot of land, among the higher groups perhaps rent, interest, or profit from some less clear-cut source. That, too, is true, but the question as to the number of these double-wage-earners, or the proportion of single-wage-earners remains unanswered. In the town of Uelzen in Lower Saxony a census was taken of all the persons who could be described as 'true proletariat in the modern sense of the word', that is to say people possessing neither land nor taxable income, but living only from contract or day-wages or by casual labour: they amounted to 35 per cent of the total population (Woehlkens, 1954). In eighteen small and middle-sized towns of the electorate of Saxony the 'disinherited' formed 30 per cent of the population (Stoy, 1935). In Stralsund the proportion of this lowest social stratum (described by Marxist historians as 'plebeian', not even 'proletarian'), to the population as a whole, taking only the group included in the tax registers of the first half of the sixteenth century, was 55.3 per cent, while in Rostock the comparable figure was 63.6 per cent (Fritze, 1967:157ff.). Probably the actual proportion of this social group was even greater. Those are very high figures, and when it is further remembered that many people in receipt of extra income depended in the last resort on their wages or salary, it will be seen that the effects of the falling wage level were widespread indeed.

Until recently it was assumed that the decline in wages described above was general all over Europe. Some evidence from the ports and industrial towns of Brabant and Flanders, however, seems to contradict the assumption. It will have been see in figure 24 above that in parts of what is now Belgium the rise in wages temporarily overtook the rise in cereal prices. In Antwerp, as we learn from both Verlinden and van der Wee, a mason's wage during the sixteenth century sank in relation to rye or rye-bread by about one-quarter to one-third. That is a great deal less than in the rest of Europe. Perhaps, even at that time, labour had achieved greater productivity in this industrially- and commercially-advanced north-west corner of our continent than anywhere else.

But a glance at the distribution of wages in Europe presents us with an even harder puzzle. Figure 32 shows a journeyman mason's summer day-wages in twelve European towns between 1551 and 1600.[19] As would be expected, wages in most of Europe were lower than in Antwerp. The Antwerp wages exceeded those in England in both silver and corn values (by 46 per cent and 54 per cent respectively), of Strasbourg (46 per cent and 54 per cent), Valencia (77 per cent and 41 per cent), Florence (51 per cent and 34 per cent), Augsburg (38 per cent and 46 per cent), Leipzig (36 per cent and 50 per cent), Xanten (49 per cent and 78 per cent), Vienna (35 per cent and 64 per cent) and Danzig (42 per cent and 89 per cent). On the other hand, in Cracow and Lemberg wages were inferior to those paid in Antwerp only when reckoned in silver content (35 per cent compared with 42 per cent) and far surpassed them in corn value

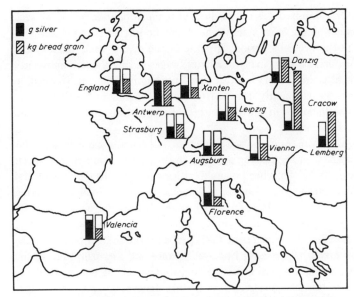

Fig. 32 Summer day-wages of a journeyman mason in 12 European towns.

(233 per cent to 138 per cent). It is hard to say why this was. If, as we have every reason to suppose, the authors have worked out the true wage and price figures for Cracow and Lemberg, the answer may well be found in the low price of grain in those two towns. It did, indeed, rise considerably as the century advanced, pushing down the purchasing power of wages, but it remained low in comparison with the rest of Europe. This may have been due to the high cost of shipping grain to the ports of north-western Europe, and, in the case of wages, to the land/labour ratio in Poland. There, on the fringes of the European economy, the law of diminishing returns from the land may not yet have applied, and labour was even more scarce than land.

The overall economic structure

The search for an interpretation

Sée and Hauser traced the fall of real wages in France back to the levying of a tax on earnings. Sée thought that if economic forces had been allowed free play wages would undoubtedly have risen, and perhaps have kept pace with the fall in value of money (Sée, 1929:195; and Hauser, 1927:102). Government decisions offer an easy explanation of events that developed in the direction the government desired. Such explanations, however, are threadbare when applied to a period when political rulers still lacked executive power, or to a phenomenon that continued for over a hundred years regardless of national boundaries. If we seek a practical argument on the other side, we need look no further than the development of wages in the previous period. In spite of the severe wage taxation and labour regulations prevailing in many countries, wages during the late fourteenth century and early fifteenth century increased not only nominally but also in relation to silver and grain. Consequently it must have been economic forces that caused the relative decline in wages in the sixteenth century. No law or agreement can adequately account for it.

We need not, therefore, examine the numerous other reasons put forward for the increasing beggary, or the decline of wages in this or that country or district. In England, enclosure has long been blamed, at least in part, for the agricultural unemployment but, in fact, the demand for labour on the enclosed land during the sixteenth century may well have increased rather than diminished. Moreover, a similar fall in wages occurred in Germany, France and other countries where no land was enclosed. Schmoller (1914:545), probably the first to point out the parallel direction taken by wages in England, France and Germany during the sixteenth century, thought it was caused by debasement of the coinage and the 'non-recognition' of this circumstance. It is hard to believe, however, that wage- and salary-earners failed to observe the debasement and the consequent rise in prices. The multitude of complaints, petitions, protests and even revolts scarcely bears out Schmoller's theory.

Some authors regarded the decline of real wages as a sort of natural phenomenon needing no explanation. They thought a monetary inflation must necessarily be followed by a fall in wages as surely as lightning is followed by thunder. The inflations of the twentieth century or the fluctuations of the nineteenth-century industrial boom (Juglar cycle) may have given rise to this theory, but these events, with their very short-lived fluctuations, cannot be compared with long-term developments. The effect of debasement on wages depends – apart from the official wage restrictions mentioned above – only on the duration of the wage period (days, weeks, months). It is in relation to these periods that prices in the labour market diverge from prices in the commodity market, for in these markets the time lapse between action and reaction can dwindle to nothing. That could cause wages and salaries to lag briefly behind prices, but it does not explain why wages could not adjust to prices for more than a hundred years.

In 1929 Hamilton, to whose research we owe a precise knowledge of the Spanish price revolution, published an article which advanced beyond the subject of prices and wages into the hitherto-neglected territory of profit and investment. It was his opinion that for many decades the low rate of labour costs brought the employer high profits. These gains had led to an accumulation of wealth which, in the hands of daring entrepreneurs, had become big investments (1929:388f.). John Maynard Keynes seized on this theory and gave it his support (1930:152f.). Since then a large number of economists and historians have thought of the sixteenth century as a century of 'profit inflation'.

Nef contributed a variant to this theory (1937:155f.; 1953:292f.). Starting from the inflation of profits, of which he also was convinced, he attributed this and the opportunities for investment less to cheaper labour than to innovations in techniques and organization. If wages, he argued, had really lagged behind prices to that extent, there would not have been the purchasing power to buy the extra goods put on the market by the old and new industries. Therefore the decline of wages had been exaggerated and the saving of cost through technical innovation underestimated. He quoted some facts to support his theory. Among other things, he examined the contents of the working-class shopping basket, in which he found bread in place of corn, probably because it was relatively cheaper, and supposed that there would be more meat there than formerly, because cheap meat would have taken the place of dear bread (?). He also supplied some information about new industries and enlarged ones, about technical advances and improved organization. Unfortunately he failed to extend these data from isolated reports into the realm of quantities and orders of magnitude.

On the whole the new discussion refreshingly widened the scope of the old subject of the sixteenth-century 'price revolution'. Consumption and investment were brought into it, helped by the high authority of Keynes, although it had its drawbacks, because henceforth the words 'profit inflation' distracted historians' attention away from the key question. That was and is – Nef notwithstanding – the question of *why* real wages in central and western Europe declined so much.

Population, consumption and investment in the sixteenth century

We must remember Ricardo's words:

> As population increases, these necessaries will be constantly rising in price, because more labour will be necessary to produce them ... money wages ... would rise; but they would not rise sufficiently to enable the labourer to purchase as many comforts and necessaries as he did before the rise in the price of those commodities ... the condition of the labourer will generally decline, and that of the landlord will always be improved.

But consumption did not decline absolutely during the sixteenth century; the growth of population was too great for that. People have to live, and food-stuffs made up a large part of their total expenditure. But consumption was sharply differentiated: there was less to consume for some, while for others there was more, and a third group wanted to keep to the old way of living that had been handed down to them, but could no longer afford to.

The wage-earner had no choice but to limit himself to the barest necessities of life. For instance, during the late sixteenth century a building worker in Uelzen (Lower Saxony) received 4 schillings daily for a twelve-hour working day. In Uelzen that would buy 7 kilograms of rye or 5 kilograms of buckwheat groats or 1.6 kilograms of fat bacon or 625 grams of butter (Woehlkens, 1954:100f.).[20] For a modest lodging, comprising a living room, kitchen and bedroom, the worker had to pay about 80 schillings a year; wood fuel cost about the same amount, clothes and other needs somewhat more.[21] That comes to 250–300 schillings annually, or one schilling for every working day, which leaves 3 schillings a working day for food. If the man had to provide for a wife and children their diet can have consisted of little more than bread, groats and coarse vegetables. At the end of the century an official of the Mansfeld copper mines (a post that seldom puts its holder on the side of the worker) declared that the miners' weekly wage was not enough even to provide a family with its 'beloved bread' (Paterna, 1960:535).

By a lucky chance there is a similar but more detailed budget referring to the north-western corner of the continent, where wages were the highest in western or central Europe. Scholliers (1960:174) investigated the incomes and household expenses of working-class families in Antwerp. The earnings were based not on the working day but simply on the day (consumption day). For an assistant mason in 1596–1600 these came to about 29 denari a day, which was the approximate equivalent of 7.4 kilograms of rye-bread. According to the available data the expenditure on food provided a family with a daily 12,000 calories, or 2,440 calories per head. The separate items of expense are shown in figure 33. Of the total

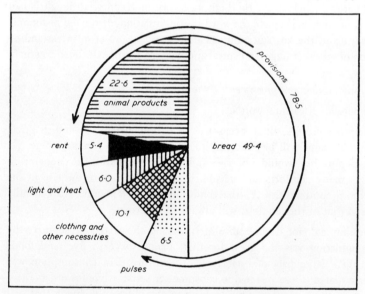

Fig. 33   Living expenses of a mason's family of five.

expenditure, 78 per cent was on food, and of this 49.4 per cent was on bread alone. For comparison it should be observed that in West Germany today a family of four spends only a third of its income on food and only 6 per cent on bread and other bakery products. To find a budget today similar to that of the Antwerp family of five in 1600 we should have to go to one of the so-called under-developed countries such as India, Persia or Ceylon. There one still finds wages with a purchasing power equal to or perhaps slightly higher than that of European wages three and a half centuries earlier.[22]

People were better fed when they lived in hospitals, almshouses or other such institutions, or if they ate with farmers or burghers, or served in noble households. For instance, in the almshouses of Göttingen at the end of the sixteenth century the inmates had meat thrice weekly, and on other days fish, eggs, cheese, bread, butter and plenty of vegetables (Wellschmied, 1963:126f.). We learn this from a petition in which the inmates maintain that they have a right to meat on all the days of the week. The master declared (in 1601) that for 6 kreuzers' housekeeping money he could not put meat on their plates every day (C. L. Sachs, 1922:207).

In the diet sheet issued in 1569 for farm servants on the royal estates of Saxony, meat appears two or three times a week, accompanied by plenty of bread, cheese, soup, vegetables, fruit and milk distributed over four meals a day. The following menu is reproduced only slightly abbreviated (from Ermisch and Wuttke, 1910), because it gives a very good idea of a typical diet for farmhands on a demesne in Saxony, and in other places.

SUNDAY	Morning:	(after prayers) meat soup, meat and vegetables
	Afternoon:	bread and cheese
	Evening:	Stewed fruit, swedes, buttermilk
MONDAY	Morning:	beer soup, bread and cheese
	Midday:	peas and carrots, milk
	Afternoon:	bread and cheese
	Evening:	groats, turnips, buttermilk
TUESDAY	Morning:	soup, bread, cheese
	Midday:	soup, meat or pancakes, oat porridge
	Afternoon:	bread and cheese
	Evening:	barley groats, stewed fruit, milk
WEDNESDAY	Morning:	soup, buttermilk, morning and afternoon bread as above
	Midday:	peas, vegetables, milk
	Evening:	buckwheat groats, swedes, buttermilk
THURSDAY	Morning:	soup, morning and afternoon bread as above
	Midday:	meat soup, meat, carrots
	Evening:	rye broth, swedes, buttermilk
FRIDAY	Morning:	soup, morning and afternoon bread as above
	Midday:	millet gruel, swedes or greens, milk
	Evening:	oat porridge, swedes, buttermilk
SATURDAY	Morning:	soup, morning and afternoon bread as above
	Midday:	peas, swedes, milk
	Evening:	buckwheat gruel, carrots, buttermilk

On high feast days such as Christmas, Easter and Whitsun, it continues, as well as on Church festival days and Shrove Tuesday, the food would be somewhat better, with roast meat, vegetables, cakes and tarts. In addition the farm servants would have sufficient small beer with their meals.

In other countries conditions were similar (for England see Drummond and Wilbraham 1958).

Everyone has heard of the feasts given by farmers, burghers and gentlemen to celebrate special occasions such as weddings, guild banquets, and dinners in honour of new doctorates. When in 1591 three doctors of theology at Cologne University gave a feast for a few hundred guests to celebrate their new dignity, the party consumed, among other things: 1 ox, 3 stags, 106 partridges, 106 hens, 106 capons, 16 young chickens, 2 swans, 2 peacocks, 62 pounds of salmon, 55 pounds of carp, 42 pounds of sturgeon and 50 pourds of pike, as well as pastry, bread, vegetables, etc. (Bianco, 1855: appendix, 95). The burghers were no less hospitable. In 1571 the Cologne merchant and councillor, Hermann von Weinsberg, entertained a few friends and dignitaries of the town, seven altogether, on the occasion of joining the corporation of 'standard-bearers', and gave them the following menu:[23] For the first course there was a great dish of baked ham surrounded by ten dishes containing beef, mutton, tongue, chickens, soused meat, Bingen sausage, sauerkraut, lamb pasties and so on. The second course consisted of another great dish with baked hares, venison and wild pig accompanied by ten smaller dishes bearing rabbits, capons, hens, woodcocks, quail 'and the like'. For the third course the great dish held three kinds of pie and the other ten dishes carried crabs, pike, carp ('seethed in bacon fat'), marzipan, lampreys, pickles etc. There were also 24 bowls filled with honey cakes, Nuremberg tarts, apples, pears, hazel nuts and walnuts, grapes, chestnuts, almonds, dates, candied fruit, aniseed, cinnamon and similar dainties. Two waiters served at table and poured wine generously from silver jugs.

*

Men of the sixteenth century scorned the pleasures of table and bottle as little as had their fifteenth-century forebears. They also spent freely on clothes, jewellery and the furnishing of their houses. A wealth of relics from the sixteenth century, the treasures in our museums and the surviving town and country houses all bear ample witness to that. So what was left, we may well ask, out of the incomes of individuals, groups or society as a whole for the maintenance and expansion of the economy, in other words for those famous investments?

In the wage- or salary-earning classes certainly very little. The majority of townspeople, including the small artisan and the pedlar, had difficulty enough trying to stretch their incomes to cover the rise in the cost of living. Among those who worked for profit the situation was different. The merchant, the manufacturer and the many speculative traders of the sixteenth century sometimes earned large sums that they used for expanding their trade or industry. But profits as a whole, and the investments they nourished, did not play a great part in the social economy or social production of pre-industrial society.

The bulk of income consisted of wages and similar payments, and rents. Rents in particular amounted to vast sums, probably not much less than the whole capital invested in the so-called industries of the time.[24] There remains the question of what happened to all this rent. A part of it was spent on administration, jurisdiction and arms for the benefit of church or court. Another part accrued to the middle stratum of society, whose consumption was even more conspicuous than at the top.

That can often be deduced from the peasant's payments and services, which in their character and extent were earmarked for the landlord's establishment. Account books and lists of expenditure tell the same story; still more convincing is the testimony of trade, at least in central Europe. The eastern territories exchanged the corn that they exported in such great quantities for spices, wine, jewellery, arms and munitions, Italian silks, Flemish brocade and English cloth, paper and glassware.

All over Europe a great deal of building was in progress. In eastern Germany 'fortified houses' on a palatial scale were replacing the homely timber-work and gloomy towers of the colonial period. In the Weser Valley rose the splendid Renaissance palaces that still delight the traveller's eye. The same thing was happening along the Loire. These buildings were not, properly speaking, investments. At Quesnay we find an example of self-sufficient economy. The landowner received 1600 livres in rent, which he spent on building a country house. In this way the rents were turned into builders' wages. The builders used their earnings to buy grain from the farmers who paid the rents. Thus the circle was completed and, it may be added, the agricultural surplus transformed into a mansion.

Of course a certain amount of the wealth derived from agriculture did find its way into industrial and commercial enterprise. In Germany the Mecklenburg and Holstein nobles dealt in grain and cattle. Count Anton I von Oldenberg had agents in Cologne who kept him very well informed about the prices and turnover of oxen on the Cologne market. In sixteenth-century Lower Saxony a certain section of the nobles had been dubbed, not without justification, 'the capitalist nobility'. Nevertheless, nearly as much money flowed back from urban industry to the land as the landowners invested in the town. The prospects held out by the agrarian boom, the desire for security, social advancement or political influence directed much of the wealth gained in city, court and military circles into the purchase of land and manorial rights. Perhaps the two counter-flowing streams of capital balanced each other, but in all probability the current flowing towards the land was the stronger.

Ricardo was observing the same phenomenon in the much more advanced England of two hundred years later. It must have been his observation of how much rent was spent on conspicuous consumption that led him to write that rent contributed nothing towards the national wealth, but was only a transfer of money, always favourable for the landowner and relatively unfavourable to the consumer, and that the country would benefit if the soil were more fertile, labour more productive and rents lower.

The essential cause of the declining real wages of the late fifteenth and the sixteenth centuries lay in the disparity between the rapid population growth in western and central Europe and the development of its economy. That may sound strange, since it was not only England that displayed signs of a marked economic upswing. In Germany, too, despite the shifting of important trade routes and the collapse of a few north German finance and trading houses, trade and traffic definitely increased during the second half of the sixteenth century. Some industries became more active and farming flourished. Even so, production could not keep up with the growth of population. Although production figures to prove it are not available, that is the only possible explanation – at least in the author's opinion – of the falling standard of living of the wage- and salary-earners, and the sharp rise in rents.[25]

5 Slumps, wars and the long-term downward trend

The agrarian market in the first half of the seventeenth century

Trade and credit recession in the early seventeenth century

At the beginning of the seventeenth century the long-term agrarian boom came to an abrupt end. Prices had been going up for decades. Land was cleared, farming was intensified, territory was reclaimed from the sea, and agriculture in the east of Europe was reorganized. Trade turnover accelerated and the trading area expanded. Ever-growing quantities of grain from the Vistula basin and increasing numbers of cattle from the land bordering the corn belt flowed into the cities of the west. A *fièvre agricole*, as d'Avenel put it (1894–1926, 1:28) seized our ancestors during the last years of the boom. The supply of farm produce began to approach the demand. A few good harvests – in the years 1598, 1599 and 1600 – were enough to bring in a prolonged fall of prices.[1]

The decline in cereal prices, reckoned in five-year periods, and expressed in 100 kilogram units and reichsmarks (1 RM = 5.5 grams of silver) went as follows:[2] wheat prices sank between 1596–1600 and 1616–20 in France from 24 to 14, and in England from 19 to 15.75; the price of rye in the same period dropped in Strasbourg from 8.50 to 5.80, in Basle from 8.35 to 5.80, and in Lübeck from 10.80 to 7.65. The Utrecht tables show that 6.82 in 1606–7 and 6.38 in 1619–20 were the lowest rye prices since 1560–1. Peters' *Eiderstedt Chronicles* give the price of rye in 1606 as 3.90, the lowest since 1549. And in 1607 rye in Stettin was worth only 3.65.

Tooke and Newmarch (1858:1, 12f.) quote some contemporary witnesses to describe the crisis years in England. For instance, on 12 February 1620 a country squire wrote:

> We are here in a strange state to complain of plenty; but so it is, that corn beareth so low a price that tenants and farmers are very backward to pay their

rents, and in many places plead disability.... England was never so generally poor since I was born as it is at present; inasmuch that all complain they cannot receive their rents. Yet is there plenty of all things but money, which is so scant, that country people offer corn and cattle or whatsoever they have else, in lieu of rent, but bring no money.

We hear of a gentleman of Herefordshire named Vaughan who observed in 1610 that foodstuffs in his neighbourhood were very cheap, but that the local inhabitants could find no work. Stretching for a mile and a half on either side of his house, he tells us, were five hundred poor cottagers, who were entirely engaged in spinning flax, hemp and tow, but when the harvest was over he had seen no fewer than three hundred people gleaning in one field. His suggestion was that some thirty looms should be set up and worked by the water power of a nearby river. This, he thought, would create a better market for agricultural products, which could then be grown to advantage.

The evidence from Germany is scant and neglected, although it took many generations to erase the memory of that period of stagnation. A report by Hieronymus Sancke (1694–1739), deacon of Herzhorn in the Stormarn region, east of the lower Elbe, is rather long-winded, but not without its interest for the theme of this book.

> Once, when I was called to a sickbed, the old man who took me there told me of what he had heard from his mother when an old woman. Before the Imperial Wars, she said, there had been several very bad years when corn was exceedingly cheap and some folk had to leave their farms and houses. Oh, then the people cried to God to bring back better times so that they could keep what was their own, and God heard their payers and the corn regained its former worth. Whereupon the inhabitants became arrogant. Instead of thanking God, they grew proud and vain and thought only of decking themselves in belts of chain two fingers wide with silver daggers. They cast off their old clothes and put on new raiment of silk and scarlet, in which they strutted about and showed themselves off. But the Imperial Wars took all their pride and vanity away and to many of them it gave a beggar's staff instead. (Cited in Detlefsen, 1892:191f.)

That colourful report is handed down from oral tradition. The chroniclers confine themselves to unvarnished words and a few figures, but are almost as informative. Thus the Peters chronicle from Eiderstedt in Holstein records that after 1601 many formerly-prosperous landowners had to leave their estates. Owing to having bought too much land, they had fallen so heavily into debt that they had to yield it up to their creditors at a very low price. According to the chronicler Peter Sachs, the price of land on the west coast of Schleswig-Holstein fell in a few years to a third of its former price. One reads again and again of those years that people were frequently forced to quit their farms because of debt. Ivan Peters surmised that within a short time some of them had nothing left at all. In former days they had acquired hundreds of demats of land, but now it was clear 'that luck could change, as it has now done with the aforesaid persons'.

In Pomerania and Mecklenburg, too, there were numerous bankruptcies like those of Philipp Adrian Borcke of Castle Pansin with its thirty villages, and of the Mecklenburg landowner, Maltzan of Kurzen-Trechow. It was in Mecklenburg, too, that the feudal estate of Gottin and the neighbouring property of Tellow, which later belonged to Johann Heinrich von Thünen, got into difficulties. In 1618 in Lower Saxony, Stats von Münchhausen, the builder of Schloss Bevern on the Weser and owner of many landed estates, blast furnaces and ironworks, had to suspend payment on debts of over ten tons of gold, or more than one million thalers, and allow insolvency proceedings to be started.

To give further instances would be superfluous. The evidence quoted is enough to show that during the peak of the agrarian boom in the last years of the sixteenth century landed property was bought on credit. No doubt the purchasers hoped that the price of corn, cattle and land would rise still higher so that it would not be difficult to cover their debts. As grain prices went down and net profit dwindled it was no longer possible to pay the interest on the mortgage. The creditors foreclosed and the owners lost their land. It was a sequence of events often repeated during the centuries to come. In times of booming agriculture landed property was overvalued and too heavily encumbered with debt. When prices or credit receded, bankruptcies proliferated. The chronicler's adage that 'luck can turn' took centuries to sink in.

It may be that this slump in northern Europe, which particularly affected the wealthier classes, also caused a recession in the spice and textile trades. The price of pepper, one of the most sought-after luxuries in both town and country, fell sharply in Augsburg and Vienna (in the latter it fell from 112.5 kreuzers the pound in 1600 to 45 kreuzers in 1607) (Pribram, 1939:221; see also Mauruschat, 1975:124ff.). In northern Italy the silk and woollen textile trade, so prosperous in the last decades of the sixteenth century, stagnated. The number of weavers' looms in the Genoese republic dropped from 16,000 at the end of the sixteenth century to 3,000 in 1608. In Florence, where 120 firms connected with the wool industry had flourished during the last decades of the sixteenth century, a 'drastic decline' set in as early as 1604 (Cipolla, 1952–3:178f.). Unfortunately, although Europe was already fairly well integrated through trade and credit, we lack enough information about interconnections of this kind to form any but the vaguest conjectures.

The rising agrarian prosperity of western and northern Europe during the Thirty Years War

The trade stagnation of the seventeenth-century's first decade was soon overcome. The long war started and, though it did not at once produce strong effects everywhere, as it continued grain prices rose steadily throughout western and central Europe, especially in Germany (see figure 34).

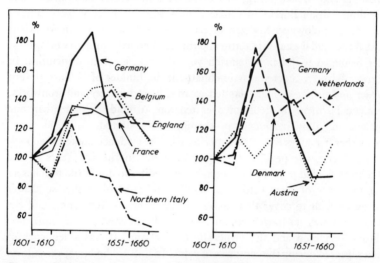

Fig. 34   Grain prices in western and central Europe 1601–70.

The course of grain prices varied greatly from country to country. In England, Belgium and Austria prices continued to rise until the 1640s, going up to 147 per cent, 150 per cent and 118 per cent respectively of their 1601–10 level. In Germany and the Netherlands they rose until the 1630s (to 186 per cent and 148 per cent respectively), while in France, northern Italy and Denmark they stopped going up in the 1620s after having risen by 136 per cent, 123 per cent and 177 per cent respectively. Moreover, as the graphs show, the amount of the increase was very different.[3]

Among some French historians the date when the long-term downward trend of grain prices began is a matter of debate. It is not easy to place that point in time, for the price curves are affected not only by the various methods of calculation and the gaps in the source material, but also by regional differences. It is hardly possible to make international comparisons using averages for any period of fewer than ten years. Annual averages will serve for individual regions or towns, but even then there are local variations. In the case of the Beauvais district north of Paris, Goubert (1960:460) thought the reaction had set in in 1630, but from his own calculations, represented in figure 35, it seems more likely that the peak of the inflation was not reached until 1650. The French Physiocrats and their forerunners, especially Boisguillebert, thought that French agriculture began to go downhill in 1660. Perhaps one should not concern oneself too much about establishing the turning-point. It might be better to speak of a turning-space which, with slight fluctuations, covered quite a long period.

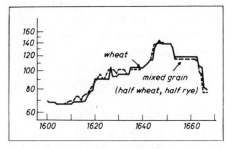

Fig. 35   Grain prices in Beauvais 1600–70.

Generally speaking, the price of cereals in western and central Europe stayed high till the middle of the century. The high prices, however, prevailed in very varied agricultural circumstances. Whereas in England and large parts of France the agrarian boom of the last century continued unabated, in Germany the Thirty Years War, in spite of the high prices, brought farming to a complete collapse.

*

Rents were still rising in England till the 1660s. Kerridge (1953–4:17) reports that arable rents in Norfolk and Suffolk increased sixfold between 1590–1600 and 1640–50, while the rent of meadows and pastures went up two or threefold. In Warwickshire between 1613 and 1648 some rents rose to about three times their former value. Rogers tells us much the same (1866–1902:V, 809).

Among contemporary witnesses, Davenant wrote in a paper first published in 1699, that English rents in 1600 scarcely amounted to half the sum usual in his day (1771 edn:221). Since it can be established fairly certainly that the upward movement of rent came to an end during the second half of the seventeenth century, this evidence can be ascribed to the first half. In the 1660s, Child (1694:44)[4] maintained, 'any gentleman or nobleman ... will find that the manors or farms ... bought fifty years past ... would now yield at least treble the money ... or even sixfold what they were then bought and sold for'. This inflation of the cost of land may have been partly the result of the changing rate of interest, which dropped from 10 per cent in 1600 to 6 per cent in 1660 (Child, 1694:40; MacPherson, n.d.:325, 482), but it was much more the result of the increased rents. Child also observed (pp. 45, 47, 49) that most leasehold rents had gone up in the past decades, more especially in the 1620s and 1660s. The conditions that had led to the agrarian boom of the previous century had not altered. The English population continued to grow rapidly after the turn of the century. In fact, it was Rogers' opinion (1866–1902:V, 782, 788) that the population of England doubled during the seventeenth century. Though it is doubtful whether the increase maintained its earlier rate during the second half of the century, it is certain that the number of inhabitants went on increasing till mid-century and perhaps later. According to Marshall (1905:223) the increase slowed to a halt in 1660.

We know that the area of cultivation expanded, that woodland was cleared, marshes drained and common pasture enclosed and put under the plough. Davenant wrote (1771:221) that there had been far more waste land in 1600 than there was in his time. Then woods, copses and commons had extended over wide areas. 'As we grow in riches,' he added, '... those many millions of acres which are now barren will by degrees most of them be improved and cultivated (see also Child, 1694:44 and Gras 1915:243).

In Belgium, too, after the severe recession in the early part of the seventeenth century had been overcome, rural income made a strong recovery. Polder rents from near Antwerp provide an example. With 1569 as the index base year, they rose from 54 per cent in 1595–6 to 146 per cent in 1601, and after the recession of 1602–5 (when they dropped to 119 per cent), they rose again to 401 in 1627–32, the final years of the series (van der Wee, 1963*a*:1, 481ff; see also figure 29).

The same goes, to a lesser extent, for the price of landed property and rents in France. According to d'Avenel (1894–1926:11, 508), the average price of a hectare of ploughland over France as a whole increased from an average of 227 franks[5] in 1601–25 to an average of 307 franks at the end of 1649–50 and to 491 franks by 1651–75. The same author informs us that the rent for one hectare of ploughland during the corresponding period rose from 14 franks, through 15.50 franks to 19.30 franks. The last average may overlap the period in which rents and land prices stagnated. From Zolla's researches (1893) and other sources it is known that rents reached their peak in 1660. The revenue from leasehold accruing to the landowning corporations in various parts of France increased from 100 in 1600–10 to 128 in 1650–60 (see Zolla, 1893).[6] According to Goubert (1960:524) the seigneurie of Catenoy in the Beauvais district that was leased for 1,300 livres in 1603 fetched 2,100 livres in 1642, representing a rent increase of 60 per cent in forty years. The leasehold of another estate in the same neighbourhood was worth 500 livres a year in 1612, but went up by 40 per cent to 710 livres in 1661. Since Goubert did not take the devaluation of money into account and Zolla did, the real increase, reckoned in the amount of silver contained in the coinage, may have been much the same in both cases.

In France, too, a growing population was the basic reason for the rising rents and cereal prices and for the continued increase of farming activity. The peaceful reign of Henry IV (1589–1610) probably encouraged a rapid population increase that may have continued, though at a slower pace, into Louis XIII's reign. Internal unrest and wars must have checked the rise to some extent, but apart from a setback as a result of the *Frondes* (1648–53) the number of inhabitants went on rising steadily, to reach its peak between the 1660s and 1680s (Levasseur, 1889:494f.).[7]

Le Roy Ladurie, from whose splendid work on the Languedoc peasants we have already quoted several times, was in agreement. Using only sources from his chosen area, he arrived at the conclusion that there was a *grand cycle agraire*. In order to illustrate the situation over a wider field he also quoted from my works. The depression of the late Middle Ages was followed by the prosperous sixteenth century and then, between 1600 and 1670 by a third phase, described by the author as the *phase de maturité*. In Languedoc the population increased, as it also did in Provence, the Loire Valley, Holland and England. Rents went up too, but certain tensions were already indicating the long-term recession (*reflux*) to come, which will be dealt with hereafter.

The *phase de maturité* (or *Umschwungsspanne* in my words, 1974:130ff.)[8] over most of France lasted into the third quarter of the seventeenth century. It seems that neither the costly policy of Richlieu's rising taxation nor the areas laid waste by the wars of the *Frondes* substantially inhibited the steady rise in rents. The position was different on France's eastern borders, which where more vulnerable to the effects of the Thirty Years War under which Germany was suffering. There is a series of land prices from Lorraine that reflects the falling agricultural income of that province. The cost of a hectare of ploughland sank from about 500 francs in 1600–10 to about 200 francs between 1640 and 1650 (Zolla, 1893:442). This decline in price has some connection with the situation in Germany, where land was practically worthless.

The Thirty Years War in Germany

Hunger, pestilence and trade stagnation

The war that was to become the Thirty Years War did not affect the agrarian market at first. Prices, which had recovered from the nadir of 1605–7, stayed at much the same level until the critical days of the war set in. Through coin-clipping and other manipulations the silver content of the currency in some German states dropped to 10 per cent or less of its former value, which naturally sent prices up. But the first inflation that was not merely due to the debasement of the coinage occurred in 1624–5; the second, and far more severe, occurred in 1637–8. Between those dates prices were occasionally lower – indeed, in the opinion of some knights and farmers, too low.

It can be seen from figure 36 (from Abel, 1967:262) that in 'cheap' periods the price of rye always fell lower than that of wheat, whereas in the lean years the two were almost identical. The reason, of course, was that in hard times the difference of taste mattered little, what mattered was to fill one's stomach; in a cheaper period the consumer preferred the more delicate wheaten loaf. This observation is supplementary to the Labrousse–van der Wee cycle (see above, p. 60). A glance at figure 36 at once suggests objections to the theory that after recovery from harvest failures prices, incomes, etc. tended to return to a 'normal

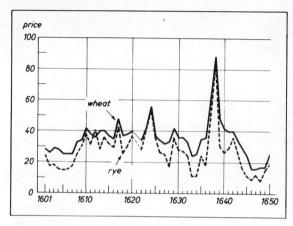

Fig. 36   Martinmas prices for wheat and rye in Halle.

level'. Rather it was as if the marketable quantity fluctuated in one direction to the consumer's disadvantage, in the other to the producer's.

In particular, the price of corn in 1625 struck contemporaries as exceptionally high, although later it rose even higher. At Solling, a little town near Dassel, there are three stones known as the Rye Stones, on which the price of rye has been carved. The first was set up in 1557, the second in 1625 (and the third in 1923). In 1625 the two town councillors, Hinrich Reckersch and Caspar Rover, recorded that in Dassel rye was worth 3 state thalers. The event was considered important enough to be commemorated on stone. But the inflation of 1637–8 was far worse. From those years a few letters survive, written by General van Werth as he and his troops invested the fortress of Herrmannstein (Ehrenbreitstein). When the general received an order from his commander-in-chief, the Elector of Bavaria, to proceed with his 4,000 men from the Rhine into Burgundy, he replied that without supplies of bread he could not let his troops march through a land where 'many thousands have died of hunger and no living soul is to be seen for miles on end'. The villages and countryside of the Palatinate and the Grand Duchy of Baden had been plundered for provisions 'only from the greatest need and poverty lest the regiment be destroyed and all die ... but the soldiers moved on, for in all these places they found nothing but ruined, broken houses, and the few subjects that remain to overwinter there will surely die of hunger'. The general stayed on the spot, and when winter came (December 1637) he saw that 'it often happens that, when they have eaten no bread for ten or twelve days, not only the musketeers but the cavalrymen, too, will eat horses that have died of horrible diseases' (Abel, 1967).[9]

The famine was accompanied by an epidemic, probably bubonic plague once more. It began in south-eastern Germany in 1634, and from 1636 to 1640 spread over the greater part of central, west and south Germany with terrible results. In some villages and towns it claimed half the inhabitants or more as its victims. From the little town of Wetter in Hesse we have a reliable report that 'because of the plague that has so long afflicted Wetter, hardly a fifth of its citizens, thus not more than sixty ... have survived and are still here' (Probst, 1963:48).

But not all the war years were as hard as this (as popular literature would have us believe). After years of inflation prices began to drop and, though the townsfolk could breathe freely once more, the farmers felt aggrieved. In the autumn of 1645 the estates of Brandenburg petitioned their duke to let them pay their contributions in corn rather than in money. The privy council refused their request because corn could be bought more cheaply in the market, whereupon the landed gentry wrote again, complaining that a farmer could not exist on the prices offered in the cities. They and their dependants, with their cartloads of grain, were left to cool their heels in the market place for up to two days before any burgher would condescend to buy, and then he expected to pay no more than 6, 7 or at most 8 groschen for a scheffel of rye. At that rate three to four scheffels were scarcely enough to buy one pair of shoes in the town. On the other hand, the brewer still sold his beer for 2 to $3\frac{1}{2}$ thalers a ton, just as he used to do, so that he could well have affored to pay double for his barley. The Elector did not ignore their plea. He told his councillors to fix fair prices for grain as well as for other goods. Whether these regulations were in fact imposed and, if so, whether they were obeyed, we do not know. 'The chief cause of the very low grain prices', proclaimed a Berlin privy council judgement in 1645, 'lies herein, that the towns, with few exceptions, have been destroyed, and so few inhabitants are left that they need no corn from the open country, since they can grow enough on their own land' (Naudé, 1896; see also Abel, 1967:262ff.). Price regulations were of no avail in that situation.

The enduring effects of the war

Gunther Franz (1961:47) estimated that about 40 per cent of the rural population and 33 per cent of the urban inhabitants of Germany fell victim to the Thirty Year War. Although marriages increased after the war, and more children were born, it was many years before such losses were made good. Wherever the torch of war had flared prosperity was burnt away. In July 1647 the landowners of Nieder-Lausitz complained that their farms were 'miserably decayed and laid waste, some consumed in flame and smoke'. They added that

> many of the nobility ... overburdened by the continuing monthly payments, have abandoned their estates and gone away, or else, because they can no longer afford servants, work the land themselves. With their children, their ploughs and harrows they scrape a bare existence with their own hands, pushing

wheelbarrows, making their own bread and fetching their own water – and that is to say nothing of the poor widows.

Farmhands were scarce and demanded high wages. 'In our common sorrow and need,' a Black Forest farmer declared in a pamphlet dated 1653, 'only the servants are in good heart; we must allow them to be the masters, when we pay them we almost have to hand them the purse along with the money; they must be full fed though we go short' (quoted in Erdmannsdörfer, n.d.:106; see also 105). In the district of Hadeln it became customary for farmhands and serving maids to work without contracts because they could easily earn enough to live on from casual day or weekly labour. This infuriated their rulers. A regulation of 22 December 1653 threatened punishment for laziness or unjustified changes of employment. There it says of the maidservants that 'they sit on their hands, as the saying goes, with the insolent excuse that, corn being cheap, they can eat their fill of wheat and rye and do not need to drudge and toil for others. Thus many cannot find servants enough and the maids are encouraged in their wantonness and petulance' (in Runne, 1956:69f.).

The news from the towns was much the same. Wage regulations were issued all over Germany, but they had little effect. The labour of furriers, cobblers, weavers, smiths, saddlers, wheelwrights and masons had become very costly. If we add to this the payments and taxes levied on landed property, it is no wonder the price of land, which during the war had sunk to a third, a quarter or, in some parts a tenth of its former value, rose very little even after peace had returned. As late as the end of the seventeenth century, an expert in Bavarian law, C. Schmid, declared (in 1694) that, in his opinion, the nobles' estates were worth no more than half, and often only a third or a quarter, of their pre-war value.

Such, in broad outline, were the enduring results of the great war in Germany. But in view of the situation described in the next chapter, one asks oneself whether the long hostilities did not produce effects that spread far beyond Germany's frontiers. Clearly that was so in the short run. When grain was scarce in Germany neighbouring countries were overrun by speculative agents from the German princes and generals. Agrarian prices, and consequently the price of land, went up. Chroniclers from Switzerland reported that the peasants' pockets were full of money, no one economized on food or clothing, if a house were burnt down a better one was set up in its place, baths and schoolhouses were built, in some villages the church tower was made higher, and some towns were 'replanned and embellished with footpaths, roads and bridges. When peace returned the profitable export business came to a halt. Many refugees went back to their homes, numerous estates and houses were up for sale. From Switzerland came comments that it was a time of 'impoverishment and tight money', and 'No one was buying anything, so the common man had to sell'.

Which leads us to suppose that, just as the short-term fluctuations of the market were influenced by events beyond national boundaries, the same must have been true of the long-term depression that weighed on the late seventeenth century and a great part of the eighteenth century. But before following that train of thought we must review the circumstances that allow us to speak of an agrarian depression in spite of its long duration.

6   Decline and depression

**Prices and wages in western and central Europe from the mid-seventeenth
century to the mid-eighteenth century**

Price trends

Figure 37 shows that the main tendency of grain price movements in western
and central Europe was in a downward direction. As with the earlier long-term
price curves, this observation applies only in relation to the weight of silver in
the relevant coinage and only to the 25-year averages marked on the graph. With
these reservations, however, it is valid for England, Belgium, France, northern
Italy, the Netherlands, Denmark and Poland.[1]

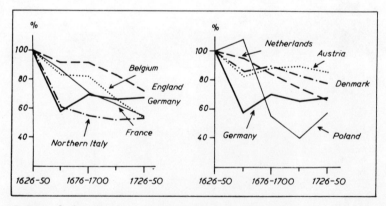

Fig. 37   Grain prices in western and central Europe 1626–1750 (25-year averages).

As can be seen from figure 37, the price of wheat in France, considered in

10-year periods, sank from 100 in 1626–50 by stages of 98, 86, 87 to 59 in the decade 1681–90. After a short rise it dropped again from 84 to 71, 60, 55, 59 and finally to 50 in 1741–50. The movement was so striking that even contemporaries were aware of it. The Physiocrats and their forerunners freely expressed their views on what seemed to them a calamitous situation. It was an eternal truth, one of them propounded in 1734 (see Melon, 1843:713), that a land with a surplus of corn must be badly governed. If the government would only leave the corn trade to its own devices the surplus would be exported, the price of corn would rise and everything would be in good order again. 'The government is to blame', was the theme of many Physiocratic writings; if hindrances to internal trade and the restriction of exports were once removed, better times would come again. But the freeing of exports did nothing to halt the long-term collapse of French prices. Herbert, one of the first French writers to undertake extensive research on the statistics of prices (1755, in 1910), Quesnay (esp. 1756:183) and other economists, with England in mind, began to have their doubts. For in England, too, the price of grain was falling, although, in contrast to the French, the English government had freed exports as early as the last decade of the seventeenth century and had, indeed, subsidized the export of grain. Today's historian, with so much more statistical material on prices at his disposal, can add that the same tendency was perceptible in southern, northern and eastern Europe.

Only in Germany and Austria did the price curves move upwards again during the last quarter of the seventeenth century. As a more detailed study of the prices would show, this was due at first to harvest failures. But the rising movement persisted, as can be seen clearly in figure 37. To supplement the graph with some figures, let us divide the century into two 50-year periods. If we take the first period, 1651–1700 as 100, the average prices during the second half-century, 1701–50, were: in Germany 104, in Austria 103, but in England 84, in France 75, in Belgium 73, in northern Italy 90, in Denmark 90, in Poland 60 and in the Netherlands 79.

It would appear that in some districts and provinces the price of cattle and animal products was better maintained, and sometimes actually rose. The matter needs more investigation, but for the present we have a graph (figure 38) from Vienna, in which Pribram shows rye and cattle price movements between 1600 and 1780. The prices show a double reciprocal relationship. When in the first half of the seventeenth century rye prices were still high, the price of oxen fell, and when there was a decline in the price of rye (interrupted only by the failed harvests of 1700) livestock prices went up. That brings us to the purchasing power of the consumer, who, when the price of bread was high had little money left for meat, but was ready to spend more on that desirable commodity when bread prices dropped.

Wages

In England a builder's wage, reckoned in kilograms of bread grain, rose from an average of 100 in 1626–50 to 129 in the next quarter-century and then from 168 and 177 up to 199 in the years from 1726 to 1750 (see figure 39).[2] The wages of an unskilled labourer in England did not rise at quite the same rate but they, too, were 50 per cent higher in the second quarter of the eighteenth century than

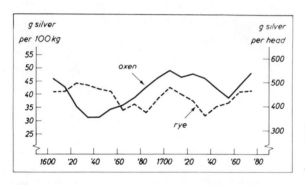

Fig. 38   Rye and cattle prices in Vienna from 1600 to 1780 (trinomial 10-year moving averages, silver per 100 kg rye or per head of cattle).

they had been in the same quarter of the preceding century. The slight flattening of the English wage curve in the first twenty-five years of the eighteenth century manifests itself in the French curve as a decline.

However, wages also increased in France over the whole period, rising from 100 in 1626–50 to 151 (for an artisan builder) and 160 (for an unskilled labourer without board) in 1726–50. Admittedly these figures are according to d'Avenel, whose calculations tend to be a little uncertain. All the same, it once more appears that the general trends are correctly outlined. In Languedoc, according to Le Roy Ladurie's research (1969:592ff., figure 36), agricultural cash wages went up 'spectacularly' (by about 30 per cent) between 1640–55 and 1686, while the price of corn sank or stagnated. For Beauvais, Goubert assembled some records of wages and presented them as a closed series which, though based on rather few and unrepresentative crafts, led the author to maintain that during the middle of this period (not the famine years, of course) the labourer was in a favourable situation. As an instance, he cites a group of labourers set to gather fuel (faggots). A graph (no. 125) shows that whereas in the years 1580–1650 it took them from two to ten working days to collect the equivalent of 1 mine (33 litres) of wheat, in 1650–1735 it required only one and a half to five days; thus, if we disregard Goubert's calculations of averages, there was a considerable drop (Goubert, 1960:558ff.).[3]

For Germany it was possible to calculate a more complete index. It shows wage movements diverging from those of England and France. After a steep rise in the first decades after the Thirty Years War, wages fell sharply, yet the wages of an artisan builder and an unskilled labourer there in 1726–50 were 111 per cent and 125 per cent respectively above their 1626–50 level.

It was also reported from northern Italy (Cesse, 1921:18) that the cost of labour increased relatively more than the price of cereals up to the early eighteenth century. And from England we have a report (from an Englishman who tended to exaggerate) stating that the annual cash wage of a farm labourer rose in the last decades of the seventeenth century from £5 to £10 (Brewster, 1695:199f.).

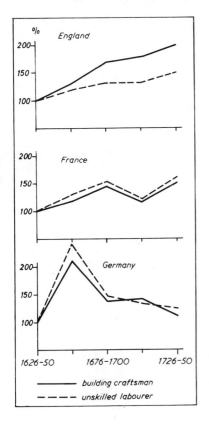

building craftsman
– – – – unskilled labourer

Fig. 39   Wages in western and central Europe 1626–1750 (per day, in kg of bread grain).

The decline of French agriculture

The long-term effects

'It is without precedent since the creation of the world', declared Boisguillebert in 1697,

> that a rich nation should lose half its wealth within thirty or forty years without having suffered plagues or wars or any of the other disasters that usually

bring countries to their ruin.... All landed property has sunk to half its former price.... France's wealth began to dwindle in 1660 and grew less from day to day, because its cause did not abate, that is to say the decline of revenue from the land [*revenu des fonds*], whose mean value today is scarcely half what it used to be. (in Daire edn, 1843:253, 173)

About fifty years later Forbonnais expressed the view that landed property was being sold dirt cheap and 'many nobles with vast estates are extremely impoverished' (quoted in Taine, 1908:387; d'Avenel, 1894–1926:11, 508).

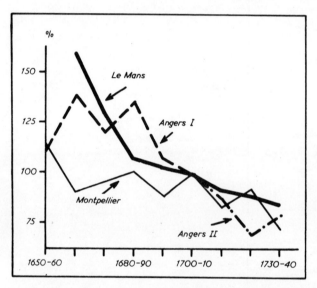

Fig. 40   Leasehold rents of French landed estates 1650–1740 (silver content of coinage 1700–10 = 100).

Having heard contemporary witnesses, let us see what some French historians have to say. *La terre n'est plus rentable* was the heading Le Roy Ladurie gave to his chapter dealing with the years around 1660 (1966: part V, chapter 4). According to d'Avenel (1894–1926:11, 508), the average leasehold rent per hectare for the whole of France sank from 12.80 francs (1 Fr. = 0.80 RM) in the years 1651–75, to 12.30 francs in the next quarter-century, and then to 7.50 francs in 1701–25. As d'Avenel's results were derived from very varied, hardly compatible, fragmented data, it will be useful to supplement them with some leasehold rents published by Zolla (1893:322–4, 691–4). The movement of these rents, depicted in figure 40, agrees with Boisguillebert's statements. As the 1650s gave way to the 1660s the rents began to go down and continued to do so without interruption for nearly a hundred years, reaching their lowest point in the third or fourth decade of the eighteenth century. During those years the sum realized from letting the estates shown in the graph was not much more than half the former amount. The decline in rents may have been even greater in other parts of the country. Taine (1908:373f.) reported that in the district of Confolens in central France a piece of land that had brought in 2,956 francs in 1665 was let in 1747 for only 900 francs. Another demesne in the same region, which in 1660 supported two noble families in comfort, had become by the mid-eighteenth century no more than a 'tiny, unproductive leasehold'. Traces of the old furrows were still visible on the neglected fields. In the district of Berry and Sologne in central France, Quesnay and Dupré de St Maur (Quesnay, 1757, in 1888:202).[4] inform us, it was hard enough to let ground of medium quality, meadows, fields and waste all together, for 15 sols the arpent.[5] Even with this meagre rent, coming to about 1.40 francs a hectare, the landlord had to supply a part of the stock. Land and soil in those regions had become practically worthless, and yet at the end of the sixteenth century prices as high as 320 francs for a hectare of ploughland and 2,000 francs for the same area of meadowland had been paid.

Land prices for the whole of France, as assembled by d'Avenel, sank from 260 francs per hectare in 1651–75 to 175 francs in 1701–25. Admittedly, d'Avenel's figures can be referred to only for the general direction of the price movement. They have little to tell us of its intensity, based as they are on all too many widely-scattered instances. In another passage of his works d'Avenel suggests that during those years landed property in France lost 80 per cent of its value.

Such a precipitous drop in land value and rents cannot be explained entirely by the counter-currents of grain prices and wages or, speaking more generally, of farming production and farming expenses. Added to these were the taxes demanded by the state. As a result of Louis XIV's costly wars, the burden of taxation resting on French agriculture had grown considerably heavier. It is true that in the course of the previous farming boom, probably between the end of Henry IV's reign (1610) and the death of Mazarin (1661), taxes rose faster than during the eighty years of the ensuing farming depression (Zolla, 1893:447f.) The relative burden, however, that is the proportion of taxation to net agricultural yield, was inconsiderable during the boom and only began to grow after 1660 as rents went down. There is no end to the complaints in the contemporary literature about the severity of taxation at that time. One of the basic principles of the Physiocratic doctrine was to censure the taxation policy of the exchequer and clergy in the stongest terms. For Quesnay who, as one of the earliest political economists, sought to disentangle the intricate skein of socio-economic relations, reproachful words were not enough. He tried repeatedly to gauge the distribution of income in his time, either as a whole or in part. In an article entitled *Grains*, written in the 1750s he estimated that the total yield of French cereal farming came to about 600 million livres. From that sum, in his opinion, about 70 per cent went on farming expenses while 13 per cent each went to the landowner as rent and to the treasury in tax, leaving barely 4 per cent with the tenant for upkeep and profit (in 1888:206). In the *Tableau Economique* he supplemented this information with figures which, he stressed, were in no way hypothetical but, on the contrary, 'copied down from life'. According to these data, which have not received their due attention from historians and theoreticians, the total production of French industry in the mid-eighteenth century amounted to 700 million livres, of which 500 million came from farming. Out of this 500 million worth of agricultural produce 200 million was used in agriculture itself as food, seed and fodder, 100 million went to buy industrial products, and the remaining 200 million, or 40 per cent, went to the landlords, the king and the Church. The landlords received 57 per cent of the payments, the king 29 per cent and the Church 14 per cent.[6]

These are doubtless only rough assessments, but they are not as entirely 'hypothetical' as modern dogmatic historians would have us believe. François Quesnay who, in his youth as a simple country doctor, came to know the life of the French peasant intimately, used to work out now and again an economic calculation comparing the profits and coast of the ordinary farm he knew so well. He came to the conclusion that, with contemporary prices, taxes and expenses, the farmer could barely cover the costs of his enterprise and, with no chance of building up a reserve fund, was helpless in the face of the inevitable emergencies such as crop failures and cattle diseases (Quesnay, 1756, in 1888:177f.).

Later research has added to Quesnay's facts. Pierre Goubert, who made an impressive study of agriculture in the Beauvais district north of Paris, estimated the charges on a smallholding of not more than 8 hectares (often only 4–5 hectares) in extent as follows (1960:180f.): The 'taillage' tax came to 20 livres, as much as the price of a good cow or five or six calves, six or seven sheep, 5 hectolitres of wheat in a good year or 2 hectolitres after a poor harvest when prices went up. The taillage alone claimed the entire production of $1\frac{1}{2}$ hectares and, together with the other taxes claimed 20 per cent of the gross yield. To that must be added the tithe and other ecclesiastical charges, amounting to a further 12 per cent, and the tenant's rent amounting to about 20 per cent; thus altogether 52 per cent of the gross yield. Goubert reckoned that the seed-born and the upkeep of the farm would cost another 20 per cent of the gross yield, so that little more than a quarter was left over for the maintenance of the farmer and his family.

To provide a family of six with bread even on a very modest scale (4 kilograms per day) took 20 hectolitres of wheat. At that rate, even when no rent had to be paid a harvest of at least 40 hectolitres from the wheat field was required to supply the family needs. In a good year $3\frac{1}{3}$ hectares would yield 40 hectolitres of wheat. Thus, under a three-course rotation in Beauvais, even an owner-farmer could not grow enough bread grain for his own family on less than 10 hectares. Most Beauvais farmers did not own that much land.

In droves the peasants abandoned the land that 'brought them as much misery as the city displays wealth' (Herbert, 1910:111). Whole districts turned to wasteland. 'Many regions that could well be cultivated are left half-desolate waste', and 'hundreds, nay, thousands of morgens of bleak moorland lie one by the other'

are among the descriptions by contemporary witnesses (Taine, 1908:379).[7]
Quesnay estimated, though he may have exaggerated, that in his day (the mid-
eighteenth century) half the cultivable area of France was quite untilled, the other
half insufficiently so (see Bauer, 1890:116f.).[8]

The harvest cycle

Quesnay and his friends related their observations to long-term trends. The prices
and crops they presented were (estimated) mean values – but the mean values
of statisticians are fiction. The actual harvests were sometimes above and sometimes below those values and, in either case, if the divergence was considerable,
brought the peasant only further distress. When the crop was poor the peasant
had little or nothing to sell and he and his family went hungry; when the crop
was plentiful the price went down, so that he could not fulfil his obligations to
landlord and state. The peasant's plight has already been pointed out by Marc
Bloch, who described the decline of prices in the later seventeenth century as
'the main feature of France's social development' at that time. Whether the years
were bad or good the French peasant had cause for complaint: in one event he
had nothing to sell and little to eat, in the other event prices were too low to
support him.

It is relevant here to describe the course of a harvest cycle in France. The
years from 1685 to 1694 have been chosen because the correspondence carried
on during that time between the Controller-General of Finance and the provincial
intendants throws some light on the subject (de Boislisle, 1874). But first this
harvest cycle must be set in its long-term context, and to that end in figure 41 we
present Usher's graph of annual wheat prices in Paris, Rozoy and Douai between
1520 and 1788 (1930:162). By comparing the price of wheat in Paris with the
London and Berlin prices (shown below in figure 42) it can be seen that the fluctua-

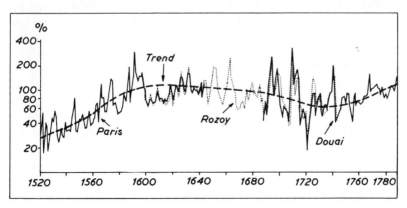

Fig. 41 Wheat prices in Paris, Rozoy and Douai, 1520–1788 (silver content of
coinage, relative value with trend superimposed, log. scale 1596–1643 = 100).

tions largely agree in time but not in their intensity. More will be said of this later.

The harvest cycle begins with the high prices of 1685 (on evidence from Rozoy alone in figure 41) and ends with the high prices of 1694. It is situated on the downward slope of the line representing long-term trends. The individual Rozoy prices are shown in table 18.

Table 18   Wheat prices in Rozoy en Brie, 1685–94 (grammes of silver per setier)

Year	Price
1685	135
1686	85
1687	90
1688	59
1689	66
1690	71
1691	75
1692	96
1693	186
1694	275

Here are some extracts from the controller's correspondence with the intendants (de Boislisle, 1874:1): On 15 March 1685, when the price of wheat in Rozoy still stood at 135 grams of silver per setier, the intendant of Rouen wrote to the controller-general: 'The poverty is such that a farmer who bought a woollen garment had to do without a linen one. The peasant women, who used to love wearing red and blue petticoats, seldom have them now. They are very poorly dressed and mostly make do with white linen'. To which circumstance the intendant was not slow in attributing the declining turnover of Rouen's textile industry.

The next year in Rozoy the wheat price went down by about a third. On 9 May 1686 (de Boislisle, 1874:I, 70) the intendant reported, 'The price of grain has dropped to an amazing degree. What cost 10 livres last year is now offered for 50 sous and still finds no buyer.' The intendant of Flanders wrote on 11 July 1686 (I, 77) that the taxes, both customary and special, were in arrears, 'due to the low value of corn'. During the following year prices remained at about the same low level. In a letter dated 31 January 1687 (I, 96) the intendant of Flanders asked for a higher import duty on foodstuffs as the only way to support the province, to raise the king's revenue, revive trade and encourage farming. Similar requests came from other provinces. During 1687 higher import duties or prohibitions and the easing of exports were demanded by, among other towns: Bordeaux, in March, where the wine trade was at a standstill (I, 97); Berry, in

May and June, with a complaint against the large import of sheep from Germany (I, 103); Limoges, in June and July, where the cattle market was stagnant (I, 106); and Tours, also in June and July, on the grounds that 'the wine trade is almost ruined' (I, 106).

The year 1688 brought the lowest prices of the whole 10-year cycle. It can be seen from the material assembled by Goubert that eighteen farms were in arrears with their rent for an average period of four and a half years. For that part of the country, Goubert observes, 'that was a long time; in the comparable year of 1646 the same farms were, on average, only twelve months behind with the rent' (Goubert, 1960:529). More interesting still is the Flemish intendant's remark on 25 May 1688 (I, 151) that the cheapness of grain had forced the peasants to grow more rape than ever before. This throws some light on the way the Flemish peasants' farming programme reacted to prices at a time when this sort of reaction was, till recently, hardly supposed to have existed. The peasants had adjusted their plans to the relative prices of rape and cereals, and now the government wanted to draw some advantage from the situation. An export duty on rape was suggested. The intendant resisted the measure not, true to his time, for the sake of the peasant, but for the sake of the trade balance. He urged that although the domestic soap-making industry might benefit from a tax on the export of rape, the Dutch, who hitherto had imported a great deal of it, would make up the deficit by growing it themselves, 'and nothing would do the country more harm'.

On 10 January of the following year, 1689, when prices were still low, the Archbishop of Aix wrote:

> The provinces have no money with which to pay the king's taxes because oil and grain, the only commercial crops of the countryside, find no buyers. The peasants abandon their farms and tenant farmers cannot pay their rents. Now, when a deserted farm reverts to the landlord, the custom of this province relieves him of all tailage-taxes. It must also be observed that it is of advantage to the people when corn is sold for a fair price [*honneste prix*], for when it is too cheap the landowners cannot afford to keep up their farms, till their fields or give work to the poor. (I, 170)

One would think a Physiocrat were talking. It was with almost the same words and reasoning that Boisguillebert, Quesnay and many other writers attacked the excessively low price of cereals.

In 1690 grain prices began to rise, and this recovery continued. In 1691 the province of Limoges had to distribute alms to 7,000 poor people. In Burgundy the distress was so great that some families had been without salt for six months. During the following year (1692) the intendant of Limoges reported, 'after careful investigation', that more than 70,000 persons had been forced to beg their bread. People ate ferns that had been dried in the oven and then crushed. Bread was so scarce and of such bad quality that 'men grew weak and the weak died'. Sad stories like these reached Paris from every part of France. In Paris itself the price of bread was so high that people banded together in protest. The authorities were no longer in a position to suppress the unrest (1, 301). A survey of grain stocks was ordered and heavy punishment threatened to anyone who sent in false returns. The burghers were to disgorge their hoarded corn. Those incapable of work were to return to their homes and the farmers were ordered to till their fields. None of this was of much avail. In Rozoy the price of wheat went up nearly threefold between 1692 and 1694, while in Paris it almost doubled.

We will now leave this evidence,[9] to turn our attention to some contemporary reports from England.

Critical years in England

Documentary evidence

English writings of this period are a more fertile source for the economic historian than those of France. Boisguillebert, who knew a great deal and wrote down some of it, had to publish his later works abroad because they were banned in France. The English wrote more freely, though, admittedly, they were less biased against the government. They, too, sought for the cause of the depression afflicting their country in the measures and omissions of the government – that was a sign of the times – but they also looked for other circumstances and conditions that might share in the responsibility and, in so doing, they made some observations that are still interesting to the historian.

Before quoting from the old writers, however, there are two comments to be made. The first concerns price fluctuations. Just as in France, the price of grain in England manifested short-term fluctuations. Plentiful harvests were accompanied by low prices, poor harvests by high prices, and this occurred in a pattern that followed the continental harvest cycle very closely, as can be seen in figure 42.[10]

The graph shows that English wheat prices fell particularly low in:

1 the 1660s, the lowest point being in 1666
2 the 1680s, with the lowest point 1688
3 at the beginning of the eighteenth century, with the lowest point in 1706.

Following on this came a longer-lasting, three-phased downward trend, with low points in 1723, 1732 and, with the lowest wheat price for the whole 80-year period, 1743.

It is also clear from figure 42 that the English and Berlin price movements, at first almost parallel, became more divergent as the century advanced until in the mid-1740s they appear to be quite independent. The long-term separate trend of German grain prices during the eighteenth century has already been indicated when discussing the grain price movements of central Europe. It will be touched on again when we come to agrarian developments in Germany.

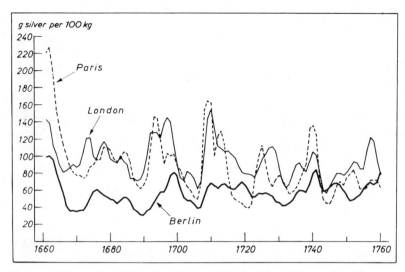

Fig. 42 Wheat prices in London, Paris and Berlin (trinomial annual moving averages).

Contemporary grievances will be better understood if we consider the cost-structure of the numerous tenant farms then in England. On the evidence of some old account-books Rogers (1866–1902:V, 816) has tried to reconstruct the production costs of such a farm during the second half of the seventeenth century. Worked on the usual three-course rotation system, a 200-acre English tenant farm of that period was supposed to produce £225 sterling gross yield annually. This gross yield was distributed as shown in table 19. A farm in such a position was at risk. If prices fell and nothing could be spared from either wages or tenant's capital, the farmer could choose only between lowering his family's standard of living still further or falling into arrears with rent. Understandably, both prospects were viewed with dread and resentment.

Table 19 Expenses of an English tenant farmer in the second half of the seventeenth century

Expenses	£	% of total expenditure
Wages	78	35
Taxation	20	9
Maintenance of the tenant and his family	30	13
Depreciation and interest on tenant's capital	37	17
Rent	60	26
TOTAL	225	100

The trade crisis of the 1660s

Rents in England had been rising steadily for decades, but in the 1660s the upward movement came to an abrupt halt. Macaulay (1849), who had noticed the event (and did not deem it too insignificant to find a place in his *History*), wrote:

> The income of every landed proprietor was diminished by five shillings in the pound. The cry of agricultural distress rose from every shire in the kingdom; and for that distress the government was, as usual, held accountable. The gentry, compelled to retrench their expenses for a period, saw with indignation the increasing splendour and profusion of Whitehall, and were immovably fixed in the belief that the money which ought to have supported their households had, by some inexplicable process, gone to the king's favourites.

The economists and politicians of the time were already trying to explain the 'inexplicable'. It occurred to them that the trouble could have arisen from the import of livestock, which had much increased in recent years. In the face of opposition from the cattle trade and fatteners, in 1666 the import of livestock from Ireland was banned. The hoped-for improvement, however, did not eventuate. Coke's treatise on the subject appeared in 1671, saying:

> That the ends designed by the acts against the importation of Irish cattle, of raising the rents of the lands of England, are so far from being attained, that the contrary hath ensued. And here I wish a survey were taken how many thousand farms are thrown up since this act; how many thousand farms are abated, some above one-sixth, others about one-quarter, others about one-third; some I know which after two years lying wasted are abated one-half. (in anon. 1750:50; and Select Committee report, 18 June 1821:230)

Josiah Child, in an essay written in the 1660s, but not published till thirty years later (1694), devoted long passages to the fall of rents. He suggested many reasons that are no longer of interest to us here, but also a few others that are worth our attention. Thus, in noting the recent huge land taxes and the inordinate raising of rents during the last years of the late agrarian boom he called attention to 'the late great improvement of Ireland ... the consequence whereof is that that country now supplieth foreign markets as well as our own plantations in America with beef, pork, hides ... and corn at cheaper rates than we can afford, to the beating us out of those trades'. He added, further, that the Great Plague of 1665 had depopulated the country, and noted, finally, 'the usual plenty of corn, which hath been for these three or four years past in most parts of Christendom, the like whereof hath been seldom known'.

The agrarian recession of the 1680s

The trade recession was overcome. Prices began to rise again and in Tooke's opinion (Tooke and Newmarch, 1858:1, 14) the favourable prices of the 1670s had led to a new expansion of English arable land. That cannot be proved, as there is no evidence available either on that subject or on the rent movements of the 1670s.

In the mid-1680s the relatively advantageous effects of the grain prices petered out in England, as in France. John Locke wrote an essay entitled 'Some Considerations of the Consequences of lowering of Interest and Raising the Value of Money' (1691), in which he preached 'An infallible sign of your Decay of Wealth is the Falling of Rents, and the raising of them would be worth the Nation's Care ...' (1727 edn:34). Of course he knew that if the landowner's lot had not improved during recent years, it had not been for the want of the English government's trying. Many years earlier when the first signs of an agricultural surplus had appeared, Cromwell's parliament had passed 'An Act for the Exportation of several Commodities of the breed, growth and manufacture of this Commonwealth' (27 November 1656). The act included the words, 'And forasmuch it hath pleased Almighty God to bless the industry and endeavours of the People of these Nations, in the great improvement of Fens, Forests, Chases and other Lands, with a great redundancy of Corn, Cattel, Butter, Cheese and divers other considerable commodities ...'. Various measures were enacted to facilitate export; four years later, when these proved ineffective, import duties were imposed. The keystone of this trade policy, adopted two years before Locke published his essay, was the corn export bounty of 1689. A bounty of five shillings was promised for every quarter of wheat exported whenever the home price fell below a certain level.

The price did fall below that level, the export bounties were duly paid, and yet rents and the price of grain and land sank. John Locke greeted the fall of land prices during those years with several long essays in which he said that the price of land, like the price of other articles, was determined by supply and demand. The supply of land was over-plentiful. During recent years bad management, luxury and absenteeism had resulted in many estates getting deeply in debt. When the burden of interest became too heavy to bear, the owner was forced to sell his land. How different it had been, he wrote, in Queen Elizabeth's day. Then the value of land had risen steadily and landed property had fetched a good price. Demand, on the other hand, was small, because a merchant who was doing well in trade was not eager to invest his money in real estate, with rents falling and likely to fall still lower.

When a Nation is running to Decay and Ruin, the Merchant and Married Man, do what you can, will be sure to starve last: Observe it where you will, the Decays that come upon, and bring Ruin to any country, do constantly first fall upon the Land: And though the Country Gentleman (who ... thinks his land an unmovable fund for such an income) be not very forward to think so ... yet he is more concerned with Trade ... than even the Merchant himself. For he will certainly find, when a Decay of Trade has carried away one Part of our Money out of the Kingdom, and the other is kept in the Merchant and Tradesman's hands, that no Laws he can make ... will bring it back to him again: but his Rents will fall, and his Income every Day lessen, till general Industry and Frugality, joined to a well-ordered Trade, shall restore to the Kingdom the Riches and Wealth it had formerly'. (1727 edn:26f.)

This passage, once the theory and style of the period have been subtracted, gives us a clear picture of the agrarian slump during those years. Trade attracted money: for some reason (not pursued further) the price of farm produce was too low. This low price depressed rents and made it difficult for the owner-farmer to carry on his business. If the property were encumbered with debt, the interest could no longer be paid and house and land were lost.

The credit crisis of the early 1690s

The crisis in farming credits already foreshadowed in Locke's essays grew more serious during the ensuing years. After the French wars both land taxes and the rate of interest on loans were increased. A large part of the farming industry, weakened by loss of income, could no longer support the new burdens. Arrears of interest and rent piled up; forced sales, bankruptcies and cut-price selling of landed property were on the increase. About this time Briscoe published an article, which is no doubt somewhat exaggerated, describing the desperate situation of English agriculture. He introduces a freeholder who makes a speech to parliament. A part of the imaginary discourse goes as follows:

And so there are not a few Gentlemen in the Nation who have large and noble Estates, without the least encumbrance upon them, yet ... many of our Estates ... are charged with no small Sums for Portions for younger Brothers and Sisters ... So that what with the Interest of Money which we pay, and the Taxes raised upon us, very many of us (though of considerable Estates) are reduced to the last Extremity: and to consummate our Miseries, our Creditors will not be satisfied, nor stay any longer for our Money, tell us they can make a better Advantage of it by lending it to the Government.... If we do not comply with their unjust Demands ... we are forced to part with that little Remainder which we had left to us to buy Bread for our Wives and Children to satisfy those devouring Harpies, without which ... we must have been imprisoned and outed of our Estates. (1696:25)

Never before had so many estates been put up for sale owing to the calling in of loans. The landowners were forced to part with their land dirt cheap. 'We have done all we can to sell our Estates, but everyone we ask tells us, they had rather sell than purchase Land upon which there are so many Taxes.'

In another paper written in the same year (anon. 1696:25) it was said that an estate which had cost a father 600 guineas was now being sold by his son for 450 guineas. Perhaps, he adds, had he offered it for sale six months later, only 300 guineas would have been bid. In 1695 a third author (Brewster, 1695:122) reported that some land was let for no more than five or ten shillings an acre and still the tenant could not pay the rent.

The crisis in the first decade of the eighteenth century

In the early 1690s the price of grain had begun to rise again in England, yet it was just at that time that the English farmers were complaining most bitterly of their poverty. The rising rents and taxes must have wiped out any advantage gained by the higher prices, while the debasement of the currency no doubt also played its part. The situation began to change, however, somewhere in the mid-1690s. During the last five years of the century a real shortage of wheat prevailed in England. Cereal prices reached a level higher than anyone could remember. Some landowners and tenants began to hope that the trade recession had been overcome at last. But their hopes were in vain. Neither the outbreak of war with France nor the subsidizing of grain exports could prevent a renewed fall in the price of corn. In January 1703, Evelyn wrote in his diary: 'Corn and provisions so cheap that the farmers are unable to pay their rents' (in Tooke and Newmarch, 1858:I, 19).

The agrarian depression of 1720–50

The harvests were bad from 1708 to 1710. In some parts of Europe there was serious famine. The price of grain went up everywhere, then fell again as quickly as it had risen. After a few quite abundant years the autumn of 1726 produced a bumper crop, according to Robert Loder, a Berkshire farmer known for the account-books he bequeathed to posterity: for every quarter of seed-corn he harvested 14.55 quarters of wheat and 8.43 quarters of barley. Wheat tumbled to half its 1612–17 price. It was reported from Norfolk that farmers were once again prepared to give the owners back their leases (see Bowden, 1967:631f.).

In England this fall in prices ushered in a long period in which, according to contemporary witnesses, the price was seldom high enough to allow a tenant to pay his rent. In 1734 Allen wrote in his *Landholder's companion*:

> The interest of our British landholders has been declining several years last past; it has been a general observation, that rents have been sinking, and tenants unable to make as good payments as formerly.... Wheat this year and last never mounted, in some of the extreme parts of the kingdom, to above three

shillings and eightpence per Winchester [bushel].... Before they can pay their
rents, wheat of middling goodness ought, I think, to sell for about four shillings
and threepence per Winchester, not in a few places but throughout the kingdom ... iron, timber, harvest people and servants being much dearer than here-
tofore, will not yield sufficient profit to the occupiers of them, unless they can
have such prices, particularly as cattle, pigs, sheep, butter and cheese are now
one-third cheaper than formerly. (quoted in the Select Committee report,
18 June 1821:230)

Three years later (1737) an anonymous writer pointed out that never before had
tenants been so much in arrears with their payments. A number of landlords
had already remitted a large part of these debts in the hope of keeping tenants
to the old rents and persuading them to go on trying for a while longer (in Mingay,
1955–6:323f.). A third author (Trowell, 1739) declared that at that time many
farmers had so come down in the world that they could not support their families
even in a normal year. In the same year a fourth writer – again anonymous –
pressed for an act of parliament, because 'many farms are unoccupied', while
still another anonymous author, writing in 1737, lamented: 'But how shocking
must be the daily Instances we have of the unfortunate Farmers!' As a deliverance
from their misery he suggested his own patent manure, for, he added, 'It's
generally agreed that this is [sic] at this time more Farms in the hands of the
Landlords than ever before, and that many more are daily falling into the like
Circumstance of Impoverishment for want of proper Manure to improve the
same'.

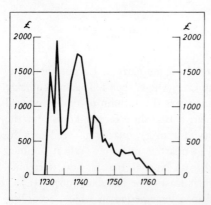

Fig. 43   Rent arrears on the Duke of
Kingston's estates.

Mingay, from whose work (1955–6) these last quotations were borrowed, investigated the arrears of rent on the Duke of Kingston's estates during those
difficult years (see figure 43). He found that these debts increased in 1730 and
again in 1740. After that date the arrears gradually diminished, but it should be
noted that the diminishment shown in the graph (and in the accounts it represents)
was only in the annual *increase* in the size of the debt. The arrears themselves

were still high and probably decreased far more slowly. As late as 1750, according to a contemporary, arrears of rent all over England represented a huge sum. Numerous leasehold farms had reverted to their owners because the landlords had refused to reduce the rent. They had tried running the farms themselves, but only very rarely had they made a profit that even approached the old rent in value. Finally the property became so overburdened with debt that in not a few cases it had to be put up for sale (anon., 1750:4, 70).

At the end of the 1750s the price of grain began to rise. There were, admittedly, setbacks in the 1760s and 1770s, but the real distress was past. The revenue of tenant and landlord began to flow in more regularly and more abundantly. New prosperity spread over the countryside, new land was put under the plough, new methods of cultivation and animal husbandry were introduced. The sap was rising through every branch of agricultural activity. A new – and until now the latest – long-term upward trend of European farming had set in.

The causes of the slump in prices and trade

Thomas Tooke, one of the earliest writers to look for the causes of the slump, attributed it to abundant harvests (Tooke and Newmarch, 1858:1, 14ff.). Although the link between price fluctuations and agricultural yield is so clear as scarcely to require proof, the harvest cycle is not enough in itself to explain the intensity and long duration of the price deflation. Both phenomena are related to the long-term downward trend of prices which, made up of short-term fluctuations though it was, needs a separate explanation.

It is equally mistaken to blame the slump on the activities of the English farmers. Although a few farmers here and there sought to beat the stagnant market by means of lower costs and higher production, they were isolated cases. The progress often given the somewhat-exaggerated title 'agricultural revolution' did not really set in until 1760 or even 1780 (Ernle, 1961).

In 1730 Lord Townshend had introduced a form of crop rotation on his Norfolk estates. Still earlier had Jethro Tull preached the use of sainfoin and invented his famous drill, but it was not until the second half of the eighteenth century that he found many followers. Nor should the subsequent advances be overestimated. Mingay underlines the need for caution in using the term 'agricultural revolution' (1963:123f.).

Up to the middle of the eighteenth century extensification often offered greater rewards. In a paper published in 1699 Davenant cites the opinion of one of his contemporaries that 'the profit of one acre of pasture in the flesh, hide and tallow of an ox, or in the flesh, wool and tallow of a sheep, or in the carcase of a horse, is of so much greater value abroad than the yield of the earth would be in corn' (in 1771:228). In the following year it was announced that 'the inhabitants are all turning their fields into pasture because the raising of cattle and sheep brings more gain than tilling the soil' (quoted in von Schröder, 1713:204). To halt the decline in corn-growing an act of parliament was passed, stipulating that the area of arable must remain in a certain proportion to that of pastureland.

Neither can England's trade policy be held responsible for the English farmer's troubles. It was during these years that the agricultural trading policy of England reached the point of impeding imports and subsidizing exports. It is true that, with the help of the export bounties, 450,000 Winchester quarters (100,000 tons) were exported annually between 1711 and 1740 (Naudé, 1896:97f., 112). This dumping did not greatly help the English farmer and only aggravated the situation on the continent.

To clarify the causes of the secular agrarian depression of the early modern era, we must turn again to the question of demand in the agrarian market. But before doing so there is evidence from other countries to be considered, as well as some short comments on Ashton's theory of depressions.

Inspired by Labrousse, Ashton developed a theory regarding English economic conditions. It culminated in the principle that before the industrial era economic slumps went with high grain prices, economic booms with low prices (1959:146f.). Both Labrousse and Ashton attributed these counter-movements of grain prices and economic activity to the low elasticity of demand for corn. If the price of grain were high, its absolute indispensability forced the consumer to economize on industrial products in more elastic demand, such as textiles, buildings, household utensils, beer and so on. Conversely, when grain prices were low there was an increased demand for these goods, and therewith for labour and capital.

There is some evidence in favour of this correlation. Thus, in 1731, when arrears of rent from the Duke of Kingston's estates were piling up (see figure 43 above), an English diarist recorded that the spinning industry was busy. In the following year it was observed that the industrial workers were doing well. The year after that (1733) he noted that, while many farmers were being ruined by the low price of corn, local industry was flourishing and the spinners and other workers were earning good wages. But Ashton's evidence is not so unequivocal in regard to the next rise in cereal prices, which occurred in the early 1740s. Admittedly English exports reached a peak in 1743, but when these exports are analysed it is seen that far the greatest increase, from 45,000 quarters in 1741 to 370,000 quarters in 1743, was in wheat subsidized by the export bounty. The wool industry and the arsenals were, indeed, fully employed, but that was because of France's demand for military cloth and England's preparations for war. During these years public expenditure began to exceed public revenue by ever-growing amounts. It seems not unlikely, therefore, that public enterprise to some extent compensated for the decline of demand caused by falling cereal prices and loss of farming income.

Here we must leave this interrelation: it requires further proof, for which, as indicated at the beginning (p. 10), we must also consider the intensity of harvest fluctuations, the prevailing size of farm, and the level of farm prices, i.e. the long-term average of real agricultural prices. In this context we are concerned only with following the effects of harvest fluctuations on farming income, and that in a given time and place.

Stagnation in north-western, northern and eastern Europe

The Netherlands and Belgium

The north-western part of the continent, which since antiquity had been deeply involved in the world market, was one of the areas hardest hit by the general agrarian depression. England's export policy aggravated the situation still further. The farmers of Flanders and Brabant, once the pioneers of agricultural progress, had little to contribute to its further development during the hundred years between 1650 and the Peace of Aix-la-Chapelle (1748). In van Houtte's opinion (1920:403f.) that century brought 'retrogression rather than progress' to Belgium and the Netherlands (see also Slicher van Bath, 1960, where the chapter dealing with this period is entitled 'The Depression'). This applies particularly to agriculture, and more to the coastal regions than to the interior. The winning of land from the sea came to an end. The dykes were repeatedly broken by flood tides (1655, 1686, 1701–3, 1714–16, 1717). Repairs to the dykes and damaged fields cost the farmers more than they could afford to pay. To make matters worse cattle epidemics broke out, especially in the years 1714–15 and 1745–6. In some parts of Friesland the stock of cattle sank so low that there was enough hay left in the meadows, neglected though they were, to send to the town for sale. Further inland the signs of recession were not as common. The population increased, sometimes quite considerably. Intensive cultures, tobacco-growing in particular, were doing well, and the textile industry's demand for raw materials and labour indicated a certain degree of prosperity (Slicher van Bath, 1965).[11]

The above verdict on technical progress also needs some qualification. Van Houtte's description, 'retrogression rather than progress', applies more to the economics of cultivation per unit of area than to the manner of cultivation, that is to say technique and organization. It seems that innovations were not entirely lacking during the depression. Improved tools and crop rotations may have raised the yield, but not enough to overcome, for the average farmer at least, the handicap of the existing price/cost situation. Leasehold rents are a more dependable witness on that score. The series of west Flemish leasehold rents compiled by Verlinden (1959:229, 237f.) shows a steady decline, with only slight interruptions, continuing right into the 1740s. Figure 44 illustrates Verlinden's figures for leasehold rents in Koeklare (group 1) and Skipje, Saatland.

Denmark and the Scandinavian countries

Land reclamation from the sea had ceased in the Friesian region of Germany too. Arrears of rent from the farms mounted up in spite of repeated wage reductions (Swart, 1910:209). The situation was much the same on the west coasts of Schleswig-Holstein and Denmark. Records of rent and tax arrears begin to multiply as early as the 1640s. The war against Sweden (1657–60) brought additional burdens, but its effects must not be exaggerated. What is significant, however, is the length of time it took to recover from those effects. The low prices prevented the accumulation of reserve funds that would have helped the farmers to withstand crop failures, cattle disease and heavy taxation.

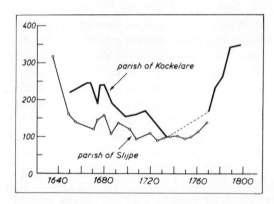

Fig. 44   Leasehold rents in west Flanders, 1635–1797.

Then the export trade in cattle from Denmark began to decline. Turnover stagnated and prices fell. The bulk of the Danish cattle sent abroad had to pass through the Rendsburg tolls. In the spring of 1612 as many as 165 herds, comprising 43,724 beasts in all, were driven through, but by spring 1659 the number of herds had fallen to 5, and toll was paid on only 634 animals. Admittedly that was a war year and thus exceptional, but figure 45 (below) shows that the pre-war peak level was not reattained. Reckoned in 10-year averages, the number of cattle passed annually through the Gottorf and Rendsburg tolls dropped from over 40,000 in the early seventeenth century to a mere 10,000 in the mid-eighteenth century (Wiese, in Lütge, Franz and Abel, 1966:XIV, 92ff.).

Signs of the long decline appear in contemporary notes such as the following, taken from ecclesiastical reports of 1690 (Hansen, 1964:67): 'Only half the arable has been sown', 'Many farms are empty', 'Many [peasants] have fled', 'deserted and impoverished farms'. An Englishman who visited Denmark in 1692 found that memories of the 'good old days' were still alive. He wrote: 'within Man's memory the Peasants lived very happily; there were scarce any Family of them that was not Owner of a large piece of plate or two, besides Silver Spoons, Gold Ringes and other odd knacks ... but now it is a great rarity to find in a Boor's House anything made of silver' (Molesworth, 1697, cited in Lohse, 1957).

In Sweden, Norway and Finland the symptoms of depression were less pronounced. That may have been because subsistence agriculture still played a larger part in the management of farms and estates there than in the neighbouring countries. In 1696–7 Finland was afflicted by a serious famine. The poor harvests of those years were felt in western and central Europe as well, but there they interrupted the downward course of agrarian prices for only a short time. In Finland the famine was seen as a symptom of over-population in an as yet underdeveloped land (Jutikkala, 1955:63).

East Germany and Poland

The grain export trade from east Germany and Poland petered out. Bad harvests in 1622–4 and the Swedish blockade of the mouth of the Vistula in 1627–30 were the first setbacks. The following decades brought a fluctuating decline. By the last decade of the eighteenth century the average volume of grain sent out from Danzig, by far the most important grain-exporting port on the Baltic coast, had sunk to below 20,000 tons (Hoszowski, 1960:117f.). Baltic grain and Danish oxen shared the same fate (see figure 45). The trade in both commodities (providing much the biggest turnover in the international agricultural trade of the time) reached its lowest level in the eighteenth century.[12]

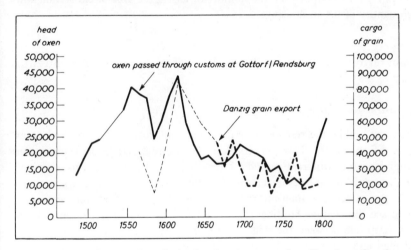

Fig. 45   Cattle exported from Jutland and grain export from Danzig, 1480–1800 (decennial averages).

Polish historians have investigated the economic development of their country at the time of central Europe's long-term agricultural depression. Topolski (1958:409 and 1962:28ff.) demonstrated that in 1685 on the landed and knightly estates (the so-called reserves, meaning properties not owned by peasants) grain production was only 65 per cent of what it had been in the mid-seventeenth century, and 60 per cent when compared with the years 1620–40. Hoszowski divided Polish agricultural history into two periods: the first a time of farming prosperity that lasted till the middle of the seventeenth century; the second, 'a long period of economic depression' that stretched into the mid-eighteenth century. The slump was attributed by Hoszowski to the long wars against the Cossacks (1648–76), the country's occupation by the Swedes and the 'negative features of the feudal agrarian system and the socio-political situation that prevailed in Poland'. The peasant worked under conditions of intensified serfdom that offered no incentive to higher productivity, while the townspeople, 'entirely subordinated to the selfish class interests of the gentry', lacked all opportunity of expanding trade or industry. On the contrary, both were drawn into a process that narrowed their lives down to agriculture alone. Topolski's views are similar. Whether the emphases are always correctly laid may be open to question, but the facts that these Polish scholars have assembled in their thorough and valuable works of documentation are undisputed. There we can also find evidence of the population movement that Hoszowski described as follows:

> Recent research has established that the population and labour force [of Poland] was reduced to a half or even a third.... It was not until the second half of the eighteenth century that conditions returned to the early seventeenth century level in regard to population, the number of farms, the area of cultivation and the quantity of urban housing.

German farming between the Thirty Years War and the mid-eighteenth century

The persistent post-war depression (1650–90)

In Germany, unlike the rest of western Europe and Poland, the hundred years between the end of the Thirty Years War and the mid-eighteenth century can be subdivided into different periods. Langethal has already made us aware of this in distinguishing the severe agricultural slump of the post-war years 1650–90 from the period between 1690 and 1740 when 'the first signs of recovery appeared' (1854–6: see the chapter headings). It is certainly difficult if not impossible to draw a sharp line between the stages of growth, which varied in time and place and shaded into one another, but there is no doubt that the situation in the first half of the eighteenth century had become very different from that of the post-war decades. Somewhere around the end of the seventeenth century, earlier here, later there, conditions were beginning to improve. To us, looking back, the brighter prospects may appear dim when compared with the later boom period, but they shone encouragingly against the dark background of German farming in the decades after the Thirty Years War.

The seventeenth-century depression was long and bitter. Wherever the war had passed, villages were burnt to the ground, livestock were destroyed and the fields were laid waste. When peace returned the prosperity of lord and peasant was gone, and for many years the strength to build it up again was paralysed. How unimportant it sounds that here and there farm buildings were repaired or a piece of waste land was ploughed up when one remembers that even in the 1690s at least a third of the land cultivated in north Germany before the Thirty Years War still lay untilled (Inama-Sternegg, 1864:38).

It has often been maintained that Inama-Sternegg painted the economic effects of the Thirty Years War too black. That may be true for some other parts of his picture, but his evaluation of Germany's lost acreage is not set too high. In 1700, according to Luben von Wulffens (quoted in Stenzel, 1841:175, 411), a third of the former arable land in the Brandenburg Marches was uncultivated. During a tour of Prussia in 1718 Kaiser Friedrich-Wilhelm I observed that 'countless fields, farms and villages are still deserted'. From the duchies of Schleswig-Holstein, too, the General Superintendent reported that in 1710 a third to a half of the formerly-cultivated fields remained unploughed (von Hedemann-Heespen, 1914:334).

In the German territories, as in other countries in the late seventeenth century, farming was trapped between the pressures of agricultural prices, wages and the cost of farm equipment and household goods. In Bavaria the churchmen lamented (1669)[13] that 'Because of the cheapness of the precious corn the poor peasant earns very little money. He has to labour hard to get enough to pay the annual taxes, the wages and such goods as he cannot do without.' In east Germany the peasant's post-war situation was further aggravated by the victory of hereditary bondage. It must be stressed, however, in the face of Georg Friedrich Knapp and the authors who adopted his ideas for Marxist reasons, that the growth of serfdom on the estates was only one of the roots of peasant distress (Knapp, 1887:67f.).[14] To no small extent the oppressed condition of the east German peasant, especially in the case of the bigger farmers burdened with cash payments, was due to the price level of agricultural produce. Langethal (1854–6:IV, 69f.), who unlike many other authors assigned these factors their due importance, considered that owing to the low price of agricultural produce the profits on a late seventeenth-century German farm when taxes, rent and services had been deducted were as a rule barely enough to support a family, even with great economy. There was certainly no net profit. For that reason the price of land was very low and 'dissuaded the capitalists from investing their money in farming. Farms whose rent included a good deal of personal service fetched no price at all. After the Thirty Years War a number of untenanted farms were let without money payment to anyone who would guarantee to maintain the services attached to the lease.'

The landlords as well as the peasants suffered from the unfavourable conditions of the post-war decades. Even in 1695 Caspar Schmid, the clerk to the Bavarian law courts, observed that there was hardly one among the richest families of Bavaria whose estates were not several thousand guilders in debt. During the same period it seems that the heavily-mortgaged estates of Further Pomerania often fell into the hands of the creditors – dealers and other townsfolk – through non-payment of interest (Malotki, 1932*a*:34). The peasants had to have their rents remitted, explained some deputies of the Knights of the Marches, or they would not stay on their farms. 'What income we do get from the peasants goes mostly on repairing the buildings and providing the necessary cattle.... It is not easy to keep ourselves or to bring our children up to knightly virtues and goodly arts' (quoted in von Ranke, 1930:319). 'The previous corn' was priced too low, the knights complained to their Prince Elector. That made life particularly difficult when iron, metalwork, glass, leather, tobacco and sugar, as well as lime and mill-stones, were so dear. Thus it was that many of their people could no longer make a livelihood, and with much lamentation, doubt and loss 'left their houses and land to take up a beggar's staff' (Deeds and official documents, 1880: see knights' votes of 23 March 1683 [p. 602f.] and 13 April 1683 [p. 610]).

Whereas in France, Belgium, the Netherlands, England, Denmark and Poland the severe agricultural depression of the late seventeenth century continued or even grew worse well into the first half of the eighteenth, there were parts of Germany where the post-war paralysis began to wear off. It was a result of contemporary price movements. As already stated on p. 159, and as figure 46 (from Abel, 1967:271) shows still more plainly, rye and cattle prices in the first

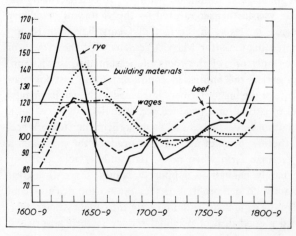

Fig. 46   Prices and wages in Germany 1600–9 to 1800–9.

half of the eighteenth century had been above their late seventeenth-century level. Wages and the price of building materials, on the other hand, swung downwards and remained at what was, in comparison with the earlier price-relation, a very low level. The rye prices shown in figure 46 represent inland markets (Munich, Augsburg, Würzburg, Speyer and Silesia), because in coastal towns the price of grain was more affected by the English price (see Riemann, 1953).

The beginnings of recovery

As farming prices rose and the ploughland began to produce a modest profit, care and enthusiasm were once more lavished on the neglected soil. Reclamation came into fashion again; heath and hunting grounds were made fit for cultivation, swamps were drained and the fields were tilled more intensively. When Friedrich Wilhelm I died in 1740 his realm presented a very different picture from that of forty years earlier. In 1753 Eckhart, an agronomist from Jena, wrote:

> People with a clear memory of fifty to sixty years ago will know what derelict areas have been brought back into cultivation and use. Neumark, Kurmark, Pomerania, Prussia, and especially Lithuania can show more than fifty estates that have been cleared within the last thirty years and so well managed that they often bring in rents of 20,000 to 30,000 thalers a year. Indeed, I know of districts, for example, the Lebus estate on the Oder, which in 1709 were worth hardly 12,000 thalers a year, but which now, divided into three and with thousands of their morgens reclaimed, bring in annual rents of 90,000 thalers. (quoted in Langethal, 1854–6:IV, 108)

The estates Eckhart had in mind were demesne lands in Brandenburg-Prussia. Nothing reflected the upward trend in east and north German farming more clearly than the rapid increase of yields from these estates, which in the time of the Electors had produced the scantiest of surpluses.

According to Stadelmann (1878:7f.) the meagreness of the revenue from the demesnes, which were very large even in the days of the Great Elector, was in no small part due to the poor yields so general at the time (see also Schmoller, 1886:341f. and Breysig, n.d.:1f.). At the end of the 1690s a new regulation concerning leaseholds resulted in considerable harvest surpluses, and in the early eighteenth century profit from the demesne properties rose still higher. Another reason, however, was that after 1701 these estates were divided into smaller units and let to the peasants as copyholds. In the first joy over their secure tenure and freedom from various irksome obligations, the new copyholders had agreed to pay higher rents. But, contrary to Luben von Wulffen's prophecy,[15] the price of grain went down. Numerous copyholders went bankrupt and had to be forcibly reminded of their financial obligations. Hardly had ten years gone by before it was evident that the policy, which had started with such high promise of profit for the state treasury, had failed. At the end of 1710 it was decided to re-introduce leasehold tenure.

Between 1710 and Friedrich Wilhelm's death the rent revenue of the Brandenburg and Prussian demesne lands increased considerably, partly because they had grown in value and partly because more favourable leasehold agreements could be drawn up. It is true that in the 1720s the Pomeranian Chamber of Deputies reported that the peasants were suffering from the 'swollen rents', which even the more capable farmers were unable to pay, and that in not a few cases distraint was in vain (Stadelmann, 1878:109; see also Naudé, 1901:11, 235). But, generally speaking, the peasants were not in actual want. Thus, behind the considerable rent increases of those years, for which Schmoller, in particular, has supplied statistical evidence (1886:343) there must have been an appreciable improvement in the economic conditions of the tenants on the estates.

Reverses and difficulties

How far the land-owning farmers benefited from the increasing agricultural yield is hard to say, for the peasant's situation was greatly influenced by the varied extent of the payments and services expected of him. In some parts the slowly rising price of agricultural produce resulted in increasing prosperity for the peasant. An agronomic writer of the period (von Rohr, 1722, quoted from Langethal, 1854–6:IV, 248) tells us that in the district of Strehla in Saxony there were 'rich barley-growers' who could dower their daughters with 'something like a thousand thalers'. Since the farms of that region usually passed down intact to the male descendants, this report must have meant that the farmer had enough spare cash to give that amount to his daughters as a marriage portion. To set against that, a contemporary witness described the peasant's situation in the Kurmark as follows:

> It is well known that the peasant lives from hand to mouth and considers himself lucky if he can manage to pay his manorial and public charges. He has no chance of saving up for the coming year. Let the slightest emergency arise, such as a poor or failed crop, the loss of one of his herd, a cattle disease, fire-damage or hail, and he has to seek for remission of his payments both to his landlord and the state. The state must do without his contribution and the landlord without his rent and services. (von Thiele, 1768:416, in Knapp, 1887:I, 72)

It may seem as if only extreme cases were being cited. To some extent that is true, but the graduation from want to prosperity was very unevenly distributed. Where the soil was good, the estate large and the dues small, peasants as comfortably situated as the rich Saxon farmers could be found in other parts of Germany, but they were exceptions to the rule. Marc Bloch's words about the French farmers of that time apply equally to the majority of German farmers: 'Whether the harvest were good or bad, they had cause for complaint, for when the crop was abundant prices sank so low that they could not pay their debts, while if it was meagre they could not afford bare necessities for their own households.'

Limiting ourselves to only one of the many harvest cycles of the seventeenth and eighteenth centuries, the following evidence gathered from various parts of Germany seems the most worth quoting. The cycle chosen starts soon after the end of the century with rich harvest and very low prices, includes the crop failures of 1709, and ends in the 1720s with a rapid price decline in England

and France, and a more leisurely one in Berlin (see figure 42 above). A summary of the situation follows, partly illustrated by examples from other countries.

In 1704 in England tenants could not pay their rents; leases for the rich lands outside the gates of Antwerp went down in price; in the Baltic ports and hinterland the grain export trade stagnated; while in East Prussia and Lithuania in 1706–7 farmers were feeding grain to their cattle, so abysmally low was the price (Grähmer, quoted in Naudé, 1901:II, 158). The autumn of 1708 brought losses and in the following year there was a harvest failure. Hunger and disease spread through Brandenburg-Prussia; many thousands died. The epidemic (possibly plague, possibly some other pestilence) penetrated as far as Pomerania. Schleswig-Holstein was spared, but the crops failed there too. In some villages of the Bordesholm district in Holstein the peasants were forced to buy bread grain and seed-corn at a high price. 'What are we supposed to pay our dues from,' they demanded angrily, 'when even in a good year we cannot afford all the payments and services owed?' A later calculation shows these payments and services amounted to 25 per cent of all the farm produce in an average year (Steinborn, 1973). Similar reports came from the farmers' deputies in Bavaria. The land was stripped bare, they said, not only by war and taxes, but also by harvest failures, crop disease and cattle pest. When, nevertheless, new taxes were imposed, we read once again (16 February 1713) that money would be difficult to collect. Poor crops and cattle disease had brought the peasants to misery. 'In the district of Vilshofen the people are staying their hunger with chopped straw. The few property owners are no longer in a position to pay for the most needy' (*Pragmatische Geschichte*, 1836:123ff.).

Those were the years of failed harvests. But in the autumn of 1713, when the corn crops were more profitable, the Bavarian provincial diet was once more driven to protest. The harvest, it reported, had turned out good enough for everyone to have ample bread to eat. But .the payments had risen sky-high, for besides the ordinary taxes there were 7 guilders to pay towards the new barracks building, 7 guilders towards the land reclamation fund and 1 guilder towards costs connected with the pestilence. The final outcome of all this was to drive the subjects and their children in distress from house and home. A glance at a short report from eastern Germany tells us that in the 1720s when the price of corn was at its lowest ebb, grain prices in the east of Brandenburg-Prussia had fallen to a point where it was not worth gathering the harvest, and the crops rotted in the fields. Estimates of the yields from farms of various sizes, laid before Friedrich Wilhelm I by the presidents of the Prussian Council during those years, all agreed that the revenue from peasant farms was not nearly enough even to pay rent and.taxes and provide for the minimum farm maintenance or the barest necessities of life (A. Skalweit, 1906:212; see also Naudé, 1901:II, 209f.).

Since the dues, taxes and services, even purely physical ones, were more than the peasants could manage, there was no chance of wealth accumulating in the middle strata of that feudal state. The price of landed property was still very low. Weyermann (1910:60f.) made a study of the price movements of knightly landed property in the Marches during the eighteenth and nineteenth centuries; von Arnim (1957:66) added a few more prices. Scanty though these records are, they do lead to the conclusion that while the really big price increases did not occur until the second half of the eighteenth century there were already signs of recovery in the first half of the eighteenth century when compared with the later-seventeenth-century prices. This contrasted with the contemporary fall in rents and the price of land to be observed in France and Belgium.

The following prices of landed estates come from the collections of Weyermann and von Arnim. In 1726 the knight's estate Wartenburg in the Brandenburg Marches fetched a price of 7,000 thalers; in 1750 the price had risen to 10,050 thalers. The price of the Brandenburg estate of Diedersdorff rose from 16,000 thalers in 1714 to 20,000 thalers in 1727; the knightly estate of Britz, which cost 36,000 thalers in 1719, was sold for 42,000 thalers in 1753. In Schleswig-Holstein the following sales occurred: the Elspeniss estate in 1672 for 3,200 thalers, and in 1721 for 5,000 thalers; and the Karlsburg estate for 36,400 thalers in 1671, 61,000 thalers in 1720 and 71,000 thalers in 1727. The Koselan estate was let from 1667 to 1699 for 1,900 thalers; this rent went up to 2,600 thalers in 1700–6, to 3,700 thalers in 1731–7, and then went down to 3,000 thalers in 1738–48.

The causes and main features of the agricultural depression

Economic theories of money and goods

D'Avenel (1894–1926:I, 29) sought to trace the price curve of this period back to monetary causes. He quotes a letter from Madame de Sévigné dated 18 December 1683, in which she says, '200,000 francs was always a good dowry, and it is true that the sum is now worth more than it was twenty years ago'. However, this testimony does not tell us much. Madame de Sévigné merely announces that during those twenty years the value of money had gone up, or that a number of prices she happened to have in mind had fallen. It may well be that other prices, less important to her, had remained static or even risen.

To explain the monetary causes of the movement of prices we must fall back on the production of precious metals and the probable circulation of money. It does now seem as if, in the period under consideration, bullion production had hardly increased at all, it may perhaps even have diminished (see Sombart, 1919:I, 2, p. 352). The Potosi mines became less productive in the second half of the eighteenth century and production fell in other mines as well. On the other hand, the yield from the Brazilian goldfields had been increasing since the beginning of the eighteenth century, although the rising gold production can hardly have made up for the decline of the silver mines as far as the bullion reserves and money circulation of western and central Europe were concerned. It seems likely, therefore, that the circulation of money in Europe did, in fact, decrease, thus putting pressure on the price level.

One could also point to the declining volume of international trade in foodstuffs (see figure 45). In the east-west corn and cattle trade the quantities transferred dwindled to one-quarter or under between the early seventeenth century and the mid-eighteenth century; the value of the goods sank even further. In this not-insignificant sector of inter-regional trade, at least, far less money changed hands than previously.

Once again, however, as during the depression of the late Middle Ages, the scatter of prices (and wages) cannot be explained by the financial aspect of the economy alone. Forces on the economy's commodity side must also have been at work, that is to say where the supply and demand of certain goods and groups of goods were concerned. Superabundant supplies from other countries could depress the market, and indeed Hungarian grain and cattle forced down the prices in Bohemia, Moravia, Austria, and Styria (Langethal, 1854–6:IV, 125f.). Saxony and Brandenburg banned the import of Polish grain, which was cheaper than their own (Naudé, 1901:11, 107, 206f.; also Langethal, 1854–6:IV, 68). In the west, as we have seen, the growing cattle export from Ireland put the English farmers in difficulties (Quesnay, 1756, in 1888:183; Child, 1694:45f. Rather than beginning with supply, we could begin with demand, affected as it is by population and incomes. We shall start with prices, however, as they will bring us nearest to the heart of the matter. They offer the best viewpoint from which to survey the changes in farm production and, in the author's opinion, they offer the best viewpoint from which to survey the deciding causes of the agricultural depression in the seventeenth and eighteenth centuries.

Price ratios and farm production

The relative prices of rye and cattle during the seventeenth century and the first half of the eighteenth century have already been discussed above (p. 182). The Vienna prices shown there in figure 38 were not an exceptional case. In all the German towns for which the prices of corn and livestock products are available, livestock prices lagged behind those of corn, as can be seen in table 20, which uses Riemann's figures (1953:136, 139, giving sources). The grain and meat prices come from six German towns and from Silesia, the wool prices from three towns and districts (Amsterdam among them). The somewhat primitve arithmetic used to obtain the averages on which the indices are based may give rise to doubts, but at least the table tallies with the main price movements, which is all that concerns us.

In other countries too there were similar price movements, as was seen with the Amsterdam wool index. No further figures will be quoted here, as exceptions were not rare, the most significant being on the fringes of the central and west European corn-growing areas, especially in Schleswig-Holstein. There, between

Table 20   Prices of farm products in Germany.

Period	Grain	Meat	Wool
1590–1640	100	100	100
1640–1690	56	89	101
1690–1740	70	99	102

1640 and the mid-eighteenth century the price of fat stock fell even more rapidly than that of rye (Wiese, 1966:104f.). The cattle export trade was now facing formidable competition. In many parts livestock farming was holding its ground or even increasing.

In England during the seventeenth century and the first three-quarters of the eighteenth, as Lord Ernle established, enclosure was at its most profitable where arable land had been converted to pasture. A great part of the Midlands grazing land was the result of such practical considerations and of no small profit to the landowners' and farmers' bank balances. Defoe observed as early as 1730 that a large proportion of the land that had once belonged to England's richest corn-growing region was now turned into pasture: 'Even most of the gentlemen are grasiers, and in some places the grasiers are so rich that they grow gentlemen' (Ernle, 1961:168; see also Jones, 1967:152ff. and bibliography). In parts of the Netherlands, too, the arable-cattle balance swung towards stock-breeding, as we learn from Slicher van Bath (1957:439). However, Slicher van Bath's information, especially about Twente, cannot be accepted as a generalization (see Faber, 1972: part 1, 206ff.). In the Netherlands, as in Germany, commercial horticulture was also proving quite profitable. Wine-growing had got over the setbacks of the sixteenth century and, last but not least, wool was selling well. Sheep farming, with its added advantage of manuring poor soil, was still a very flourishing concern.

Such were the shifts and transmutations in land use, referred to here only in passing (see further Slicher van Bath, 1963). They indicate changes in demand. Farm products in income-elastic demand, a category to which not only meat but most of the industrial raw materials belonged, fetched good prices; although corn was an indispensable commodity, its price depended less on available income than on the number of consumers, and hence it came under strong pressure. The agrarian depression of the seventeenth and eighteenth centuries, being above all one of corn-growing, turns our thoughts to the changing density of population.

The population curve

The changing density of population was particularly evident in Germany. The people living at that time had little doubt that the root of all their troubles – including the high wages – lay in the great loss of inhabitants due to the Thirty

Years War. Historians and political economists were of the same mind (see Hermann, 1832:127; Helferich, 1843:102; Langethal, 1854–6:IV, 66; Roscher, 1857:469). But in other countries, too, the rapid population growth evident in the sixteenth and early seventeenth centuries did not continue into the late seventeenth and early eighteenth centuries.

As early as the end of the seventeenth century Boisguillebert (1697:209f.) emphatically put forward the idea that the low price of cereals was not caused by the reduced money reserves but by the decline in consumption, which had decreased by half in the last forty years. In 1760, in an article entitled 'Hommes', known to us only from extracts (see Bauer, 1890:116f.), Quesnay wrote that a hundred years earlier France had had 24 million inhabitants. By 1700 the figure had dropped to 19.5 million, and at the time Quesnay was writing the population was no larger than 16 million. The administrator of Orléans reported in 1700 that 'the number of inhabitants and the production have decreased by a fifth in the last thirty years'. Another report said that 'the population has greatly declined in numbers' (Zolla, 1893:417f.).

Observations of this sort, surely true in principle, if perhaps exaggerated in degree, led to extensive discussion on urban and rural depopulation.[16] 'The real reason for the loss of inhabitants', Mirabeau the elder maintained (1756:39), 'is the decline of agriculture on the one hand and of luxury on the other.' The French peasant was under pressure from both taxes and slow turnover. 'It is no longer worth marrying and bringing children into the world; they will only grow up to be as miserable as their parents' replied the young men and women in the French villages when they were asked why they remained single and childless (d'Argenson, quoted by Taine, 1908:I, 375). The peasants migrated to the towns in the hope of getting better fed, but that only resulted in the situation deteriorating still further, for the urban birth-rate was, with few exceptions, falling steadily and, in some places, rapidly. This led numerous authors to inveigh, in every manner they could think of, against the luxury, selfishness, immorality and profligacy of the towns:

> It is in the towns, especially the capital cities, that morals are declining and people going to the dogs. With its insatiable appetite for men and women, the city affects the provinces in the manner of a colony. As Rome needed regularly to replenish her stock of slaves, so Paris, London and other great cities demand a steady influx of new blood. (Diderot, 1778:815f.)

It was Montesquieu (1784:247) who likened the population decline to 'an inner evil, a hidden and secret poison, a protracted illness', which had crept into the body of the French people. 'If the decline does not cease,' he said, 'the world will be a desert in a thousand years.'

Population was falling in other lands during the seventeenth century, as it was in France. It can be accepted that in parts of Belgium the number of inhabitants decreased in the second half of the seventeenth century and the first half of the eighteenth. In other parts of the country the population may have remained at its old level, or even increased slightly, but Mols estimated that in Belgium as a whole (within its present-day boundaries) the population between its peak period in the seventeenth century and 1714–15 fell from about 2 million to 1.75 million (Mols, 1959:491f.; see also Inama-Sternegg and Häpke, 1924:681).

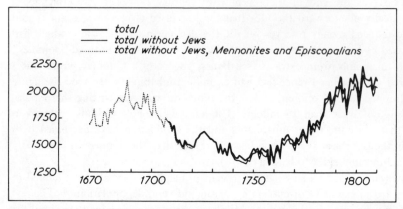

Fig. 47   Number of children baptized in Rotterdam 1670–1810 (after Mentink and van der Woude).

The decline in the number of children baptized in Rotterdam is astounding (see figure 47). These figures, a most welcome contribution to the history of population, are confirmed by information from the province of Holland that between 1650 and 1750 the population there dropped by 40–45 per cent, 'quite independently of force of arms or famine years' (van der Woude, 1972:613). It is impossible to generalize, however. In the Netherlands the movement varied from one province to another. In the east of the country the population was growing, while in the west it declined. Taking the average of all the provinces together, the population may have maintained its seventeenth-century level or even grown a little, but certainly not very much. Recent estimates based on a wide range of material state that the Netherlands population increased from 0.9 or 1 million inhabitants in 1500 to nearly double that number (1.85 to 1.9 million) by 1650. It was, however, still only about 1.95 million in 1750, after which it grew to 3 million in 1850 and 10 million in 1950 (Slicher van Bath, 1965:110).

In a mid-eighteenth-century paper worth serious attention it was asserted that the population of Sweden had been declining for several generations (see Mombert, 1931:488f.). At the same time Denmark was complaining of the shortage of manpower. 'We', wrote a Dane, 'whose huge population in the old days enabled us to conquer and occupy all Europe, can now barely defend our own frontiers. We, who swarmed into England, Switzerland, Germany, Italy and France and peopled all those countries, now find ourselves reduced to bringing in members of other nations to give our dwindling race new life and strength.' In Switzerland the parson Muret testified that in a group of seventeen villages in Waadtland from the late seventeenth century to halfway through the eighteenth, the number of births had declined absolutely (188:33f.). The Italian population had already stopped growing in about 1600, as Beloch has long made us aware. It has recently been established that in Poland between the mid-seventeenth and mid-eighteenth centuries the population declined by a third or even a half.

Quesnay had already recognized the relationship between population and agriculture. It was estimated, he said (1756, in 1888:171f.), in the case of France, that there existed about 50 million arpents of land suitable for tillage, of which more than a quarter were not used. The cultivated land produced 42 million setiers of grain, but the whole requirement of the 16 million inhabitants of France was only about 36 million setiers. What would they do with all the surplus corn, if the rest of the potentially-fertile waste were sown with cereals? 'It is hardly likely that such a great quantity could be sold abroad for an acceptable price.' In saying that Quesnay was unquestionably right. England was already choking the shrinking world market with her state-subsidized grain exports: there was no room for increased grain exports from France in the contemporary world.

But England, too, was hard pressed. There, too, the demand on the home market was smaller than the potential production of the farming industry. On the evidence of tax and parish registers King assessed England's 1688 population at 5.5 million inhabitants (quoted in Davenant, 1771:182). Since other estimates for the same period range from 5.2 to 5.8 million (see R. Faber, 1888:5), King's figures can be accepted as fairly accurate. According to well-based calculations the population of England and Wales in 1740 was not much over 6 million, very little more than fifty years earlier (see figure 51). A preliminary estimate included in the material collected by the Cambridge Group for the History of Population and Social Structure reveals that in a high percentage of English parishes the excess of births over deaths in the second half of the seventeenth century and the first decades of the eighteenth was far lower than before or afterwards, while in a sizeable minority of parishes the change was so conspicuous that the death-rate exceeded the birth-rate during all or most of the decades of that period. In a more-exactly-evaluated case this change can be illustrated by a graph, as in figure 48 (Wrigley, 1966:82f.). Wrigley did not see the causes of the shrinking birth-rate in Colyton to be connected with the economic situation (which he considered was more likely to have led to an increase in births) but to a process which he called family limitation. He could not find a rational explanation of the phenomenon. As we have seen with the late medieval decline in population, long-term movements of population pose riddles to which no solution has yet been found.[17]

Thus in England, too, the demand for grain stagnated, less dependent on income though it was. Export proved an inadequate outlet for the regular excess production released by that inherent tendency to expand, from which farming was no more exempt than any other industry. The meagre grain export –

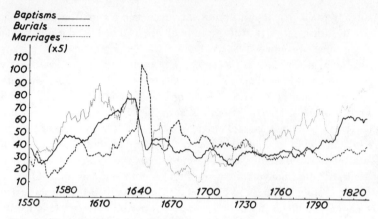

Fig. 48   Baptisms, burials and marriages in Colyton (9-year moving averages).

scarcely 100,000 tons during the years 1711–40 – was enough, however, to close the international market not only to the French but also to the Germans. From the lower Rhine Valley the Cleves Chamber of Deputies reported: 'Holland is so cheaply supplied by England that we can sell them little or nothing from here' (quoted in Heuser, 1916:11). Almost the only grain shipped down the Elbe during the 1730s was the corn supplied to the Hamburg markets (Naudé 1901:II, 255). During the 1720s the Pomeranian Chamber recorded that their overseas grain trade was practically at a standstill (Stadelmann, 1878:109). Danzig's export figures have already been given above (p. 179). The Königsberg merchants were lamenting that they could not remember a time when trade had been so stagnant; wheat and rye were so absurdly cheap in Holland that they could not get rid of their stock. From Reval not one scheffel of wheat was exported between 1700 and 1711 (Naudé, 1901:II, 164).

*

The stimulus to the new upward trend in German agriculture did not come from the international market but from within the country itself, that is to say from the increasing demand of a growing population. For in Germany, and especially in Brandenburg-Prussia, the population was getting larger, while in other countries it remained static, or even shrank. The people's natural recovery in number after the terrible losses of the Thirty Years War was aided by various population policy measures, especially in Brandenburg-Prussia. At the death of the Great Elector the population of the two provinces was estimated to be 1.1 to 1.66 millions. When Frederick the Great came to the throne there were at least 2.4 million inhabitants in his united kingdom, and at least 2.1 million within the 1688 boundaries of the old provinces. Between 1688 and 1740 Berlin, the capital, had grown from a city of 20,000 people to one of 90,000 (Behre, 1905:197f.).

Not without reason Naudé saw the capital's expanding population as the cause of the rising price of cereals on the Berlin market. It must be observed, however, that London's population was also increasing at that time, but English cereal prices were going down. For the greater part of Brandenburg-Prussia, Berlin's demands were of less importance than the increasing number and size of the small- and middle-sized towns scattered over the countryside, whose prosperity Friedrich Wilhelm I made his special concern.

The national grain trade policy turned this expanding domestic demand to good account. Saxony, to which cheap Bohemian corn could so easily be transported, had levied its first import duty in 1656. Brandenburg-Prussia followed suit in 1721 to keep the low-priced Polish cereals out. For a number of years Friedrich Wilhelm I adhered to this formerly well-thought-of policy, in spite of vigorous opposition from his ministers. To keep foreign competition at a distance and the home markets open for domestic production became the prime motive of Brandenburg-Prussia's agrarian policy. It explains how agriculture began to flourish in the German territories while in France, England and northern and western Europe the farming depression dragged on.

Part Three

The agrarian economy of western and central Europe from the mid-eighteenth to the mid-nineteenth centuries

7 The upward trend of agriculture during the second half of the eighteenth century

Prices and wages

The reciprocal relationship between agricultural returns and costs

After the 1730s or 1740s European grain prices, generally speaking, began to rise. This is evident in figure 49.[1] Between the 1730s and the first decade of the

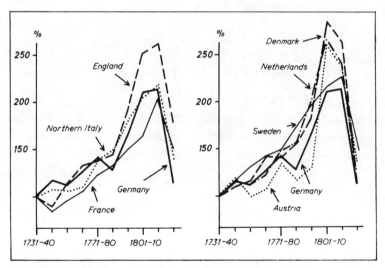

Fig. 49 European grain prices 1731–1810 (decennial averages).

nineteenth century the price of the chief bread grains, taken in 10-year averages, went up by about 250 per cent in England, 205 per cent in northern Italy, 210 per cent in Germany, 163 per cent in France, 283 per cent in Denmark (on somewhat doubtful data), 265 per cent in the Netherlands, 259 per cent in Austria and 215 per cent in Sweden. In Denmark, the Netherlands and Austria this was the highest point reached in the long-term ascent of prices. In other countries the increase continued into the next decade, bringing the increase from the 1730s in England to 262 per cent, in northern Italy to 217 per cent, in Germany to 212 per cent, in France to 202 per cent, and in Sweden to 218 per cent. Reckoned in silver content of the coinage, grain prices all over western and central Europe had doubled or more than doubled.

Figure 49 also shows that until the 1780s the price increase was quite moderate; only in the Netherlands and Denmark did it exceed 50 per cent of its original level (by 157 per cent in each case). After that date the upward movement of prices accelerated, obviously affected by the war. The war, however, was only one of the secondary causes of the secular price trend.

The graph depicts the European price movements in rough outline only, because it is divided into 10-year periods, which ignore that short-term price fluctuations, and because, wherever possible, indices based on large areas have been used. It does not exclude the possibility of regional and temporal variations such as those to which Verlinden (1959) has called attention. Until the 1780s Netherlands prices went up more slowly than Belgian prices because, as Verlinden argued, Belgium was more dependent on grain imports than the Netherlands. Also, prices rose faster at first in France than in the Netherlands, but after the turn of the century the Dutch prices seem to have overtaken the French.

If grain prices are assembled into long periods, their movement can be compared with those of manufactured goods and wages. Obviously the results can be influenced greatly by the selection of data. To avoid this, either very specialized and local data must be chosen or, as here, the widest possible range of information. Some of the conclusions that can be drawn regarding western and central Europe as a whole are, as figure 50 shows, hardly open to debate, so closely do the separate graphs agree.[2]

In all the countries of western and central Europe the price of grain went up more rapidly than wages and the prices of manufactured articles. There is no doubt that in England, and to a lesser degree in France, industrial goods were relatively the cheapest of the three items, whereas in Germany, Austria, Poland and Denmark it was wages. This was probably due to the varying levels of industrialization in the different countries. However that may be, the purchasing power of wages sank all over Europe.

From eastern Germany in the late eighteenth century Professor C. J. Kraus of Königsberg produced some disturbing evidence of the poverty of 'the most numerous of all a nation's classes, the class of the working man, of no matter what kind' (1808:164f.). Farmhands and servants were subject to strict rules; rural working conditions included forced labour and taxed wages. The people cast envious glances at England, where things seemed to go better for the workers. 'Nowhere', it was said in late eighteenth-century east Germany, 'does the working

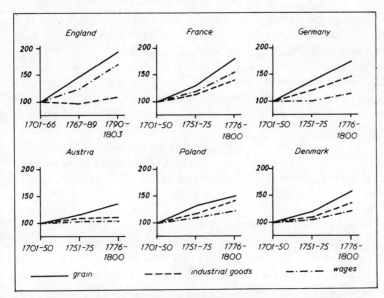

Fig. 50   Some European price and wage movements in the second half of the eighteenth century.

class live as well as in England' (Kraus, 1808:177). But English wages were often inadequate, too, as Steffen has shown (1901–5:11, 31f.; see also below, page 250). In the case of France, Hauser's notes, which have been used in the graph, bear witness to the gap between wages and the price of grain. Labrousse's information (1933:11, 599f.) ends in 1789. According to him the purchasing power of French money wages between 1726–41 and 1771–89 dropped by 25 per cent in comparison with the proverbial 'basketful of commodities'.

   In the graph for Germany urban wages only are included. From contemporary reports and farm account-books, however, one gathers that the cash wages of both serfs and free farm labourers lagged behind the increasing cost of grain. It is true that in 1816 Schwerz recorded from Westphalia that harvesters' day-wages had risen 'in the last fifteen to twenty years', and, in another case, in 'the last twenty-five years' (quoted in Neumann, 1911:87), but cereal prices had been climbing for much longer than that. At the end of the century Gülich (1830:11, 327) and Thaer (in Neumann, 1911:86) reported wage increases in Lower Saxony. On the other hand, at the farms of Goertz-Wrisberg (Goertz-Wrisberg, 1880:70–3, tables 137f.) and the Marienrode monastery in Hanover province (*Landwirt-schaftlich-historische Blätter*, 1907:IV, 99) day-wages for casual labour did not change at all during the eighteenth century; in fact, the wages of the regular Goertz farmhands were slightly reduced. Thaer, too, who in 1799 had spoken of 'large and disturbing' wage increases throughout Lower Saxony and especially in the region of Hanover, considerably qualified his statement a few years later (see Neumann, 1911:86f.).[3] In 1809 Thaer wrote that farmers everywhere had been grumbling about the higher wages for some time, but 'for the most part their complaints are quite unfounded and the rise in wages is merely nominal, not real, because while the value of money has diminished in relation to everything else, the price of all those commodities, especially corn, now stands in a more favourable proportion to the cost of labour than formerly' (see Neumann, 1911:106f.).

In north and east Germany, too, cash wages lagged behind the price of grain. According to G. Hanssen (1880:25f.) farm wages in Schleswig-Holstein were not raised even in the 1790s, when the cost of living soared. In Mecklenburg-Schwerin, Brandenburg, Saxony and Silesia the agricultural labourer's wages remained constant almost without exception until the end of the century (Neumann, 1911:84f.; Westphal, 1925a:86). Although on the demesnes of the Count von Stolberg the threshers' pay was increased, there were parts of Brandenburg where the cash wages of reapers were actually reduced (Neumann, 1911:84f.). In 1799 Kraus wrote of East Prussia that 'during the last fifteen years the price of corn has risen incomparably more than the average cost of labour' (C. J. Kraus, 1808:11, 177; 1, 164f.). Day-wages on a Bohemian demesne stayed at the same level till 1810 in spite of rises in the prices of the chief agricultural products (Neumann, 1911:64f.).

All this adds up to the conclusion that, with few exceptions, western and central European wages between 1740 and 1800 were left far behind by the rising price of cereals. Since the same was true of the prices of the more important industrial products, the ratio of agricultural income to agricultural costs was in favour of the farmer, and most of all, as will be seen, of the arable farmer.

Why prices rose

Even at the time the causes of the rising grain prices were debated endlessly. At first there were a number of Frenchmen who believed that the freedom to export granted by the government was responsible for the price inflation in their country. At the same time, some Englishmen were blaming the export restrictions then prevailing in England for the same effect (Tooke and Newmarch, 1858:1, 34). However, when it quickly became evident that prices were rising all over the continent in spite of widely-differing trade policies (see Young, 1812), the old argument reared its head once more. Some considered the fall in silver value to be the cause of the inflation; others thought it the consequence of a growing population. Both groups were able to produce impressive evidence to support their opinions.

Bullion production must have increased considerably during the second half of the eighteenth century. Although the Brazilian goldfields became exhausted at about the mid-century, the deficit was more than made good by the newly-opened silver mines of Mexico, which doubled their yield in the course of the eighteenth century (Sombart, 1919:1, 2, p. 533f.). Apart from this, the Spanish and Portuguese mines in South America, and the mines of Hungary, Russia, Saxony and central Germany produced important quantities of precious metal during this period. A good deal of the newly-won metal was used for coinage, so that, according to a calculation by Bucher (1805:9), the amount of money circulating in central and western Europe towards the end of the eighteenth century was increasing by about 1.5 per cent yearly. The volume of cash was also considerably supplemented by the paper money and bonds issued by various states – the period was, indeed, nicknamed 'the paper age' (Büsch, 1802). These circumstances could well have had an inflationary tendency.

Meanwhile the other side could point out with equal justice that during the sixty years between 1740 and 1800 changes had taken place in the food supplies of Europe's population that were bound to lead to higher prices. 'The true cause of this rise of price', Sir Edward West propounded, 'was the increasing population, and the increased cost of providing the additional produce for that increasing population' (in Tooke, 1858:1, 35). Indeed the population of western and central Europe grew rapidly during the second half of the eighteenth century. From the number of recorded births or baptisms, marriages and deaths Talbot Griffith reckoned the population of England and Wales in 1740 to be 6 million, though Brownlee put it at little more than 5 million. Both authors, however, agreed in estimating that in 1800 there were about 9 million inhabitants (see figure 51). Although the above calculations are open to some objections, they were generally approved by English historians. They show a very slow rate of increase for the first fifty years of the eighteenth century but after that there is a strong upward movement that continued into the nineteenth century. France's population in

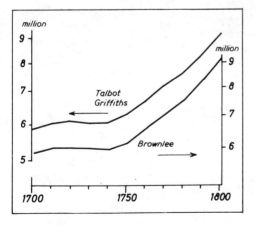

Fig. 51 The population of England and Wales, 1700–1800 (from Tucker, 1963: 207).

1740 was probably under 20 million; by 1811 it had grown to almost 30 million, half as big again (*Statistique de la France*, 1, ser. 3, 1837:10; also Levasseur, 1889:215). Hertzberg (quoted in Preuss, 1834:291) calculated that in 1740 the old provinces of the Prussian state contained about 2.2 million inhabitants; by 1786 there were already 4 million. According to Behre's rather more dependable tables (1905), the population of the Prussian states, including Prussian Lithuania, grew from 3.5 million in 1748 to 5.7 million in 1805, an increase of two-thirds or, if one takes the period 1740–1811, just double.

The coincidence of rapid population growth with the increase in cereal prices was so obvious that it clearly suggested a connection between the two. The idea that the inflation had been caused by the rising demand for foodstuffs was not current in England alone: shortly before the Revolution in France the same explanation had occurred to people in many different walks of life (Young, 1793:11, 270f.). From Russia von Schlözer (1807:17) reported: 'Here nearly everyone is complaining of the excessive rise in the cost of food. The politicians almost all blame it on the increased amount of bullion in circulation. I believe that circumstance by itself has very little to do with it. The growing population is a far more decisive cause of the high food prices.' The reason why the greater demand could only be met at an ever-increasing cost was a problem that Turgot and Anderson had tried to solve as early as 1777, without, however, arousing much contemporary attention. It was not till the peak period of the inflation that there appeared in England almost simultaneously the books and pamphlets of Torrens, West, Malthus and Ricardo, whose solution had become a matter of the keenest interest. Agriculture, they concluded, was subject to the 'law of diminishing returns from the land'. At a certain stage of its development, the yield from the land failed to keep up with the cost of production, whether the cultivation was on hitherto untilled ground or whether the object was to wring increased yield from already-exploited land by means of an added outlay of capital and labour. The rising purchasing power of farm produce was based on the growing cost of its production.

Counter-movements involving income

The price of foodstuffs during the second half of the eighteenth century increased not only in relation to goods that could be produced at a falling or constant cost but also in relation to wages, which led to anomalies in income that many writers of the time saw as grave social injustices. In 1805 Bucher, the German political economist, wrote,

> In our day the gap between rich and poor is becoming ever wider, and the impoverished classes feel it the more deeply when they can so plainly see the growing wealth of landowners and tenant farmers who, according to their different tastes, education, principles and habits, either save and hoard treasures

and capital, or spend it on excessively sumptuous food, drink, entertainment and clothes, costly furniture, carriages, gambling and so on. To what fearful explosions such disparity can lead we know, not only from ancient history but, by bitter experience, from very recent events. (1805:34)

Here Bucher was referring to the price riots that had broken out in Rostock in 1802 and been repeated in several German states during the following two years (see Weber, 1807:31). An anonymous journalist writing in the *Schleswig-Holsteinische Provinzialberichte* of 1797 (11, 64f.) declared, 'The working man's earnings do not keep pace with the cost of food ... the farmer, on the other hand, whose income depends on foodstuffs, never fails to make a profit.' One would almost think one was listening to Ricardo, who was to write a few years later in his *Principles of Political Economy*: 'The condition of the labourer will generally decline, and that of the landlord will always be improved.'

If the discrepancy between prices and incomes in the late eighteenth and early nineteenth centuries was so great that it could no longer be ignored by anyone with a seeing eye, it was but a short step to recognizing the inner connection between the two. Arthur Young had already pointed out in his *Travels to France* (1793:11, 270f.), speaking of pre-Revolutionary days, that 'the continuing distress of the poor working class' lay in 'her too great population'. Malthus and Ricardo brought the interdependence of population growth and the movement of prices, wages and rents into sharper focus, as follows: since the demand of an increasing population could be supplied only at the cost of rising prices for staple foodstuffs, the owner of favourably-situated and fertile land was able to exact a rent. The labourer's wage, on the contrary, could not keep up with the cost of living because it is determined by the productivity of the soil most recently exploited to supply the rising demand.[5]

As is clear from the above exposition, the much-quoted theories of Malthus and Ricardo were influenced by contemporary conditions. At the end of the eighteenth century numerous authors, often little-known even then, produced theories to account for the emerging disparity of price and wage movements. These theories differed from those of the classic English writers only in so far as the majority of the former theorists were concerned solely with the circumstances of the moment, whereas the latter, by postulating certain allegedly 'eternal truths', advanced from the particular circumstance to a general, unavoidable conclusion. How very arbitrary were their assumptions as to population growth and declining agricultural yield is clearly demonstrated in the above paragraphs. Nevertheless their theories of declining yield, rising purchasing power of farm produce and differential movements of wages and rents have historical interest because they were once very close to reality. The economic historian who renounces these theories entirely is cutting himself off from a rich vein of knowledge.

Expanding agriculture

The causes of the new upward trend

The relation between the price of farm produce and that of manufactured goods and wages, for which the general economic interpretation is that there was a growing imbalance between population and cultivatable area, provides from the viewpoint of farming economics an inducement to plough up more ground and spend more capital and labour on land already in cultivation. For as long as farming costs, consisting of capital outlay, amortization, interest payments and wages, lagged behind receipts it was expedient for the landowner or tenant farmer to raise expenditure till his last thaler or shilling brought no further profit. Those, in a nutshell, are the market-orientated forces which contributed to the remarkable expansion and intensification of agriculture in the second half of the eighteenth century.

But just as this agricultural expansion was accompanied by changes in farming systems and methods, so did the economic motives join with intellectual and political movements in their effect on late eighteenth-century farming in western and central Europe. The economic conditions did no more than determine the general direction. Individuals, contemporary trends and political measures gave the development its special stamp. Farming pioneers appeared in every land, treading new paths in the field of agriculture. These pioneers included Tull, Townshend, Bakewell, Young and Coke in England; von Eckhart, Leopoldt, Hagedorn and Schubart von Kleefeld in Germany; Patullo and Duhamel du Monceau in France. The Physiocrats and Cameralists advocated the abolition of the bonds that inhibited progress in farming systems. A great number of agricultural societies and economic associations were founded during those fifty years, and a flood of agricultural journals flowed through the various countries. Agriculture became the centre of interest among the educated classes so suddenly that even contemporary opinion was startled. Voltaire made fun of the French who, after visiting the Opéra Comique, turned the conversation to corn. 'In about 1750,' he wrote, 'the nation, satiated with verse, tragedies, comedies, novels, operas, romantic histories, and still more with romantic moralisings, romances and theological squabbles, began to discuss the question of corn' (quoted in Petzet, 1929:44; see also Walters, 1905:148). Looking back, a Schleswig-Holstein journal recalled that 'Farming had become the subject of conversation and amusement even in the highest circles' (*Schleswig-Holsteinische*, 1811:255). The strength of this 'agrarian movement' can be gauged by its effect on the courts of Europe. In Versailles, under the patronage of Madame de Pompadour, research on the preparation of seed-corn was undertaken; Marie Antoinette decked herself with potato flowers and milked and fed the cows at Trianon. Joseph II ploughed the fields in person; Friedrich of Bavaria appears in history as a Physiocrat, while George III was proud to be known as Farmer George. All the world, from princes down to the more enlightened farmers, took an active part in achieving agricultural improvements and reforms in systems of farming.

The interest in agrarian development felt by the wielders of political power expressed itself in comprehensive and positive agricultural policies. Whereas in the earlier part of the century the chief object of any political agrarian measures was usually the fiscal advantage of the ruler, now their aim was more often to advance agriculture itself. Just as in Brandenburg-Prussia, where Friedrich Wilhelm I had acted largely from motives connected with crown land policy, and Frederick the Great's later agrarian measures were the first to deal with the estates of the nobility and landed gentry and various farming matters (see A. Skalweit, 1910:6), so in other lands it was noticeable that the aim of agrarian policy was changing. That naturally influenced the direction taken by farming.

To describe these measures in detail would be outside our terms of reference. It must suffice to devote a few words to *agrarian reforms* because, of all governmental measures, they played the greatest part in the intensification and expansion of agricultural production.

The personal bond between the peasant and his manorial or territorial lord, entailing labour services and manorial levies, had held back, if not completely suppressed, technical progress for hundreds of years. The liberation of the peasants from the fetters of feudal law was as successful as the Physiocrats and Cameralists had prophesied: the peasants' interest in work increased and so did farming yields. This was especially obvious in France, where the Revolution abolished the seigneurial system with one blow. In 1819 Chaptal (quoted in Tessier, 1819:210) gave it as his opinion that

> the changes that have taken place in land ownership during the last thirty years, and the rise of a numerous class of smallholders, have contributed to the improvement of agriculture. The new owner works the land more carefully than the old farmers did. He cultivates all the ground that seems to him worth the ploughing and tills every plot capable of bearing a crop. He cannot rest till he has carried out every possible improvement. (See also Sée, 1927a:106; Bourgin, 1911:157f.)

Thus many things came together to bring about a new upsurge in European farming. But chief among the forces that produced this growing prosperity was the pressure of population and the price and wage movements that followed on its heels. This could be seen most clearly in England.

The expanding arable area

In England we learn about the farming activities of these years from statistics showing the extent of enclosure. In particular, much-used meadows and waste were turned into ploughland. From 1702 to 1714 a yearly average of only 110 acres was enclosed, and between 1724 and 1727 it was still no higher than 1,260 acres over the whole of England. During the next period, 1727–60, the figure gradually rose to 9,780 acres, while between 1760 and 1800 something like 70,000 acres were enclosed every year (Gulich, 1830:1, 109).[6]

These enclosures, which could not be carried out without the concurrence of the landlords, those entitled to tithes, and four-fifths of the commoners, show clearly how the price/cost ratio affected farming. Everyone agrees that the rising price of grain was the immediate cause of the enormous spread of enclosure.

It may well be that agriculture was expanding at a similar rate in the regions of the Maas, Scheldt and lower Rhine. In the opinion of van Houtte, who made a study of this movement in the area of modern Belgium, farming activity began to increase directly after the Treaty of Aix-la-Chapelle in 1748 (1920:420f.). A great deal of heathland in the poorer parts of the Campine and Ardennes districts, and extensive fens and moors in the richer countryside of Flanders, Brabant and Hennegan were ploughed up during the ensuing long period of peace. The Duc d'Aremberg, for instance, had more than 600 bonniers of bog and marshland drained in 1785–6; in 1809 the Abbe J. Thijs certified that during the last thirty-five years alone Tongerloo Abbey had converted at least 300 bonniers of waste into good agricultural land.

France shows us the same picture (see Wolters, 1905:196f.; Taine, 1908:1, 387; d'Avenel, 1894–1926:111, 80; Kulischer, 1965:11, 54f.; Toutain, 1961:37f.; also Bourde, 1967).[7] Even in 1677 and 1713 anyone who would cultivate fallow demesne land was granted tax relief and rights of possession, but so meagre was the response that it was possible for Quesnay to write in the mid-eighteenth century that out of all the cultivable areas of France half were entirely neglected and the other half inadequately exploited. A very different outcome awaited the proclamations of 1766–76, in which the government promised renewed and increased tax benefits for the cultivation of virgin land. Taine reports that as a result of the edict of 1766 about 400,000 morgens were reclaimed in twenty-eight provinces during the next three years. Companies with abundant capital were formed for converting wasteland to arable. In Bordeaux a company of this sort acquired 24,000 morgens, a great part of which they turned into ploughland. Going on the most reliable contemporary evidence, Toutain estimates that the arable area (*terres labourables*) of France increased from 19 million hectares in 1751–60 to 23.9 million in 1781–90.

And so a great expansion of arable farming took place all over Europe during this half-century. Sometimes on the farmer's own initiative, sometimes through governmental action, held back here by outdated farming systems, accelerated there by agricultural reform, great expanses of heathland were ploughed up, marshes drained, forest cleared and pasture converted to arable. In France it was said that a large section of society had been seized by a *fanatisme de l'agriculture*; *Ackergier* (greed for soil) and *Ackersucht* (ploughing mania) were new-coined words in the German literature.

In a 'Description of the recent improvements in Schleswig-Holstein agriculture' written in 1811 (in *Schleswig-Holsteinische*, 1811:233f.), we find the following passage:

> Wasteland has been ploughed; by means of ditches, sour, marshy fields have been rendered sweet so that rye can now be planted where nothing but sad-looking reeds once grew....We can well believe that in this duchy, from the beginning of this prosperous time until recently, the area of cultivated and useful farmland has increased by a fifth.

The arable area of Silesia grew by 15 per cent between 1721 and 1798 (M. Müller, 1897:86f.). In further Pomerania during the 1760s and 1770s, when the state offered easy credit for land improvement, some 480,000 morgens (which amounts to 10 per cent of all the farmland existing in the 1930s) was tilled for the first time (von Malotki, 1932b:117). And this does not include areas improved by farmers with money out of their own pockets: such independent land reclamation was also very extensive. The owner of the Stargord estate in the district of Regenwalde recorded that in the 1780s, by converting pasture to arable, planting clover fields, increasing his livestock and similar expansion and improvement of his farm, he had been able to raise his net profit from 700 thalers in 1770 to 3,000 thalers fourteen years later (von Malotki, 1932b:127). According to the Schleswig-Holstein journal quoted above, it was mainly the rising price of cereals that led to this continual expansion of the ploughland.

No small proportion of the new arable area was contributed by drainage schemes inaugurated and financed by the German princes. Thus, with the aid of state funds, the Danube bogs in Bavaria were drained and the Warta Bruch and Oder Bruch, among other regions, reclaimed. Although these and similar undertakings were doubtless partly inspired by political motives, most of them became highly profitable. Frederick the Great continually urged that profit must not be forgotten in any of his land-winning ventures. 'We next desire to hear what the enterprise will cost and how much it will bring in', was a remark Frederick II repeatedly wrote in the margins of the reclamation proposals put before him. Nevertheless, a return of 14 per cent on the invested capital, as assumed in the estimate prepared by the Stettin Chamber of Deputies for reclaiming 25,000 morgens of the Great Kamin Bruch in Pomerania, was probably exceptional (see von Malotki, 1932b:127; and for further information Abel, 1967:294ff.).

The intensification of agriculture

Important progress in farming systems was made at this time. Flanders took the lead in the later eighteenth century, as it had in the sixteenth century. European travellers in 1800 all agreed that Flemish agriculture was once more the most advanced in Europe.[8] Although signs of crop rotation had already appeared in this densely-populated area at the beginning of the modern era, it was only the first stage of a greater variation in crop sequences. By 1800, however, a visitor to Flanders might have found, for example, a twelve-course rotation including clover, flax, potatoes, hemp, rape and turnips. In England, the Norfolk system of convertible husbandry prevailed: turnips, barley, clover and wheat. In the rest of western and central Europe a crop rotation of the Flemish-English type was confined to a few areas especially suitable climatically or commercially, although several princes were in favour of its introduction.

In most of western and central Europe the old farming system evolved in other ways. In parts of France, central Germany, Austria and Denmark the old three-course rotation developed into the improved three-course rotation. Although the three-year system was retained, crops were planted on part of the fallow. Roots, peas, vetch, buckwheat, clover, lupin and sainfoin were grown as fallow crops more and more often during the last decade of the eighteenth century. From England and Switzerland potato-growing spread to France, Germany and Denmark. Once resistance to this vegetable, supposed at first to be poisonous, had been broken down by the famine of 1770–2, its cultivation spread so rapidly that in east Germany, for instance, both Lithuania and East Prussia were soon producing, in addition to their rye harvest of about 210,000 wispels (one wispel = approximately 24 bushels), a potato harvest weighing about 175,000 wispels (A. Skalweit, 1910:55).

In north-west Germany rape-growing was at a high peak. It seemed at one time as if rape, in alternation with corn, was close to supplanting pasture in this stronghold of convertible husbandry. It is significant that this region, once an importer of grain, now had a grain surplus. Unfortunately, reliable data on the subject are hard to come by, but it is evident that during the later eighteenth century regulated convertible husbandry spread out from the North Sea coast towards the north and east. By 1800 it was quite established on most of the manorial estates in Denmark, but the peasant-owned farms were to a great extent still at a transition stage between the new and the older systems. Mecklenburg and some of the areas bordering the Brandenburg-Prussia kingdom had also changed to a regular alternation between arable field and meadow, usually with the emphasis on cereal-growing.

Further east and on poorer soil the old three-course rotation was still predominant; in some remote regions even the three-course rotation had not yet been established. Benekendorf reported in the 1780s that 'many of the fields are in such poor condition in the summer that they cannot produce a summer crop, and so are left untilled and unsown' (quoted from A. Skalweit, 1910:37; see also Thaer, 1809:138, 1810:318; and Abel's summary, 1967:306ff.). Similar descriptions come from the less fertile regions of other lands, such as the central and southern provinces of France (see Sée, 1927:107; Zolla, 1893:200f.; Yvarts, 1807:32f.). All the efforts of enthusiastic agricultural improvers miscarried in the face of the peasants' resistance and the unfavourable conditions, natural, social and economic. It was not until the nineteenth century that a more intensive form of agriculture penetrated these fastnesses. The right conditions were not there in the early eighteenth century.

The new farming systems benefited stock-raising. In areas of convertible husbandry or improved three-course rotation the greatly-increased production of fodder crops made it possible to keep larger herds. Livestock inventories of the kingdom of Brandenburg-Prussia enable us to follow the development of stock-raising there (Behre, 1905:463f.).[9] The number of cattle in the western and central provinces of the kingdom rose by more than one and a half times (153 per cent) between 1756 and the end of the century; in the eastern provinces, where, unfortunately, directly comparable figures are lacking, the stock rose by 10 per cent in the short period of 1776 to 1800. Sheep, on the other hand, following the advance of intensive farming from north-west to east, migrated to the eastern provinces. Between 1756 and 1790 the number of sheep in East Prussia and Lithuania increased by 70 per cent. In contrast, the total sheep population of the provinces of Pomerania, Courland, Neumark, Magdeburg and Halberstedt sank by 4 per cent during the same period, and in Tecklenburg-Lingen, in the west, the number of sheep went down by as much as 18 per cent. Travellers who visited western Germany in 1800 noted that the extensive pastures, once the mainstay of local sheep farming, had disappeared (see Nemnich, 1809:68).

The increased numbers of livestock naturally produced a larger quantity of dung, which improved the soil. At the same time artificial manures increased in importance. The use of calcium sulphate, marl and lime became customary in many places. Progress was also made in land-drainage methods. From England, Denmark and north-western Germany we hear of improved drainage by ditch and canal. It is of no small importance that farm implements became more efficient. Here, too, England, the most industrially-advanced of European countries, rendered pioneer service. From the 1770s onwards the new English drill-ploughs and ridge-drills became renowned (Thaer, 1798a:485). In north-west Germany, too, contemporary reports testify to 'better farm tools of every kind' (*Schleswig-Holsteinische*, 1811:255), and the same was true of France. Deby, one of the best judges of French agriculture at the end of the century, published some years later (1825:236f.) a comprehensive list of the new or improved ploughs, harrows, carts and other farm equipment introduced into French agriculture at the time of the agrarian boom. Deby wrote his treatise in the 1820s, under the influence of one of the severest agricultural crises that European farming had every been through. He sought to explain the overabundance of farm produce, so plainly obvious at the time, and believed he had found its chief cause in the technical advances of agriculture. For, he reasoned, the progress in farming methods had made it possible to achieve a greater yield for the same cost as before.

But those are considerations induced by a slump. In the later eighteenth century the thought of over-production as a threat had not yet entered anyone's mind. The sale of agricultural products was no problem.

Trade routes

The great bulk of the surplus yield produced by the expanding arable areas and more intensive farming methods was, in most of the countries of western and central Europe, consumed by the native population. The population had grown, especially in the cities. At the end of the century London had 800,000 inhabitants, Paris over 400,000, Amsterdam and Vienna each over 200,000. Berlin's 1740 population of 90,000 had, by 1800, grown to 140,000. Moreover, four German towns (Breslau, Königsberg, Munich and Dresden) had passed the 50,000 mark, and some eighteen towns had between 20,000 and 50,000 inhabitants (Aix-la-Chapelle, Altona, Augsburg, Brunswick, Bremen, Danzig, Frankfurt am Main, Hamburg, Cologne, Leipzig, Lubeck, Magdeburg, Mainz, Münster, Nuremberg, Potsdam, Regensburg and Würzburg). There were also many smaller places that could not do without provisions and raw materials from the countryside, even when they carried on a certain amount of farming themselves within and without their walls.

However, a not insignificant proportion of the agricultural surplus found a sale on what was then the world market. In spite of increasing her production of grain, England found herself in the 1760s becoming a grain-importing country instead of a grain-exporting area. With 1 million quarters of wheat imported yearly, at the end of the century she was the foremost grain-importing nation. Between 1801 and 1805 about 50 per cent of these imports came from German and Prussian ports, 19 per cent from Ireland, 11 per cent each from the Netherlands and North America and 6 per cent from Russia. The insignificant remainder came from other countries.[10] Other import areas were, as of old, the densely-populated north-west of the continent and the Scandinavian lands, as well as some parts of the Mediterranean coast and the West Indies. From 1800 to 1805 the latter received a large part of the United States' annual export of wheat and wheat flour, averaging 314,000 quarters (according to the expert Jacobs before the Select Committee, see report, 18 June 1821:370).

The chief grain exporting areas were the German and Polish regions bordering the Baltic Sea, although the trade from Odessa and other Black Sea ports was growing in importance, and the United States and Canada were already shipping wheaten flour as far as England. The greatest grain exchange was, as ever, Amsterdam. The Amsterdam grain merchants of 1800 listed according to quality and point of origin no fewer than twenty-eight distinct kinds of wheat and twenty-four distinct kinds of rye. (Nemnich, 1809:111, 166f.).

In 1800 the Danish islands and the North Sea coastal regions were still the chief exporters of cattle and animal products, as they had been in 1600, but some changes in quantity and location had taken place during the seventeenth and eighteenth centuries. At the time of the severe depression in the late seventeenth and early eighteenth centuries the once-flourishing Danish cattle trade had gone steeply downhill: from 55,000–60,000 beasts in 1600–20 to only 20,000–30,000.

Certainly the Danish cattle trade recovered somewhat after the mid-eighteenth century, but even at the century's end it came to little over half the peak figures registered at the toll-houses in the early seventeenth century (Wiese, 1966:93).

The toll register at Tönning shows that it was now Schleswig-Holstein that plied the larger trade in cattle, whereas its cheese exports, which in 1600 had amounted to an annual 1–1.5 million kilograms, had now sunk to almost nothing (Volkmar, 1795: appendix).[11] The principle cheese-exporting area had moved westwards. At the end of the century Holland and Friesland were exporting huge quantities: from there more than 15 million kilograms of cheese would be sent abroad in a good year around 1800. Friesian butter was another very successful export. It was shipped in special kegs to America and India, although of course only in small quantities (Nemnich, 1809:111, 13f., 17). By far the largest part went

Table 21   Butter prices in Hamburg and London (annual price)

Period	Correlation
1736–1757	r = 0.458
1758–1779	r = 0.766
1780–1801	r = 0.866

to Hamburg, Bremen, the German interior and England. In 1800, a source from Aurich tells us, London was 'the biggest and best market for butter'. That the connection with the London market was a close one can be deduced from a correlation of butter prices in Hamburg and London, as shown in table 21. The extent of agreement in annual price (co-variation) nearly doubled between 1736–57 and 1780–1 (Bölts, 1966:246f.).[12]

The huge east-west cattle trade had declined even more sharply than that of north-west Europe. Oxen bred in Poland were still fattened on the grazing lands of the Oder, Warthe and Netze, but the great days of the east-west cattle droving were over, and those few oxen that reached Germany from Hungary, Poland and Russia were nothing to the enormous herds that had crossed the frontier two and a half centuries earlier. In 1800 Brandenburg, Prussia, Saxony and the larger part of west Germany were practically self-sufficient in meat. Some districts were even able to sell cattle abroad, as did the Hohenlohe Plain, from which in 1800 a considerable number of cattle were exported to France and as far as Paris. As late as 1865, when this cattle trade had also passed its peak, it was said in a description of the Öhringen district that 'In Paris to this day *boeuf d'Hohenlohe* is a synonym for good beef. Never a week passes but on two or three days strings of oxen are driven through Öhringen on their way to Frankfurt, Strasbourg and Paris' (quoted from Abel, 1967:316).

Agricultural rents and wages

Rents and the price of land

Considerable though agricultural and commercial progress was during the second half of the eighteenth century it was still not enough to supply the growing demand for foodstuffs at the old price level. From a general economic point of view, the supply and preparation of farm produce could be said to be affected by the diminishing growth-rate of yield. That did not prevent the great majority of agricultural estates in western and central Europe, with all their improvements, and with the price and wage situation as it was, from continuing to make rising profits. And, in fact, the net profit of farming often rose even more than the price of farm produce. Arthur Young, who appears to have been astonished at the exaggerated increase of English rents, hit on the right reason when he declared (1812:104):

> The implements have been rendered more effective, the expense of tillage reduced: shorter ways of arriving at the same end have been discovered; draining, irrigation, and manuring, have been extended and improved; in a word, new energies have been brought into activity, and a spirit unknown to preceding periods has animated the industry of the farmer: these have enabled the landlords of the kingdom to appropriate in rent 38 per cent more than would appear at first sight to be their proportion.

In England the agrarian slump continued into the 1740s, as we have seen in the preceding section. Young thought that during this period of stagnation there was never any question of increased rents. Grandfather, father and son followed one another under the same leasehold agreement without the subject of a rent increase ever arising. The landlord was more likely to be afraid of losing his tenant at the old rent than hopeful of obtaining a higher one. Young added that in some parts of England leasehold rents had risen 'considerably' during the Seven Years War, but that the upward trend did not set in generally till the war came to an end (1812:60, 104).

From the voluminous material published by the various House of Commons committees during the agricultural crisis at the end of the eighteenth and beginning of the nineteenth century one gets the impression that the upward movement of rents was very slight until the 1790s, after which it soared rapidly. The land agent, Wakefield, giving evidence before the Select Committee of 1821, said that he could quote hundreds of instances of rents being increased threefold between the 1790s and 1813. A few examples will serve to illustrate the degree of increase in rents (from Select Committee, 18 June 1821:207, 212, also Levy, 1902:7; Chambers and Mingay, 1970:106ff.). During a 33-year period from 1772–3 to 1805 the rent of some Northumberland estates went up as follows:

East Lilburn	from £360 to £1,600
Wooperton	from £240 to £1,200
Wilfield	from £250 to £900
TOTAL	from £850 to £3,700

thus about fourfold. The rent of Hollywell Farm in Essex, which had been let
for £90 before 1790, went up to £240 in that year and to £689 in 1811, a sevenfold increase in the space of eighty years.

In France, too, after a long period of stagnation, leasehold rents began to rise
again in the middle of the eighteenth century. According to d'Avenel (1894–

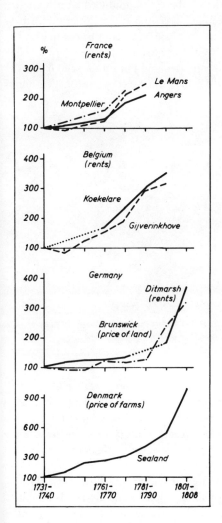

Fig. 52   Rents and prices of farmland in
western Europe, 1731–1808. Silver content
of coinage 1731–40 = 100.

1926:11, 508), in the second quarter of the eighteenth century the average leasehold rent of farmland per hectare for the whole of France came to 62 grams of silver; in the third quarter it rose to 81 grams of silver and during the last quarter-century it rose to 117 grams of silver. Since d'Avenel's periods overlap the turning-point of the rent movement and also need some supplementary information, we will turn to Zolla's date (1893:691f.). To avoid obscure and tedious tables, these will be shown in the form of a graph and compared with similar data from other countries (see figure 52).[13]

When the leasehold rents collected by Zolla are calculated from the average for three French farm-leasing estates, their increase between 1731–40 and 1771–80 amounts to 208 per cent. As the figure shows, the 1780s produced a further rise. Then there was a sudden change in direction. Lavergne averred (1877:38f.) that 'all contemporary documents agree that in 1795 and 1796 land prices fell by 50 per cent'. This drop in value was caused by the upheaval of the Revolution. The estates of the clergy and nobility were expropriated and put up for sale. A fourth to a fifth of all France's farmland changed hands during those years. The huge supply of land pushed down land prices and rent.

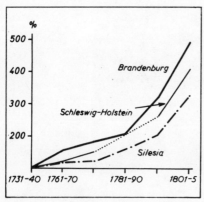

Fig. 53   German land prices.

From the few and incomplete data collected by van Houtte (1920:576f., 407f.) we gather that in neighbouring Belgium rents and the price of land continued to rise during the 1790s. Verlinden's figures, which have been used in the graph, confirm the assumption. The last of his eighteenth-century series of leasehold agreements (1794 at Gijverinkhove and 1797 at Koekelare) stipulate rents more than three times higher than those of 1731–40.

The rents and land prices recorded in Germany went up rather more slowly until the 1780s or 1790s, but after that gained impetus and by the beginning of the next century had also increased to about three times their level in the 1730s.

For Denmark we have only those farm prices supplied by Falbe-Hansen. In the same period of seventy-five years they increased tenfold![14]

Still richer material is available in the price statistics of German estates, which already have been assembled elsewhere (see Abel, 1967:330ff.). A few examples – the clearest and most typical instances of the rising prices – are presented in figure 53. Land prices which were obviously affected by important changes on the estate or special sale conditions have been omitted from the graphs.[15]

The prices of landed property in the three provinces of central and east Germany illustrated in figure 53 show the same tendency and the same change of tempo in their ascent as the Ditmarsch rents and Brunswick land prices shown in figure 52. Until the 1780s and 1790s the price of landed property rose slowly and steadily to two or two and a half times its average value in 1740–60. After that it gathered speed. Between 1781–90 and 1801–5 the price of Silesian estates doubled, while Brandenburg landed property went up two and a half times in value.

The farmer's income

Even today farming income is difficult to determine. It depends on the size of farm, its organization, type and location. Moreover, the figures conceal a considerable amount of income in kind derived from the farm itself. It was no different in 1800, except that during the last days of the *ancien régime* the matter was further complicated by the wide range of peasant dues and services still in existence. In Brandenburg-Prussia in 1800, Krug's Prussian statistics inform us, there were agricultural estates worth 20,000 thalers or more and some that – to their owners at least – were beyond price. This came about through the relatively high payments and services exacted from the peasants. Thus we read in a Brandenburg-Prussian edict of 14 September 1811 of a measure affecting copy-holders which presupposes 'the usual conditions, according to which it is accepted that the tenants' payment shall be to the limits of their capacity'. In 1809 the Pomeranian government reported to the Ministry of the Interior regarding the farming nobility of the country that

> if one estimates the revenue the landlords draw from their farms: payment in kind, cash rents and services, and, especially in the last instance, their cost to the peasant, and then compares it with the lot of their tenants, nothing is more certain, generally speaking, than that the landlords get the bulk of the farm production, while the tenant is a mere servant, living on a pittance. (in Knapp, 1887:75f.)

What makes farming income particularly difficult to estimate are the *services* that the majority of peasants in east Germany and the whole of eastern Europe were obliged to render. One Polish historian gets round this difficulty by not including services in his assessment at all, because, in his opinion, they affected the farmer's revenue only indirectly. He came to the remarkable conclusion that the free peasants were far more encumbered with payments than the serfs.

That verdict is not realistic. But, as Rosdolsky explained in his instructive treatise on the distribution of agricultural production in the feudal age (1951:247f.), it is also somewhat unsatisfactory to convert the compulsory labour into cash and subtract it from the gross or net farming yield for then the peasant's share can drop to nil, or even less than nil! As a relevant example Rosdolsky quotes an account concerning the Galician peasants submitted in 1820 by Philip Kraus, governor of Galicia (Poland). Kraus estimated the net agricultural production of Galicia at 9,369,101 guilders (presumably on the basis of the land register compiled under Joseph 11 between 1785–9). From this sum, according to Kraus, 5,806,226 guilders had to be subtracted for services, feudal dues and tithes for the landlords and a further 2,909,817 for highway tolls, taxes and other payments, making 8,716,043 guilders in all, so that only 653,058 guilders remained. About 3 million people, or 336,888 peasant families, had to share the last sum between them. Thus, even before deducting tithes and other payments to the church, compulsory transport labour and a few other items, a single household would receive 'a yearly income of 1 guilder 57 kreuzers'. If these figures are analysed regionally, it will be found that in the Tarnow district peasant dues and services came to 101 per cent in the Stryj district to 107 per cent and in the Sanok district to as much as 111 per cent of the farm's net output (gross yield minus seed-corn and fodder).

Rosdolsky suggested that the villein services should be included in the farm revenue, on the grounds that they were a 'main source of peasant income', since they paid for his land. But, quite apart from its doubtful basis, this argument serves only to bypass the awkward question of 'negative income'. Be that as it may, the peasant of Galicia – and other eastern regions – was indeed, as the Pomeranian government had declared in 1809, a 'mere servant living on a pittance'.

In sharp contrast to the above account of a peasant's lot east of the Elbe are the contemporary reports from those areas where free peasants farmed their own land. From the marshes of north-western Germany in the 1790s comes the following description:

> Rich harvests and high grain prices brought a new ease into the marsh-dweller's life at that time. The houses grew finer, the furniture grander, the carts handsomer, the clothes more fashionable, family life more elegant, speech more affected, the bosom higher, the hand softer and always full of silver thalers. That makes a gentleman out of one who was no more so than his father before him. But who are the first to turn round and call the country bumpkin 'Sir' now he is so changed? Why, the innkeeper, the artisan, the pedler of spices and stuffs, and anyone else who sees those silver thalers in his hand and hopes to get a share by flattering him with that title.

So wrote Pastor Harms, a cleric who lived in the same village of Ditmarsch from which a rent series has been given above (Rolfs, 1891:84f.). In an article written in 1789 and bearing the significant title *Holstein und Luxus* we read: 'Our beauties dress themselves up in diaphanous gauzes.... Tableware, once made of pewter or, if you were rich, of silver, must now needs be faience or porcelain, and though their cost is much the same, the metal can at least be melted down if it grows bent or dented, whereas the latter, once broken into pieces is not worth a farthing' (*Schleswig Holsteinische*, 1789:1, 218f.). It is reported from the Kronprinzen Polder near Büsum in Schleswig that a farmer who was entertaining a distinguished guest ordered two dozen mahogany chairs to be made at eight thalers apiece (*Schleswig Holsteinische*, 1796:1, 184). A visitor to the Haldeln district in the department of Stade declared that Brabant lace, spices, wine, brandy, sugar, tea, coffee etc. were consumed in great quantities by the country folk: 'Where luxury is concerned, Hadeln is approaching its highest peak. In fact, in my opinion, it has reached that peak and *ne plus ultra*' (Beckmann, 1788:126).

When Albrecht Thaer visited the north-west German marshlands in 1798 he heard people say that the inhabitants' luxurious living was 'a great misfortune, and would bring the marshes to ruin'. Thaer rejected this gloomy prognosis. He considered that the high net profit earned by the marshland farms justified the owners' extravagance (1788b:1, 433). But the expenditure ate into the profits and little was saved. Other farming areas presented the same picture. 'On the so-called gentleman-farmers' estates there are usually coach-houses, gardens, hunting for pleasure and so on, which is all utterly incompatible with true farming economy: what the latter builds up, the former all too often pull down': so ran an article published in 1804 (*Annalen der Niedersächsischen Landwirtschaft*: VI, 1, p. 280f.).

We can deduce from the above evidence that during the last years of the eighteenth century there were often too many expenses being taken out of the farm returns. The rising standard of living and the higher state taxes, as well as the increased business costs due to intensified farming methods, were founded on high agricultural boom conditions. Any deterioration of the economic situation was bound to lead to trouble. Moreover, at the end of the eighteenth century most of the cultivated land was heavily encumbered with speculative mortgages.

The traffic in real estate and mortgages

'Thirty or forty years ago', wrote G. Hanssen, the agricultural historian, in 1832 (p. 240), 'our whole nation got into a frenzy of buying and selling real estate in a way now reserved only for government stocks.' Hanssen was thinking of the situation in northern and eastern Germany, where speculation in landed property was at its worst, but speculative real estate business and over assessment of land value were not unknown in other lands.

It appeared at its most harmless in the widespread landhunger of France. Land was cheap there, because after the Revolution the estates of the Church and nobility were redistributed. For that reason the land bought by the peasants and towns-people was seldom encumbered with debt. Reports from the Netherlands and

Belgium give a very different impression. An eye-witness wrote that in 1780 for every saleable plot of land there were four or five would-be purchasers bidding against each other. Whenever a plot of land was put up for sale the peasants snapped it up and paid more than it was worth (van Houtte, 1920:405). In England, too, after the 1790s, the price of leasehold farmland was driven sky-high by eager bidders. Freehold farms, which had often been in the same family for generations, changed hands more quickly; quite often they became the objects of speculation. The English select committees that were appointed early in the new century to look into agricultural distress published testimony showing that, during the last phase of the agrarian boom, land and leasehold prices were no longer based on the long-term production values of past years, but on the hoped-for and greatly overestimated yields of the future. The report of the 1833 Select Committee on Agriculture described this state of affairs as 'speculation' (p. ixf.).

But nowhere did this traffic in real estate, aptly defined by Kraus, the political economist, as 'land purchase for resale' (1808:11, 41f.), have such unfortunate consequences as in the farming areas between Denmark and Schleswig-Holstein in the west and Silesia and East Prussia in the east. 'There are estates', wrote a contemporary in 1807, 'which have been in the same family for two or three hundred years ... but which, in the last ten to fifteen years, have changed hands three or four or even six times, and always at a higher price' (Weber, 1807:57f.). A good example is furnished by the noble's estate of Goddentow in the Lauenburg district of Pomerania, which had five different owners within four years, and whose purchase price went up, admittedly after considerable improvements to the property, from 24,000 reichsthalers to 70,000 reichsthalers. In the Grand Duchy of Mecklenburg-Schwerin only 49 feudal estates were sold in 1771–9, whereas in 1790–9 the number was 327. 'In Silesia they traded in landed property almost as if it were horses', noted the Breslau Councillor for War and Crown Lands, van Kloeber, as early as 1788. The East Prussians compared the commerce in real estate with the Dutch tulip fever that had once set the world on fire. During the 1790s Seetzen, a farmer from the Netze district, reported that 'the nobles' old estates are continually being bought and sold. They are treated as mere articles of trade, for many of the purchasers buy them not to keep but to sell again immediately for profit. Thus a property may pass through several hands within a single year. Every estate is for sale if the price is high enough' (Seetzen, 1801:1, 89).[16]

It is not to be supposed that the writer was exaggerating in order to expose an abuse. He was no opponent to this traffic, but its supporter, for in his opinion it did away with the old humdrum way of farming, aroused interest in agricultural matters and encouraged technical improvement. What he and most of his contemporaries overlooked was that the mobilization of land resources would harm not only the state and society but finally the farmer himself. For as land speculation increased, the proportion of debt in the purchase price grew larger, since the trade in real estate was financed only to a small extent by private means, far more by the taking up of credit. Credit flowed freely during those decades, especially in Brandenburg-Prussia, where the rural credit organizations formed after the Seven Years War allowed great estates to accumulate more debts than their actual production was worth. In the *Annalen der Niedersachsischen Landwirtschaft*: 1801, 111, 89) we read that 'families of modest means buy a number of large estates on pure speculation. For they buy, or perhaps own, a first property, have it valued, raise as much money on it as they can, buy a second estate, once more get a valuation and raise money on that, until they are in a position to buy a third.' That transactions of this kind had already become an accepted method of business is amply supported by Weyermann's history of land credit in Prussia (1910). In the spring of 1806 the knights' estates of Neumark, as Weyermann discovered from his researches, carried an average debt amounting to 72 per cent of the last purchase price and 106 per cent of the provincial assessed value.

These burdens were becoming increasingly hard to shoulder during the last years of the agricultural boom, yet speculation drove the price of land still higher. In 1800 the Schleswig-Holstein estates, for instance, were producing an interest of only 2 per cent of the last purchase price. It was about this time that a Jutland squire wrote to one of his compeers in Iceland:

What can be the cause of the – I can only call it audacity – with which people have lately bought properties for more than double what they are worth in the opinion of men who have managed them or are practical farmers? Does it not strike you as very risky, especially when most of the purchase money is borrowed? What prospects has a man who can do such a thing in spite of having all his senses?

Alas, we do not possess the Seeland squire's reply, but the author of an article published in the *Schleswig-Holsteinische Provinzialberichte* of 1811 seems to have hit on the right answer. For him the reason that the price of farmland was rising above the value of its yield lay in 'the speculation of greedy buyers who hoped for still higher prices in the future'.

These areas where landed property was so heavily weighed down with debt became focal points of potential crisis, ready to break out at the first whisper of economic disturbance. Even in the 1770s, when the price of corn suffered a slight setback, many farmers were unable to pay the interest on their loans. In the 1780s signs of a credit crisis were already perceptible, and by the end of the 1790s the annual reports of the kingdom of Prussia were issuing warnings against over-confidence in the agricultural boom, for, with the price of grain declining and the rate of interest rising, the tenants would not be able to pay their rents and real estate would topple from 'the summit of its artificial price'.

But up to that point the threats of trouble went unheeded. They were, indeed, a mere prelude to the great agricultural slump that was to ruin so many over-encumbered farmers after the turn of the century.

8 The agrarian depression of the early nineteenth century

The three phases of the crisis

The first phase (1801–5)

After an almost unbroken ascent lasting nearly fifty years the price of wheat in England and at the export ports of Germany reached its highest point in 1801. Then with the peace English wheat prices suddenly began to fall.[1] Protests at their abrupt descent arose from every county. A flood of petitions poured into parliament. The House of Commons immediately ordered an inquiry, which produced a report containing the following passage: 'The recent high corn prices led to an increase of farming activity; extensive areas of waste were brought into cultivation, and their production during the last two harvest years has caused so great a decline in the price of corn that agriculture is certain to fall into deep distress if not assisted by the state.' Parliament decided to increase the duty on imported wheat. The resolution remained on paper, however, because the increase was only to come into force if the market price sank to a certain minimum level. That minimum was never reached. Some poor harvests during the next few years, followed soon afterwards by the cutting-off of England's sources of supply (with the renewal of war), led to a recovery in the price of grain (see figure 54).

In France the price of cereals continued to rise until 1804, but the more abundant harvest in that autumn was enough to arouse complaints of trade stagnation and inadequate prices. The farmers maintained that farming costs were too high and that the low prices did not cover the costs. Moreover, taxes had almost doubled within the previous few years (Harouard, 1805:28f.).

Along the borders of the Baltic Sea the price of cereals followed the same downward curve as in England. The decline of prices in eastern Germany, however, was to some extent held back by the harvest failures that occurred in the interior of the country at that time. If a number of east German farmers, nevertheless, got into financial difficulties, it was due not so much to low prices as to the excessive debts raised on the estates during the years of prosperity. In Silesia, where agricultural credit had been easiest of all, there were a 'considerable number of bankruptcies' as early as 1801, in spite of the still-rising prices. These failures arose through property having been too heavily mortgaged (Weyermann, 1910). In Mecklenburg in 1804, according to the anonymous author of an article that appeared a few years later (anon., 1813, in *Neue Annalen*, 4 January 1813:3) there was already a danger of collapsing credit because, the high price of grain notwithstanding, it was becoming difficult to pay out of the farming returns the high interest on the heavily-indebted estates. In the duchy of Schleswig-Holstein the number of bankruptcies among the landed nobility rose from twelve in 1802 to twenty in 1804 (*Staatsbürgerlichen Magazin*:IV, 824f.).

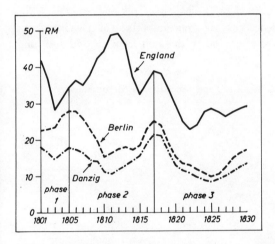

Fig. 54 Wheat prices in England and Danzig 1801–30.

There can be no doubt that the financial difficulties of the landowners were due to the cumulative burden of debt weighing on the estates. All over Germany at this time the price of grain remained high, farming returns were abundant, and the credit market was relatively fluid. Professor Kraus of Königsberg, one of the best economists of his day, wrote at the end of October 1805 that though the landed proprietors, deeply in debt as they were, might complain, there was still plenty of capital about, which would be lent willingly to certain farmers at very moderate rates of interest (1808:11, 33f.).

In the first official Berlin stock exchange list of 9 August 1805, in which mortgage deeds are given a good deal of space, we find the old 4 per cent mortgage deeds of Pomerania, Silesia and West and East Prussia quoted on the stock exchange at between 103 per cent and 107¼ per cent (Mauer, 1921:44). On a good security the landowner, so Kraus assures us, could get as many mortgages as he liked at 4.5 or 5 per cent.

West and south Germany were spared such troubles, as the quarterly reports that Thaer regularly contributed to the *Annalen der Niedersächsischen Landwirtschaft* bear witness. Most of the quarterly reviews he wrote at that time can be described in Thaer's own words as 'material that had to be whipped up into a foam before it would fill a few pages'. Very little occurred that was 'remarkable or would affect agriculture'. Only a few years later Thaer had more than enough material to fill his 'Annals'.

The second phase (1806–17)

The second phase of the early nineteenth-century agricultural depression began with the good harvests of 1806 and 1807. The fall in English grain prices was brought to a halt through the continental blockade ordered by Napoleon in his Berlin decree of 1806 and intensified by the Milan decree of December, 1807. England was forced to replace her German grain imports, which had made up half of all the cereals she got from abroad, with grain from Ireland and other countries (see table 22).[2]

Table 22   England's grain imports in 1801–5 and 1806–12 in 1,000 quarters

Land of origin	*1801–5*		*1806–12*	
	1,000 quarters	*% of total imports*	*1,000 quarters*	*% of total imports*
Prussia	489	50	77	15
Other parts of Germany	255		101	
Ireland	287	19	598	49
North America	158	11	111	9
Netherlands	156	11	150	12
Russia	83	6	47	4
Other lands	44	3	131	11
TOTAL	1,472	100	1,215	100

Because German grain could no longer be sent to England, the price of grain in the ports and hinterland of Germany began to fall. The German farmers' revenue diminished while their expenses, owing to the war and the heavier taxation it entailed, increased. The money-lenders were less sympathetic to farmers' requests for loans, assessing the financial risk to be greater in such uneasy times. Moreover, the border zones were directly affected by the war. Troops, fighting or passing through, devastated the countryside or imposed taxes on it. However, the more general economic evil was the falling price of grain, a point emphasized by Thaer in 1809, when he wrote, 'The abrupt decline in the price of corn, which has entirely upset the balance between the countryman's income and costs, is undoubtedly the gravest trouble that has befallen us for many years.... It is not impossible that these unfavourable circumstances will end in the downfall of agriculture, so newly come into its own.' The bankruptcy statistics of the duchies of Schleswig-Holstein indicate a gradual increase between the years 1806 and 1809, after which the numbers rose steeply. By 1812 the number of nobles' estates that had gone bankrupt was 113, five times more than in 1805. A year later, in 1813, the trade in landed property and mortgages was practically at a standstill. Such buyers as were to be found were offering up to 75 per cent less than the price the same land had fetched a few years earlier (*Staatsbürgerlichen Magazin*: IV, 1824f.; see further 'Chronik des Jahres', 1807, in *Staatsbürgerlichen Magazin*, 1823: 111, 395; *Schleswig-Holsteinische*, 1814:147).

In Mecklenburg, by January 1813, land had sunk to half its former value. Farming, lamented a contemporary, was 'a bread-losing occupation' (anon. 1813:1f.). From Silesia it was reported in January 1810:

> The farmer is in a grievous situation, and needs a deal of courage not to give up. Deprived of vital capital, burdened with debt, his farm, its natural and financial yield diminished by these unhappy conditions, cannot produce enough to cover its expenses. The lack of ready cash is serious, credit can be obtained only on exorbitant terms.... It is not always possible to maintain the concern properly, to say nothing of improving it. A sombre outlook for countrymen and patriots. (*Annalen der Landwirtschaft*, XI, 352)

In the leasehold-farming areas of Germany the sudden reversal of the agrarian boom was felt no less sharply. 'Only a short while ago', it was stated in an article published in 1808 (Schmalz, p. 452), 'the tenant farmer was regarded with envious eyes, and many wished to be in his shoes. But now – now he deserves the most heartfelt sympathy.... So many people rushed to buy a leasehold and get rich quick that there were not enough farms to go round. So of course they overbid wildly to join the fortunate few as soon as possible.' There were also many laymen, unfamiliar with farming finance, who took on leasehold farms. The experienced husbandmen carried on in the hope that cereal prices would not fall too low, but many of these, too, were soon 'forced to quit with lock, stock and barrel'.

In sharp contrast to the falling prices on the continent, the price of grain in England began to climb as soon as the blockade was imposed. In 1812 a hundred kilograms of wheat cost the equivalent of 56.30 RM. Reckoned in the silver content of the coinage, that is the highest price to be found in the English price tables dating from the thirteenth century. Admittedly the price conversion does not take the devaluation of the English currency fully into account. In 1812–16 the suspension of cash payments and the increased circulation of bank-notes in England had led to a 25 per cent depreciation in the English rate of exchange. As even during the blockade England was involved with foreign countries, the drop in her monetary standard may have contributed to the rise in prices that occurred during the same period. One thing is certain: the price of agricultural produce rose far above farm wages and other farming costs, though those too were climbing, so that once again the area and intensity of cultivation were growing and rents soared to dizzy heights. 'Nothing', an English author wrote a year later,

> was considered inaccessible to the plough; the tops and sides of hills, the unsound and rushy beds of morasses, the thin-skinned and flinty downs, the drifting sand and most tenacious and ungenial clay, were all alike subjected to its power. Capital was heaped upon the land, the most expensive draining was undertaken, the most costly manure purchased, the most prodigal expenditure of labour incurred, exorbitant rent was paid and purchases of land made at prices which would, if anything could, have caused our ancestors to start from their graves in astonishment. (Whitmore, 1822:23, in Levy, 1902:7f.)

*

The reopening of navigation and the abundant harvest of 1813 combined to bring down the house of cards. Between March and December 1813 the price of wheat fell by more than one-third. Panic broke out among the tenant farmers. On the strength of the prices of the preceding years they had agreed to rents which they could no longer afford. The better soil yielded less profit, while the recently-reclaimed sand dunes and marshes produced none at all. The pressure of the landed interest induced parliament to pass a new Corn Law in 1815. The importation of wheat was prohibited so long as the price of domestic wheat was below 80 shillings a quarter; for colonial grain imports the limit was 67 shillings a quarter.

However, before this law came into force continental agriculture had already seized the opportunity of supplying the English market. Since the reopening of navigation the Prussian seaports had enormously increased their export trade to England, as had many other ports, though to a lesser extent. The result was that while the price of corn was falling in England, it began to recover on the continent. From 1811 to 1815, that is to say, from the worst year of the blockade to the new regulation of English grain imports, the price of wheat in Hamburg climbed from 15.95 RM to 20.75 RM per 100 kilograms. In Rostock it rose from 14.40 to 19 RM, and in Danzig from 8.80 to 16.20 RM.

East German agriculture's future prospects were not rosy. The lowest price at which foreign grain might be sold to England was double its price at the continental seaports. It was feared that the export of wheat to England would come to a halt, and prices at the grain ports would collapse once more. But that did not happen. Harvest failures drove prices up. The harvests of 1815 were only fair, and in the following year harvests failed all over western and central Europe. In 1817 they were still only fair to middling.[3] Owing to the inelastic demand for grain, these crop failures led to a rise in price that more than compensated the large- and medium-sized landowners for the meagreness of their yield. Contemporary witnesses report that this was a time when wage- and salary-earners suffered but farmers made big profits. The correspondent to the *Conseil Royal d'Agriculture*, for instance (in Romeuf, 1902:24), declared that the period between the conclusion of peace and 1817 was a prosperous one for French farmers. The excessive prices obtained through the bad harvests enriched the growers, and this encouraged the landowners to put up rents. In England leasehold land was in high demand and pastures were once more converted to arable use. In eastern Prussia there was even a new wave of land speculation in which, now that the restrictions on land-owning had been lifted by the edict of October 1807, ordinary citizens were free to join and to bid for knights' estates.

Farmers everywhere took new heart. The English Corn Law of 1815 was extolled not only in England, as would be expected, but also on the continent. It was thought that the conditional ban on grain imports was keeping up the price. A report from Mecklenburg in 1818 illustrates the mood of the landowners at that time (*Möglinsche Annalen der Landwirtschaft*, 1818:11, 546): 'After so many dark years the last two seasons have been truly favourable for Mecklenburg. Everything is coming to life and looking more cheerful. The future is full of hope.... With the European population growing so fast that we cannot keep up with it, we should have no difficulty in selling our goods.' They were wrong. The potential threat of recession that had been gathering since the height of the late eighteenth-century boom was still there. For agriculture the darkest years were still to come.

The third phase (1818–30)

The harvests of 1819, 1820 and 1821 were incredibly bountiful. The autumn of 1820 saw the farms of Schleswig-Holstein 'encircled by piles of grain almost as tall as the pyramids of Egypt (*Schleswig-Holsteinische*, 1821:I, 1f.). As a result the price of corn fell abruptly, as figure 55 shows.[4]

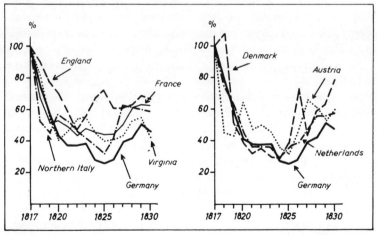

Fig. 55   The price of grain in western and central Europe and north America 1817–30.

The precipitous and persistent fall in grain prices took both farmers and agricultural experts completely by surprise. Albert Thaer, the pioneer of rational farming in Germany, had asserted in May 1807 (*Annalen der Landwirtschaft:*V, 680) that no one 'able to take a clear view of the situation can seriously believe that the price of a scheffel of rye over a number of years can ever fall as low as 22 groschen' (6.90 RM per 100 kilograms). The average price of rye in 1824 and 1825 was only 6 RM per 100 kilograms even in the big Berlin market, while in Thaer's more restricted home market of Hanover it was 5 RM per 100 kilograms. Taxes, rents, standards of living and intensity of cultivation had all been based on a much higher price level. The effect of the declining prices between 1818 and 1821 and the long slump that followed was devastating. In Germany they described the prices as 'enough to bring the growers to despair' (from the quarterly report of the *Möglinsche Annalen der Landwirtschaft*, June 1821). In Denmark, too, according to the Hamburg stock exchange list of 9 July 1824, the price of grain sank 'fearfully'. In England so many petitions from impoverished farmers were sent to parliament that once again a Select Committee was appointed to look into the depressed state of the nation's agriculture (see report, 18 June 1821). The French peasants were feeding their bread grain to the pigs because they could not sell it. The Hungarian correspondent to the Hamburg stock exchange list reported on 19 January 1824 that Hungary was 'suffocated by the blessings of Nature, which their very excess was making worthless'. Even in distant North America the farmers were becoming 'impoverished in the midst of plenty, for the sale of their produce did not bring in enough to buy the simplest necessities, such as farm tools and textiles' (Deby, 1825:202).

The tables in the appendix tell us that between 1817 and 1822 the price of wheat in England and France dropped by more than half, and in Denmark by almost three-quarters, while in northern Italy between 1817 and 1825 the price of wheat dropped by over two-thirds. In the German ports in 1825 bread grain cost 28 per cent, and inland only 23 per cent, of its average price in 1817. During the same period in Virginia, in the United States, the price of grain more than halved; the nadir there was reached in 1825 when it fell to 40 per cent of the old top price of 1817.

It may here be added that during the previous decades North America had also experienced a boom similar to the European one in its nature but far greater in its influence on the area of cultivation. The population increased about tenfold between the mid-eighteenth century and 1820. Agricultural production had risen even more, for since the peace of 1816 America's export trade had expanded rapidly. According to contemporary reports, speculation in land grew to unprecedented proportions. In Ohio and other states, from the beginning of the nineteenth century to 1818, the price of land leapt to ten times its former level. The effect of the twenty-year collapse of agrarian prices on farms so dependent on a large turnover was almost as disastrous as in Europe.

The Hamburg stock exchange list of 22 April 1862 contained a summary of world wheat prices, based on reports from British consuls abroad (see table 23).[5]

Table 23   World wheat prices in 1825
(The Hamburg Stock Exchange listed wheat prices in terms of reichmarks. One reichmark equalled 5.56 grams of silver.)

Localities	RM per 100 kg	Localities	RM per 100 kg
England	30.50	Leghorn	15.45
		Civitavecchia	10.70
Marseilles	22.80	Trieste	10.35
Bordeaux	17.60	Venice	10.10
Le Havre	17.00	Ancona	9.10
Charente	15.25	Fiume	8.60
French ports	18.20	*Italo–Austrian ports*	10.70
Washington	15.30	Danzig	9.40
Philadelphia	14.60	Emden	9.10
Norfolk	14.50	Königsberg	8.25
Rhode Island	13.85	Memel	8.20
New York	11.30	Hamburg	7.80
North American ports	13.85	*North German ports*	8.55
Antwerp	13.50	Libau	9.40
Amsterdam	10.75	Odessa	7.60
Rotterdam	10.15	*Russian ports*	8.50
Dutch ports	11.45		
		Copenhagen	7.50

The table shows that in 1825, at the deepest point of the agrarian depression, the price of grain differed greatly from country to country. In England wheat cost four times as much as in Copenhagen; a similar ratio exists between English prices and those in the Russian and north German ports. These differences had not a great deal to do with the cost of transport or commercial charges. At this time the combined transport costs, shipping charges and other expenses, not including the English customs duty, incurred in sending wheat from Danzig to London amounted to about 4.70 RM per 100 kg,[6] a mere fraction of the price difference between the two cities. England's grain trade policy was the deciding factor for English grain prices.

Since 1815 England had imposed a conditional ban on imported cereals. The limit above which wheat imports were admitted was reduced from 36.75 RM per 100 kg to 32 RM per 100 kilograms in 1822, but at the same time a sliding tariff was introduced that was almost prohibitive in the lower categories. The Corn Law of 1822 stipulated that the importation of wheat should be forbidden as long as the domestic price remained under 70 shillings a quarter. If the price were between 70 and 80 shillings the import duty would be 12 shillings, if the price were 80 to 85 shillings the duty would be 5 shillings, and if it stood at 85 shillings the duty would drop to 1 shilling. In 1828 the sliding scale was more finely graduated, but the tariff remained high, for example when the price was 51–52 shillings a quarter the duty was 35 shillings 8 pence.

In France and the Netherlands the price of wheat was affected by import duties, introduced by France in 1819 and by the Netherlands in 1824, to protect their domestic agriculture. That the price of North American wheat was far higher than that in the east European ports may have been due to the fact that the bulk of the North American wheat and wheaten flour exported went not to England but to the West Indies.

The strongest pressure on grain prices was endured in central and eastern Europe, for whom the sale of cereals to western Europe, and especially to England, was vital. In these lands, dependent on their grain exports, an import duty could be of no help in maintaining prices. Other government measures to that end were of little avail. In an address of March 1824 the provincial deputies of Nassau wrote resignedly that 'no power on earth can avert the very real damage that these almost worthless prices for farm produce bring with them'.

The Hamburg stock exchange list of 20 March 1824 said: 'The situation in Mecklenburg typifies the state of affairs in all the grain-exporting countries. Very little of her native farm produce is consumed in its country of origin. Therefore, the first condition for her prosperity is the free and unhampered sale of her produce on the international market.'

*

On the marshland farms of Schleswig-Holstein, where it had long been the custom to buy lean cattle in the spring, put them out to graze and sell them as fat cattle in the autumn, the price paid for lean Jutland oxen in the spring of 1821 was more than the farmers received the following autumn for their fattened beasts. It is said that one Eiderstedt farmer lost 50 reichsthalers on only two oxen (*Schleswig-Holsteinische*, 1822:IV, 126).[7] In the following year, 1822, the price of meat and animal products in this region was 'perhaps lower than for a hundred years'. The best beef could be bought from the slaughterer for $1\frac{1}{2}$ to 2 schillings (0.12–0.17 RM) per pound. In the smaller town markets the farmers got 2 schillings (0.17 RM) for a pound of butter (*Schleswig-Holsteinische*, 1823:I, 141).

Schleswig-Holstein, however, was a special case. Other regions, less exclusively adjusted to the export of cattle and animal products, were better able to maintain the price of those articles. As figure 56 shows,[8] the prices of wool, butter and meat declined less than cereal prices. In fact, at first the price of wool rose in England, Berlin and Mecklenburg. For Berlin, unfortunately, only the retail price of butter and meat could be discovered, which, since the cost of marketing and preparation are added to the breeder's price, makes it only partially comparable with the grain prices contained in the graph. This statistical blemish, however, hardly impairs the graph's general impression. The price ratio was not lost on

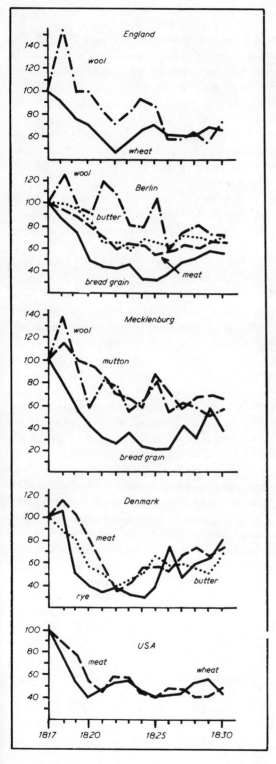

Fig. 56   Farm prices 1817–30.

contemporaries. Thus, during the worst part of the slump, Johann Heinrich von Thünen, the north German landed proprietor, recommended that grazing should be expanded at the cost of arable farming, since the price of animal products, especially wool, meat and butter, stood relatively high (1875a:11, 1, p. 22f.).

Witnesses giving evidence before the Select Committee on Agriculture appointed by the English parliament in 1833 declared that the price of cattle and animal products was closely related to the price of grain. When cereal prices were high the farmers turned meadows and grazing-land into arable fields. Conversely, when they were low, ploughland was converted to pasture. Thus, they considered, a certain balance was always maintained between the prices of grain and animal products (Select Committee report, 2 August 1833:68, 129). That was only partly true, and far from the real relationship. The witnesses underestimated the difficulty of changing a farm's whole organization, and completely overlooked the different income-elasticity of demand for the two kinds of farm product.

In the report of the Select Committee of 1833 (p. vii) we find the remark that amidst the general distress there was one comfort, namely that the farm labourer was now better off than he had ever been, because his wage now had more purchasing power. Similarly, the adviser to the French *Conseil Royal d'Agriculture* reported in 1825 (in Romeuf, 1902:24f.) that the depression was advantageous to the agricultural worker because the cost of living had sunk lower than wages. In the same year a farmer in Germany confirmed that cash wages had either remained stationary or fallen less than the price of corn (in Thaer's *Möglinsche Annalen der Landwirtschaft*, 1825:XVI, 411). On the other hand, the *Schleswig-Holsteinischen Provinzialblätter* (1824:I, 159) reported that a day-labourer's wage had sunk to less than half its former rate. Opinions are equally divided about East Prussia. Privy-Councillor Hoffman asserted in the *Möglische Annalen der Landwirtschaft* (1829:XXIII, 302) that 'relatively speaking, day-wages in East Prussia have not dropped anything like as much as the price of corn', whereas Neumann (1911:176) considers it evident, on the strength of contemporary testimony, that during the 1830s a free labourer's wage in East Prussia had fallen below the price of rye. The general impression remains that wages kept their level better than the price of cereals, because – and in so far as – non-agricultural work was available even in purely agricultural areas. Thus in Prussia, for instance, there were relatively-well-paid jobs to be had in road-building, among other things, and in England there were various opportunities for employment away from the farm. Jacob, giving evidence before the Select Committee of 1836 (1, 18), declared that even in non-industrial areas it was not difficult for a farm labourer to find other work at 'fair wages'.

There are similar reports on the price of farming requisites at this time. From England, Denmark, France and Germany we hear of farmers complaining that the prices of agricultural tools, stock and household necessities had not gone down along with the price of corn and cattle.

It is, alas, impossible to present complete series of prices of the chief agricultural necessities and farm wages. We can only show a few values for Greenwich Hospital in London concerning the wages of non-agricultural workers (carpenters, masons, etc.) and of some industrial goods (see figure 57).[9] The graph does, however, indicate the main direction of prices and wages. It is clear that during this agrarian slump, as in so many previous ones, the relation between costs and the price of the product was greatly to the farmer's disadvantage.

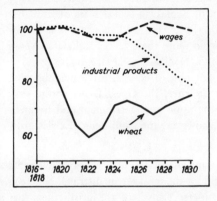

Fig. 57   Movement of prices and wages in England 1816–30 (trinomial annual moving averages).

The effects of the depression

How some north-west German farms fell victim to the slump while others survived it

We have now come to the time when our sources of information permit us to discuss the effects of depression in more detail. The size of the agricultural concern, its system of management, the taxes and costs, the living standards and enterprise of the peasant or owner, all varied greatly in different parts of Europe. The effects of the falling prices were equally various. To demonstrate these differences Stelzner, the Councillor for Economic Affairs, published an article in 1826 in which he compared the north-west German marsh country with the neighbouring district of Geest (p. 50f.).

In the fertile marshlands stretching from east Friesland to Schleswig the effects of the slump that followed the Napoleonic wars were as dire as any that occurred in other times and places. Gülich, who lived through that crisis, estimated that in some parts of east Friesland more than half the landed proprietors had gone bankrupt before the end of 1824 (1830:II, 403, note 1). In the *Schleswig-Holsteinische Provinzialberichte* (1823:I, 136) it was argued that the declining monetary value of farm produce while rents and wages remained high had produced 'impoverishment, despair, insolvency and confusion of every kind'. In a later issue we read that 'bankruptcy, arson and general despondency ... are steadily gaining ground'. The same journal reports that the accumulation of forced sales had depressed the price of land in the duchies of Schleswig and Holstein to a quarter and a third respectively of their value of twenty years before. A few years later it became hard to find a buyer to take on the ever-decreasing official payments attached to the land. The exchequer had to take over the numerous farms put up for compulsory auction. Where land prices are recorded at all they are incredibly cheap. In Maltharde, in the Rippen district, in 1829, a farm was practically given away for 112 Lübeck marks 8 schillings, although in 1802 it had fetched twenty times as much. In the Stapelholm region of Schleswig two demats of land that had been bought for 456 reichsthalers in 1807, were sold in 1834, when signs of recovery were becoming apparent, for no more than 34 reichsthalers (*Neuen Staatsbürgerlichen Magazin*, 1834:11, 390; G. Hanssen, 1884:11, 481).

The crisis of the marshland farming did not, of course, leave neighbouring Geest entirely unaffected. According to Stelzner, the Geest farms within easy reach of the trade routes often suffered the same impoverishment and frequent change of owner. As we advance inland, however, the symptoms of crisis grow weaker.

> The inhabitants of these miserable-looking places can at least pay their rents and taxes, which is more than can be said for the most fertile districts. Nineteen out of twenty bankrupts were marshlanders. Yes, there are jurisdictions that extend over both the marshes and Geest where a third of the marshland estates are insolvent, while in Geest all payment obligations have been fulfilled.

That was Stelzner's view, and he was in a position to know.

The question of how this contrast arose remains to be answered. Without going too deeply into the causes, we will mention (following in Stelzner's footsteps) that the more favourable soil, climate and proximity to trading centres had resulted in the investment of capital and labour being more concentrated in the marshlands than in Geest. More labour, stock and farm equipment were taken on, which produced a greater dependence on the structure of wages, rent and prices. It may be that during the agrarian boom some of the farms were run more intensively than was economically advisable. In any case, the costs were much heavier than on the small Geest Farms, which were worked by the farmer and his family and were thus much less affected by prices and wages.

During the boom days the marsh-dwellers' personal expenditure had become excessive. The instances of their growing love of luxury quoted in the previous chapter will be recalled. 'They say', wrote Albrecht Thaer in 1798 (1798b:1, 433) 'that many of them are addicted to luxurious living, not only eating and drinking well, but spending a great deal on furniture, silverware and other such things.' It will be remembered that Thaer defended the farmers against their critics on the grounds that their big profits justified their extravagance. But, in fact, they were taking too much out of their profits and getting into habits that were hard to break when their incomes began to dwindle. The Geest people, on the other hand, said Stelzner, remained faithful to the ways of their forefathers. The stuff for their clothes was produced from their own fields and their own beasts. Silk and cotton were used only for special trimming on the women's dresses. Their food, too, was all home-grown.

The higher the net profits became, the more debt accumulated on the farms. The increasing sale value of land together with frequent changes of ownership led to many residual mortgages and mortgages to be settled on inheritance, the interest on which was a heavy burden on the property. In Geest the big returns of the good years had been saved up as emergency funds, which made it possible to pay the rents and farm expenses when the bad years came.

Not economic conditions alone, but also the way of life and the farmers' spirit of enterprise, explain why the farms of the marshes and those of Geest were so differently affected by the depression. In 1800 the typical marshland farmer had been progressive and ready to respond to the stimulus of the agrarian boom, whereas his fellow in Geest had been a conservative peasant, living and working as his father had done before him.

A general survey of western and central Europe

A quick survey of western and central Europe at this time reveals poverty, grievances and despair everywhere, but also, occasionally, pockets of resistance like Geest, capable of surviving the direst drop in prices. In England we find the admittedly somewhat diminished class of yeomen owning their own farms. Except those whom the recent boom had lured into extravagant management of home or farm, they survived the critical years tolerably well. They economized, joined in the hard work and, their farms being unencumbered, were even able to make a profit for 'where a man has no rent to pay for stock or interest, he ought to be saving money' (Select Committee report, 1833:431, 467).

But this group of farmers was not large. In the same report (p. ixf.) we also read:

> In the counties of England where yeomen heretofore abounded ... a great change of Property has recently taken place. The high prices of the last war led to speculation in the purchase, improvement and inclosure of land; money was borrowed on the paternal estate for speculations of this nature. Prices have fallen, the debt still remains, or the estate has changed owners.

During the continental blockade English rents had gone up more than ever, but now rents were reduced, made payable in arrears or even remitted if only the tenant would stay on the farm. Thus the landlords had reason to complain, but tenants, too, often went down in the world. Some testimony given before the 1833 Select Committee illustrates this situation (report, p. 399f.). The tenant farmer who appeared as a witness had undertaken in 1815 to pay a rent of 30 shillings an acre. When the slump came the rent was reduced to 24 shillings. The tenant, however, found he was still losing money and finally gave up the farm. His successor, who agreed to pay 24 shillings an acre, lost all his fortune through the tenancy. Fifteen shillings an acre, the witness declared, was all the land would bear at that time, but the landlord refused to accept such a low rent.

During the boom period in England the old class of countrymen was joined by numerous new farming aspirants who with quite inadequate private capital had bought farms at high prices, a large proportion of which had been raised as a mortgage on the farm. It was reported to the Select Committee of 1833 that at the beginning of the century men with private capital of no more than £4,000 or £5,000 would buy landed estates costing £10,000 to £15,000 in the hope that the high interest on the borrowed remainder could be paid quite easily out of the farming returns. 'I know many', testified the witness Hancock. 'There are some that reckon upon their own estate, upon their land, and they have not calculated upon the decrease of the produce in the last four or five years; that has affected them very much' (report, 1833:431). The properties put up for sale fetched very low prices. Another witness spoke to the Select Committee of 1836 about a landed estate bought in 1811 for £42,000. The purchaser made improvements costing £30,000, and now the improved property was on the market for £37,000 (report, 4 March 1836:199). If the price of land was steadier in some parts of the country it was, as many experts have pointed out, because merchants and industrialists were buying landed property.

In Denmark the Copenhagen journal *Staatsfreund* reported in 1821 that 'the situation of the countryman, whether the greatest of landed proprietors or the humblest of peasants, has deteriorated so much since 1813 that he has lost both comfort and fortune: that, alas, requires no proof' (in *Staatsbürgerlichen Magazin*, 1821:1, 414f.).[10] Denmark had just passed through a serious monetary crisis. During the Napoleonic wars the national banknotes had fallen far below par. At first the farmers took advantage of the situation by paying off their old mortgages in devalued currency. But after 1814 the rate of exchange held its ground and new debts began to accumulate, partly because of the numerous agrarian improvements carried out and partly because of greatly increased private consumption, or so Nielsen considers (1933:386). When, in 1820, the third phase of the agrarian depression set in, the farmers' shrinking resources were faced with a rigorous campaign of deflation by the government and the national bank. Credit for agriculture dried up, the rate of interest increased and a wave of bankruptcies followed, pushing the price of real estate down to the bare value of the buildings and inventory, if as much. The Danish newspapers carried the following advertisement from the Hamburg stock exchange list of 3 January 1824:

A small farm, Lyngebeck in the district of Hirschholm, having an area of 230 tons [126.6 hectares], a garden of 6 tons [3.3 hectares] with 500–600 fruit trees, and almost new buildings, which last alone have been insured for 16,000 silver state bank thalers [38,000 RM], will be put up for auction on 5 January for the fifth time and, if no higher bid eventuates, will be sold off unconditionally for the last-bid sum of 4,000 reichsthalers.

If the thaler notes are valued at par the state bank thalers would have been worth about 9,000 RM. In fact the rate for thaler notes in that year was at least 10 per cent below par; thus the entire 126-hectare estate was sold for about one-fifth the amount the nearly-new buildings were insured for. This helps us to appreciate the words of an unknown writer in a Copenhagen newspaper (here quoted from the Hamburg stock exchange list of 3 May 1824):

> There are ladies' dresses worth twice as much as some farmers' whole estates. The price of a genuine shawl can now buy a whole property with fields, peat-bogs and appurtenances. So great is the plenty, so indescribable the super-abundance. We are almost like those native Americans, who had so much gold that, when the Europeans first came, they would give a pound of the precious metal for a knife or a little looking-glass. For corn, which is our gold, is now so low in price that a single orchestra stall often costs more than a ton of rye.... What will future generations say when they are told that in 1824 a real shawl and a place in the country were worth about the same amount?

But there was also in Denmark a group of farmers who did not get drawn into the vortex of the general collapse. As everywhere, they were the peasants who during good years had not borrowed money to enlarge their enterprises. Among these slump-resistant peasants Nielsen counted the smallholders and tenant farmers because, during the rising boom, their farms had offered no basis for 'progressive' management. Their bond to the soil and to their manorial lords, still partly of a patriarchal and feudal nature, prevented them from incurring debts during the boom period or losing hearth and home when the depression supervened.

If we turn our attention to Germany we find there, too, very varied conditions, that have called forth some widely different verdicts. While Ucke, who wrote an otherwise excellent treatise on Prussian agriculture, asserts that 'the peasants were but little affected by the slump' (1887:64), Neumann writes (1911:146) that 'the available evidence leaves no room to doubt that a large proportion of the ... farmers in the provinces of Prussia, Pomerania and Silesia were ruined'. By cession of land and the remission of their former payments and services, the peasants came into the free and exclusive possession of their farms, but now a new burden fell on them – rent. On the evidence presented Neumann would appear to be right when she states with confidence that a large proportion of these farms changed hands during the depression of the 1820s. Georg Friedrich Knapp, the best-known expert on agricultural conditions in East Prussia at that time, had already registered a similar view (1887:1, 236): 'Especially when the rent had been fixed, the tenant farmer during the years of low grain prices between 1819 and 1826 could not raise the money to pay that rent and so was ruined.'

Not only the rents but also the taxes often led to disaster. It was reported in 1822, for instance, that in the Lithuanian department of Gumbinne, out of the total number of 1,500–1,600 agricultural estates, about 1,000 had been publicly sold at unprecedently-low prices, because the owners had not been able to pay their taxes (Schmalz, 1827, quoted in Neumann, 1911:146).

Although the Prussian peasant's situation may not have been as favourable as Ucke pictured it, the reasons for East Prussia's crisis were different from those affecting the farmlands of north-west Germany. On the marshes by the North Sea the loss of house and land was brought on to some extent by the peasants' own behaviour during the preceding boom. The breakdown of Prussian farming, on the other hand, was outside the farmers' own jurisdiction. The needs of the east German peasant were simple; they were practically all supplied from the farm itself. Very little was bought on credit during the good years, so that when the depression set in the farms of East Prussia, West Prussia and Posen were almost free of private debt. That may have been due less to the peasants' own merit than to an edict issued by the Prussian government in 1811, which set a limit to loans on farm property of one-quarter of the farm's value. The effect of this edict, however, was undermined by the unsuccessful agrarian reform laws, which laid insupportable burdens on the peasants. For it is due to these and perhaps to high taxation that the depression in eastern Germany caused more distress than might have been expected on farms so free of debt.

In western Germany the depression varied from one region to the next. Neumann, who studied contemporary reports from Rhineland and Westphalia, found hardly a mention of bankruptcy among them. The farming families in those parts had been rooted on their land for generations. Here there had been no speculative changes of ownership leading to mortgages and debts. The effects were felt more severely in the smallholding areas of south-west Germany, where land-owning had been fluid for generations, and the property was usually broken up during the farmer's lifetime, or on inheritance. Georg Hanssen (1832:200) recalls how, on a journey through Bavaria and the Palatinate, he observed in one village that out of 300 smallholders, 100 had become insolvent within a short time and 100 more were in danger of the same fate. The fragmentation of the land had gone so far in these villages that 'the country folk had abandoned plough and team and taken to the spade again, like people thousands of years ago, before the plough was invented'. Capitalists bought up the derelict plots for ridiculous sums, and the former smallholder 'free of debt and worry, went back to being a casual labourer'. It is true that wages and costs amounted to little or nothing on these small farms, but even here the rents and payments had been adjusted to the former high price of corn, so that a fall in price inevitably led to forced sales. In Wurtemberg in the 1820s a morgen of the best arable land was to be had for 1½–2 thalers; in some areas plots were given away for nothing (see further Abel, 1967:341).

Complaints about the low prices and high running costs were equally insistent in France. At the opening session of the *Société Royale et Central de l'Agriculture* on 10 April 1825 the government representative said:

> There is none among you who does not know that for the last six years the farmers' fields have hardly paid for their upkeep, despair rules in the countryside and only with difficulty can the husbandman pay his taxes.... Like Tantalus surrounded by water, he is unable to profit from the wealth he has produced. He cannot sell his corn because the price is too low; he cannot store it because he must cover his expenses. (Romeuf, 1902:19)

All the same, the effects of the agrarian slump were less severe in France than in other lands.[11] The French peasants were not so often overburdened or in debt, for it was only a few decades since they had been relieved of the feudal payments and services. It was no doubt true, as Romeuf declared, that the slump of the 1820s in France was more generally critical for the *grande culture*, the big estate, which was more dependent on the wage-price structure.

The agricultural estates of eastern Germany

The *grande culture* had long been widespread in east Germany. The effects of the agrarian depression were certainly nowhere more dire than among the farming estates of East Prussia, Pomerania, Silesia and up to the borders of Mecklenburg and Schleswig-Holstein. Although the Prussian state lost millions in direct and indirect subsidies to the east German landowners in the various territories, as well as granting tax concessions and delayed payment, credit moratoria and reductions of interest rates, 80 per cent of the east German squires lost their estates during the depression, if the often-quoted but somewhat exaggerated report of the deputy, von Lavergne-Peguilhen, in 1851 is to be believed. It is a fact that in parts of east Germany the land market broke down completely owing to the over-supply of estates. In East Prussia, for example, the Perckuiken estate, six miles from Königsberg, was valued at 171,200 RM in 1805; during the 1820s it could not find a buyer at 33,000 RM. A valuation of 118,500 RM was put on the Bergenthal estate in 1798, but after 1825 it was for sale at 52,000 RM. During the boom Pomeranian landed property was bought for 50 per cent above its land valuation; in 1824 the price was two-thirds of the valuation. Between 1804–6 and the 1820s the price of knights' estates in the Brandenburg Marches sank to about half its former value. In Mecklenburg-Schwerin, from 1800–4 to 1825–9, the average price of feudal estates fell to 61 per cent, that of allodial estates to 67 per cent of their earlier value. In 1820–30, the larger properties in Schleswig-Holstein were worth less than half what they had cost in 1803–6 (Ucke, 1887; Westphal, 1925a; Weyermann, 1910; Marwitz, 1909:196f.; Oldekop, 1906–8; and Statistics office of Mecklenburg, 1858).

A number of different elements combined to produce this situation. Some of the great estates had been much weakened by the war. In particular the levying of excise duty on the land and the introduction of taxes on the para-industrial enterprises of landowners in Brandenburg-Prussia in 1810–20 hit some of the landed proprietors very hard. Moreover, the regulation of the manorial-peasant relation had brought with it a greatly-increased need for working capital to replace the now-suppressed services of the peasants and their teams and to supply the newly-apportioned farms with livestock and equipment. But the part played by these circumstances should not be exaggerated. If we look beyond the Brandenburg-Prussian borders towards the neighbouring territories, it becomes clear that there were other more important reasons for the breakdown of the farming estates of northern and eastern Europe. The dependence on the market that was a natural result of the farming system, together with the top-heavy debts incurred during the boom, were the landowners' undoing. Von der Marwitz reported in 1820 that all the bigger landed properties in the province of Brandenburg were, on the average, in debt up to half their value. This estimate may even be too low, for, according to Weyermann's information, as early as spring 1806 the average mortgage on the knights' estates of Neumark was higher than their assessed value and up to three-quarters of the last price paid for them. It was impossible, under the conditions of the 1820s, to pay the interest on such large debts out of the farming returns.

The end of the depression

The causes of the price decline

An agrarian depression has many aspects, according to one's point of view. By alternating between a chronological and a systematic presentation of the nineteenth-century agricultural slump we have tried to show a wide cross-section of the whole and at the same time to deal separately with points of special interest. The aim has been to draw in outline the varying effects that war, blockade, agricultural laws and taxation policies, excessive debt and the structure of farms, wages and prices had at different stages, in different regions and among different types of landowner and peasant. Having done at least approximate justice to the many-sidedness of the problem,[12] let us concentrate once more on its central feature, the movement of grain prices. The rising price of corn had started the agriculture of western and central Europe on the upward trend that had culminated in the excessive rents, land prices, taxation, living standards and running costs of the previous boom period. When the price of corn fell, rents dwindled to vanishing point and over-burdened farming concerns were brought to ruin. So we are left with the question of what could have caused grain prices in that part of Europe and beyond to fall to half or less their former value, and stay at that abysmal level for nearly a decade.

A contemporary writer (Müller, 1833:18f.) suggested that the fall in prices was caused by a shortage of precious metal from overseas. In 1810 there were riots in the American mining areas, and for the next few years the silver fleet stayed away from Europe. At the same time America began to siphon off European bullion in the form of loans. These difficulties reached their peak in 1825, the very year in which the price of cereals in Germany and other lands was at its lowest level. Although the above explanation, with some additions, found acceptance in the English literature and was even referred to in a report to the Ministry of Agriculture and Fisheries in 1925 compiled by the Committee on the Stabilization of Agricultural Prices, the alleged scarcity of bullion can hardly have accounted for prices declining as early as 1801 or for the later variations in price. It would seem more probable, therefore, that the determining cause of the collapse of farm prices lay on the commodity side of the price movement. Thus, once more, we come up against the question of whether the declining prices were due to the demand or the supply aspect of the market, whether, in other words, we are dealing with a crisis of under-consumption or of over-production.

This question, which forms an important part in any discussion of the agricultural depression between the two world wars, was already relevant to the slump that followed the Napoleonic wars. Neumann and Ciriacy-Wantrup, followers of the school of Schmöller, supported the theory of under-consumption. These writers maintained that it was the consumers' want of purchasing power that brought on the collapse of prices. But already, writing at a date earlier than either Neumann or Ciriacy-Wantrup, Thünen had questioned such an explanation on the grounds that the consumer (in Germany) had been perfectly well able to pay the average pre-1820 grain prices (1875a:11, 22; see also 1875b:224f., 233). Thünen's statement is borne out by the relatively high prices of animal products such as meat and butter during the depression. A further objection to the under-consumption theory is furnished by the fact that labourers' wages stayed high during the first years of the slump and only later followed the price of grain on its downward course. Wage series and contemporary evidence leave little room for doubt that the labourer's purchasing power rose rather than fell between the beginning and the nadir of the depression, which quite undermines the theory of under-consumption.

Thünen's view all along had been that the price decline was due to the over-production of cereals, a result of very abundant harvests from 1820 to 1824 and 'the expansion of agriculture in nearly all the countries of Europe, set in motion by the unnaturally high prices of the preceding era' (1875b:11, 2, p. 224f.). Extensive land reclamation and technical progress raised production to the point where the market for farm produce was more-or-less saturated. A few specially-rich harvests were enough to upset the balance between supply and demand, setting prices on a downward course from which there was no escape until a fresh impetus emerged to set them free.

The new impetus

Many writers and agronomists, recognizing over-production as the root of the agrarian troubles, recommended that cereal-growing should be cut down. Thünen was among those who declared that only by limiting production could German farming be saved. In France, Deby pointed out (1825:227) that while the markets were over-supplied with grain, the country still needed oil, silk, linen, timber and livestock. If the production of these goods were expanded, the demand and supply of more important commodities (cereals) would be restored to its proper level.

There was in fact a certain amount of crop control and change. In England the Select Committee of 1833 reported (p. iv) that fields which had been planted with wheat from time immemorial were now growing other crops. In France, according to a contemporary report (*Mémoires de l'Agriculture*, 1825:14f.), the planting of mulberry trees and the cultivation of potatoes, tobacco and oleaginous plants was on the increase. In northern Germany the grain-growing area was being pushed back by industrial crops such as rape, hemp and flax as well as by fodder plants, clover and potatoes. In an article printed in the Hamburg stock exchange list of 10 January 1826 a north German farmer declared that he used to sell 4,000 scheffels of corn on the international market, but that after the news of the English Corn Law came out in 1822 he decided to give up cornchandling altogether. Now, five years later, he was not selling a single scheffel of grain. He had switched over completely, though not without considerable expense, to horse-breeding and sheep farming, sold his products at a fair price, and was 'doing increasingly well financially'. Even in the worst years of the depression Thünen thought that 'we [the German farmers], with few exceptions, carry on our business as usual' (1875a:111, 236).

The forces that gave new impetus to prices came less from the production side than from the side of demand. The population of western and central Europe was growing fast. Consequently the demand for the staple products of the soil rose from year to year. By the end of the 1820s supply and demand were so nearly balanced that words spoken twelve years too soon at last became a reality: 'With Europe's population expanding so fast that agriculture cannot keep up with it, we shall have no worries about selling our produce' (see above, p. 225).

On the continent the fresh impetus was the better able to work in that, during the slump, wages, running costs and official and legal payments had declined, the price of land had fallen and debt had been brought down to a supportable level. The countless bankruptcies, however sad for the victims, had one advantage: the new landowners were comparatively free of interest and amortization payments. The same was true of England, but here the upward trend met with obstacles originating in the grain trade policy of the preceding years.

Obstacles blocking England's road to recovery

The English Corn Laws of 1822 and 1828 had neutralized price ratios between England and the continental markets. The English tariffs were graduated in accordance with home prices, so that when the price of domestic corn was high the import duty was low, and vice versa. But even the low duty levied when the price was high seemed all too heavy in continental eyes. For instance, after 1828, when the price of wheat was 51–52 shillings a quarter the customs duty came to 35 shillings 8 pence a quarter. The result was that between 1821 and 1830 wheat cost two to three times as much in England as it did in eastern Europe.

In 1830 two ways stood open for England's grain trade policy. By a gradual lowering of the tariff wall an attempt could be made to force the price of English corn down to continental levels. Such a policy, however, would upset England's agrarian economy for a long time. The other possibility was to stabilize English grain prices at an increased level by retaining the tariff wall. The high cost of food was rendering the price of English manufactured goods uncompetitive in the international market. As is well known, after a protracted struggle the Free Trade party won the day. The farmer had to bear the consequences. Before discussing that, however, the consumer must be brought into the picture.

9 Mass poverty

Wages and the standard of living in western and central Europe, 1790–1850

Distress in Germany

In 1845 Friedrich Engels published his *Condition of the Working Class in England*. The book aroused enormous interest that reached out far beyond its own time. Inasmuch as Engels did not limit himself to portraying the distressed situation of the English labourer on the strength of numerous individual or group examples, as many had done before him, but tried to interpret it in the light of prevailing circumstances and conditions, he arrived at a position from which he could attack the whole capitalist industrial system. This he did with lasting effect. Not in Marxist writing alone but to a great extent in the non-Marxist literature Engels' thesis went unchallenged.

However, soon after the appearance of Engels' book, Bruno Hildebrand, cofounder of the so-called older historic school of political economy, opposed Engels' theories (1922). To show that industry was not to blame for the labourers' poverty, he brought to his readers' attention the example of the palatinate province of Upper Hesse. 'In its industrial situation', he wrote,

> this province still belongs entirely to the last century. There we can see with our own eyes the economic conditions of the past. . . . What we usually consider as the causes of pauperism and the proletariat are nowhere to be found: no factories or factory workers, no steam engines or other machines, no free competition between individuals or liberty to practise a trade. Here, in the old patriarchal style, there is nothing but farming and the old handicrafts.

And how did matters stand during the year 1840 in this relic of the past? In the eleven square miles composing the district of Marburg with its two towns, eighty-eight farming communities and roughly forty thousand inhabitants, there were only four industries in which the number of journeymen exceeded the number of taxable masters. Many masters of trades worked without any assistance. According to Hildebrand, they were no more than a superior kind of day-labourer. While the ordinary day-labourer with his wife earned an average wage of 60–70 state thalers on the land, or 90 in the town, a master cobbler or tailor made about 100 state thalers. Out of this craftsman's wage, Hildebrand continued, he would have to spend an average of 12 thalers for his dwelling, 10 for wood, fuel and light and 13 for clothing, washing and other necessities, so that only $5\frac{1}{3}$ silver groschen were left for the family's daily food: thus at best, if there were no children to feed, 2 silver groschen and 8 pfennigs for each person. For that sum one could buy, according to the official prices set by the Upper Hesse police, 1.7 kilograms of plain rye bread or 0.4 kilograms of meat (beef, pork or mutton). Since the bread would contain 3,800 calories and the meat only 1,500, a meat meal must have been a rare luxury.

That was in normal years. In years of high prices, like the winter of 1846–7, we are further informed, 'the distress reached a level to be compared only with descriptions of the Irish famine'. During that winter, when the temperature was −10°C, two babies were born in the open streets of Marburg. In Hünfeld the authorities organized the beggars into processions that daily followed a fixed route through certain parts of the town and neighbouring countryside to beg for alms. Almost a third of the inhabitants were entirely without resources.

So much for Hildebrand. In direct contradiction to Engels' theory, he attributed working-class poverty to the lack of industries.

*

The facts Hildebrand presented are confirmed by documentary evidence from many sources: pamphlets, monographs, straightforward reports and more pretentious literary descriptions, statements from officials, experts, authors and poets. This multitude of writings, each composed with a different end in view, were yet united in their assement of the situation. All this evidence (not yet systematically studied, alas) on the 'pauperism' prevailing at the beginning of the century and into the 1840s brings home to us the measure of working-class distress.

The comprehensive studies by Mombert (1921:169f.) and Kuczynski (1960–3: vols 8, 10, 11, 18) contain extracts from the literature and bibliographies, but unfortunately only those concerning the situation of the labourer. Even a hasty perusal of the literature shows us that the poverty extended much further both as regards region and type of worker. Riehl (1850:211) spoke of the 'white-collar proletariat', among which he counted 'the proletariat of officialdom, schoolmasters, perennial Saxon candidates for Holy Orders, starving university lecturers, writers, journalists and artists of all sorts from touring virtuoso to strolling player, organ-grinder, and itinerant ballad-singer downwards'. F. W. Schubert, the Königsberg professor, described the miserable state of affairs in the province of Prussia, where there was as yet no industry (1847:30). 'Without exaggeration', he assures us, 'a third of the whole rural population of the province is unable to afford a daily portion of bread, and has to make do with potatoes alone.'

While we cannot enlarge on this subject here, we will quote two further examples that may better illustrate the extent of the need. In Brackwede near Bielefeld a weaving school was founded for the children of the spinners and weavers. The attendance at this school was very poor. 'When we tried to discover the reason for this scarcely enthusiastic response', runs the board of governors' report (1849)

> we found it to consist solely in the incredible poverty, and hence lethargy, of the spinners.... Most of the linen-weaving pupils (the majority being girls between sixteen and eighteen years of age) have a long way to walk to school, in some cases a journey of one or two hours. That prevents them from returning home for their midday meal, so that they have no choice but to bring it to school and eat it there. And that meal, as we recently learned, consists of an often very small piece of black bread without butter. And with no more than this meagre repast to sustain them the children, at an age when the appetite is normally at its heartiest, had to work and hold out for twelve hours, which is more than enough to explain their disinclination to come to school. (quoted in Blotenberg, 1960:61)

The voice of the poor themselves was understandably seldom heard, but there were exceptions, a notable one being Ulrich Bräker's work *Der arme Mann in Tockenburg*, issued in several editions, the most recent of which appeared in 1948. Ulrich Bräker, a small dealer in yarn, described his poverty during the early 1770s which, though admittedly exceptional, throws light on the general situation.

> I had five children and no income but for a trifle of spun yarn. Every week my little business lost more money.... We soon ate up the few potatoes and other vegetables left to us by the pilferers who robbed our small garden. I was forced to fetch provisions from the mill day after day; by the end of the week that came to a pretty sum for flour and rye bread alone.... So bitter was the need that winter [1770] that many of the poorest could hardly hold out till the spring, when they would be able to gather a few roots and herbs. But I would rather have fed my little birds on the leaves of the trees than do what I saw with my own eyes one of my unfortunate neighbours doing. He and his children hacked a whole sackful of meat from a dead horse that the dogs and crows had been at for several days.

The historian, who extends his interest from the particular instance to the general situation, will want to know how large was the group of people forced to live in such circumstances, either temporarily (because of unemployment and/or rising food prices) or permanently. Some indications are to be found in the works of contemporary authors such as Hildebrand, who estimated that in Hesse 'a third of the population was quite without resources', and Dieterici (see Conze,

1954:349f.), who wrote that in the 1840s 'at least 50–60 per cent of the population [of Prussia] were poor at the best of times and in bad years fell into desperate need and distress'.

On special occasions the numbers were more exactly assessed and classified. In November 1800 Friedrich Wilhelm III ordered cards to be issued for the 'poor' of Berlin to buy army bread at half the market price (A. Skalweit, 1931:605f., with legal supplements and price statistics). After a certain amount of discussion it was decided that the following would qualify as poor people unable to support themselves by their own exertions:

1 about 1,000 paupers who, until then, had been looked after for nothing by the workhouse at the cost of the town council
2 the poor textile workers, whose number was estimated by the ministers to be 12,000 persons, but whom the king counted as 5,000 to 6,000
3 the 'poor professionals', i.e. the craftsmen, tradesmen and others whose income was insufficient to provide them with even the barest necessities: some 2,000 persons
4 the most low-paid officials of royal and other public administrations, in particular messengers and copyists: some 1,500 persons.

That comes to about 10,000 people in all. With family dependants added, the number must have been between 30,000 and 40,000. In those days Berlin's population, without the military element, was about 150,000. Thus, in 1800, every fourth or fifth Berliner, even according to the strict standards laid down by the king, could not afford to buy the most vital necessities.

The humbler ranks of the royal civil service were also included in the above classification. According to the wage list of a Prussian Council for War and Crown Land Estates in 1800, the president of that council received a yearly salary of 3,000 thalers; a councillor earned 700 thalers, a head clerk 280 and an assistant clerk or copyist 50 thalers (see Krug, 1805:400f.). The highest salary paid to a council member or assistant was thus sixty times more than the lowest. Even in the cheapest districts the 50 thalers a year earned by an assistant clerk would buy no more than 2,000 kilograms of rye, or about 5.5 kilograms a day. Even if a man in this position, who usually had a wife and children to keep, ate nothing but bread-and-water soup, and potatoes, it is difficult to see how he could manage to feed, clothe and house his family.

Even a member of the War Council did not lie on a bed of roses. In Berlin, where prices were relatively high, 700 thalers was worth only 14,000 kilograms of rye. Converting the price of rye then to its present-day value, that amount would represent DM 600 a month in West Germany: less than half the salary of an assistant judge. How such a councillor – a high-ranking official – lived is described in a letter dated 17 September 1799 from Johann Gottlieb Fichte in Berlin to his wife.

Last Saturday half a pound of beef and six pounds of potatoes and carrots were stewed together for the Councillor and his family. But the meat was not cooked till tender; only the vegetables were eaten on the first day, while the beef was stewed up again for Sunday's dinner.... The shift the Councillor's lady will wear on Sunday is washed by the lady herself on Saturday night in her bedroom and she goes shiftless till it is dry. (see Fichte, 1925:2, p. 143)

From a memorandum on the administration of the Franconian principalities, written by Hardenberg on 10 January 1792, we learn that 'most ranks in the Civil Service are so poorly paid that they are almost forced to exact illegal fees, accept bribes and resort to various small swindles, a cancerous evil that must be stopped. Some Under-Secretaries of State get only 500 florins, for example, a salary of 100 ducats, on which they can barely live' (see Hausherr, 1963:236).

To illustrate the living standards of the ordinary labourer we will refer once more to masons' and carpenters' wages. They represent an important section of working-class income, are based on good evidence and are very suitable for comparing conditions between different periods and places. Table 24 shows the average daily earnings (as long as he was in work) of a journeyman mason or carpenter receiving no board or lodging from his employer.[1]

Table 24   Average daily earnings of a journeyman mason or
carpenter around 1800

in Strasbourg	1790 to 1850	9.9 g silver or 9 kg wheat
in Emden	1790 to 1850	8.6 g silver or 10.9 wheat
in Leipzig	1790 to 1810	7.1 g silver or 9.3 kg wheat
in Berlin	1800	5.6 g silver or 6.7 kg wheat

Taking the Berlin wage (admittedly the lowest), it is possible to estimate how it was divided among the most essential needs of life. If we presume that the man was in work throughout the year, thus earning 1,737 grams of silver or 104 state thalers, and if we further suppose that a family of five had to live from that income, his expenses would be approximately those shown in figure 58. The rent would be at least 15 state thalers and a further 7 thalers would go on heating and light. Six thalers would have to be put aside for clothing and other necessities, a meagre sum, but all that could be spared, since the rest would be required for food. Some 73 per cent of all living expenses were for provisions, especially bread. Only a third as much could be spent on meat and other animal products as on bread. Each member of the family would be limited to some 1.5 kilograms of butter, 4 kilograms of herrings, 8 kilograms of curds and 8.5 kilograms of meat annually (Saalfeld, 1964).

Wages and the cost of living in France

In Paris in 1789 a factory worker earned the equivalent of 3.8 kilograms of bread a day. If we subtract Sundays, feast days and other workless days, the average daily income drops to 2.3 kilograms of bread a day. To buy 2 kilograms of bread, which would provide a family of four with 4,800 calories, 87 per cent of the worker's income would have to be spent. That was impossible, since money had to be kept for dwelling, clothes and drink; the rent alone would be about 3 sous a day, or 20 per cent of his earnings.

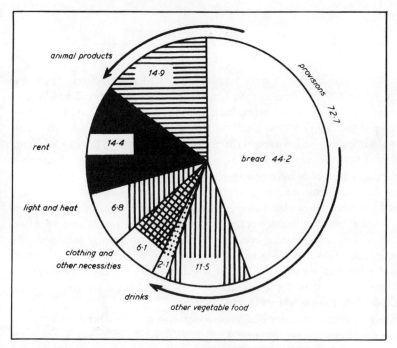

Fig. 58   Living expenses of a mason's family of five, Berlin 1800.

These figures come from Rudé (1953–4:247f.) who continued Labrousse's researches from where he left off, that is to say from the year 1789. Rudé published some further data from which we gather that the day-wage of a Paris mason was the equivalent of 6.2 kilograms of bread; stonemasons and goldsmiths, who were at the top of the wage scale, earned about 15.4 kilograms of bread per day (see table 25).

In 1806, when official wage levels were introduced in France (*Annuaire Statistique de la France*, 1905:86f.), a Parisian mason's wage per hour for casual work was fixed at 0.325 francs, rising after 1828 to 0.35 francs. The day-wages

Table 25   Paris wages and bread prices, 1789

Trade	Day wage in sous	Price per kg bread in sous	Day wage in kg bread	Actual day's earnings in sous	Actual day's earnings in kg bread
Factory worker	25	6.5	3.8	15	2.3
Builder	30		4.6	18	2.8
Mason	40		6.2	24	3.7
Carpenter, smith	50		7.7	30	4.6
Stonemason, goldsmith	100		15.4	60	9.2

(for an official ten-hour day) were 3.25 and 3.50 francs respectively. That was some 75 per cent higher than in 1789 but, on the other hand, bread had become more expensive. In the worst years, such as 1830, it reached a level that almost cancelled out the rise in wages. During 1830, when a Parisian mason's day-wage for casual work was 3.50 francs, and the price of bread was 0.55 francs a kilogram, the value of his earnings was 6.4 kilograms of wheaten bread, little more than during 1789, a year of hunger and revolution.

When estimated from long-term averages, however, the wage-earner's position appears in a more favourable light. The wage and price accounts of the Paris hospitals show that the average wage of a mason between 1824 and 1855 was worth about 11.7 kilograms of bread a day. In the provinces it does not seem to have attained that level. Taking the average from 86 *départements* for which wage and price data are available, a mason halfway through the 1824–50 period earned the equivalent of 8.3 kilograms of wheat (or about 9.3 grams of silver) (*Statistique de la France*, 1863:XII, 162, 192).

It is more difficult to determine the *development* of wages between 1790 and 1850, because there are no complete wage series covering those years, nor is the period long enough to even out all short-term fluctuations. If we confine ourselves to the years 1815–50 data are more plentiful, but then the search for the general trend has to be made from an even-narrower base. Nevertheless, it would appear that Dunham was right when, after a most careful examination of the available material, he concluded that wages in France between 1815 and 1850 'did not appreciably rise, but rather stagnated, with a tendency to fall' (1943:117f.).

Contemporary literature, however, is very informative. Beside Balzac, whose *Comédie Humaine* was particularly appreciated by Friedrich Engels,[2] we have Eugène Sue (1804–57), who so vividly depicted the life, and poverty, of the simple working man. Many other, less celebrated, authors are worth consulting, but not without a certain caution. That was the opinion of Heinrich Heine, who spent some time in Paris during the 1830s and 'found it hard to track down the truth where all parties sought to deceive and one could not even trust the evidence of one's own eyes'. Heine related (25 March 1832) how one of his friends, a wealthy man, took him round Paris so that Heine could see for himself how happy and content the people were.

> Merrily he took my arm and merrily he hurried me along the streets.... On the damp pavement by the Porte Saint-Martin lay a man, deathly pale, with a death-rattle in his throat. The surrounding onlookers declared he was dying of hunger. My companion, however, assured me that these people 'died of hunger' in a different street every day and made their living by it, for they were paid by the Carlists, in the hope that such sights would turn the public against the Government.

But, thought Heine,

> the job cannot be very well paid since so many are really dying of hunger. It is a curious thing about starvation. One would see thousands in that condition every day, did the condition but last longer. However, the sufferers usually die after three days without food, and they are buried and one hardly notices that they have gone. (1862:135)[3]

Heine's observations of the city's poverty were confirmed from official quarters. Chevalier (1959) quotes the following instances. The deputy of the Jardin du Roi district declared that the situation of the Parisian labourer, especially when given notice at the month's end, was desperate. 'Yesterday I visited some artisans living in my district', he wrote. 'I saw unfortunate families with four or five children, who had no bread in the house and did not know how they could get food on the next day.' The deputy of the Popincourt district, where four-fifths of the population were working class, reported: 'One cannot imagine the distress of these unhappy people. They have had to sell or pawn all their possessions, even the tools of their trade. Having parted with all their furniture for miserable prices, they live in mean and dirty lodgings.' 'The labourer has lost everything', wrote the Louvre district deputy. 'He has no bed, no clothing, no shelter, no wood for the winter.... How he will get through the winter at all no one can tell.'

English wages compared with those of other nations

Eugene Buret, one of the first French writers to compare the situation of the French labourer with that of his counterpart in England, expressed an opinion in a sentence that was short and to the point: *La France est pauvre, l'Angleterre est misérable* (1841:237). He was able to refer back to the classic English economists, who lent him evidence enough for his assertion. Later a friendlier view of English conditions prevailed, but it has not gone undisputed. As Hobsbawm pointed out, the favourable opinions of Clapham, Ashton and Hayek have come increasingly under attack (Hobsbawm, 1962:104f; 1957:46f., with further bibliographical references; supplemented and summed up in Cole and Postgate, 1964).

Hobsbawn himself, who may fairly be counted as one of the 'Neo-Pessimist' group, points out among other things that meat consumption stagnated until the 1840s, if it did not actually decline. Statistics referring to Bradford-on-Avon in the west of England show that in 1841 the 8,309 inhabitants of that city consumed 9,497 pounds (approximately 400 grams per head) of meat a week, but that two-thirds of it was eaten by a minority of only some 2,400 people. All the sources of information agree that the factory worker's usual weekly diet consisted of bread and potatoes, tea with a little milk, small amounts of meat and fish, especially herrings, and a few eggs. In ten out of forty-six places investigated the poorer classes had no fresh meat at all, even in small quantities. Inadequate nourishment accounts for the many deficiency diseases of the time, in particular rickets, which became known in Germany by the sad name of 'the English disease'.

As to furniture, Hobsbawm reports that in Sheffield around 1850 the qualified and better-off working-class family had beds, but not for all the children, tables, chairs and cupboards, cutlery and dishes, but no carpets, curtains or blankets, and very little linen. The husband had two suits, one or both of which he replaced every year, the Sunday suit being then downgraded to everyday use. This working-class aristocracy even had clocks or watches, of which one only hears when some crisis forced their owners to pawn them. The really poor existed in far more distressful circumstances, in which the more prosperous workers all too frequently joined them when hit by unemployment.

There is no doubt, Hobsbawm added, that the material level of life in England improved after 1840. Sugar consumption rose from an annual average of 20 pounds for the years 1831–50 to one of 35 pounds in 1851–70, while between 1841 and 1851 the consumption of tea increased from 23 ounces to 24 ounces and that of tobacco from 13 ounces to 18 ounces.

Hobsbawm has little faith in estimates of real wages. He has reason on his side in that for the 1860s (a period that particularly interested him) a clear-cut calculation of trends is hardly possible. Rougher methods, however, can at least give some idea of the English labourer's position in the late eighteenth and first half of the nineteenth centuries. Tucker's frequently-quoted wage index for London craftsmen rises by 0.2 per cent a year from 1793 to 1847. That, admittedly, shows only variations between two quite arbitrarily-fixed points (see Gayer, Rostow and Schwartz, 1953:626), but comparable series indicate the same tendency, for example, Steffens' carpenters' wages, when converted to corn values,[4] as well as the southern English builders' wages compiled by Phelps-Brown and Hopkins from much wider sources of information (1956:296f.). These equivalents come near enough to real wages, since they are based on 'packages of commodities' containing not only foodstuffs but also expenses for clothing, fuel, light and similar items. Starting from an average 100 between the years 1740 and 1749, these equivalents fell by stages of 96, 87, 84, 88, 82, to 66 per cent during the decade 1800–9, then rose again by stages of 77, 99 and 105 to an average 107 per cent from 1840 to 1849. Thus we cannot avoid the conclusion that during the first half of the nineteenth century English wages recovered from the 'Asiatic level' (to use an expression of Colin Clark's) to which they had sunk in 1800.

But the question of the development of English wages from 1790 to 1850 must be put aside for the moment. It is less relevant to the comparison of international wages attempted in the ensuing paragraphs than is the mean level of those wages converted into values in universal – even if not exclusive – demand, namely the corn values already selected by the classical economists as a criterion of the purchasing power of wages. First, however, let us consider money wages. According to Steffen (1901:471; 1904:13, 30; 1905:19, 25), the average day wage in England for a carpenter over the whole 1790–1850 period was 46 pence; Phelps-Brown and Hopkins (1955:195f.) give the corresponding wage for a builder's labourer at 44.5 pence, while Bowley (1900) estimates the corresponding wage for a mason in Manchester at 45.8 pence and for a carpenter at 48 pence.

We would not be far wrong, then, in setting the mean wage of an English building labourer between 1790 and 1850 at 46 pence, which, converted according to the wheat prices given in the appendix, produces an equivalent value of 13.3 kilograms of wheat.

Bruno Hildebrand attempted a comparison of English and German wages based on the prices of the most essential foodstuffs in the two countries. He showed that prices in England were about half as high again as in Germany. It should be noted, however, he added, that wages were more uniform throughout England, though also more fluctuating, than in Germany, where they varied more from place to place but remained at the same level for longer. He thought that the wages of railway signalmen, 'whose number was already considerable in both countries, and increasing daily', would form the most reliable base for his comparison because it was a job for which the pay was fairly level all over Germany and, in England, was the least liable to fluctuations. In Germany a signalman received 120–144 thalers a year, and sometimes there was a house that went with the job, but most of the railway companies deducted 22 thalers from his salary for the uniform they supplied. In England, 'according to information obtained by myself on the spot', a signalman's pay was £52, or 346⅔ thalers, as well as the uniform and sometimes a house, thus almost three times as much.

While these observations were not without interest, Hildebrand did not suppose that they completely answered his question. He examined the wages of a number of other workers such as craftsmen, textile workers, domestic servants and 'ordinary labourers'. It would take too long to give all the details; it must suffice to quote his conclusion:

The overall result of my rather numerous and extensive investigations has convinced me that the average pay for a day's work in England during the last three years [1844–46] comes to 3 schillings a day or 300 thalers a year, whereas in Germany it is at most 100 thalers. Thus, at the present rate of exchange between the two countries, the English workman can buy twice as many necessities as the German. Even if the average wage is taken as 2½ or 2 schillings, the worker in England is still better situated than his counterpart in Germany.

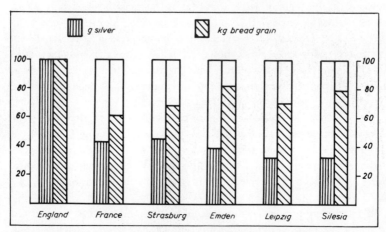

Fig. 59   Day wages of a journeyman mason or carpenter, 1790–1850.

Hildebrand's observations are still valid today, but that does not free us from the task of making a new comparison of international wages, a somewhat hazardous undertaking for, in spite of the rich material concerning wages and prices that has come to light since Hildebrand's book was published, there are still great gaps in our knowledge. That is particularly the case in France before 1824 and Germany after 1810, the last year of the Elsas collections. For that reason figure 59, which is based partly on facts already familiar,[5] can do no more than indicate orders of magnitude, and will soon, we hope, be supplemented by more complete information. It can, however, be maintained with some certainty that English wages were not, as so often is supposed, especially low. They were higher than continental wages, just as the continent lagged behind England in its degree of industrialization.

The historical context of pauperism

Stages in the decline of real wages after the Middle Ages

In presenting the history of the decline in real wages, those living at the time relied on data going back only a few decades, or at most a few generations. This is very understandable. The figures were easily available and plentiful enough

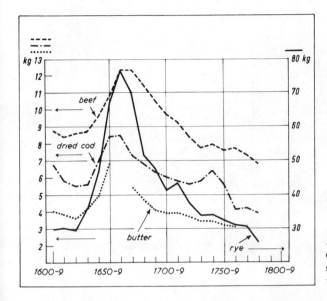

Fig. 60 Food obtainable for a stonebreaker's weekly wage in Würzburg.

to make further research seem unnecessary. We might here refer back to the price and wage movements well known since the mid-eighteenth century (see above, page 199), or to the decline in German 'corn wages' after the Thirty Years War (see above, page 161). It may be added that between 1660–9 and the end of the eighteenth century the purchasing power of a stonebreaker's weekly wage sank by nearly a third in relation to rye and by about a half in relation to beef, dried fish and butter (see figure 60).[6]

But, in fact, the decline in real wages set in far earlier. Looking back into the past we see real wages missing during the seventeenth and eighteenth century like a peak from the plain. Behind that nearer eminence, however, a far higher summit is hidden: the wages of the late Middle Ages. Their highest level was not regained until the 'industrial era' and then in completely different circumstances.

The decline in wages after the late Middle Ages can be represented as a series of steps leading downwards and upwards but, in the long run, downwards. Figure 61 shows such a series for England, and for Strasbourg, Vienna and Leipzig, for which continuous wage and price series exist.[7] The most pronounced falling-off all over central and western Europe occurred in the sixteenth century. The next ascent came to an end in Germany just after the Thirty Years War, but continued until the eighteenth century in other countries. To keep figure 61 simple, wages for Germany (Leipzig) were also chosen from the first half of the eighteenth century. They, too, were higher than during the second half of the sixteenth century

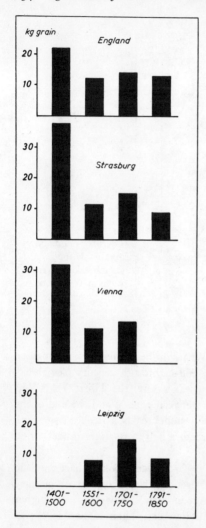

Fig. 61   Stages in the decline of real wages in western and central Europe.

but considerably lower (though unfortunately that cannot be demonstrated in the case of Leipzig) than during the fifteenth century.

Changes in the consumption and production of foodstuffs

Connected with the decline in real wages came changes in the composition of the people's diet and in farm production. That has already been described quite frequently for separate areas and periods, but it is not until the late eighteenth century and early nineteenth century that the situation can be seen, in spite of some exceptions, as a whole.

The development of food consumption can be summed up briefly as the victory, despite their rising prices, of comparatively cheap and bulky foodstuffs, rich in carbohydrates, over foods that, although more concentrated, protein-rich and savoury, were dearer per unit of nourishment. That was especially so in the case of meat. It would not be far wrong to estimate the annual meat consumption of late medieval Germany at over 100 kilograms per head of population (see above, page 71); at the beginning of the nineteenth century the amount of meat eaten in Prussia, Saxony, and Germany as a whole must have sunk to something under 20 kilograms per head per year (Abel, 1937:444f.).

Even in the Netherlands where, thanks to better conditions for industry and production, meat consumption was less affected, the average amount eaten annually in the years 1801 to 1804 was only 27 kilograms (beef, veal and pork together) per person (van der Woude, 1963:149).

At the end of the eighteenth century and beginning of the nineteenth century the consumption of eggs, butter, poultry, game and wine (which was supplanted by cheap beer and spirits) had likewise fallen much below its late medieval level. In a German town chronicle written in the fifteenth century, when the city was under siege, it was reported that 'the rich still had plenty to eat, but the poor were short of several commodities, especially butter' (in Heyne, 1901:310). At the beginning of the nineteenth century it would never have occurred to a writer to include butter among the foods that 'the poor' particularly missed. The idea of a food shortage had changed. It came to mean a lack of cereals, common vegetables, pulses and, as the nineteenth century advanced, the cheapest of all vegetables, the potato.

Naturally there were circumstances that allowed, even invited, exceptions to the general rule. Four instances are worth mentioning:

1. The households of people who grew their own food in country or town. Goethe reported from Heilbronn that along the streets and lanes beside the city wall and away from the main thoroughfares 'every small householder kept some livestock'. In 1786, Hanover a bigger town even then, contained 365 cows and oxen to its 20,000 inhabitants.

In the country it was the rule to eat meat produced on one's own land or on the farm where one rendered service. Where circumstances permitted, the table was as plentifully-spread as ever. The farmers on the North Sea marshlands in 1800 enjoyed the same diet as they had had for centuries, perhaps better, supplemented as it now was by coffee, tea, sugar and fine wines. In some places even the farm workers had their share of these good things. Von Justi reports from central Germany (1755:481) that the employees' diet, though it consisted chiefly of bread with butter, cheese, soup and vegetables, did include half a pound of meat twice a week for each person.

There were other farmers, however, who had to make do with less. Among these were the peasants of the border country high in the Steigerwald, where the 'poor people had no small difficulty in finding a miserable patch of grazing large enough to feed their beasts for a day', or on the Spessart heights where, another writer tells us in 1800, 'A broth of bread and water with a little milk was their breakfast, boiled potatoes with curds their midday meal, and bread-and-water broth once more their supper' (Abel, 1964:245). Others in the same plight were the smallholders in the richer villages, and all over Europe, whether on poor or fertile soil, peasants whose payments and services left them without the very necessities of life.

It is not hard to find examples. Even a hasty selection from the information available could fill many pages. That is unnecessary here, but it might repay us to cast an eye on a part of the world to which this book has hitherto paid little attention. In Switzerland, it is said, in about 1820 (Brugger, 1956:13), the country folk ate chiefly bread, farinacious foods, oat porridge, pulses, fruit, milk and milk derivatives. Even prosperous households had meat only once or twice a week, fresh meat usually being reserved for Sundays, while the poorer families ate meat only a few times in the year. Abbot Maurus of Moudsee in upper Austria (1652) declared that 'for all their hard work parishioners with their wives and families could not get as much oaten bread as they needed'. In 1655 the priest at Ternberg wrote 'a peasant and his family eat no more than a pound of meat in a quarter-year'. Baron Hoheneck reported in 1742 that, except in the more prosperous districts, the majority of his subjects by the river Enns in Austria were reduced to satisfying their hunger 'almost exclusively with oat bran bread, or, in times of poor harvest and high prices, bread baked from straw, acorns, hayseed and husks' (see Grull, 1963:53f.). Life was still harder for the Polish peasants who, in feudal times, stood on the very lowest rung of the long ladder of social dependence. Johanna Schopenhauer says in her memoirs (1958 edn:37f.) that she often came across these people in Danzig when they brought their great shiploads of grain down the Vistula to the city. Of their lives at home in winter, she wrote, she knew nothing, but she could tell something of their situation in summer:

Their food, day in day out, is a very thick porridge made of dried peas or buckwheat, which they cook for themselves in a huge cauldron hanging from a cross-beam. Should they manage to scrounge a few tallow candles to flavour the thin broth they consider it a most delicate meal. There they sit at midday, close by one another in truly picturesque groups, holding the great wooden spoons that are among their dearest possessions, and ladling, gulping and chattering as fast as they can go. ... One morning, while walking through the lanes between the warehouses, I noticed a polsky in the distance lurking in front of one of the stores and casting covetous glances at the various provisions on display. My companion, Jameson, and I stopped for a minute to see what the fellow was up to, when he suddenly darted towards a barrel of herrings that was standing in the doorway and seemed to be planning to steal one. Instead of that he took a huge slice of black bread out of his pocket, dipped it deep

into the brine and fled without looking round, as if he had just got away with
the most delicious booty.

2. Meat seems to have been plentiful enough in monasteries, hospitals,
infirmaries, and institutions generally till far into the modern era. As late as 1800
in some households of this sort even the most frugal menu allowed each person
about half a pound of meat a week, seldom less, usually more. Eggs were often
served as well as fish, cheese, butter and bread (Ilzhöfer, 1942:150f.).

But the expenditure of such establishments depended on their income, and
not all of them were as well endowed as those whose menus have come down
to us. There were almshouses, workhouses and similar institutions that had to
live hand to mouth on public charity or even on the money earned by the inmates.
There the diet was more austere.

A not unamusing example that will serve to illustrate the conditions is the
Rumford soup that enjoyed a certain renown in Germany. It was named after
the Count Rumford who laid out the English Gardens in Munich, reorganized
the Bavarian army and founded a workhouse to receive the Munich beggars. As
a diet he recommended a soup which, according to his own recipe (in Larsen,
1961:91f.), consisted of the following ingredients: 'Two quarts of pearl barley,
two quarts of peas, eight quarts of potatoes, slices of fine wheat bread, salt, 24
measures of weak malt vinegar or sour beer, about 560 measures of water'. There
was neither fat nor meat in the soup; it would not be very highly thought of
nowadays. According to the 1956 edition of the Gross Brockhaus encyclopedia,
a modern Rumford soup contains, in addition to the barley, peas and potatoes
prescribed by its inventor, a strong bone stock and some pork. Even new ways
of making soup can reflect the economic development of a nation!

3. Somewhat apart from the two preceding groups is consumption on special
occasions such as weddings, christenings, admission into a guild, and so on. For
such celebrations the food was still abundant even in the eighteenth century. But
estimates of everyday consumption cannot be based on banquets of this kind,
even if the occasion celebrated was not always a very important one.

Sometimes money was spent on extra consumption for the sake of the rewards
it would bring in. For instance, in 1571 when the Cologne merchant, Hermann
von Weinsberg, celebrated his enrolment in the Corporation of Banner Knights
of Cologne by entertaining some friends and gentlemen of the town to a lavish
meal (already described above, page 143) he noted in his memorandum book that
although the dinner had cost him 64 guilders, he was glad that 'it had happened
as it had to, for henceforth I shall be free. I shall be excused twelve excise services
every year as long as I live, have two free dinners each year, be exempted from
guard duty and enjoy other privileges and exemptions into the bargain' (1887:223).

4. Finally, we must consider cases in which incomes were so high that
expenditure on food was not an important item in the budget, so that the income-
elasticity of demand for food reached zero level. The rich did not actually limit

their consumption of foodstuffs, but in so far as they maintained a normal meat consumption they narrowed still further the already tight supply of animal products available at prices which that immensely larger group, the working class, could afford to pay.

Von Thünen, writing at the time, has already described this situation in reference to his 'isolated state' (Waentig edn, 1930:256). He suggested that we should drop for the moment the assumption that agriculture in the isolated state must necessarily remain in a constant condition, and suppose that the concerns hitherto devoted exclusively to livestock-breeding gradually go over to arable farming. Then, firstly, the quantity of animal products sent to market would decrease and, secondly, the question would arise as to how the reduced amount of animal produce should be distributed among the now greater number of consumers. 'When buying meat', he replied to this question,

> people with small incomes can afford only the price it is worth to them when compared with other provisions. If the price goes up they must do without meat or, at best, eat less of it. The rich, on the other hand, are prepared to pay more for the pleasure of eating meat than its money value in relation to grain would indicate. And since it is these same high prices that prevent the poor from buying meat, the rich man's table can bear as much flesh food as before, while the working classes must make do with the cheaper but less nourishing vegetable foodstuffs.

From this Thünen concluded that the transition to a higher state of civilization can mean a most unwelcome reduction of living standards to the worker.

*

Since Adam Smith's day political economy, and agricultural economy, too, since the time of Albrecht Thaer, have distinguished different stages of animal husbandry and meat supply. In the first stage, when a small population makes extensive use of the land possible, animal husbandry is by far the most important farming activity. In Germany, as in the rest of western and central Europe, this phase began in prehistoric times and ended in the late Middle Ages. Cattle, sheep and pigs found good grazing on the numerous meadows, pastures and in the woods, and a plentiful supply of fodder in stall or sty. In both country and town meat formed an important part of the human diet. In many places even the villeins had two abundant meat meals a day ('so much that the dishes overflowed').

In the second stage animal husbandry dropped behind arable farming in extent. A moderate-sized cornfield, Adam Smith expounded, produced more human nourishment than the same area of the best meadow-land. Although its cultivation demanded far more labour, the surplus left after subtracting seed-corn and labour costs was also much greater. Meat, though its price probably rose more slowly than that of cereals, was beyond the means of most people. Seeing that, the farmer preferred the opportunities offered by agriculture. Cattle, which in the pastoral era had seemed to provide the most rewarding and labour-saving form of land exploitation, were now valued chiefly for their contribution to the soil's fertility by means of their dung, and for their usefulness as draught animals. In that period animal husbandry dwindled away.

There followed in the West, though not in the ancient civilizations along the Tigris, Euphrates and Nile or in Greece and Rome, a third stage, during which the two forms of farming were mutually helpful and some arable products were grown to feed cattle. The industrialization of the West brought this phase to an end.

The first German 'handbook of the theory and practice of improved stock breeding' worthy of the name (Weber, 1810) appeared during the second phase, when arable farming was still predominant. In this work we read that 'only on the so-called stock farms situated on grazing land whose low fertility renders it useless for agriculture do cattle continue to provide a true net profit. It is hardly ever so on the ordinary arable farms, where they are kept only because they are indispensable to the working of the farm.' Contemporary statistics confirm that view. Incomplete though they are, the picture of Prussia for which they sketch the rough outline is undoubtedly a good likeness. Grain was by far the most important product of Prussian-German farming in 1800. According to Leopold Krug (cited in Abel, 1967:325) cereals represented some 53 per cent of the monetary value of the entire food production, other vegetable produce about 23 per cent and animal products a mere 24 per cent. In West Germany at the beginning of the 1960s the position was completely reversed: in 1959–60 animal products made up 72 per cent of farm production.

The end of an era

The phenomena depicted above fit into the pattern laid out by Malthus, Ricardo and, later, Thünen for a population whose rapid growth was exerting considerable pressure on agriculture. Real wages sank or, when they reached the minimum for existence, stagnated. Consumption was concentrated on the land-intensive vegetable foodstuffs, meat-eating declined and animal husbandry became unprofitable. Farming activity shifted to growing vegetables, chiefly cereals and pulses and, later, potatoes, which yielded more calories per area of land. Food resources shrank because science and technical skill were not as yet sufficiently advanced to overcome the natural obstacles that stood in the way of human progress.

It may be added that the Labrousse cycle, postulated by its author for the *ancien régime*, continued well beyond 1789. In Prussia a significant relation between rye prices and marriages was evident right up to the 1860s (Wagemann, 1928:146f.; 1929:56f.); in Bavaria the curve representing pauperism and the movement of rye prices followed a parallel course until 1858–9 (Laves, 1884:208).

These circumstances contradict Engels' theory that industry was responsible for the poverty he observed in England. If we look beyond the city and its factories to the countryside, and past the nineteenth century to earlier times, it becomes clear that poverty existed before the industrial age, and was rooted, though not of course in all its manifestations, in pre-industrial conditions. Its origins and development belong to a dying phase of western history.

Another question is why mechanized industry, which started very early in England, took so long to free the western peoples from a shortage of food resources. The usual answer is that each country's industrialization meant a shift of national income from consumption to investment, and that took time. But it is a solution that postulates an indefinite period of hunger and thirst and pays too little attention to the fact that not only were wages and profits available for financing the industrial breakthrough, but also rents, which in early-nineteenth-century England constituted a sixth of the national income (Marshall, 1885, in Hamilton, 1960:160). In the case of Germany, an answer which does take rents into account has already been given elsewhere (Abel, 1964:252f.).

Hobsbawm has tried to do as much for England (1962:1047f.). He stresses that in England, too, by far the largest part of the rents was used to finance the landlord's consumption of goods and services, especially the rents accruing to the four thousand or so big landowners. Such wealth as was reinvested went into the land, trade and certain colonial and financial ventures. Industry was neglected. 'For every pound invested in industry, many more simply accumulated.'

Hobsbawm emphasizes that the 'relatively enormous amount of capital' at England's disposal in the eighteenth and early nineteenth centuries was enough to provide the modest investments required by industry in those days, without depressing the living standards of the people as a whole. The small yield derived from investment in industry meant that the entrepreneurs were continually in need of capital. This atmosphere encouraged a puritanical idealization of money-saving, a hatred of unprofitable outlay, blindness to everything that did not produce money and a growing lack of sympathy with the artisan class. Consequently the inland market was very limited, especially for the working classes. About 60 per cent of the entire production of cotton, the chief industry of the first period (1780–1850), was exported (thus, incidentally, spoiling the market for home industries on the continent). Consumer goods such as clothing, shoes and furniture were seldom made by machinery or mass production methods before 1850. Moreover, the way in which public finance was organized tended to make the rich richer and the poor poorer. 'In short, the organization of industry was a permanent conspiracy to hold down the living standards of the working class' (quoted from O'Brien, 1959:267).

Which may explain why industry took so long to fulfil its appointed task of raising those same standards.

Part Four

The agrarian economy of western and central Europe
in the industrial age

Preface to the final part

The nearer we get to our own day, the richer becomes the material and literature relating to the food and agrarian economy of our chosen area. To evaluate the statistics and relevant writings in the same way as we have done in the foregoing chapters would be impossible. Bounds must be set to the amount of the available evidence used.

The selection of material, so difficult for the historian in this sort of situation, is here made somewhat easier by the limited subject matter and definite question posed at the beginning of the book. Both concerned prices and their relation to the quantity of money and goods in the economy. It was postulated that certain correlations between these prices and quantities and the level of costs and incomes had existed since towns were first built on European soil, but that the strength and nature of this interdependence were still an open question. To examine them and, if necessary, modify our conclusions was the object of the exercise.

That this history has now arrived at the age of the mature market economy is no reason to alter the formulation of our question. It still concerns agricultural depressions, understood as slumps in farming economy, and the agricultural situation understood, if not hitherto strictly defined, as of farming in conjunction with markets; but remembering, however, that the situation is continually changing, like the positions of the stars to which astronomers first applied the word 'conjunction'.

Accordingly, in this final section only those prices, incomes and marketed quantities which are part of the agrarian economy will be discussed. That in so doing consideration must be given to the shifting combinations of qualities and goods goes without saying, but whether changes in the economy's structure necessarily call for new deductions or theories is another question that must be approached with an open mind. To attempt an answer before examining all the evidence – in other words from pure speculation – would be against the character of this work. The problem will be put aside, but not forgotten.

10 The solution to the problems of inadequate food supply

Prices, wages and living standards since the mid-nineteenth century

The rise in real wages

The movements of prices and wages after the first half of the nineteenth century are depicted in figure 62. The graph continues on from the preceding diagrams and calculations dealing with earlier periods, the effects of nineteenth century currency changes being eliminated as far as possible (see appendix). Once more four groups are examined: wages, grain prices, the prices of animal products and those of industrial products. The groups are made up of numerous but unweighted series of individual prices and wages.[1]

Wages went up in all the countries, but to varying extents. How much they rose may have depended partly on the level from which they started. English wages during the first half of the nineteenth century, it will be remembered, were higher than on the continent (see figure 59). The price of animal products followed wages at some distance, grain prices lagged still further behind, while, except in England, the gap between the price of cereals and that of industrial products was yet more pronounced.

Such, in rough outline, are the price and wage movements of the industrial era. They can be subdivided and they can be clarified visually, for example by presenting them in the form of linear trends, though at the cost of suppressing any intervening fluctuations. Some German prices are shown in this way in figure 63, which comes from Feilen (1935–6:33).[2]

Wage groups can also be considered separately. It can be shown that some industries forged ahead, others followed in their wake and finally agriculture moved in the same direction, although it was kept back for long periods by the pressure of prices. The investigation will not be attempted here, however, since the general principle is unassailable even without such refinements: it was technical and industrial progress that sent wages up. Other factors contributed, but in the final analysis it was the growing productivity of human labour, measured by any standard, that turned the scale.

Thus wages rose in relation to prices. In other words, the purchasing power of wages increased, but to what extent real wages went up cannot be learned from the available graphs and statistics. The classical writers of political economy,

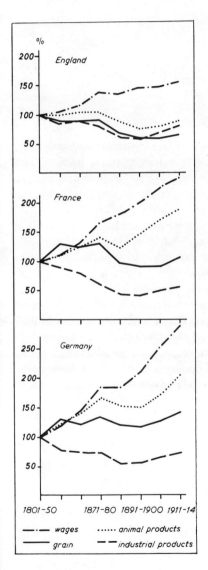

Fig. 62   Movements of prices and wages in western and central Europe 1801–1914.

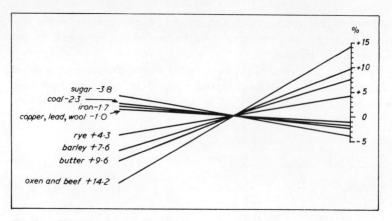

Fig. 63   German price-trends 1792–1913.

who studied the fluctuations of real wages in the late eighteenth and early nineteenth centuries, were content to compare nominal wages to the price of corn. That was probably accurate enough for their own time and its preceding periods, because in the pre-industrial era grain, with its derivatives and substitutes, was one of the chief items in a working-class family's budget.

That has now changed. Proportionately less is spent on food. Other kinds of goods and expenses have come to the fore and must be included in our 'shopping basket' and, what is more, their changing amounts and distribution must be reviewed from time to time. In spite of these efforts, the 'true' value of a rise in wages can only be conceived in the vaguest terms since there is no standard by which the objective worth of an article can be compared to its subjective worth. As a concrete example, how much improvement does a 1960 working-class family's possession of a car signify, in view of the fact that a hundred years earlier there was no such article? The increase of convenience cannot be measured, because it corresponds to no lesser convenience of the same kind. For the ancestors of today's car-owners a horse-drawn carriage would have been a possession beyond their wildest dreams.

The exact extent to which real wages went up in the industrialized countries of Europe is, therefore, a question to which there can be no categorical answer. Nevertheless, some calculations relating to the subject have been carried out (for England see Cole and Postgate, 1938) and more will probably follow.[3] Here it will suffice to indicate that real wages did, in fact, increase, and to sketch, if only in outline, the attending circumstances and conditions.

However, one document of the period may perhaps be quoted to breathe life into the dry bones of tables and figures. A report from the Bielefeld Chamber of Commerce in 1872 – admittedly a boom year – tells us:

Only twenty years ago things were so bad in the linen industry, that the weavers' poverty was a running sore in public life and, as recently as 1849, the state, at the request of the National Assembly, subscribed 35,000 thalers to relieve the most acute needs of the spinners and weavers in the Bielefeld administrative area. Today (here at least) there are twice as many hands employed in the linen industry as there used to be and there is no more talk of the weaver's bad or inadequate pay. Now we hear nothing but complaints about the labour shortage. It is typical of the situation that the present-day mechanical looms can procure the weaver three times the money he earned fifteen years ago, and yet it is impossible to find enough people to occupy the 200-odd weaving stools that stand empty out of a total of 520, although there would be a good turnover for all they could produce....

The German linen industry reached its nadir some fifty years ago. The recovery began when the industrialists replaced spinning and weaving hand-workers with spinning jennies and mechanical looms. (in Blotenberg, 1960:68)

The development of foodstuff consumption

Exactly when the supply of foodstuffs in Germany reached its lowest point of the century is hard to determine, for the long-term trends are obscured by short-term fluctuations which are not easy to distinguish, even if one confines oneself to one series, such as meat consumption, and one country only. During the first two decades of the nineteenth century there were some disastrous harvest failures (1805–6 and 1816–17), to which were added the effects and after-effects of the Napoleonic Wars. Esslen (1912:247) reckoned that Prussia's meat consumption in 1816 was 14 kilograms per head, and that Germany's in the same year came to 13.6 kilograms per head. The 1820s were marked by a severe agricultural depression accompanied by the stagnation of urban industries. It is uncertain whether meat consumption sank still lower as Ciriacy-Wantrup thought (1936:72) or rose as Soetbeer's Hamburg figures would lead one to suppose (see, Schmoller 1870:206, 234). Relative meat consumption in Prussia and Germany may have increased slightly from the early 1830s to the middle of the century. The figures for Prussia arrived at by Dieterici and Engel Ernst show an ascent with slight fluctuations from 16 kilograms per head in 1831 to 18 kilograms per head in 1863; Esslen's figures for German meat consumption rise from 21.6 kilograms per head in 1840 to 23.3 kilograms per head in 1861 (Dieterici, 1846:13f.). The change probably occurred in the 1850s. According to Esslen's reckoning, which concerns only the consumption of domestic produce, the amount consumed per head of population was already 29.5 kilograms in 1873. By 1892 it had increased to 32.5 kilograms, and by 1904–5 to 46.8 kilograms (further, see Abel, 1937:445; Schmoller, 1871:284f.; Saalfeld, 1977:244–253).

That is only one series from the history of food consumption. Others stand in different degrees of positive and negative correlation with it. Compared with the Germany of 1909–13, people in West Germany in 1958–9 consumed about 50 per cent more edible fats, 92 per cent more eggs and 156 per cent more fresh and dried fruit, while the consumption of potatoes fell by 29 per cent and the consumption of cereals by 30 per cent (Thiede, 1955; supplemented from the *Statist. Jahrbuch. f. d. Bundesrepublik*).

The same differences in consumption that we have seen developing through the years also exist between one part of the world and another. If we look beyond the development of consumption to the explanation for it in different nations, we see a gradation corresponding to different periods in western history, and behind those varying conditions the same group of causative forces. What determines the differences in quality of diet is the level of real income per head of population. In India and Pakistan, where the people's per capita income is under DM 300, the consumption of animal protein is minimal (6–7 grams per person per day), in Turkey, where the income is DM 825, consumption of animal protein is slightly higher (15 grams per person per day) and in Spain and Greece, with an average income of DM 1300, consumption is higher still at 22 grams per person per day.

The results are similar when meat consumption is compared with the national income per head of population (see figure 64).[4] The horizontal axis indicates annual

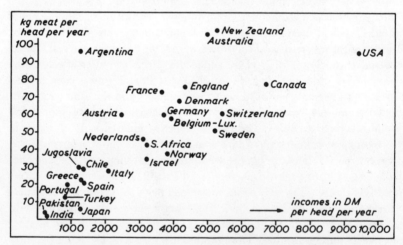

Fig. 64   National income and meat consumption in various countries.

income per head in DM, the vertical axis indicates annual meat consumption per head. A diagonal line could be drawn from near zero and across the graph to the consumption and income of the United States. Well to the side of this line lie three countries, Argentina, New Zealand and Australia. They have a relatively sparse population per unit of food-producing area, accompanied by advanced technical proficiency and organization.

How difficult it is to feed an undernourished but rapidly-increasing population and at the same time to raise the quantity (of calories) and quality of its diet is exemplified by Hanau with the help of the following calculation. Since the preparation of animal products involves an average loss of 80 per cent of calories originally present, the area of yield has to be five times larger than would be needed for directly-consumed plant products. Consequently, the number of primary calories per head to be produced must be increased by 54 per cent per head if the daily diet of 2,000 calories together with 10 per cent of consumable calories from animal products (making a total of 2,800 primary calories) is to be improved even to 2,400 calories, together with 20 per cent of consumable calories from animal products (making a total of 4,320 primary calories).

This calculation is relevant to present-day problems of the so-called developing countries, but it is also meaningful to the historian studying the history of western food economy.

Agricultural production

Farming structure

In the central and western Europe of 150 years ago there was little room left for the further expansion of agricultural land. In England the Continental Blockade had led to even the poorest soil being cultivated ('flinty hillsides and drifting sands', see above, page 224). On the continent the shortage forced the peasants to abandon their traditional farming system with its extensive permanent pastures and frequent fallow periods.

Thus the cultivation of hitherto-untilled soil could do little towards feeding the growing population. More important than the expansion of farmland was its optimal use, i.e. increasing the yield of soil already in cultivation. That is easily said, but such progress demanded a great deal. New methods, tools and systems had to be devised and human endeavour freed from its shackling bonds; land had to be transferred to the peasants and capital to the land; then all these innovations had to be set within a legal framework that would ensure a lasting and ever-increasing exploitation of the economic possibilities. That was the task tackled by the movement for freeing land and peasants on the continent, by the Enclosure Acts in England and by the new regulations for trade, industry, taxation and finance – in short, by the great reforms that were carried out in Europe in the late eighteenth and early nineteenth centuries and even later.

These reforms were also concerned with one of the most important and basic factors in agricultural activity: the size of farms. But history had already played its part. It may be of some use here to write a few words on the distribution of farm sizes in Europe and illustrate them with a map (figure 65). Since the international statistics available permit only an approximate picture, we must confine ourselves to a phase diagram. It represents the distribution of farms of

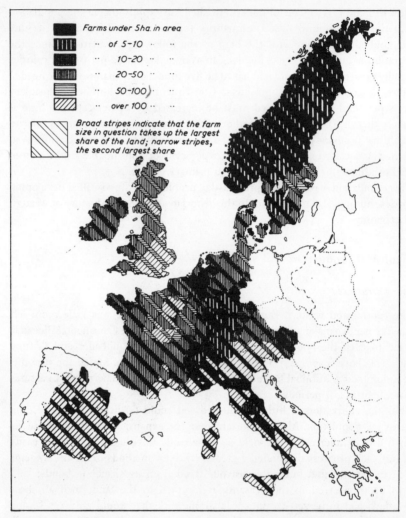

Fig. 65   The distribution of farm sizes in mid–twentieth–century western Europe.

various sizes in the mid–twentieth century. Admittedly, it does not give an accurate picture of the present situation, or of that of 150 years ago, but the important point is that during the whole of that long period the distribution of farm sizes in general did not alter greatly. Eastern Europe has been omitted because the agrarian reforms and revolutions since the first and second world wars have entirely changed the traditional farming structure there.

Figure 65 requires some explanation. The farms have been graded into the various size–divisions according to area farmed. Only for Norway and Sweden were they classified by area of arable and pasture (Norway) or by area of arable alone (Sweden) because the proportion of wasteland and rough grazing in those northern territories is disproportionately high. Farm sizes have been grouped into six different divisions. The statistics for the United Kingdom, Denmark and Italy are classified differently, but have been adjusted to fit in with the above scheme as far as possible. In general, as with the German figures, only farms of over 5 hectares have been taken into account. When it was not possible to keep within that limit, the established statistics for the nearest size groups were used. That was necessary in the case of Great Britain and Ireland (from 0.4 hectares upwards of the total area of land in agricultural use), Norway (from 0.5 hectares of arable and pasture), Sweden (from 0.25 hectares of arable), Denmark (from 0.55 hectares of farm area), the Netherlands (from 0.5 hectares of the total area of land in agricultural use, or 0.2 hectares of arable land and smallholdings used for horticulture or keeping one sheep, one horse or one cow), Belgium and France (from 1 hectare of farm area, under 1 hectare being professionally-managed specialized concerns) and Spain (all farms).

To arrive at the predominant divisions of farm sizes, the proportion of agricultural land falling into the various divisions had to be established. In France and Spain areas of cultivated land in the departments had not been classified by size, or else figures were not available. For that reason, and because the proportion there between farm sizes and the area of land in agricultural use on farms of up to 200 hectares is very stable, we have used the farm areas for classification in both those countries. In some countries agricultural land is not classified in the same way as is usual in Germany. Thus, to obtain comparable figures, the rough grazing in the United Kingdom and the mountain pastures in Switzerland have been separated from the land in agricultural use. The same could not be done for Austria, so that in figure 65 the Austrian farms appear larger than they should in comparison with those of other countries.[5]

The farm sizes represented in figure 65 can be divided roughly into four zones:

Zone 1 on the eastern border of the map, shows a type of distribution in which farms of 20–50 hectares in area take up the largest share of land in agricultural use. This zone stretches from southern Sweden over Denmark, Schleswig-Holstein, Lower Saxony, part of the Netherlands and, with a few interruptions in the central area of West Germany, to south-eastern Bavaria and beyond. In southern Sweden there are some administrative areas in which farms run by managers take up over 40 per cent of the land in agricultural use, in the districts of Göteborg, Malmöhus, Östergötland, Gotland, Västmanland and Uppsala. In second place come farms of 50–100 hectares in Östergötland, or smaller farms in the neighbouring districts. In Denmark farm sizes tend to fall somewhat under the 20–50 hectares limit, while in parts of the Netherlands (Groningen, Friesland, Drenthe, North and South Holland, Zeeland), as also in north-west Germany and south-east Bavaria, sizes gravitate more to the centre or upper limit, but here too the same group remains in first place. The situation persisted through all the changes in property management (grazing was predominant in Sweden and

Denmark in 1700) and agricultural economy. Certainly there were shifts within the group, but only quite recently have those trends intensified to a point where a considerable number of farms have grown beyond the upper limit of the group in question.

In *Zone 2*, adjoining the first zone on the west, farms of under 5 hectares claim the largest share of the land in agricultural use, followed by those of 5–10 hectares. The zone includes Norway, parts of Belgium, the West German wine-growing areas and reaches into France and Italy. It contains farms existing under very varied climatic and socio-economic conditions. In the north and in parts of the Alps the climate and relief set a limit to the size of farms. Flemish Brabant and the Rhineland, with their many towns, have long offered opportunities for intensive cultivation whereby a small area can produce a good yield, and made it possible for small farmers to find secondary employment in industry. The custom of dividing an estate among heirs, to which German historians have often attributed the fragmentation of landed property in western Germany, is of only minor importance in the heart of this region (though not always so along its borders).

That can be seen when we examine *Zone 3*, in which once more farms in the 20–50 hectares division predominate. This group includes most of France, where, the Civil Code having long ago legalized the distribution of land among living owners or as an inheritance, the dividing-up of landed property was quite usual. Nevertheless, it is middle-sized farms that still predominate in French agriculture today. In northern and central England, too, and in Ireland, a large proportion of the land in agricultural use belongs to this group.

In south-eastern England farms tend to be bigger. English statistics being based on other size categories, that part of the map had to be prepared from estimates only, but even so it is clear that the greater share of the land in agricultural use is occupied by farms of over 100 hectares. In exceptional cases the farm area is as much as 1,000 hectares. This phenomenon is connected with enclosure, which extended over waste and rough pasture, and with the English rental system. It secures, in fact if not in law, the tenant in the possession of the farm and any additional rented land for many years.

In France there are also farms with an area of over 100 hectares, especially in the Ile de France (with a share of the land in agricultural use amounting to 52.4 per cent in the *département* of Seine-et-Marne, 48 per cent in Aisne, 43.1 per cent in Oisne); in central France the proportion is 30 per cent (Cher 36.7, Indre 27), while many are found in southern France in a long strip covering nine *départements*, with a share in the total land in agricultural use ranging from 25.3 per cent (Aude) to 54.8 per cent (Bouches-du-Rhône). The origin of the large concerns in some parts of France (as in England, and in the region of great landed estates east of the Elbe and Saale not included here) goes back to the period of deserted villages in the late Middle Ages, when property became concentrated in a few hands. Even there the matter is not simple: capital and feudal power, in varying forms and with fluctuating importance, also played a part.

In the surroundings of Paris medium-sized farms began to decline in number
as early as the sixteenth and seventeenth centuries. They were broken up by the
pressure of rapidly-increasing population; smallholdings multiplied. It is said that
even at the start of the seventeenth century 1,133 such holdings were under
cultivation (Le Roy Ladurie, 1975:139ff.).[6] In many cases the larger farms were
able to maintain some 40 hectares (Dion, 1946, in Meuvret, 1971:177), but even
that did not last long. They seldom increased in size till the nineteenth or twentieth
century. Between 1830 and 1943 in the department of Oisne the number of farms
over 150 hectares rose from 55 to 124; in one canton of the *département* Aisne
Chézy-en-Orxois at the end of the century there were 25 farms, fifty years later
there were only 15. Sugar-beet-growing combined with modern technology
emptied the farmhouses. Agricultural concerns of up to 1000 hectares and over
– more than 2,500 hectares in a few cases and often with factories on the premises
– spread over the land.

Centrifugal developments of this sort, displacing the tradition of the medium-
sized farm, were also found by Le Roy Ladurie in the regions of great estates
in southern France (1966:1, 150ff.). Here too there had been extensive domains
ever since the fifteenth and sixteenth centuries. More modest estates were broken
up into 'micro-properties', incapable of supporting their owners and leading to
the 'pauperisation of the masses'.

Perhaps the situation in southern France was a presage of that in *Zone 4*, which
starts in Spain and spreads to southern Italy. Latifundia, much larger than in
France, extended over the countryside, while most of the peasants sank to the
level of a rural proletariat.

But those are marginal phenomena, both in the geographical and socio-economic
sense, in central and western Europe. It must be repeated that the distribution of
farm areas of such very different natures is hard to express in graphs and statistics
when the comparison extends over such a vast territory. The varying proportion
of rough grazing, woodland and waste does not make it easier. If one considers only
the intensively-tilled areas, as was done with Norway, Sweden and Switzerland,
the farms tend to look like smallholdings. If, on the other hand, we take the whole
area in agricultural use, as with Austria (where it was not possible to do otherwise) the farms appear to be very big, although in both cases, according to
economic and sociological standards, we are dealing with peasant farms or, in
other words, concerns run by small farmers.

Seen from this angle, the predominance of medium-sized farms in the part
of Europe under investigation becomes still more significant. In the United
Kingdom in the 1950s about 60 per cent of the total land in agricultural use was
occupied by farms of between 20 and 120 hectares; in France some 45 per cent
had an area of 20–100 hectares, a further 45 per cent were below 20 hectares,
while only 10 per cent were over 100 hectares. In Holland, parts of Belgium,
north-west and south-east Germany, Denmark and southern Sweden the typical
farm structure was much the same. In West Germany at the same time about

25 per cent of the agricultural land fell into each of the following four groups: up to 7.5 hectares, 7.5–15 hectares, 15–30 hectares, over 30 hectares. Since then there has been a slight upward shifting among the groups, but not enough to invalidate the situation depicted in figure 65: that small and medium-sized agricultural enterprises, adapted to regional conditions, predominate in western and central Europe.

That fact should be kept in mind when we turn our attention from the size of individual farms, only one aspect of our subject after all, to agricultural yield, the progress and development of which concern us more closely. Although East Germany, hitherto excluded, must now be drawn into the picture, the scope of this book requires us, in the following chapters, to concentrate only on the more significant phenomena.

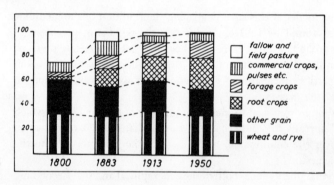

Fig. 66 The use of farmland in Germany 1800–1950

Intensification and changes in the production process

English agricultural historians sometimes describe the years between Queen Victoria's accession in 1837 and the great depression of the 1870s as the period of High Farming.[7] Those were the years when the Royal Agricultural Society of England was founded (1838); Liebig's work on the application of organic chemistry to the chemistry and physics of agriculture was translated into English (1840); new and better farming equipment came into use; older methods of land drainage were replaced by pipe drainage; and manuring, seed and livestock underwent great improvement – when, in short, farming innovations were introduced in profusion.

All this had a momentous effect on the extent and cultivation of agricultural land. Rough grazing dwindled. Fodder and commercial crops invaded the fields, potato-growing, already extolled by Adam Smith, covered ever more acres. The same phenomena, with modifications and to varying degrees, appeared in other lands. In many countries, up to the 1870s, agriculture became steadily more intensive, which meant that it required a greater investment of capital and/or labour to a given area. After that divergences set in between different lands and regions: in England there was a sharp decline in corn-growing, in Denmark and the Netherlands the changeover to intensive cultivation and livestock production was accelerated, in Germany, France and Italy, where corn-growing was protected by import duties, agriculture moved in the same general direction, but to a lesser degree.

Figure 66, which is drawn from Bitterman's figures (1956), illustrates the situation in Germany. It shows that cereal-growing remained more or less at its 1800 level. Since then it has declined by a small percentage (partly owing to the change in national boundaries). The area of root-crop cultivation expanded from 2.3 per cent of the arable area to 25.5 per cent, the fodder-crop area from 3.9 per cent to 13.5 per cent. This expansion took place at the expense of fallow land and leys which fell from 25 per cent of the farmland to 0.9 per cent.

At the same time animal husbandry increased (see figure 67). Between 1800 and 1935–8 the cattle population of Germany rose from about 10 million to 20 million and the pig population from 3.8 million to 24 million. Goat-keeping also increased considerably, but the number of sheep declined owing to the more intensive arable farming. Other branches of stock-breeding, however, were not adversely affected and the total number of livestock increased threefold between 1800 and 1935–8.

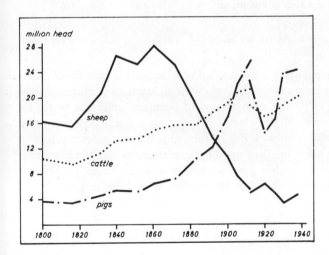

Fig. 67 Changes in livestock in Germany 1800–1938.

Increased yields

It will suffice to quote a few statistics for Germany. At the end of the eighteenth century and beginning of the nineteenth a hectare of land yielded some 10.3

double zentners of wheat, 9.0 double zentners of rye and 6.8 double zentners of oats. In 1950 the corresponding amounts were 27 double zentners, 22 double zentners, and 23 double zentners. The milk production per cow rose from about 860 kilograms to 2,400 kilograms. The dead weight of oxen went up from around 160 kilograms to over 300 kilograms, yet the time taken for the beasts to reach that weight was reduced by one fifth. The time taken by pigs to reach their full weight was reduced greatly: by roughly one half.

These figures can be combined with the aid of the 'grain value' devised by Woermann and his colleagues. The term 'grain value' (GV) includes nutritional content (with most plant products), relative yields (as with vines, hops and tobacco) and fodder norms (with animal products) in relation to grain.[8] By using this concept Bittermann, from whom the above figures were taken, reckons that during the last 150 years German farm production per unit of area has increased five and a half times. If that figure is compared with the number of inhabitants, it appears that agricultural yield was not only able to keep pace with the population explosion but sometimes even overtook it (see table 26).

Table 26 The growth of agricultural production in Germany

Production	1800	1900	1950
Net farm production in GV per hectare	4.5	13.1	23.5
Net production in GV per head of population	5.6	8.1	6.9

Net farm production = vegetable and livestock production after deducting seed, fodder for draught animals and purchases.

As the number of inhabitants increased, however, so also did their demands. At the beginning of the nineteenth century, when the annual meat consumption was about 15 kilograms per head, the population of Germany could still be fed on some 5.6 double zentners of grain units. When meat consumption rose to 40 kilograms per head and over, as it did in the industrial era, it formed part of a total consumption of more than 10 double zentners of grain value. This increased demand for the higher-value foodstuffs could no longer be supplied entirely from home territory. It had to be supplemented by imports.

World-wide division of labour

As transport grew cheaper and the political obstacles to commerce began to fade away, the local differences which had become noticeable in the sixteenth century evolved into an international division of agrarian labour. At first the thickly-populated and highly-industrialized north-western corner of Europe bounded by the triangular London–Paris–Ruhr district was regarded as 'the town' and 'the world'. Round this 'urban area', writes Schiller, (1940:11f.), spread 'an intensively-exploited zone of improved cultivation and horticulture. Next to that stretched the great east European corn-belt. The outermost ring was formed by the yet more extensive cultivated areas overseas.' Between the last two zones lay Europe's peripheral agricultural areas, especially those of the Mediterranean lands whose share in world agricultural trade consisted almost entirely of a few special crops such as semi-tropical and dried fruits. The intensive zones supplied the animal and horticultural products consumed in the industrial areas; from the extensive zones came the agricultural raw material needed for industry itself, and also the livestock products from the steppes. During the nineteenth century still other supply zones came into being, especially in America and the Far East.

In the heart of industrial Europe some areas still remained under less intensive forms of agriculture. In spite of the extensive type of farming practised in the overseas supply zones, a number of them began to manufacture dairy products which soon entered into competition with the dairy-farming areas of the old world (Denmark, the Netherlands, Sweden, Switzerland and Ireland). But on the whole this 'zonal economy' prevailed and, because of it, the peoples of Europe were better fed.

That, in very rough outline, answers the question of how the food supply problems that beset western and central Europe in the late eighteenth and early nineteenth centuries were overcome. The answer is incomplete, however, as long as only consumption and supply are considered. It is time to bring the other aspects of the economy of food supply into the picture: trade turnover, price structure, farming returns and their fluctuations.

11 Agrarian crises during the industrial era

The phase of international adjustment within Europe (1830–70)

The repeal of the English Corn Laws

At the beginning of the 1830s there were wide differences between the grain prices of the various European countries. Danish domestic prices were the lowest, English the highest. Somewhere between came French and German grain prices. In the course of the next five decades the balance changed to the point where Danish, German and French prices rose while English prices sank (see figure 68). These movements must be borne in mind if one seeks to understand the complaints of the English landlords and farmers. While on the continent, after the agrarian depression of the 1820s, the agrarian upswing that had begun in the eighteenth century continued with undiminished vigour, in England parliament was forming a Select Committee to inquire into agricultural distress.

When the price of cereals began to rise again in 1830 people in England thought the depression was over. Landlords and tenants arranged new leases based on a wheat price of 56–64 shillings per quarter; to a small extent they even began to plough the deserted fields again.[1] After a few successive harvests had fetched pitifully low prices, however, the crisis broke out once more. In May 1833 yet another Select Committee was summoned to inquire into agricultural distress, and the testimony of numerous witnesses from many countries was recorded. The same complaint came up time after time: prices were too low, costs were too high, and consequently rents could not be paid. Tenants were impoverished and less corn was being grown.

Scarcely had the 1833 Committee's report been made public, when both Houses of Parliament instituted new inquiries into the state of agriculture. No effective results, however, emerged from the voluminous evidence, confirmed though it was by documents and accounts, heard by the new 1836 Committee. The thousands

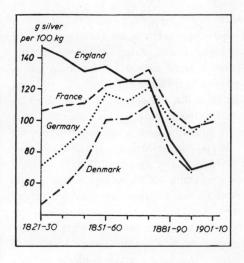

Fig. 68   Some European wheat prices 1821–1910.

of answers given by the witnesses questioned could only confirm that the tenant had indeed reason to complain. The narrow margin between farming costs and returns was not enough to pay landlord and state and to support a family.

During the next four years, from 1837 to 1842, the English farmers' lot was relatively favourable. Industry, on the other hand, had its troubles, for England was afflicted by a severe industrial and commercial crisis. It was thought that a reduction of the grain import duty might ease the situation. On Sir Robert Peel's suggestion the duty that had been fixed since 1828 was lowered in 1842, but it was hoped (or feared) that even with this reduced tax the price of wheat might stay at 56 shillings a quarter.

The first breach had been made in England's lofty tariff wall. In the ensuing years, and especially in March 1845, numerous petitions complaining of impoverishment and ruin were again being presented to parliament by landowners, tenants and tradespeople, and the government decided only one year later, in 1846, to abolish the Corn Laws altogether. A greatly-diminished tariff scale was to remain in operation until 1849 to prepare for the introduction of Free Trade. From 1 February 1849 the duty exacted for a quarter of imported wheat was only one shilling. As the sum was so small, the price of English wheat immediately adjusted to the French price and only differed from the Danish and German prices by the amount required for transport, expenses and the dealer's profit.

The 'golden decades' of continental farming

As early as 1830 Germany had experienced a slight improvement in its economic situation. In the *Neuen Annalen der Mecklenbürger Landwirtschafts-Gesellschaft* of 1832 a farmer wrote that the tenant's 'position and circumstances have improved during the last few years owing to the higher prices, whereas the landlord, who in bad times was forced to let his farms at rents far too low for today's conditions, is at a disadvantage'. In the ensuing years rents were gradually adjusted to prevailing prices, but where the landlord did not demand a maximum rent there was enough margin left for the tenant, too, to build up his resources. Thus the average rent of farms on Prussian estates rose from 13.90 RM per hectare in 1849 to 31.18 RM in 1869. Nevertheless, August Meitzen was able to say of these leasehold properties in the early 1870s that they were 'till very recently among the most intelligently-run concerns, and a big proportion of the tenants have managed to accumulate comfortable fortunes in spite of considerable expenses and improvements' (1871:419; leases in Conrad 1900:225).

Crop rotation and the improved three-course system had by now replaced the old convertible husbandry and primitive forms of the three-course rotation in Germany as elsewhere. A deeper and more thorough cultivation of the soil had become habitual everywhere; animal husbandry had undergone a sweeping reorganization and farm implements were greatly improved. The use of artificial manures, which had increased rapidly since the mid-nineteenth century, contributed still more to the gross returns so that, in spite of the steadily rising wages, net profit went up as well.

These conditions naturally influenced the price of agricultural property. Meitzen reported in 1870 that 'generally speaking' large agricultural estates were being sold for three or even four times as much as they had fetched in the 1820s. He added that ordinary farms had become relatively even more expensive. Whether or not his estimate is exact cannot now be verified. Evidence exists only in the case of a small number of properties and farming estates, and only for a few years. Thus it can be seen in the report of an inquiry instituted by the Prussian Chamber of Deputies in 1851 that farm properties rose in price by 25–50 per cent between 1830 and 1840, whereas knights' estates fetched 50, 80 and 100 per cent more than their tax valuations. The difference, however, lasted only one decade.

The following are examples of how the price of single properties developed: the estate of Naulin in the Pomeranian district of Pyritz was bought for 278,100 RM in 1838, valued at 738,000 RM on inheritance in 1871, and estimated to be worth 960,000 RM in 1894. Buchenberger quotes an estate that rose in value from 84,000 RM in 1819 to 260,000 RM in 1852, 510,000 RM in 1862 and finally to 855,000 RM in 1871 (Weyermann, 1910:182f.; von der Goltz, 1903:273; Buchenberger, 1897:60; Steinbruck, 1900:29f.).

The prices of a number of large farm complexes have been recorded. They were worked out by the Mecklenburg Statistics Bureau in 1858. According to their calculations, which go back to the 1770s, the price of these estates rose by roughly two and a half times between 1811–30 and 1851–60 (see figure 69). That increase resembled the upsurge in the late eighteenth and early nineteenth

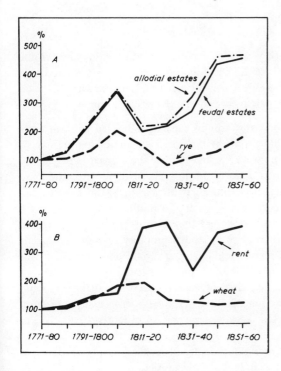

Fig. 69
Prices of farmland and rye in Mecklenburg-Schwerin 1771–1860.
The rent of a 225-acre farm in Norfolk and the price of wheat, 1771–1860.

centuries which was interrupted by the fall in land values that followed the Napoleonic wars. The Mecklenburg prices correspond in general outline to the movement of land values and rents in the Netherlands and in France.[2]

In England the change came later. England's tariff policy delayed first the onset of the depression and later the recovery of cereal prices and rents, as can be seen very clearly in the graph on Norfolk farms that forms the lower half of figure 69.[3] So it was that, after a certain delay, English farming took its part in the 'golden decades' of continental agriculture. Landlords and tenants said no more about their grievances. Capital and energy were poured into the land to such good purpose that by the 1860s the cultivated area was even more extensive than before the slump. Between 1808 and 1866 the proportion of farmland taken up by arable in England and Wales rose from 40 per cent to 58 per cent; the proportion of permanent pasture went down from 60 per cent to 42 per cent. Among the arable crops, wheat's share of the farmland increased from 10.9 per cent to 13.2 per cent, that of root crops from 4.0 per cent to 10.1 per cent. These increases are at least as impressive as their continental equivalents and may even have overtaken them in the 1850s and early 1860s (see Prothero, 1912:456, 466f.; Williams, 1960:121f.; Chambers and Mingay, 1970; among others).

Speculation in landed property; excessive debt and credit crises

The long-term nineteenth-century boom did not result in an adjustment to the conditions of the time. It culminated, as had its eighteenth-century predecessor, in excess, particularly in the price of landed property. A contemporary German witness described conditions in relatively-conservative Bavaria this way:

> The high prices obtained for crops around the year 1854 led to farm rents soaring up and up. People thought of the high prices as something permanent and the seven-league-boot progress became part of their creed. Because the release of economic forces after 1848 made progress so rapid, they supposed it would continue indefinitely, forgetting that the growth of those forces had a natural limit and would soon exhaust itself. To profit from the progress a man would have had to buy early, before the prices soared sky-high. Land fever became an epidemic. The price of landed property grew to monstrous proportions. Those who had merely sold a farm at a good profit were not considered the lucky ones, but those who by its purchase had acquired the chance to turn it into a gold mine, and that, of course, was what all farms would become in the future. Because rents had risen, the farm was worth more. Very soon the situation was reversed: because land was so expensive, rents had to be put up. Farming was pervaded by the atmosphere of the stock exchange. It was not only that the prevailing agricultural returns were considered as normal and permanent: they were looked on as a mere prelude to still higher rents in the future, and for that the purchasers were willing to pay inordinate amounts.... In short, the characteristic economy of the previous decade and the first years of the present one was, above all, one of speculation. (Ditz, 1868:142)

During the 1860s the Prussian government instituted an inquiry into the frequency with which knights' estates in their territory had changed hands between 1835 and 1864 (Rodbertus-Jagetzow, 1868: appendix, also p. 50). Out of all the estates investigated in the eastern provinces, each property had, on the average, changed ownership more than twice (2.14 times) during the thirty years: 60.2 per cent through voluntary sale, 34.7 per cent through inheritance and 5.1 per cent through enforced sales.

The over-assessment of land values led to a *growing amount of debt*. One gathers from an investigation carried out by the Prussian Ministry of Justice (dated 14 October 1857) that the 'visible assets' of landed properties in six east German districts doubled between 1837 and 1857, but that the indebtedness of the same properties more than doubled during those twenty years (see table 27).[4]

The indebtedness of the larger estates (knights' estates) in the Merseburg-Halle district of Saxony-Anhalt rose even more steeply, as can be seen in figure 70, which shows how the gap widened between the price of rye and the cost of commodities on one hand, and between the latter prices and the burden of debt

Table 27   Prices and debts of farm property in six Prussian districts between 1837 and 1857

Prices and debts	1837		1847		1857	
	Thalers	%	Thalers	%	Thalers	%
Visible assets	6,895,772	100	10,144,654	148	13,737,029	200
Indebtedness	5,498,284	100	8,787,280	160	11,076,974	202

on the other, the indebtedness being the higher value (Steinbruck, 1900:29f.; the price of rye from Conrad, 1879:83).

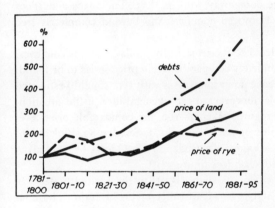

Fig. 70   Price of rye and prices and indebtedness of landed property in Saxony-Anhalt 1781–1895.

The increased land values entered in the mortgage deeds in some parts of Germany (and doubtless elsewhere) developed in a similar way. Rodbertus-Jagetzow, who had fought for credit reform in the 1860s, described the situation in the following words: 'The greater part of the increased value was no longer attached to the land as capital. It now became a burden on the estate instead of a resource.' The burden grew steadily heavier until it became insupportable. From the 1830s right into the 1860s one credit failure followed another. Most of these troubles were purely local, but at the end of the 1860s a real credit crisis spread from the large estates of north-eastern Germany to the farms of the south and west. Farm prices were high and continued to rise. The rate of interest, however, had gone up: on private mortgages it was now 4 or 5 per cent. That slight increase was enough to bring on a spate of forced sales and to push down the price of commodities in the affected areas.

The crisis soon passed. It was only a prelude to the much more harmful and long-lasting depression of prices that overtook the economy of Europe and the world during the 1870s.

The phase of world-wide crises

The agrarian depression of the late nineteenth century

The repeal of the Corn Laws in England was a stimulus to free trade aspirations on the continent. Napoleon III favoured liberal ideas. In 1856 he put a Free Trade Act before the parliament. Although his project was not accepted, wheat duties were thenceforth levied only in years of good harvest, and shortly afterwards he managed, without consulting parliament, to arrange a trade agreement, the famous Cobden Free Trade Treaty of 1860, whereby taxes on most foods and raw materials were greatly reduced or even abolished. Cavour in Italy followed the same policy. Except in the southern part of the country import duties on wheat vanished altogether after 1854. In Germany the grain import duties still contained in the 1834 customs union tariff were done away with in 1853. The 1850s and 1860s saw the grain trade of all the European countries and beyond completely free of tariffs.

The result was that cereal prices became remarkably similar in all the countries. Unfortunately, there are no completely comparable grain price series to be found, even for this period. We must make do in some cases with very roughly-estimated 'national averages'. It is possible, however, to get a general idea of the situation. If the price of wheat in Amsterdam is taken as 100, the comparable price level in other regions was: in the Baltic area – Denmark 77, Sweden 80, Finland 69; towards south-eastern Europe – Vienna 82, Budapest 68, Odessa 61; in Italy – Udine 93, Rome 89; in New York, 96 (see figure 71).[5]

The drop in the New York price was slight. By 1850 the United States was as yet supplying Europe with only a small quantity of bread grain. The total export of wheat from the United States between 1851 and 1860 was 5 million bushels compared with 41 million bushels supplied by Russia during the same period (and 107 million bushels from the United States in the years 1875–9). In the 1850s the prairies west of the Mississipi were still thinly populated and the transport costs were heavy.

After the Civil War (1865) more people began to settle in the west. The wheat-growing area of the United States doubled between 1865 and 1880, and during this period a network of railways spread across the land and shipping was vastly improved. The cost of transporting wheat from New York to Liverpool, which was 21 cents a bushel (gold currency) in 1873, had fallen to under 3 cents a bushel by 1901.

The reduction of freight charges had already begun in the age of sail. Even after 1873 sail was the leading form of transport for long voyages and bulk articles, but sailing ships had become more efficient and, moreover, the threat of steam navigation sharpened the demands of the ship-owners and captains. The cost of sea transport fell even more than the price of grain, and, relatively speaking, the

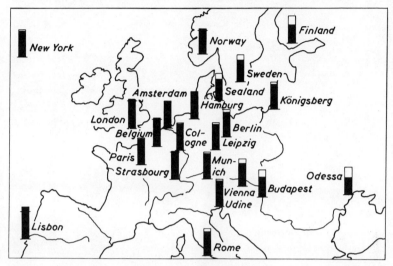

Fig. 71   Wheat prices in Europe and U.S.A. 1851–1860.

longer the voyage, the more steeply the freight charges dropped (North, 1958:537f.).

In Europe the price of cereals was forced down by the cheap imported wheat from overseas. Prices began to fall at the end of the Franco-Prussian War, were held up for a time by a series of bad harvests in the late 1870s and early 1880s (and, on the continent, by some political tariff measures) and then fell sharply again during the 1880s and early 1890s. In England, where free trade still prevailed, the rock-bottom price was reached in 1894: 22 shillings 10 pence for a quarter of wheat. English wheat had fetched about three times as much in 1867–8. The effects of the import duties imposed in 'Germany since 1879 (1 mark per 100 kilograms of wheat, 5 marks after 1880) and in France since 1885 (3 francs per 100 kilograms of wheat) were already making themselves felt. The amount by which the Franco-German price exceeded the English price corresponded more-or-less to those tariffs. They succeeded in slightly flattening the price depression, but certainly did not level it out (see figure 72).[6]

There is little out of the ordinary to report on this depression. Events followed the usual pattern: in England rents fell, and on the continent the farmers lost heavily. According to a weighted index calculated by Rhee, English rents dropped from 106.5 between 1874 and 1877 to 76 in 1894, the year when grain prices were at their lowest, then went down still further to 71 in 1899, a low-point that was repeated in 1904. The continuation of depressed rents after the price of corn had begun to recover is easily accounted for by the different structure of grain prices and the abandonment of land as a main source of income (see figure 73).[7]

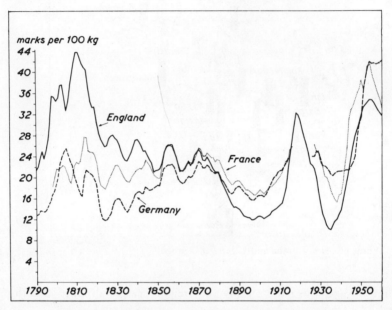

Fig. 72   Wheat prices in England, France and Germany 1790–1960.

On the continent most of the landowners managed their own farms. That must have been the situation Max Sering (one of the first historians and agrarian economists to study the phenomena of agricultural slumps) had in mind when he defined an agricultural slump as: 'a price structure with an attendant ratio of revenue to costs and burdens such as put many a farmer in danger of losing his house and land, and threatened whole districts with dereliction'. It is true that a certain number of farmer-owners lost their farms, but the 'threat' was worse than the actual losses. As far as can be ascertained, even in Germany, where the situation was as bad as anywhere, forced sales were kept well within bounds (see Conrad, 1909:206f.; further, Sering, 1887, 1935). In Baden between 1883 and 1890 about 1,600 concerns with 7,000 hectares of farmland in all were compulsorily auctioned; in Bavaria in 1890–1900 the same fate overtook 11,400 concerns with 89,000 hectares. In Prussia 5,650 farms totalling 200,000 hectares went bankrupt. That came to 0.2 per cent of all the existing farms and 0.7 per cent of the farming area. At that time Prussia contained 3.3. million farms with a total agricultural area of 28.5 million hectares.

Nor was there much sign of 'dereliction' on the continent. The grain-growing area of France hardly varied. In Germany pasture was turned over to arable (the ratio of pasture to arable was 1 : 2.44 in 1870, 1 : 2.93 in 1893 and 1 : 2.98 in 1900). Intensive agriculture and more intensive forms of animal husbandry came to the fore in Belgium, the Netherlands and Denmark. It was only in England that this type of farming became more extensive, as figure 74 illustrates.[8] Between

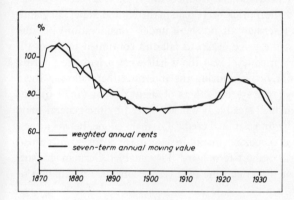

Fig. 73   Rents in England and Wales 1870–1935.

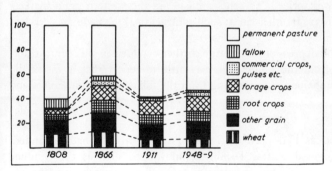

Fig. 74   Use of farmland in England and Wales 1808–1950.

1866 and 1911 the wheat-growing area declined from 13.2 per cent to 6.8 per cent of the total farmland, root crops from 10.1 per cent to 7.9 per cent, forage crops from 12.2 per cent to 10.6 per cent, pulses and commercial crops from 3.5 per cent to 2.1 per cent, and the arable area as a whole from 58 per cent to 42 per cent. The land no longer cultivated was used for grazing. The proportion of pasture rose from 42 per cent to 58 per cent of the farming area.

The agrarian depression between the two world wars

With the coming of the new century rents and land values on the continent began to rise again. At a meeting of the Prussian House of Representatives on 7 February 1907 the Minister of Agriculture, von Arnim, spoke of 'a general increase in the price of land, which is rapidly approaching a critical level' (Conrad). The First World War sent the cost of land and its produce still higher, wherever it was given free scope. The highest wheat prices were paid in the United States, England, France and other countries (Germany is not here under consideration) in June 1920. After the 1920 harvest the price began to fall and continued to do so till December 1921. In 1922 the price level was about half what it had been during the first years of the post-war boom. During the interlude that followed there were a few years of recovery (1924–5) and others of slight decline (1926–9), but on the whole the market remained steady. It was supported by the general trade boom and, to a great extent, by international credit. Germany alone, between 1924 and 1928, received some 6,000,000,000 marks in long-term loans from abroad and about 4,000,000,000 marks in short-term loans. That enabled German industry to pay the reparations and at the same time to invest a considerable amount of capital.

At the end of 1929 this relatively favourable situation deteriorated. Between November 1929 and September 1931, the price of wheat dropped to about half its former level, and from then till 1934 fell by a few more per cent, reckoned in gold currency. In the United States, which went off the gold standard in April 1933, the lowest price – 50 cents a bushel in the western grain markets – was recorded in 1932. In other lands, such as Argentina, the nadir was reached in 1934.

The effects of the depression will not be further explored in this context, for, once again, apart from the timing, there is little to report that is essentially different. Its more obvious causes sprang from the following circumstances and events:

(1) New land areas had been cultivated. Wheat-growing had expanded, especially in the United States. Technical innovations such as the combine harvester driven by its own motor or power take-off, the tractor, dry farming, and new varieties of wheat facilitated that expansion, or indeed made it possible at all in the semi-desert regions of the west.

(2) The automation of farming had freed great tracts of farmland for the production of food. It is estimated that in the United States nearly as much land was gained through the diminished need for forage crops as through new cultivation.

(3) Instead of taking advantage of the fact that debts had been transformed into demand and modifying their trading policy, the United States heightened

their tariff wall, thus preventing the debts from being repaid in the form of goods.

(4) The United States farmer no longer ruled the world market. He was threatened by competition from the farmers of Canada, Australia and South America. They could produce more cheaply than their United States rivals, perhaps to the same not insignificant degree as, two generations earlier, the Americans' forebears had been able to undersell the Europeans.

(5) Under the auspices of Lenin's New Economic Policy the Soviet Union began to export grain once more. Europe's domestic production also increased. The wheat yield of Europe without the Soviet Union, which had amounted to 37 million tons in the years 1909–13 and then dropped to 30 million in 1920–3, had increased by 1933 to 47.5 million tons, thus by roughly 10 million more than before the First World War.

Doubtless the list could be extended. It does not claim to be complete. But if more points were added, we should lose track of the phenomenon we seek to interpret as a unity.

The causes of the depressions

There have been repeated attempts to account for the last two or even three depressions by some theory resting on a unified basis. Unfortunately these theories do not agree with each other. As on earlier occasions, a monetary theory has been advanced, in addition to theories of under-consumption or over-production.

The monetary explanation, especially popular among wide and influential circles in the Anglo-Saxon countries,[9] centred round the apparent coincidence in time between agrarian slumps and certain currency manipulations supposed to diminish the circulation of money. Great Britain went on to the gold standard in 1819. In the early 1870s many countries, including Germany, Italy, the United States, Austria-Hungary, Russia and Japan, followed her example. The consequent growing demand for gold put up the price of that metal or (which came to the same thing) caused the price of commodities to drop. After the First World War the situation repeated itself. The gold standard, suspended during hostilities, was reinstated and led once again to a rise in the value of gold or, alternately, a fall in the value of goods.

The monetary theories are contradicted, however, by the fact that prices had begun to decline *before* the currency manipulations (before 1819 and 1925, that is to say). Nor can they explain the way prices were scattered during the deflation. Even when incomes and the income-elasticity of the demand for goods are called in to aid the argument, it is hard to see why a shrinkage in the circulation of money (and consequently in incomes) should hit grain prices first of all, in recent slumps just as it had in the past. If the price-reducing impulse had stemmed from reduced incomes, one might suppose that the cost of goods in income-elastic demand, such as meat, butter and so on, would be the first to fall. Those, however, were the commodities whose prices remained steadiest in recent as in earlier slumps.

The price of manufactured goods reacted similarly. Kondratieff spoke of a 'relative boom in industry'. When farm prices went up, he reasoned (1928:56f.), so did the purchasing power of farming produce: when prices fell it declined. This process took the form of long-term waves that, between the late eighteenth century and early twentieth century, rose three times to a crest and twice sank to a trough. These 'long waves' of Kondratieff's can be discerned in the graph of grain prices, figure 72.

Kondratieff's description and interpretation of the long-term waves gave rise to extensive discussion – summarized by Imbert (1959) in 532 pages! The discussion centred mainly on the question of what relationship existed, or could have existed between these trends and the short-term fluctuations of the industrial age, known as the Juglar Cycle. As far as historical evidence is concerned (see Spiethoff, Schumpeter, and others) it could be established that the phases of the long-term trends influenced the duration and intensity of the short-term fluctuations (or vice versa), not only in prices but also in volume of production. Schumpeter went a step further. He thought that the causes of these movements, whatever their duration, were connected, indeed were basically one and the same, namely 'innovations'. The curves rose to a peak at the time of the industrial revolution (the end of the eighteenth century and the first half of the nineteenth) when the textile industry was mechanized, and again when railways were invented and first spread over the land between the 1840s and the 1870s. The third upsurge, from 1870 to the First Wold War, coincided with the introduction of electric power and improvements in mining, in the iron industry and in communications. Between these upsurges came periods of stagnation during which the innovations were digested, the obsolete discarded and the next upswing prepared for.

This school of thought pushed the agrarian cycle into the background or even quite out of the researcher's field of vision. Most authors now felt it unnecessary to discuss the subject (as even Kondratieff had done). The few who continued to study it did so quite aside from the mainstream of research, and thus not under the most favourable circumstances. That was true of Ciriacy-Wantrup (1936) who took up the discarded theory of under-consumption once more and sought to explain the earlier and steeper falls in the price of grain by the activities of commerce, and of Sirol (1942), who, on the contrary, pointed out that the 'long-term rise and fall of the European and American economy since the end of the eighteenth century' had been largely determined by agriculture.

Of course there are connections, but they are specific and not as yet explained. One has but to think of farming incomes and the degree to which they were spent on either consumption ('when the farmer has gold, the world's his oyster') or investment. Without doubt the railways in the 1830s and 1840s were largely financed out of rents, but, as agriculture's share in the national income diminished, the influence excercised by agricultural revenue grew weaker. Conversely, consumers' incomes were vital to the farmer. When 60 per cent or more of the net farm profits come from the sale of animal products in income-elastic demand, that much is plain. However, that level of production and consumption was not reached until our own century. As long as cereals or potatoes were the basic foods a decline in consumer purchasing-power could not make people turn to still 'cheaper' provisions. Consumption could not be reduced; need had to be satisfied at the expense of industrial products in income-elastic demand, as has been observed time and time again in the comparable case of harvest failures.

It is not irrelevant, therefore, to look for a basic endogenous reason for agrarian depressions during the nineteenth and twentieth centuries. Until further research discovers a more convincing link between the industrial sector's long-term trends and the agrarian cycle, the theory of over-production seems to offer the most likely explanation of farming depressions and their related booms.

When prices sank after the Napoleonic wars Thünen observed the coincidence of a series of good harvests with an increase in farming activity 'due to un-naturally high land prices' characteristic of the years just before a slump. At that time the farmers of Europe, with English tenants, Flemish peasants and east German landowners in the vanguard, were driving up production, abetted after the mid-century by the still-more-energetic overseas farmers.

In 1800 the chief burden of increased production fell on human labour. Freed from many of their bonds, the peasants gave of their best and produced more. In 1850 the centre of gravity shifted to the land; in our own century it shifted to capital, in the form of technical aids at the disposal of the farmer before the production process begins: improved machinery, plants, animals and farming methods. All these changes threatened future depressions with longer duration, wider fluctuations and greater severity, for the potentialities of technical and scientific research are almost boundless.

Nevertheless the essential character of the depressions did not change. At the heart of all their manifestations lay the fact that they were crises of over-production or, more accurately, the alternating phases of inflation and readjustment appertaining to an agrarian cycle that accompanied and upheld the vast expansion of European and overseas agriculture from the end of the eighteenth century onwards.

Summary and conclusion

Long-term trends in the agrarian economy of western and central Europe since the high Middle Ages

We have come a long way. It has led us through periods and associations hitherto seldom explored. The economic historian, in Germany at least, has preferred to study the systems, laws and institutions of the economy; the taxonomist has been content with structures and data, hardly reaching back beyond the nineteenth century, viewing what lay further in the past as arcane knowledge.

Yet there has been no lack of material or of questions. Since the time of the classic economists there have been theories of diminishing returns from the land, declining food resources, the rising purchasing power of agricultural products and the differential movement of wages and rents. For a long time scholars have carried out research on the history of prices, wages, population and production. In essence, it only remained to relate the material and the questions to each other and by purposeful research to add a little here and there to the fund of knowledge.

In the forefront of the investigation stand the long-term trends in the price of grain. They cannot be explained adequately by fluctuations in the circulation of money, though that has been attempted often since the time of Jean Bodin (1568). Even when improved forms of the simple quantity theory are summoned to the rescue, the discrepancies of time apparent in the course of the price movements remain inexplicable. Wages in the fourteenth and fifteenth centuries followed the downward curve of grain prices only very slowly. In the sixteenth century they lagged well behind, and during the next price deflation the purchasing power of wages went up again.

The prices of animal products and manufactured goods moved in a similar way. They can be thought of as the point at which lines extending from the movements of grain prices and wages would intersect. Connected with the price of cereals, the basic price of all pre-industrial goods, was the exchangeability of household commodities (bread in place of meat, for instance) and the possibility of changing the direction of production (grain instead of cattle, or vice versa). Wages were related to the income-elasticity of demand and, in the case of industrial goods, to the cost structure of supply. Thus it could happen that when wages began to diverge from the price of grain a reciprocal relationship was formed between the prices of grain, animal products and industrial goods, in which grain prices rose furthest during a boom period and fell furthest during a slump.

That suggests that behind the price and wage curves stood changes in the structure of supply and demand. Until the nineteenth century the density of population can be seen developing in more-or-less the same direction as the price of grain and in inverse ratio to wages, as far as the latter can be measured in units of commodities (see figure 75).[1]

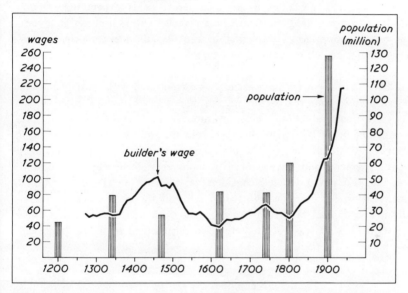

Fig. 75   The population of western and central Europe and builders' wages in southern England from the thirteenth to the twentieth century.

The effects of the changes in prices, wages and population on agrarian production and returns are hard to separate from one another and far from easy to distinguish from the immediate consequences of contemporary events such as wars, feuds, domestic unrest and so on. Their influence can also be obscured by factors seldom recorded among the data of economic theory (meagre market quotas from peasant farms, and social obligations, for instance). Exactly how close the connection was between prices, farming activities and the income derived from farming remains unproved. It is certain, however, that there were parallel movements.

This can be seen, firstly, in the extent and expansion of the farming area. In the words of Schülter, the geographer: 'As if Europe were alternately breathing in and breathing out, we see periods in which the people feel an urge to settle on the land in great numbers and cultivate it, and others in which they tend to concentrate on a few points and lines, while the rural population shrinks or increases relatively slowly' (1903:209). The reclamation and rural settlement of the twelfth and thirteenth centuries were followed in the late Middle Ages by the period of deserted farms. Another outbreak of agrarian expansion accompanied the higher prices in the sixteenth century and extended far to the east and north of Europe, while a third wave of farming activity broke out in Germany soon after the end of the Thirty Years War and spread to other lands a few decades later.

Secondly, the long-term trends of grain prices affected the intensity of agriculture. No matter whether we are considering yields, expenditure, farming systems or farming techniques, the decisive advances always occurred in a period of long-term rise in prices. Times of falling agricultural prices were characterized by recession, stagnation or, at best, by very modest progress in farming development.

Thirdly, these long-term price-trends were connected with farming incomes. That had been so from the beginning, and indeed was so by definition, for that part of the agricultural output which, measured in market values, can be counted as a source of profit derived exclusively from the soil, or, in other words, for the rents of Ricardian theory. It also applied, if only in a diluted form, to the stipulated payments and services of an economic system in which not only the market but also power exerted considerable influence on the distribution of income, that is, for example, the feudal rents of the early market economy. Finally it also applied to peasant wages which, although made up of earnings and rents did, in the case of medium-sized farms, tend to follow rents when wages and rents diverged.

The mid-nineteenth century break in development

Malthus and Ricardo had a long-term evolutionary development in mind when they referred to the difficulties involved in feeding a growing population. They thought that the price of farm produce would undoubtedly go up in relation to that of industrial goods. Wages would go up as well, but only cash wages. Real wages, measured in corn value, would sink, because they were dependent on the marginal profit of labour, which, in farming, decreased as cultivation expanded. Rents, on the other hand, would rise in both cash and corn value, so that agricultural progress would inevitably be accompanied by

1 rising rents
2 the price of grain lagging behind rents
3 the price of industrial goods lagging behind grain prices
4 workers' wages bringing up the rear

The evidence shows that until the mid-nineteenth century prices and income developed exactly as Malthus and Ricardo had predicted. Rents, judged by the rents of unencumbered farms, and the price of land, taking the rate of interest into account, both increased considerably; wages lagged behind, and the price of cereals rose absolutely in relation to the price of industrial goods.

On the threshold of the industrial age, however, a break in the development was plainly visible. This can be represented in a series of graphs, as in figure 76.[2] The presentation may seem questionable in that it spans the centuries, paying no heed to periodic fluctuations, but it is acceptable as an illustration of the basic principle. In that period when farming was dominant the price of wheat in England increased more than fivefold, wages threefold and the price of iron by 4 per cent. In Germany the price of rye went up barely fourfold, wages by 50 per cent and the price of iron by 70 per cent. When we take the last prices of the agrarian age as the starting prices of the industrial era, the relationships are reversed: wages have now far outstripped prices.

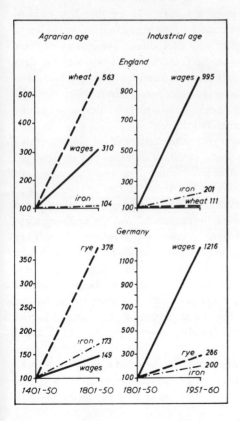

Fig. 76 Price and wage movements in England and Germany.

The causes of the changeover of price and wage curves have already been discussed fully. During the industrial age agriculture lost the function assigned to it by the classic economists of acting as an indicator of wages and a regulator of prices. Industry took the lead and freed wages from the fetters of the 'diminishing returns from the land' and made possible or enforced a change of emphasis combined with an extraordinary upsurge of agrarian activity. In the pre-industrial age every measure for increasing production was aimed at the land itself and at labour. Those measures were relatively cheap but not highly effective. Now the main expenditure had shifted to the means of production, i.e. capital in the rapidly-changing and ever more productive forms in which it became available to the farmer.

Agricultural depressions

Such is the background against which the agricultural slumps must be assessed. Buchenberger (1897:201) defined them as 'circumstances characterized by a persistent recession of farming returns, rendering the owner's position more difficult and involving the great mass of the agricultural classes'. According to Sering (1925:1) they consisted of 'a price structure with an attendant ratio of revenue to costs and burdens such as put many a farmer in danger of losing house and land, and threatened whole districts with dereliction. The history of these depressions went back far beyond the nineteenth century. It began in the days when towns first grew too big to supply their demand for farm produce from their own fields. It was at that early stage that rural industry lost the self-sufficient independence of primitive times. Landlords and peasants became dependent on the market, if only to a limited degree.

However, if one looks beyond the outward manifestations of the slumps, which were much the same throughout the years, certain differences can be observed between the early depressions and those of more recent date. The price recessions of the fourteenth and fifteenth centuries, like those of the seventeenth and eighteenth, were the consequence of a standstill or decrease in population caused by plagues or wars, thus the causes were 'from outside' and not endogenous in the Malthusian sense, although they operated according to Malthusian laws. They alleviated, to some extent, the pressure of population on food supplies, although price inflation and famine never entirely disappeared. The rising wages, falling grain prices and the less-marked fall in the cost of products in price-elastic demand (meat, wool, hops, dyes etc.) can be interpreted easily according to the laws of agricultural returns as understood by the classic economists: as a natural barrier holding back an economy that was still largely static, a restriction to be eased only by changing or reducing demand.

The agrarian slumps of the nineteenth century occurred in a period of population explosion. In so far as one can speak of primary causes at all, they appear to lie in the tremendous drive of expansion that set in after the technical-social revolution of the late eighteenth century in agriculture, as in other fields. They were phases in a cycle formed not only by external circumstances such as war or commercially-oriented policies, but also by forces inherent in agriculture itself, and by the pressure of agricultural production striving to anticipate demand.

Appendix

Conversion of currency and measures

Notes on the tables

The price series from various European countries reproduced in the text and appendix are taken from the list of references. From 1911 onwards the prices come from official sources. For the years 1911–33 they are drawn from the international price surveys contained in the *Statistischen Jahrbuch fur das Deutsche Reich, 1915–1939*. They consist of wholesale prices already converted to RM per kg by the State Department of Statistics. The years 1915–23, being unsuitable for purposes of price comparison, are omitted. The averages for the second and third decades of the twentieth century are therefore reckoned only from the 1911–14 and 1924–30 prices. The prices for 1934–60 are taken from the FAO *Production Yearbooks*, Vol. 1, 1951, and 15, 1961. The Yearbook quotations are given in the currency of the country and in U.S. dollars per 100 kilograms. In order to compare these recent prices with earlier ones expressed in the silver content of the amounts, all the prices are converted according to the official rate of exchange of the currency concerned in relation to the German Reichsmark, allotted the imaginary silver content of the old reichsmark, i.e. 5.56 grams.

Conversion Table   Rate of exchange between the U.S. dollar and the German Reichsmark

Period	U.S. dollar : RM/DM
1934–1938	1 : 2.48–2.51
1939–1943	1 : 2.50
1944–31.10.1949	1 : 3.33
1.11.1949–1.3.1961	1 : 4.20

Notes on table 1 of appendix: Wheat and rye prices in western and central Europe between the thirteenth and twentieth centuries (ten-year averages, in grams of silver per 100 kilograms).

(1) *England*: The English wheat prices for 1259–1702 were taken from Rogers' book: *A history of agriculture and prices in England* (1864–87).

For the period between 1702, the last year of the Rogers series, and 1770, the first year of official English grain price statistics, the Eton and Oxford tables assembled by Tooke (1858) are used. These tables contain annual average prices calculated from the mean of the Lady Day and Michaelmas market quotations and given in Winchester quarters and shillings. Both price series have been compressed into a single series by means of finding a simple average.

From 1771 onwards we follow the official English price averages for the year and the Winchester quarter, published in the *Statistical Abstract for the United Kingdom*. They are averages of the quoted prices published weekly by the Inspector of Corn Returns for England, Scotland and Wales in the London Gazette – hence the official expression 'average Gazette prices'. The imperial quarter was slightly bigger than the old Winchester quarter. It had a capacity of 290.8 litres. That has been taken into account. As already noted, all information relating to events after 1911 has been drawn from international publications.

(2) *Belgium*: The Belgian wheat prices were provided by C. Verlinden's price and wage collections from Flanders and Brabant. The price series in the tables were assembled out of the simple mean values of wheat prices from six Belgian towns. The sources of these figures are:

for *Bruges*,	1401–1500:	G. Croisiau's *Prijzen in Vlaanderen in de 15ᵉ ecuw*
for *Bruges*,	1564–1604:	A. Wyffels' *Prijs van tarwe te Brugge*
for *Bruges*,	1601–1705:	J. Vermaut's *Prijzen uit Brugse instellingsrekeningen, 17ᵉ ecuw*
for *Ghent*,	1400–1500:	Croisiau
for *Diksmuide*,	1482–1615:	*A. Wyffels' Prijs van tarwe te Diksmuide*
for *Nieuwpoort*,	1591–1792:	J. Vermaut's *Prijzen van tarwe en rogge te Nieuwpoort en gewicht van het brood*
for *Antwerp*,	1429–1600:	E. Scholliers' *Prijzen en lonen te Antwerpen*
for *Brussels*,	1568–1795:	J. Craeybeckx' *De prijzen van graan en van brood te Brussel.*

(3) *France*: The French wheat price series from 1200 to 1500 are based on d'Avenel's average annual prices. While d'Avenel's series go up to 1800, for the years 1501–1760 H. Hauser's price data from Paris and Grenoble have been called in to supplement them. From 1756 onwards the French Ministry of Agriculture itself has published the apparently reliable wheat price quotations from which we have been able to calculate the average French wheat prices used in this text and appendix (*Archives Statistiques du Ministere des Travaux Publics de l'Agriculture et du Commerce*, Series I, 1837, p. 1f. *Annuaire Statistique de la France*). They have been employed in preference to privately collected price series. The years of the *assignats* (1791–6) had to be omitted, because no prices were quoted during that time.

(4) *Northern Italy*: The evidence for the north Italian wheat price series was gathered from several different publications. Prices from Genoa, Piedmont, Portogruaro, Arezzo, Florence, Brescia and Milan have been arranged in annual and ten-year averages and, after a certain amount of adjustment, made up into a small number of series.

Genoese wheat prices for 1190–1330 were published in 1878 by Magalde and Fabris.

Prices for 1501 and 1599 have been taken from those published by Bartolini in 1878 (from Portogruaro), by Fanfani in 1940 (from Arezzo), and Parenti in 1939 (from Florence).

The Italian Ministry of Agriculture published the Udine wheat prices from 1600–1875. Once more the more recent prices are from international sources.

(5) *The Netherlands*: The Dutch rye prices have been calculated as a mean value of the

prices from three towns: Utrecht 1461–1644 (from Sillem, 1901), Arnhem 1544–1901 (from the Survey of Market Prices ..., 1903) and Amsterdam 1620–1904 (from Posthumus, 1946).

(6) *Germany*: The German series of rye prices is made up of prices from thirteen different German towns. It begins in the mid-fourteenth century with rye prices from Brunswick and Frankfurt-am-Main. By 1400 five towns in all were included in the mean value, and by 1500 there were nine. After 1630 it comprises data from thirteen towns. Most of these series come to an end at the beginning of the nineteenth century. In only five towns (Hamburg, Munich, Königsberg, Leipzig, Berlin), which were, however, the most important centres of the grain trade, could they be continued until 1940. For dates later than 1934 international statistics from the FAO Yearbooks have been drawn upon. Up to 1944 they apply to the old national area, since 1945 to the Federal Republic of Germany. Further details about the price series (origin, length and conversion methods) can be found in the notes to table 2 of the appendix.

(7) *Austria*: The Austrian series is based on Pribram's price and wage collections (1938). Averages were calculated for rye prices in five towns: Vienna, 1431–60 and 1521–1920; Klosterneuburg, 1441–1650; St Pölten, 1731–90; Wels, 1471–1760; and Weyer, 1621–1790.

(8) *Poland*: In his series *Badania Z dziejow spolecznych i gospodarczych* (volumes 4, 13, 14, 15, 16, 17, 21, 22, 25 and 33, 1928–38 and 1949–50) F. Bujak has supplied the world with a rich source of price data for Poland. The prices for bread grain, however, are sadly deficient. The oldest are the relatively complete prices from Cracow. Apart from a few gaps, they stretch from 1360 to 1795. The series shown in table 1 of the appendix refers only to these prices. Unfortunately the Cracow price-level was considerably lower than that of the other Polish towns, and that has to be taken into consideration when comparing Polish (i.e. Cracow) prices with other European prices.

Records of oat prices are much more plentiful than those of rye in Cracow – as in other Polish towns. Where the two series can be compared their development runs parallel. It seems, therefore, a good idea to bridge the gaps in the Cracow rye prices series by means of oat prices. In years when there are oat prices but none for rye, the three preceding and the three following rye prices are expressed as a percentage of the corresponding oat prices. Subsequently, the oat price in question is multiplied by the index number thus obtained, and the resulting value inserted into the series for the year in which the price of rye is missing.

If the price of rye in the years 1, 2, 3, 4, 5, 6, 7, 8, etc. is called A, B, C, D, E, F, G, H, etc. and the oat prices a, b, c, d, e, f, g, h, etc., the missing rye price E in year 4 can be determined by the following equation.

$$\frac{B + C + D + F + G + H}{b + c + d + f + g + h} . e = E$$

The rye price obtained by this method is put between brackets in table 1. The original quotations have already been converted to their silver value by the compilers of the Cracow grain price statistics (J. Pelc, 1369–1600; E. Tomaszewski, 1601–1795). The grain measure used (the *cwiertnia*) contains 360.3 litres.

Notes on table 2 of the appendix: Rye prices in Germany between the fourteenth and twentieth centuries (ten-year averages, in grams of silver per 100 kilograms).

So many rye prices are available for Germany that some have had to be left out. The selection is determined by the nature of the data and by their suitability to our purpose of assembling the individual series into one set of index numbers. Only complete price series for more than two hundred years have been used, and then (except for Brunswick) only if there are at least seven annual prices for each decade. Furthermore, care has been taken that the places of origin are so distributed as to be truly representative of 'German' rye prices. For the more distant past, it must be owned, these are counsels of perfection, for the further back one goes, the scantier grows the evidence. In cases where the grain measure's capacity, or the source of that information is not disclosed, we have referred to Noback.[28]

(1) *Brunswick*: The Brunswick series are taken from documents in the archives of the city of Brunswick.[29] They consist of prices charged by the monks of St Blasius for the corn they sold in Brunswick market. Between 1374 and 1445 there is no mention of prices; from 1330 to 1374 and from 1445 to 1480 the evidence is very incomplete. The prices in the series diverge very little (3.7 per cent) from those in the official surveys between 1692 and 1730, which the Brunswick town council ordered to be made 'truly and faithfully by the most recently appointed senators of the time' in order to find out 'how much grain, that is to say, wheat, rye, barley, oats and peas ... was worth in the open market' (Brunswick city archives, Doc. C I 5 No. 18).[30]

(2) *Frankfurt-am-Main*: The Frankfurt rye prices have been supplied from the Elsas collection.

(3) *Xanten*: Beissel (1885) assembled the Xanten rye prices.

The earliest information on the Xanten coinage was provided by Beissel and later supplemented by Kruse[34] and Schrötter.[35]

(4) *Strasburg*: These prices come from Hanauer's *Economic History*. Those of the nineteenth century are based on the official records of the Strasburg municipality. For his 1591–1793 information Hanauer depended chiefly on the Strasburg town archives, with additions from the account books of a few charitable institutions in the town. He was also able to find still earlier price quotations in the accounts of a number of monasteries and other foundations.

(5) *Schleswig-Holstein*: The Schleswig-Holstein rye prices were collected by Waschinski (1959) from many different sources (official documents, treasury accounts, estate books, ecclesiastical account books, market quotations from various towns, etc.). Until the end of the fourteenth century there are not many quotations, but after 1391 they grow more frequent. That is the year in which Waschinski began to utilize the material to calculate mean values extending over periods of five and ten years. After the middle of the sixteenth century the rye prices of Rendsburg are recorded in their entirety up to the year 1793, but only those between 1550 and 1790 have been used. From 1791 onwards we have drawn on the Hamburg prices quoted by the State Statistical Department.[37] They diverge from the Rendsburg figures during the overlapping years by only 2.6 per cent so it is quite permissible to continue the series with the prices from Hamburg.

(6) *Göttingen*: Kullak-Ublick (1953) was responsible for collecting the Göttingen rye prices.

(7) *Munich*   (8) *Augsburg*   (9) *Wurzburg*   (10) *Speyer*   (12) *Leipzig*: The prices and the details of the coinage and measures needed for conversion have been taken from Elsas (*loc. cit.* I, II, A).

(11) *Danzig/Königsberg*: The Danzig prices up to 1700 are provided by J. Pelc (1937), from 1701 to 1815 by T. Furtac (1935).

(13) *Berlin*: The Berlin grain prices 1631–1806 come from the volumes on grain trade policy (*Getreide handelspolitik*) in the Acta Borussica, which were written by Naude and Skalweit and published by the Prussian Academy of Science. In the second volume of *Getreide-handelspolitik* Naude presents a table of the 'highest and lowest prices paid in the Berlin market from 1624 to 1740', from which he has worked out a series of annual averages by converting the yearly quotations into simple averages. In the subsequent volumes Skalweit gives the Berlin grain prices between 1740 and 1806, and these have also, where

necessary, been turned into averages for the calendar year. After 1806 the figures are taken from the *Jahrbuch für die amtliche Statistik des Preussischen Staates* 2, 1867, p. 112f., and from later regular publications by the Prussian Statistics Department.

The wheat prices of Rostock and the rye prices of Schwerin come from H. Westphal's collection.

The Danzig prices for wheat and rye can be found in the Report from the Select Committee ... 18 June 1821, p. 365.

Table 1 Wheat and rye prices in western and central Europe between the thirteenth and twentieth centuries (ten-year averages, in grams of silver per 100 kilograms)

Year	Wheat				Rye				Year
	England	Belgium	France	Italy	Netherlands	Germany	Austria	Poland	
1201– 10			19.6	21.5					1201– 10
11– 20	26.2		21.8	23.0					11– 20
21– 30	35.1		25.6						21– 30
31– 40	28.6		28.5	18.5					31– 40
41– 50	28.8		37.0	27.9					41– 50
51– 60	38.0		23.7	33.9					51– 60
61– 70	35.3		28.6	26.1					61– 70
71– 80	42.0		27.1	45.7					71– 80
81– 90	37.8		30.5	53.3					81– 90
91–1300	45.3		52.8	59.3					91–1300
1301– 10	41.1		41.9	49.8					1301– 10
11– 20	58.1		66.2	53.5					11– 20
21– 30	50.5		43.3	80.4					21– 30
31– 40	34.7		29.6	67.3					31– 40
41– 50	35.7		59.0	69.1		16.9			41– 50
51– 60	38.0		52.6	63.0		21.1			51– 60
61– 70	46.4		54.9	66.2		28.7		(3.4)	61– 70
71– 80	36.3		45.7	72.8		21.6		6.5	71– 80
81– 90	30.8		22.7			20.7		3.5	81– 90
91–1400	30.8		30.9			20.8		3.5	91–1400
1401– 10	35.1	27.9	25.0			24.2		5.3	1401– 10
11– 20	28.3	28.1	38.6			19.2		(5.0)	11– 20
21– 30	26.8	31.4	59.3			18.6		(3.7)	21– 30
31– 40	34.3	47.1	50.2			21.3	18.9		31– 40
41– 50	25.4	34.4	21.7			16.9	13.4		41– 50
51– 60	27.5	35.9	21.6			19.6	8.4		51– 60
61– 70	21.0	23.1	16.2		15.8	14.6	19.4		61– 70
71– 80	21.2	26.9	18.1		29.2	15.3	12.0		71– 80
81– 90	25.0	36.2	26.6		31.0	21.1	13.9	(3.0)	81– 90
91–1500	20.1	26.4	17.7		21.5	23.6	18.5	1.6	91–1500
1501– 10	21.5	24.4	28.8	51.3	20.6	20.6	14.0	3.2	1501– 10
11– 20	26.7	28.5	29.9	49.9	23.9	17.8	13.2	(3.2)	11– 20
21– 30	28.0	27.5	48.2	80.3	43.4	19.5	13.1	4.6	21– 30
31– 40	27.2	41.0	48.6	72.3	31.1	26.1	17.0	2.9	31– 40
41– 50	20.8	48.3	50.2	55.4	31.5	25.7	15.0	5.5	41– 50

Year									Year
51– 60	35.9	52.9	54.2	90.2	42.0	31.2	17.5	9.3	51– 60
61– 70	33.9	60.6	81.7	90.5	43.5	39.9	34.6	8.6	61– 70
71– 80	47.5	79.1	98.1	102.7	70.2	51.5	44.5	12.3	71– 80
81– 90	63.3	123.3	141.2	110.4	52.1	48.6	35.3	8.9	81– 90
91–1600	91.4	92.6	187.4	157.5	65.6	52.6	38.0	12.9	91–1600
1601– 10	83.0	79.7	91.6	123.0	49.2	45.5	40.1	27.1	1601– 10
11– 20	93.3	71.1	96.4	106.5	51.0	52.5	47.8	19.0	11– 20
21– 30	107.3	105.6	124.6	151.6	72.3	76.0	40.5	26.3	21– 30
31– 40	109.5	118.6	123.3	109.9	73.0	84.5	46.8	(17.6)	31– 40
41– 50	122.3	120.4	116.5	105.7	67.8	54.8	47.3	17.8	41– 50
51– 60	104.3	103.9	118.7	73.0	72.3	40.2	34.2	23.5	51– 60
61– 70	103.3	90.2	104.3	64.8	67.4	40.8	44.7	(17.0)	61– 70
71– 80	107.6	97.1	80.7	79.2	58.8	42.4	29.0	15.2	71– 80
81– 90	83.7	76.3	71.8	57.3	44.6	35.9	36.4	7.2	81– 90
91–1700	124.0	115.2	102.0	63.7	75.2	66.7	50.4	14.7	91–1700
1701– 10	91.3	91.7	85.4	67.7	58.2	44.0	38.8	9.3	1701– 10
11– 20	98.8	73.2	72.5	59.9	51.6	51.0	46.1	10.6	11– 20
21– 30	91.5	58.9	66.6	46.9	45.2	42.4	35.1	4.8	21– 30
31– 40	82.8	62.2	70.8	63.9	44.3	45.2	36.5	11.9	31– 40
41– 50	74.6	66.4	60.2	69.1	50.6	52.7	43.5	11.8	41– 50
51– 60	95.6	60.6	68.8	67.5	49.7	51.1	36.2	9.3	51– 60
61– 70	109.2	69.4	74.7	70.2	54.4	58.1	39.1	12.2	61– 70
71– 80	113.1	72.8	86.9	87.6	65.9	62.5	48.6	13.3	71– 80
81– 90	118.8	82.7	93.1	93.7	69.6	57.5	43.2	13.8	81– 90
91–1800	157.4		106.4	116.1	88.4	75.4	47.4	14.6	91–1800
1801– 10	208.0		115.8	130.8	117.5	95.0	94.5		1801– 10
11– 20	216.8		143.9	138.6	103.9	96.1	84.9		11– 20
21– 30	147.2		107.0	86.0	56.1	51.4	49.4		21– 30
31– 40	141.1		110.2	93.2	71.6	62.7	49.2		31– 40
41– 50	132.1		111.5	107.0	81.5	72.4	63.5		41– 50
51– 60	135.3		123.5	123.0	98.0	84.4	80.0		51– 60
61– 70	126.4		125.8	115.8	90.2	85.4	76.4		61– 70
71– 80	126.5		133.0		91.1	95.9	101.7		71– 80
81– 90	88.6		107.6		76.9	85.0	93.8		81– 90
91–1900	69.9		96.5		63.3	82.4	94.0		91–1900
1901– 10	74.1		100.4			87.8	104.2		1901– 10
11– 20	89.9		90.8			105.8	123.0		11– 20
21– 30	119.2		138.2			112.9	101.7		21– 30
31– 40	64.6		87.4			99.7	64.6		31– 40
41– 50	135.1		159.4			116.8	112.7		41– 50
51– 60	187.3		216.2			216.2	210.4		51– 60

Table 2 Rye prices in Germany between the fourteenth and twentieth centuries (ten-year averages, in grams of silver per 100 kilograms)

Year	Braun-schweig	Frank-furt	Xanten	Stras-berg	Schles-wig-Hol-stein/Ham-burg	Göttin-gen	Munich	Augs-burg	Würz-burg	Speyer	Dan-zig/Königs-berg	Leipzig	Berlin	Mittel der Preis-reihen	Year
1341– 50	16.9													16.9	1341– 50
51– 60	13.0	29.2												21.1	51– 60
61– 70	15.0	41.4												28.7	61– 70
71– 80	14.3	28.6	21.9											21.6	71– 80
81– 90		21.7	21.1		12.9									20.7	81– 90
91–1400		24.9	24.1	19.4	12.5									20.8	91–1400
1401– 10		26.2	27.8	21.6	14.7	35.3								24.1	1401– 10
11– 20		21.6	18.0	19.2	13.6	22.2								19.1	11– 20
21– 30		19.4	24.0	19.2	9.5	16.6								18.6	21– 30
31– 40		29.3	20.7	19.4	9.1	24.5								21.3	31– 40
41– 50	11.4	20.5	22.0	19.6	9.3	18.5								16.9	41– 50
51– 60	12.0	26.6	22.7	17.7	10.1	17.9	31.3							19.6	51– 60
61– 70	12.4	13.9	14.2	12.7	17.9	13.2	26.1							14.6	61– 70
71– 80	12.1	13.0	16.8	11.6	16.7	9.8	23.3	20.2						15.3	71– 80
81– 90	18.7	23.5	29.9	19.7	29.6	14.5	31.3	20.1	12.9					21.1	81– 90
91–1500	20.2	19.6	25.9	16.2	20.6	15.0	40.1	26.9	15.2					23.6	91–1500
1501– 10	10.1	20.3	19.4	13.6	23.5	9.0	43.4	25.2	18.7					20.6	1501– 10
11– 20	8.8	14.6	15.5	14.8	23.6	11.5	31.8	21.5	18.2					17.8	11– 20
21– 30	13.0	17.5	15.5	14.9	21.7	13.6	36.4	25.7	15.2					19.5	21– 30
31– 40	13.2	24.7	17.4	22.2	17.9	16.8	56.3	31.7	33.4	23.9				26.1	31– 40
41– 50	14.9	36.4	24.1	25.9	27.0	18.7	42.8	32.0	26.2	25.7	17.7			25.7	41– 50
51– 60	19.5	40.9	33.8	29.8	26.5	22.4	45.3	33.8	33.4	35.9	21.7			31.2	51– 60
61– 70	22.4	45.5	36.0	41.1	34.0	26.4	76.9	50.3	45.7	42.9	25.5			39.9	61– 70
71– 80	30.6	53.7	53.2	54.2	34.0	34.4	95.8	63.7	70.7	57.4	28.9	40.9		51.5	71– 80
81– 90	29.1	68.3	41.7	60.2	27.9	34.0	74.3	53.9	62.9	51.7	31.2	47.6		48.6	81– 90
91–1600	39.0	59.1	35.8	54.8	39.4	33.3	93.4	60.4	61.4	58.4	44.2	52.2		52.6	91–1600

Period													
1601— 10	33.7	52.0	25.0	49.3	28.9	31.9	78.4	53.9	61.6	48.3	34.2	48.5	45.5
11— 20	35.1	58.8	29.0	45.4	36.2	36.7	84.5	62.2	75.7	56.1	38.0	71.9	52.5
21— 30	43.4	93.3	47.9	77.1	67.5	67.8	112.3	128.2	91.2	52.8	53.7	76.3	76.0
31— 40	56.8	106.2	45.2	140.6	50.4	79.5	76.7	103.1	85.7	194.8	43.5	63.8	84.5
41— 50	50.5	69.5	43.8	63.5	57.5	52.8	65.1	66.3	48.7	63.1	46.8	40.1	54.8
51— 60	44.7	52.3	35.1	31.1	54.5	36.7	38.9	28.5	27.5	32.6	55.5	34.1	40.2
61— 70	36.4	45.0	36.8	33.8	52.3	36.7	51.2	40.6	32.2	31.4	45.8	42.4	40.8
71— 80	38.9	53.4	31.0	63.9	38.8	39.9	42.8	42.9	38.8	51.4	37.6	37.0	42.4
81— 90	34.5	53.9	26.2	41.7	34.4	38.0	46.7	34.5	37.8	27.5	28.6	30.4	35.9
91—1700	89.4	106.2	48.3	70.8	58.3	54.6	83.4	65.6	75.9	66.2	47.3	49.8	66.7
1701— 10	36.8	62.8	36.1	55.7	45.8	38.4	46.7	58.4	43.9	41.7	35.0	35.8	44.0
11— 20	48.9	67.8	34.3	45.3	53.8	54.5	52.8	69.5	59.5	44.5	36.7	43.9	51.0
21— 30	41.1	68.4	31.3	30.1	46.0	44.9	41.7	52.8	50.0	35.0	29.5	40.0	42.4
31— 40	44.0	59.5	27.4	39.1	45.2	42.9	50.0	69.5	51.2	40.0	33.9	38.4	45.2
41— 50	43.0	82.3	20.9	45.3	40.9	46.1	63.9	91.0	63.9	55.0	36.1	38.9	52.7
51— 60	46.2	88.4	34.3	39.3	43.2	55.3	48.9	79.9	54.5	50.0	36.1	40.0	51.1
61— 70	62.4	95.6	42.5	44.4	63.2	58.1	53.9	78.5	57.3	53.9	37.8	56.7	58.1
71— 80	56.7	120.7	34.1	46.8	58.5	59.8	70.6	79.9	65.1	61.7	45.0	56.7	62.5
81— 90	58.9	92.9	35.9	53.2	66.5	54.8	60.6	69.5	51.7	51.2	51.7	45.6	57.5
91—1800	73.3	135.9	46.2		87.1	65.1	65.6	104.3	80.6	67.8	61.7	53.9	75.4
1801— 10	107.3	145.7	73.0	64.7	110.2	84.2	95.6	117.5		53.9	87.3	98.4	95.0
11— 20		151.7	87.8	101.0	93.2		98.7				61.3		96.1
21— 30			58.4	64.7	48.8		49.2				36.9	75.1	51.4
31— 40			61.8	77.8	61.5		52.7				47.0		62.7
41— 50			73.6	86.1	68.7		75.1				59.1	88.8	72.4
51— 60			92.8	93.7	96.1		82.1				85.1	100.4	84.4
61— 70			90.1	92.5	92.2		81.3				66.4	88.3	85.4
71— 80			101.5		100.7		95.7				81.1	84.0	95.9
81— 90					88.9		90.2				74.8	89.4	85.0
91—1900					85.2		87.9				74.6	96.5	82.4
1901— 10					89.4		90.0				82.9	98.3	87.8
11— 18					98.2		124.1				92.5		105.8
24— 30					115.6		114.6				107.5		110.7
31— 40					100.9		101.5				96.5		99.7

Table 3 Wheat and rye prices in Europe and America 1791–1830 (German marks per 100 kilograms)

Year	*England*	*France*	*Italy*	*Virginia (USA)*	*Denmark*	*Germany*										
						Hamburg	*Rostock*	*Schwerin*	*Danzig*		*Berlin*		*Breslau*		*Münich*	
	Wheat	*Rye*	*Wheat*	*Rye*	*Rye*	*Wheat*	*Wheat*	*Rye*	*Wheat*	*Rye*	*Wheat*	*Rye*	*Wheat*	*Rye*	*Wheat*	*Rye*
1791–1800	28.30	19.14	20.88	–	–	19.14	–	–	12.72	7.95	15.24	11.38	11.16	9.50	15.85	11.71
1801	53.10	23.46	37.98	23.42	–	33.78	34.18	25.69	20.71	10.76	22.35	14.38	14.92	11.25	18.20	11.14
1802	31.03	25.47	30.83	15.41	–	24.94	27.47	21.79	15.44	10.24	22.94	17.20	16.69	12.75	26.70	20.69
1803	26.20	25.72	25.17	16.49	–	24.94	26.39	24.95	13.64	9.76	23.53	16.88	18.80	13.38	27.70	21.54
1804	27.72	20.10	22.86	19.26	–	25.08	22.36	16.78	15.51	9.04	23.84	17.83	23.97	18.25	24.90	18.75
1805	39.97	19.94	26.81	22.04	–	26.25	32.28	25.80	20.08	13.38	32.66	25.63	39.48	35.75	33.50	26.71
1806	35.22	20.25	21.85	17.26	–	36.54	31.38	28.42	17.73	–	27.29	24.50	18.33	17.50	28.55	23.36
1807	33.92	19.78	17.63	15.56	–	26.97	29.25	28.17	14.04	–	23.53	20.00	19.04	13.75	18.25	13.06
1808	36.22	17.32	15.24	12.17	–	26.25	23.57	21.07	17.38	–	26.59	25.00	–	–	15.95	9.11
1809	43.35	15.57	15.49	15.56	–	20.00	19.84	17.55	12.40	5.43	17.88	15.00	14.57	11.50	18.25	11.10
1810	47.40	20.54	21.32	21.73	–	16.24	17.06	9.58	12.23	5.28	14.12	8.00	11.52	7.75	15.90	11.62
1811	42.42	27.37	27.03	21.88	–	15.95	14.39	6.91	8.77	3.11	14.35	9.50	11.30	8.70	15.05	9.64
1812	56.34	35.97	23.93	22.34	–	24.36	16.70	18.48	11.30	8.89	20.24	15.75	16.66	14.55	25.05	14.42
1813	48.89	23.58	20.29	16.02	–	26.54	18.50	12.83	–	–	17.65	12.75	12.85	9.20	21.90	14.81
1814	33.11	18.57	24.82	12.63	–	21.10	16.19	12.83	15.27	12.00	16.00	12.50	16.19	11.35	16.95	13.24
1815	29.21	20.46	33.89	19.57	–	20.74	19.00	17.82	16.19	12.90	17.88	13.75	18.45	13.98	19.25	15.04
1816	34.97	29.65	41.03	25.73	–	19.29	18.27	13.38	15.46	11.93	21.41	15.75	18.28	15.00	31.95	29.01
1817	43.17	37.88	30.93	29.74	15.45	32.34	35.31	23.18	25.15	15.00	29.41	20.50	22.25	17.10	52.25	45.71
1818	38.41	25.82	16.20	24.35	16.60	28.28	32.36	22.99	23.29	13.13	24.71	17.75	18.14	12.75	23.40	18.52
1819	33.18	19.29	13.58	16.02	7.82	20.45	25.80	19.76	15.09	10.83	18.12	13.75	13.40	10.75	13.50	8.74
1820	30.21	20.04	17.47	12.02	5.93	16.53	15.83	11.38	12.40	7.75	14.35	10.00	10.60	8.70	12.95	6.90
1821	24.98	18.63	16.24	13.71	4.88	13.49	12.90	7.45	11.13	6.28	13.65	7.75	14.24	8.43	15.00	7.91
1822	19.78	16.23	14.08	15.87	5.48	12.04	14.26	5.92	10.88	7.43	12.47	8.50	13.70	10.45	14.00	8.44
1823	23.75	18.35	13.03	16.18	4.64	11.75	11.44	10.10	10.29	7.90	12.71	10.00	12.76	11.45	12.20	8.42
1824	28.47	16.99	11.63	13.09	4.38	10.00	10.61	5.86	8.29	4.23	10.12	6.00	7.94	5.40	10.35	6.39
1825	30.51	16.49	9.82	12.02	5.82	8.84	10.02	4.75	8.06	4.68	9.41	6.00	6.44	4.10	9.70	7.40
1826	26.13	16.60	13.07	12.17	11.28	8.26	8.91	5.79	8.88	7.20	10.12	8.50	7.87	6.95	8.20	6.67
1827	26.05	19.06	19.06	12.63	6.72	12.18	13.54	13.37	10.15	8.88	12.00	11.75	10.53	10.85	10.35	7.33
1828	26.91	23.08	18.54	15.56	9.00	13.63	11.69	10.70	10.76	7.48	14.59	11.00	12.71	10.45	16.50	11.85
1829	29.51	23.66	18.40	16.18	9.68	19.86	24.52	11.84	12.64	7.35	17.41	10.25	13.23	8.45	16.10	11.76
1830	28.61	23.45	18.03	12.63	12.09	17.26	17.91	9.65	13.75	7.78	16.71	10.75	12.10	10.28	14.10	11.44

Notes to the text

Introduction

1 The values in figure 1 are taken from table 1 in the appendix. Also to be found in the appendix is information regarding the conversion factors of currency and the sources from which the prices in this figure have been compiled. The trinomial ten-year moving averages were calculated from the tables in the following manner: if a, b, c, d, etc. represent the successive ten-year averages, $\dfrac{a+b+c}{3}$ replaces b, $\dfrac{b+c+d}{3}$ replaces c, and so on. Since the above calculation was worked out, further prices series have appeared. Although they have now been included in the select bibliography, they have not been used to supplement the above figures or table 1 in the appendix. The labour involved would have been too great, while the main features of the long-term fluctuations of grain prices, which alone concern us here, are already clearly shown.

2 The above reasoning was in part only indicated by Ricardo. It was more clearly defined by Mill (1852) and Dietzel (1901) where the theory of diverging wages and rents in particular is worked out more fully.

3 See Helferich (1843:4). Since 1935, when this book was first published, the view of price history developed above (and in Helferich's text) has gained a considerable number of adherents. We have only to mention Beveridge who, in his *Prices and Wages in England* (1939:xxvf.) declared: 'In the study of modern prices, determination of the "general level" of prices and its movements has bulked largely, perhaps at times too largely. Prices have been considered mainly as a means of throwing light on monetary problems. . . . In the present work the emphasis is different. Price-relatives for single commodities rather than index numbers for commodities in combination are the main objective. Index numbers do not appear . . . in any of the first three volumes.'

4 The discussion of trade development during the last centuries of the first millennium, which was carried on under the heading 'Natural or Money Economy', reached the conclusion that the decline in trade and barter that had already begun in the days of imperial Rome sank to its lowest ebb between the eighth and tenth century: see von Inama-Sternegg (1879:I, 465; 1891:II, 365f.), Sombart (1919:I, 94), and Sée (1930:21). There is disagreement as to the extent of this decline at the end of the first millennium.

Contrary to previous opinion Dopsch (1928:307, 345, 560) and Kötschke (1924:296f.) stressed that there was at no time a complete collapse of internal economy.

To give references for the following statements is superfluous for they are common knowledge, even if the viewpoint from which they are seen is an unusual one.

5 This estimate is based on Schmoller (1896:699f.) and on the figures of yield per hectare in the bishopric of Winchester which are quoted below.

6 Lamprecht believes, on the evidence of some accounts found in the Moselle district, that grain prices rose at the turn of the millennium, only to fall again during the twelfth century (1885:333; 1886:11, *passim*).

7 These relationships have already been explained more than once, first in Abel (1936:7ff.), but have hitherto received scant attention from historians and theoreticians of the harvest cycle. For this reason they are repeated here.

Chapter 1   Rising agrarian prosperity during the high Middle Ages

1 In this calculation the slight long-term decline in the value of English currency was taken into account to facilitate the comparison of Farmer's figures with those of Rogers.

1 Until the end of the Middle Ages transport costs were too high to permit more than a sporadic export of grain from the eastern shores of the Baltic Sea to western Europe. See Lesnikow (1957–8:613f.), whose objections, directed chiefly against the ideas of Naudé, do not apply, however, to the towns between the Elbe and Oder. That the cereal trade from this region to the west was more than occasional even before the end of the thirteenth century is indisputable. In the fifteenth century towns still further to the east participated to quite an extent in the east-west grain trade, as Tits-Dieuaide (1975) has pointed out.

3 Thus in St Marien-Aix in 1232 the levy for the building of the new Traben church was reduced from 20 measures of wine to 12 measures, which corresponds to a 66 per cent increase in the price of wine (Lamprecht, 1885–6:11, 616).

4 For criticisms and evaluation of Lamprecht's estimates see Mombert (1929:31) and Abel (1967:26f.).

5 Baratier establishes a considerable increase of population over a large area until about 1320, then a decline followed by a further increase after about 1470. Working on an even wider base, Fierro came to a similar conclusion.

6 Inama-Sternegg's article remains the best collation of the old literature on the subject, and the estimates and calculations are still valid today.

7 Marc Bloch himself inclined more to the opposing view.

8 It is superfluous to give further references as Duby's work is the most comprehensive. It might, however, be worth mentioning the author's own *Geschichte der deutschen Landwirtschaft*, 3rd edition, 1978 which there has not yet been time for Duby to study.

9 The newer English literature of medieval agriculture is so abundant that it is impossible to name all the authorities.

10 See evaluation in Abel, 1967: table 6. The prices are made up from average prices per farm divided by the number of sales in order to balance the variable frequency of the sales.

11 It may be that these were exceptional cases, for fifteen to twenty-five times the value of the harvest seems high even for a purchase price.

12 The wage figures are based on Rogers, 1866–1902:1, 303f., arranged in annual averages. The mason's wages represent the average of all the figures from all over England, the

carpenter's (highest rate) likewise; the thresher's rate of pay per quarter is an average made up from all the available wage entries in the Midlands.

13 The expression was first used by either Schmoller or Philippi (1909).

Chapter 2   The fourteenth-century recession

1 Graus reviews the literature on the late medieval depression, and the place of the present book within it.

2 Thus in the penetrating, and to me most welcome, foreword by Ruggiero Romano to the Italian edition of this book (*Congiuntura agraria e crisi agrarie*, Turin, 1976:xiii–xxv).

3 See also the old but still valuable article by Lucas (1930:343f.); further, van Werveke (1950a:5f.), Abel (1976:74f.), with evidence from contemporary writers cited in the following quotations, and Graus (1963:720f.), a supplement to Carpentier's paper.

4 Postan's thesis that the disproportion between population and food-growing area was certainly one of the causes, even the main cause, of the most important phenomenon of the fourteenth and fifteenth centuries, the downward turn of the population curve, was an opinion shared by Genicot (1962:5f.).

5 Unless otherwise stated, sources for the passages and records quoted will be found in Carpentier and, with additions, in Abel (1976).

6 The French population data extending over the mid-fourteenth century was collected by Le Roy Ladurie (1966:1, 140ff.).

7 See Helleiner (1967:5ff.) for a summary of the available evidence with critical notes, which, unfortunately, lack of space prevents us discussing here.

8 It is difficult to represent the medieval movements of industrial goods accurately in a graph or table, since differences in quality and wide variations of price make it hard to arrive at averages. Thus in figure 8 the price of iron includes prices for various kinds of wrought iron, although Rogers' compilation of relatively numerous single prices has to some extent smoothed out extremes of price and quality. For the average cost of 'Iron, 108 lbs', and his own collected wheat prices, see Rogers (1866–1902:1, 478). The day wage of a mason was selected to avoid overloading the graph. The wages of other groups, such as carpenters, threshers, and reapers, moved in a similar way.

Chapter 3   The late medieval agrarian depression

1 Hegel converted the original prices into a 'gold value', estimating the rate of gold to silver as 1:15.5, although the ratio at that time was only 1:11. The conversion has been reversed and adjusted to determine the value of the actual Nuremberg grain prices in silver. Hegel's conversion methods are fully explained by Schmoller (1871:319).

2 The old Königsberger scheffel had a content of 51.4 litres.

3 The series represented in figure 10 are arranged as follows:
   ENGLAND (Rogers, 1866–1902:I–IV):
      Grain: wheat, rye, barley, oats
      Livestock and livestock products: oxen, sheep, butter
      Building materials and iron: roofing tiles, bricks, wrought iron
      Textiles: canvas, table linen
      Wages: day-wages of masons; piecework wages of threshers, reapers and hay-makers
   FRANCE (d'Avenel, 1894–1926:II, III, IV, VI):
      Grain: wheat, rye, barley, oats

Livestock and livestock products: oxen and cows, calves, wethers, sheep and pigs, beef, pork, veal, mutton
Building materials and metal: roofing tiles, bricks, limestone, iron, carpenters' nails, door locks
Textiles: clothing, stockings, boots and shoes
Wages: day-wages of masons, carpenters, painters and farmhands
FRANKFURT AM MAIN (Elsas, 1940:II A):
Grain: wheat, rye, oats
Building materials: limestone and bricks
Metal: only horseshoes
Wages: Day-wages of casual farm labourers in summer. These wages, like those of navvies and canal-diggers, remained nominally the same throughout the period.
CRACOW (Pelc, 1935, 1937):
Grain: wheat, rye, barley, oats
Livestock and livestock products: horses, cattle, calves, pigs, butter, also butter and pig lard
Building materials and metals: rafters, shingles, tiles
Leather goods and skins: boots, shoes, furs
Wages: Wages of carpenters, masons, unskilled labourers and other salaried groups, including city officials. A mean value has been extracted from Pelc's wage series which he has already arranged in groups and converted to a relative value. As there are no data on our base period (1351–75), wages and salaries from 1381–1400 have been taken as equalling 100.

4 The figures in table 9 have already been used by Postan (1950:II, 221f.).

5 Data for table 10 as follows:
England (Rogers, 1866–1902:I, 234; IV, 322): Rogers gives mason's wages as a ten-year average (1371–80). For the conversion of coinage and measures Rogers' data have been supplemented by information from other sources: 1 quarter = 218 kilograms, 1 penny = 20 troy grains, 1 troy grain = 0.064179 grams silver.
Antwerp (van der Wee, 1963a:I, 174, 457, 336): masons, 9 Flemish groats; one Antwerp quarter = 77 litres or 56 kilograms; 1 Flemish groat in 1379 = 1 gram silver.
Rostock (Hauschild, 1973:57): 1 scheffel of rye in Rostock in 1379 was worth 2s. 6d.; 1 scheffel = 40 kilograms (average figure from F. Engel's tables of old coins, weights and measures (1965:9), confirmed by Hauschild), 1 Denar = 0.203 grams silver. For a day's work, tips included, a mason earned 27¾ denars or 5.6 grams of silver.

6 Based on van der Wee's appendix 48, entitled 'Real daily income of masons and masons' labourers ...'. In response to my inquiry Mr van der Wee told me that the table's heading contained an error and should read 'real weekly income ...'. Furthermore, I learnt that a 'week' was determined by the number of working days per year, 210 on average, divided by 52. According to that, the daily wage we are concerned with could be reckoned as a quarter of the weekly wage.

7 Hauschild contradicts my theory of agricultural depressions and my belief in the 'golden age' of the craftsman, but the wages and prices she has so industriously assembled do not support her contradiction, as can be seen above.

8 Data for table 11:
Alsace: see Hanover (1878:II, 421, 555).
The Coblenz Valley area: according to Lamprecht (1885–6:II, 613) the average price of rye per measure (malter) during the fifteenth century in the Moselle region was 27.1 grams of silver, a malter at that time containing about 200 litres (II,510). The wage

data for masons and carpenters refer to the years 1431–2, 1444–6, 1464–5 (II, 538), those for unskilled labour to these and other years of the first half of the century, converted to a total average of 1.89 grams of silver (II, 612). The food rations were added to the money wages as 1.92 grams of silver per diem (II, 612). The above calculations are confirmed by Schönfeldt's work on the same material (1903:I, 60).

Saxony: according to Falke (1869:393f.), nominal wages during the second half of the fifteenth century in Saxony were 3.5 groschen for masons, 2 groschen 2 pfennigs for carpenters, 1 groschen 2 pfennigs for day labourers. A Dresden scheffel of rye, which Falke (1869:367) considers to have contained 103.8 litres cost on the average 6 groschen 4 pfennigs between 1455 and 1480 (1869:371).

East Prussia: see Aubin (1911:97).

Holstein: von Buchwald (1881:173, 190, 191) holds that average nominal wages at the Preetz monastery (Holstein) during the fifteenth century were: masons, 3 schillings; carpenters, 2 schillings 4 pfennigs; day-labourers 1.75 schillings. Waschinski (1952, 1959) estimated that the price of rye in Schleswig-Holstein in the second half of the fifteenth century, the period of most of these wages, was 12 schillings a tonne (= 100 kilograms) This 'rye value' of the Holstein wages coincides with the estimate of von Buchwald (1881:174) that the free labourer of Schleswig-Holstein earned half a measure (scheffel) of rye a day during the fifteenth century.

9 If enough time remains to me, I intend to deal with the subject in greater detail and in a wider field under the title 'Strukturen und Krisen der spätmittelalterlichen Wirtschaft'.

10 The conversions were done according to the rule indicated in the appendix.

11 A plaphart or 'thick pfennig' was worth 7 ordinary pfennigs.

12 Further details of living standards and wages in Constance are to be found in von Richenstal, pages 86, 153. In autumn there was a plentiful harvest 'and the people's wages had become high'. As in other places, wages in Constance did not follow the downward drift of prices. This was no doubt related to the shortage of labour in the late Middle Ages.

13 Some of the data that follow without further reference will be found in Abel (1976: 150f.).

14 From the archives of the Teutonic Order, Reg. No. 8599 in the Göttingen archives. Toeppen (1888:II, no 388) gives a short summary, from which Aubin (1911:58, note 1) quotes in passing.

15 Even in 1480 the complaint was 'if the coinage remains so base, it will bring ruin to this land' (Toeppen n.d.:V, no. 121).

16 Le Roy Ladurie has more than once commented in *Annales* on climatic (and weather) changes, first in his essay *Histoire et climat* (1959:3ff). See his summing up in *Times of Feast, Times of Famine* (1971), a book discussed in detail by Post (1973:721ff.).

17 See Abel (1967:127) for a map showing the boundaries of German wine-growing at the time of its greatest expansion in area.

18 Miani describes the agricultural advances in northern Italy as the 'defensive reaction of a privileged region (a meeting point of the chief trade routes) to the all-European depression'.

19 Authority for ensuing statements will also be found in Abel (1976a:138ff.). Since only a short summary can be given here, it is not possible to acknowledge all the authors to whom the writer is indebted for his material. Only some of the newer works have been cited.

20 Maschke considers, with every reason, that he has established the spiritual stagnation, the diminished social status and the economic impoverishment of the Teutonic Order during the fifteenth century.

21 For Flanders this is stressed by van der Wee (1963a:65), but it remains valid for other parts of western Europe. Kriedte, Medick and Schlumbohm (1977) have dealt with the basic problems of secondary rural occupations.

22 In Sweden, according to a manuscript in the diocese of Funbo near Uppsala, the accounts for the years 1395–1483 disclosed that the peasants were burdened with tithes and rent amounting to 25–30 per cent of the gross corn yield (Andre, 1965:385–400).

23 C. A. Christensen's phrase, used to describe Danish farmers, but applicable to the great majority of German, English and French farmers.

24 Figure 17, as well as the above calculation of averages for Germany, is based on the work of Pohlendt (1950:69f.). The lost-village quotients he has assembled for various districts (106 certain, 43 probable, thus 149 in all) have been supplemented by the results of more recent research (65 quotients) so that altogether 214 lost-village quotients for Germany are available. The quotients were entered on cards. To obliterate chance variations of situation, to level out the quantity of local data and to obtain a better overall view of Germany, the quotients for areas of similar natural environment and comparable trading situation were converted to averages. By this means some regional differences were lost, especially total losses in woodland districts but, on the other hand, differences involving extensive areas, which were more important for our research, were brought into prominence.

25 For English research on lost villages (Beresford and others) see page 82 above. An admirable bibliography of the more important publications on this subject is presented by Hurst (1974:237ff.). A good general view of the progress of research in several countries was afforded by the Third International Congress of Economic Historians and published as a collection in 1965. Current information on English and other research is provided by the annual reports of the Medieval Village Research Group, London, e.g. No. 23, 1975, also reports on France, Italy and Norway.

26 Of the voluminous Nordic literature on deserted villages, there is space to mention only Holmsen's *Eidsvoll Bygds Historie*, 1950–61, one of the few really great local and regional histories in the international literature; also, Holmsen (1962:165f.), Sandnes (1970), the volume of proceedings of the Northern Historians' Conference in Bergen, 1964; and Gissel's report on the Nordic Ødegard Project in the five northern countries (1976:43–54).

27 See Abel (1976a:29f., 98ff.) for the works of the above-mentioned Norwegian authors, as well as for evidence in support of the ensuing paragraph.

28 *A Discourse of the Commonweal*, now thought to have been written by Sir Thomas Smith, first appeared in 1581 but had been written in 1549. In the interval agrarian conditions had changed somewhat, especially in that wages had fallen steeply in relation to the price of cereals. Although the work was composed at a time when the agricultural slump was almost at an end, the dialogues entirely reflect the conditions of the fifteenth century depression. The list was supposed to have been given by a 'husbandman' in reply to the 'doctor's' question as to what articles a farmer needed.

29 A general survey of the present state of research is to be found in Abel (1935:670f.; 1976a:84ff.). Inama-Sternegg and Häpke (1924:671f.) also made a summary of the international research of their day, and had already drawn the conclusion that 'every-where' (i.e. in all the chief European countries) 'there was, during the fourteenth century, a decline, or at any rate a standstill, of population'. More recent literature on

individual countries and regions can be mentioned here only in particular cases. For further information refer once more to Helleiner (1967:5ff.).

Chapter 4 Farming and the standard of living in the sixteenth century

1 Further information on the population of northern Europe, including the period of rehabilitation, is expected from Scandinavian research on lost villages.

2 In table 15 Le Roy Ladurie's figures have been slightly altered as the sums given did not correspond.

3 Further references to the literature can be dispensed with, except to mention a few works dealing with the Baltic trade: Jeannin (1956:334f.), Malowist (1959:178f.), Hoszowski (1960:123f.).

4 To O. Pickl (1973:143ff.) we also owe a comprehensive survey of the results of the international research to date, with a map of the north and east European cattle trade in 1600, showing grazing areas, quantities and main routes.

5 The quantities, values and routes of the ox trade were taken from Wiese (1963, 1966). The grain trade figures used for comparison were calculated from works by Bang and Korst (n.d.), and A. E. Christensen (1934:94). The grain prices are derived from the Danzig grain prices compiled by Pelc (1935, 1937).

6 The information on prices in England came from Rogers (1866–1902:IV, 333; V, 354); that for Antwerp from Scholliers (1959:309f., 393f.); for Strasbourg from Hanauer (1878:197); for Spain from Hamilton (1934:335–54); for Florence from Parenti (1939:39); for Vienna from Pribram (1938:I, 581, 583, 621, 623); for Münich, Leipzig and Würzburg from Elsas (1936, 1940:I, 590, 642; II, A, 524); for Hamburg and Jutland from Wiese (1966:82); for Danzig and Cracow from Pelc (1935:121f.).

7 Hausherr (1954) devotes an impressive chapter to the latifundia and sheep farming of south-western Europe.

8 It would be irrelevant to enlarge upon this question here. However, Hoszowski (1961:441f.) and Mankov (1957) have contributed papers containing additional material on the subject.

9 Figure 24 is based upon the following:
ENGLAND (from Rogers, 1866–1902:IV, V):
Grain: wheat, barley, oats in southern England
Industrial products: charcoal, firewood, lime, iron, roofing tiles, bricks, sailcloth, linen, paper
Wages: day-wages for carpenters, masons, sawyers, tilers, metal workers and unskilled labourers
BELGIUM (from Verlinden, 1959:241f.):
Grain: wheat, rye, barley, oats
Industrial products: soap, paper, sailcloth
Wages: journeyman mason, unskilled mason, stonemason, journeyman tiler, journeyman paviour, journeyman carpenter, master carpenter, sawyer, thatcher, unskilled labourer
FRANCE (from d'Avenel, 1894–1926:II, IV. It has already been pointed out that d'Avenel's figures are not entirely to be trusted. For this period, however, they are largely confirmed by Hauser's reliable price series. Unfortunately Hauser gives very few examples from the industrial products of this period and none at all of wages):
Grain: wheat, rye, barley, oats

Industrial products: men's outer clothing, hats, shoes, boots, stockings, soap

Wages: farmhand, mason, carpenter, vineyard labourer, smith, painter

GERMANY (from Kullak-Ublick, 1953; Beissel, 1885; Elsas, 1936, 1940:1, 11A; Pelc, 1937):

Grain: wheat, rye, barley, oats in Danzig (except wheat), Göttingen, Xanten, Augsburg (except wheat), Munich, Frankfurt am Main, and Würzburg

Industrial products: firewood, planks, charcoal, bricks, tiles, slates, lime, lead, nails, iron, horseshoes, wax, wax candles, ticking, linen, gloves, shoes, paper from seven different German towns (as above)

Wages: Mason and carpenter (master and journeyman), stonemason, unskilled labourer and builder's assistant (handyman to prepare mortar etc.), sawyer, raker and haymaker, reaper, thresher, straw-cutter, maidservants, farmhands, town surgeons and physicians, town clerks, from the same seven towns

AUSTRIA (from Pribram, 1938:1):

Grain: wheat, rye, barley, oats from Vienna, rye and oats from Klosterneuburg

Industrial products: lime, building stone, roofing tiles, firewood, boards, roofing shingles, vine stakes, twine, paper, wax, nails, candles in Vienna and Klosterneuburg

Wages: day-wages for masons, tilers, journeyman mason and carpenter, handyman, vineyard labourer in Vienna and Klosterneuburg

POLAND (from Pelc, 1935; and Hoszowski, 1954):

Grain: wheat, rye, barley, oats in Cracow, oats in Lemberg

Industrial products: woollen cloth and blankets, boots, firewood, tiling battens and shingles, bricks, lime, iron, roofing and batten nails, paper, wax, furs, linen in Cracow and Lemberg

Wages: mason and carpenter (journeyman and master), unskilled labourer, notary, clockmaker, porter, captains in Cracow and Lemberg.

10 This material comes from the annual accounts of the Hiob and St Georges Hospital in Hamburg. It was assembled by Dr Elsas' colleagues and transferred to London in 1933, and from thence, together with Dr Elsas' complete literary remains, it has recently been placed at the disposal of the Institute of Social and Economic History of Göttingen University. It could possibly be completed as a supplement to Elsas' *Umriss einer Geschichte der Preise und Löhne in Deutschland* (1936, 1940).

11 Figures on prices and wages from the towns of Munich, Leipzig, Augsburg, and Würzburg were taken from Elsas (1936, 1940) and adapted for the present purpose.

12 For further contemporary evidence see Brentano (1927:81f.) and Rogers (1866–1902:V, 804f.). The subject has recently been treated in greater depth, and based on more abundant evidence, by Bowden (1967:593ff.). From this authentic and comprehensive work, which we cannot begin to evaluate here, it will be enough to note that, according to Bowden, there were some estates in Warwickshire where rents between 1556 and 1648 went up by 1,000 per cent (p. 693).

13 Eiderstedt rents from Peter Sachs (1637) and Ivar Peters (n.d.). Since there are no complete series of rye prices for Eiderstedt, the price of rye in Rendsburg according to Waschinski (1959) has been used instead.

14 D'Avenel considered it advisable to omit exceptional prices from his calculations as obviously in such a wide area as France the differences in soil quality and location for trade caused wide variations in price. That he was nevertheless so nearly accurate should be mentioned, in view of his many critics. According to d'Avenel the price for a hectare of farmland (reckoned for the whole of France in grams of silver) increased between the 25-year periods 1451–75 and 1576–1600 as follows: 217, 439, 427, 541, 864, 1,317.

If these figures are compared with those in table 17, derived from smaller areas, it will be seen that the movements do not differ seriously.

15 Raveau gave his farmland prices in Tournois livres, which unfortunately cannot be properly converted by the Wailly tables to which Raveau refers. These tables are full of errors (see Wiebe, 1895). It is safer to go by the livre's silver content, as in d'Avenel's tables (1894–1926:I, 483). The Eiderstedt prices were calculated from the notes of Peters (n.d.) and Peter Sachs (1637). The chroniclers recorded the prices in Lübeck marks per demat. The present Eiderstedt demat contains 216 square rods of 21 square metres each, about half a hectare. It probably had the same area in the sixteenth century. In 1567 a new, smaller rod was introduced measuring 16 instead of 18 feet, but Sachs observed that this new measure made the demat bigger, which can only mean that its nominal content of square rods was increased and that the real content remained constant. Jesse (1928:209, appendix table) gave the silver value of Lübeck marks up to the year 1551. In 1619 the Lübeck mark was put on the 'mark standard', i.e. 27 marks were minted from the standard silver mark (233.855 grams), so that it contained about 8.66 grams of silver. It is not certain how much the Lübeck mark was worth in silver during the interval between those dates. According to Sachs 'the state thaler, hitherto valued at two marks was now set at three'. Since the Augsburg coinage decree of 1566 the state thaler had contained 25.98 grams of standard silver. Consequently the exchange rate and the proportionate silver content of the Lübeck mark was devalued from 12.99 grams to 8.66 grams of silver. In his last calculation for the year 1551, however, Jesse quotes the silver content as 17.6 grams, so it seems that a reduction of the standard must have followed, perhaps in 1572, when new coinage regulation was introduced in Lübeck. In any case the reduction cannot have occurred before 1567, for Sachs' comparison of the Lübeck mark to the gold ducat in the years 1551 and 1567 gives no indication of a devalued mark. The silver content of the Lübeck mark current in Eiderstedt does not appear to have sunk any lower after 1575. There are no further records of its devaluation in the Eiderstedt Chronicles; moreover the grain prices for the following years entered then in the Chronicles in Lübeck are perfectly compatible with the Lübeck grain prices for the same period collected by Hansen, as long as the Lübeck mark is valued at 8.66 grams of silver. Among J. Hansen's works his *Beiträge zur Geschichte* (1912) should be specially mentioned. It gives the Lübeck rye prices in Lübeck scheffels and schillings. The Lübeck scheffel was worth about 34.5 litres. Since Jesse imparts the silver content of the schilling, the Hansen prices can be used for comparison.

16 This development is well illustrated by the rich contents of the Bavarian National Museum in Munich.

17 It was not only in Pomerania that there were some prosperous peasants. Aubin (1911:142) describes the same conditions in East Prussia, and similar reports of isolated instances come from other parts of eastern Germany. Unfortunately we have insufficient evidence regarding how the two groups of peasants, the prosperous and the poor (already differentiated by Kantzow), stood in quantitative relation to each other.

18 One of my colleagues, who specializes in the sixteenth century, based his calculation on the minimum needs reckoned in calories, of a builder's family of five, and compared the purchase price of this requirement with a builder's wage. Even with that calculation, it was impossible to take into account the varying contents of the shopping basket during the sixteenth-century inflation period.

19 Wages and grain prices were taken from the following authors:
for England: Rogers, 1866–1902:IV, 524, V, 664 (wages); IV, 290, V, 268 (wheat)

for Antwerp: Scholliers, 1960:474f. (wages); 1960:200f. (rye)

for Strasburg: Hanauer, 1878:421 (wages); 1878:91f. (bread grain)

for Valencia: Hamilton, 1947*b*:397f. (wages); 1947*b*:354f. (bread grain)

for Florence: Parenti, 1939:39 (wages and bread grain)

for Augsburg: Elsas, 1936:1, 731 (wages); 1936:1, 595 (bread grain)

for Leipzig: Elsas, 1940:11A, 592 (wages); 1940:11A, 516 (bread grain)

for Xanten: Beissel, 1885:184 (wages); 1885:126 (bread grain)

for Vienna: Pribram, 1938:601, 643 (wages); 1938:571, 611, wages, pp. 601, 643; grain
  (bread grain)

for Danzig: Pelc, 1935, 1937 (wages, bread grain)

for Cracow: Pelc, wages 1935, 1936 (wages, bread grain)

for Lemberg: Hoszowski, 1954:207 (wages); 1954:192 (bread grain)

20 The himt of bread, assessed by Woehlkens as 20 kilograms, is here reckoned as 22.5 kilograms.

21 At that time (1585) 1 ell (60 centimetres) of cheapest linen cost 1 schilling; 1 ell of undyed cloth, 6 schillings and 1 pair of shoes, 7 schillings.

22 In Sri Lanka, for instance, a labourer earns the equivalent of 8 kilograms of rice a day. Rice contains more nourishment per unit than rye or rye-bread.

23 Dinners of this ceremonial kind sometimes invested the diner with some new right or relieved him of a former duty. Thus Weinsberg remarked of this meal that, although it cost him 64 guilders, it was worth the expense, as in future he would be free from guard-duties and also certain fees; also Höhlbaum (1887:IV), description of the above meal (11:223f.).

24 The word 'industry' is here used in the sense of Nef, Keynes and others to mean large-scale industry, which exceeded the ordinary handicraft businesses in the number of workers employed and the amount of capital invested (see Nef, 1953 edn:294f.). We shall return to the comparative importance of rents and industrial capital in a later chapter, but it may be observed at this point that as late as the mid-nineteenth century, within the territory of the German Customs Union without Wurtemberg and Frankfurt am Main, the whole textile industry – by far the largest German industry at that time – was supported by a business and floating capital of no more than 190 million thalers, whereas the *annual* rents of the period must certainly have been over 200 million thalers in Germany alone (see Abel, 1963:333).

25 For further information on Germany's economic development during the sixteenth century see Lütge (1958*a*:43f., 1958*b*), Abel (1961*b*:448f.).

Chapter 5   Slumps, wars and the long-term downward trend

1 The depression became more pronounced after the turn of the century, a subject discussed in Abel (1974:130ff.).

2 For sources and conversion methods see appendix notes on pp. 299–303. The Stettin prices are taken from the *Acta Borussica, Getreidehandelspolitik*, 1901:11, 610.

3 The figures are taken from: for England, Rogers (1866–1902); for France, d'Avenel (1894–1926) and Hauser (1936*a*); for Belgium, Verlinden (1959–1973); for north Italy, *Movimento dei Prezzi* (1886:XXXf.); for Germany, Elsas (1936, 1940), Beissel (1885), Hanauer (1876, 1878), Waschinski (1959,11), Pelc (1935, 1937), Saalfeld, Kullak-Ublick (1953), Naudé (1901); for Austria, Pribram (1938); for the Netherlands, Posthumus (1946, 1964), and for Denmark, H. Pedersen (1905:788f.).

4 Although Child's work bears the date 1694, the preface and the references on pp. 45f. to the Great Plague (1665) and the Great Fire (1666) indicate that it must have been written in the 1660s.

5 Pre-1914 French francs; 1 Fr. = 0.80 RM.

6 Zolla based his estimate on the leasehold rents received by the estates of the Saint Nazaire chapter at Béziers, the chapter of Montpellier and the Hôtel-Dieu of Angers. At Montpellier the entries between 1600 and 1610 are missing and have been assessed from the movement of the other two series; each of the series has been given equal weight in the averaging. Unfortunately a number of errors and misprints have crept into Zolla's work, which it has not been possible entirely to eliminate. The first edition of this book contained on page 76 the figures of the separate series and decades. It is not necessary to repeat them here as so much new information has come to light in the intervening thirty years that Zolla's figures no longer have quite the same importance. See Le Roy Ladurie, 1966:1, 477.

7 Levasseur believed that the French population attained its greatest density after the Peace of Nijmwegen (1679). According to the additional information quoted below, page 320, n. 16, the increase may have reached its peak a few years earlier.

8 Here also will be found reason for the term, which, against a background of other countries, includes the course of events in German territories.

9 See Abel (1967) for a description of the spread of the 1634–40 plague in Germany, taken from Keyser.

Chapter 6 *Decline and depression*

1 As before, the price series in the appendix have been used. Figures from: for England (wheat), Rogers (1866–1902) and Tooke and Newmarch (1858:1, 11); for France (wheat), d'Avenel (1894–1926) and Hauser (1936*a*); for Belgium (wheat), Verlinden (1959–73); for northern Italy (wheat), *Movimento dei Prezzi* (1886); for Germany (rye), Elsas (1936, 1940), Beissel (1885), Hanauer (1876, 1878), Waschinski (1959, 11), Pelc (1935, 1937), Saalfeld, Kullak-Ublick (1953), Naudé (1901); for the Netherlands (rye), Posthumus (1946, 1964); for Austria (rye), Pribram (1938); for Poland (rye), Tomaszewski (1934); for Denmark (rye), H. Pedersen (1905).

2 As before, English wages up to 1702 have been taken from Rogers (1866–1902); those for the subsequent years are derived from Steffen (1901:1, 471), whose conclusions were based on the manuscript of Rogers' seventh volume and on the notes of Young and Smith. According to Steffen, the cash wages of the English labourer remained almost static during the first half of the eighteenth century. The cash wages were converted to kilograms of wheat on the basis of the price tables in the appendix. The artisan builder's wages refer to masons and carpenters.

The French wages were borrowed from d'Avenel. Here too, masons' and carpenters' wages were used for calculating the artisan-builder wage index. The German wages represent the mean values of wages paid in Munich, Augsburg, Würzburg and Leipzig (from Elsas), and Strasburg (from Hanauer).

3 The making of 100 faggots is taken as the equivalent of a 10- to 12-hour working day (Goubert: 558, note 27). The equation seems realistic, since a labourer's day wage in 1660–1735 would be worth 6.6–22 litres or by other reckonings 5.1–17 kilograms of wheat.

4 Quesnay quotes Dupré de St Maur's information as if it were his own.

5 20 sols = 1 Tournais livre = (between 1728 and 1758) 4.27 grams of silver (according to

d'Avenel, 1894–1926:1, 483); 1 arpent = about 34.2 a; see also d'Avenel (1894–1926:1, 496f.) and Quesnay (1757, in 1888:196).

6 Quesnay's writings, with an excellent commentary, can now be found in *François Quesnay et la Physiocratie*, published by the Inst. National d'Études Démographiques, in 2 volumes, 1958.

7 Often since quoted and supplemented in the German literature assembled by Braeuer (1968).

8 Bauer quotes from Quesnay's unpublished article, 'Hommes'. Quesnay states elsewhere (1756, in 1888:171f.) more cautiously that something over a quarter of the soil suited to cultivation was wasteland. There are other writings that go more deeply into the connection between the Physiocratic movement and the difficult agricultural situation of the time: see Thiele (1906:515f.) and Weulersse (1931:244f.).

9 For further information on famine in the pre-industrial era in other years and countries, and with it a deeper, more comprehensive analysis see Abel (1974).

10 The Paris prices were taken from Hauser (1936:110f.), the Berlin prices from Naudé and Skalweit (1910:11, 568; 111, 625f.; IV, 647f.), the London prices from Rogers (1866–1902: V, 272f.) and from Tooke and Newmarch (1858:11, 512f.).

11 For Friesland see Faber's great work (1972:part 2) which extends far beyond the hitherto-known facts and deep into social history, confirming the depression symptoms that existed in Friesland between about 1650 and 1750, a matter only touched on here.

12 The Sound toll registers, the chief source of documentary evidence on exports from the Baltic zone, have been studied in great detail by Jeannin (1964:55ff., 307ff.).

13 The Provincial Diet of the Electorate of Bavaria in 1669, assembled from authentic manuscripts, 1812, p. 375.

14 Knapp sought to explain the unfavourable position of the east German peasantry solely as the result of changes in agrarian organization. His way of limiting agrarian history to the history of agrarian systems not only has determined the formulation of German farming history for decades, but also has provided welcome material for those historians who tend to see 'feudalism' as the root of all distress.

15 Von Wulffen thought that the peasants could support the rents because they no longer had to fear a drop in prices: now that the East and West Indies were within reach and the whole world within communicable distance, he supposed the price of commodities would be fixed unalterably. Von Wulffen shared the fate of many prophets: he was completely wrong. See Ranke (1930) on the discussion that preceded the copyhold regulation of the Prussian demesnes.

16 Mirabeau senior reckoned that the population of France had only sunk to 18 million, not 16 million as Quesnay maintained. See also the older literature and Levasseur (1889) who supposed mistakenly that the French population had begun to grow again as early as the 1720s or 1730s. In this supposition he was contradicted by many contemporaries. More recent research as well has confirmed decline or stagnation as early as the first half of the eighteenth century, as does Le Roy Ladurie (1966:544ff.), who estimated the decline in the Languedoc population between 1677 and 1741 at 18 per cent, in some villages even 50 per cent or more. See also Goubert (1960), especially his chapter on the *crises démographiques* of the old type.

17 The most thorough and authentic work to date on European population movements in century comes from Helleiner (1967).

Chapter 7   The upward trend of agriculture during the second half of the eighteenth century

1 The prices represented in figure 49 for England (wheat), France (wheat), northern Italy (wheat), Germany (rye), the Netherlands (rye) and Austria (rye) are given in the appendix and explained in the appendix notes. The Danish prices (rye) come from H. Pedersen (1905:788), the Swedish prices (rye) from Åmark (1921:154).

2 A considerable number of price and wage series have been used for the different countries and each of the series has been related to the base period. Subsequently these relative values have been converted to a mean value for each country. Data for the series as follows:

ENGLAND (Young, 1812: appendix):
Grain: wheat, barley, oats from various sources
Industrial goods: shoes, clothes, hats, dishcloths from Greenwich Hospital account books
Wages: various kinds of wages from different sources

FRANCE (Hauser, 1936*b*):
Grain: wheat, rye, barley and oats in Paris and Château-Goutier
Industrial goods: candles, soap, firewood, charcoal and plaster in Paris; soap, lime, slate, firewood in Château-Goutier
Wages: day-wages of navvies, masons, joiners and carpenters in St Antonier

GERMANY (Elsas, 1936, 1940):
Grain: wheat, rye, barley, oats in Augsburg, Frankfurt am Main, Speyer and Würzburg (without barley)
Industrial goods: lime in Ausburg; lime, roofing tiles, bricks and charcoal in Frankfurt am Main; lime, roofing tiles and bricks in Speyer; lime, building stone and firewood in Würzburg
Wages: day-wages of masons, journeymen carpenters and unskilled labourers in Augsburg; yearly salaries of librarians and town clerks in Frankfurt am Main; day-wages of haymakers, threshers, reapers and dairymaids in Speyer; unskilled labourers' day-wages in Würzburg

AUSTRIA (Pribham, 1938):
Grain: wheat, rye, barley (up to 1800) from Vienna
Industrial goods: lime, bricks, roofing tiles and candles from Vienna (up to 1780)
Wages: masons, carpenters, tilers from Vienna (up to 1780)

POLAND (Tomaszewski, 1934):
Grain: wheat, rye, barley and oats in Cracow
Industrial goods: linen, boots, candles, firewood, bricks, roofing tiles, lime, iron in Cracow
Wages: mason, carpenter and unskilled labourer in Cracow

DENMARK (various sources, especially Falbe-Hansen, 1904; Friis and Glamann, 1958; Nielsen, 1933:164f.):
Grain: rye, barley, oats
Industrial goods: salt, firewood, iron, tar
Wages: farmhands' day-wages

3 As chief witnesses to what she considers 'remarkably high wage increases' in north-west Germany during the last two decades of the eighteenth century, Anna Neumann (1911:86f.) calls on Gülich, Wiarda and, above all, Thaer. Gülich's sparse notes and the inaccurately-dated wage data in Wiarda (1880:65f.) hardly justify Neumann's con-

clusions, while Thaer, as mentioned, later modified his 1799 statement on wage increases.

4 It was Arthur Young, in particular, who established this fact. He was among the most distinguished agrarian experts and practitioners of his time.

5 As is well known, Ricardo put forward more than one theory of wages. The theory of 'counter-movements in wages and rents' is only touched on in different parts of his work. Its clearest formulation comes from Dietzel (1901).

6 According to Porter (1912:188), an annual average of about 80,000 acres was brought into cultivation between 1760 and 1799. The difference between the statistics quoted by Gülich and those of Porter (and a few of the more recent estimates) is less significant than the fact, accepted by Porter and many later authors, that the enclosed areas consisted entirely of hitherto untilled land, i.e. waste and commons, whereas other authors, such as B. Skalweit (1915:17), maintained that only a third of the enclosed land was of that type, and the remainder a joining-up of plots among the common fields. Unfortunately Skalweit does not cite the sources of his information. A parliamentary report of 1797, which might have had something to tell us about this question, cannot be traced. A carefully-considered picture of the advantages and disadvantages of enclosure is presented by Chambers and Mingay (1970:77ff.), while Martin (1967:19ff.) tells us of the enormous increase in the value of enclosed fields.

7 Toutain made a compilation and critical evaluation of all the obtainable evidence; Bourde's thesis supplements Toutain's quantitative data.

8 It was only hinted at in the travel report by Young and Schwerz, quoted by Kulischer (1965:11, 44f.).

9 For the western and central provinces the above calculations were based on the herds in Minden-Ravensberg, Tecklenburg-Linden, Kleve Geldern, the county of Mark, Mörs, Halberstadt-Hohenstein, Pomerania and Courland which, in 1756, contained in all 736,000 beasts, a number which increased to 1,123,000 by the end of the century. The figures for the eastern provinces came from East Prussia, Lithuania, the Netze district and Silesia, where the total cattle population in 1776 was 1,367,000, while in 1800 it was 1.5 million. The sheep populations were reckoned from lists prepared by the ministers von Hoym and von Struensee and reproduced by Behre. These tables are more complete than the so-called livestock lists.

10 The import figures are from McCulloch (1834:425). The export figures are to be found in the report of the Select Committee on Agriculture (18 June 1821:391f.). Mitchell and Deane (1962:94f.) also give import and export statistics but, alas, not divided among the different countries.

11 For 1795 and 1796 even more detailed lists are given in *Schleswig-Holsteinische*, 1797:11, 128f.

12 The co-variation calculation was prepared in the Institut für Wirtschafts und Sozialgeschichte.

13 From Zolla's work the series of leasehold rents from estates belonging to the hospitals at Angers and le Mans and the Hospice St Pierre at Montpellier have been used. The Belgian graph has been compiled from Verlinden's data (1959:229f.). The Ditmarsch rents are based on the rents produced by the inns of the community (Schülkruge) at St Anne in North Ditmarsch (Holstein) published by Rolfs (1891:86f.). Rolfs keeps his figures in schillings and scheffels as in the original documents. It appears from his additional information that a scheffel was equivalent to 848 square metres, and a Lübeck schilling contained 0.429 grams of silver. The values have been calculated from this silver content. The land prices of Brunswick farms have been taken from a work by Achilles in Lütge, Franz and Abel (1965:XIII, 11). The prices of Danish farms were taken from

Falbe-Hansen (1888:99f.). They are presented in hard corn tons, i.e. rye and barley. A hard corn ton was the area needed to produce a ton of corn and varied according to the quality of the soil. It might be anything from 6,300 to 94,500 square metres. On the average the hard corn ton measured 28,370 square metres (see Noback, 1858:347).

14 The author must accept responsibility for this graph himself, as it was he who arranged the original data into periods and converted the values into modern Danish kroners. However, the name Falbe-Hansen is enough to assure us that the series was carefully calculated and rests on a sure foundation.

15 The prices of the Silesian estates were taken from Ziekursch (1915:402f.). They refer to seventeen landed properties in the Nimptsch district, which changed hands in 1740–60 or the next few years. The prices have been calculated from the graph's base line and then averaged. The Schleswig-Holstein prices came from Oldekop (1906–8). Since they are given in various currencies, the prices have been converted according to the following rates: 1 reichsthaler (silver) = 4.55 RM, 1 reichsthaler (coin) = 3.64 RM, 1 fine Danish Kroner (pre-1726) = 2.69 RM, 1 Lübeck Mark (post 1725) = 1.21 RM. See the conversions made by Noback (1858:13f.) and Niemann (1830:143). The prices from the Brandenburg Marches (the Teltow and Nieder-Barnim districts) have already been arranged and converted by Weyermann (1910:60f.), the Brandenburg-Prussian thaler being valued at 3.50 RM from 1690 to 1749 and at 3 RM after 1750 (see also notes to tables in appendix).

16 The additional evidence on the traffic in land and mortgages came from *Schleswig-Holstein Blätter für Polizei und Kultur* (1800:I, 148, 151); *Schleswig-Holsteinische* (1811:81); Ziekursch (1915:402f.); Paasche (1881:316); and Weyermann (1910:94f.).

Chapter 8   The agrarian depression of the early nineteenth century

1 The grain prices of 1801–30 are given in RM (1 RM = 5.56 grams of silver) in table 3 of the appendix. Figure 54 is drawn from the same prices. Recommended reading on the early-nineteenth-century agrarian depression includes for Germany: Ucke (1887), Westphal (1925*b*), the corresponding section in von Ciriacy-Wantrup (1936), Weyermann (1910:I, 1) and Neumann (1911); for France: in addition to the inadequate treatment in Romeuf (1902) there is the more comprehensive work by Sirol (1942). The best English expositions are to be found in the reports of the parliamentary Select Committees of 1804, 1821, 1833 and 1836, and some contemporary writings which will be mentioned in the course of this chapter. From the more modern literature we suggest Levy (1902) and for Canada Quellet and Hamelin (1962:36f.); although it is a pity that this work does not go into the close connection between the Canadian depression and the contemporary slump in Europe.

2 Table 22 was reckoned according to the figures given in McCulloch (1834:425).

3 For further information on the harvests see Hanssen and Wolff (1832:431f.); Heunisch and Bader (1857:127f.); Torfs (1859:220); and Tooke (1858:I, 178). The famine years 1816–17 have been treated in detail in Abel (1974: 314ff.).

4 The prices represented in figure 55 are based on the grain prices in table 3 of the appendix.

5 The reporter had already converted the original prices to Winchester quarters and English currency. The figures have been converted to reichmarks (1 RM = 5.56 grams of silver).

6 According to the testimony of the London cornhandler, Solly, before the Select Com-

mittee of 1821 (report, p. 316), the loading charge and dealer's commission at Danzig came to 3 shillings per Winchester quarter of wheat, the carriage from Danzig to London was 4 shillings to 4 shillings and sixpence, and the London market and transport cost 3 shillings, thus 10 shillings and sixpence in all. For the reckoning see appendix notes.

7 It may be remarked that the same situation was repeated 110 years later in 1931.

8 The English wheat prices are from table 3 in the appendix. The English wool prices are calculated from an average of the Norfolk and Suffolk quotations for 'clothing per pound' and 'combing per pound' contained in the third report from the Select Committee 1836 (21 July 1836:543). The Berlin bread grain prices are averaged from wheat and rye prices, the meat prices from the prices of beef and pork, the wool prices are for the 'medium quality'. The prices come from the *Jahrbuch für die amtliche Statistik des Preussischen Staates* (1867:11). Unfortunately not all the prices are taken at the same level. Those for meat and butter are retail, but not the Mecklenburg prices, which were paid at the sheep farm of the Klein-Roge estate, Teterow. The latter prices for the years from 1804 to 1832 were published in the *Neue Annalen der Mecklenburger* (1834:287). The Danish prices are from Nielsen (1933:384), the meat in question being pork. The U.S. prices (bacon) were assembled by Peterson (1929).

9 The wheat prices represented in figure 57 come from table 3 in the appendix. The wages and the prices of industrial goods are in the reports of the 1833 and 1836 Select Committees. In order to compare the prices of the various commodities and the wages of the different kinds of labourers, each price and wage series was first converted to a percentage of the 1816–18 figure: the percentages were then turned into unweighted averages. Included in the indices are *manufactured goods*: shoes, stockings, hats, blankets, coats; and *wages*: carpenters, masons, bricklayers and plumbers.

10 A comprehensive description of the crisis, containing fresh price material, is presented by Pedersen (1970:174ff.).

11 It is significant that Henri Sée did not mention the agrarian depression of this period in either *La vie économique* (1927b) or in *L'économie rurale* (1927a). For him the word 'crisis' denoted the famine and inflation of 1816–17.

12 Some contemporary writers compiled whole lists of the causes to which they attributed the downfall of agriculture. Among the best of these comprehensive essays on the farming crisis of that time is a forgotten work by Lips (1830:12f.) in which is to be found a description of the depression that is in many ways still unsurpassed.

Chapter 9   Mass poverty

1 Strasbourg wages and wheat prices from Hanauer; Emden figures from Aden (1963: appendix); Leipzig figures from Elsas (1940:11, 593, 519f.); Berlin wages from Krüger (1958:324). Berlin wheat prices from *Acta Borussica, Getreidehandelspolitik* (III).

2 In a letter to Miss Harkness, Engels remarked that he had learnt more from Balzac, even in regard to economic details (e.g. the redistribution of land and personal property after the Revolution) than from all the professional historians, economists and statisticians of the time put together (cited in Kuczynski, 1964:11).

3 This reference was called to my attention by Chevalier's *Classes laborieuses et classes dangereuses* (1959:317), a work in which he has brought together a great number of contemporary voices which, taken all together, leave a strong impression.

4 Quoted in the appendix of the first edition of this book. Later research, especially Phelps-

Brown and Hopkins' calculations here quoted, has rendered its further reproduction superfluous.

5 The values for England come from Steffen, those for France come from *Statistique de la France* (1863:211), for Strasburg from Hanauer (1878:11, 99f.), for Emden from Aden (1963), for Leipzig from Elsas (1940:11A, 520f., 593) and for Silesia from Heisig (1884:140, 188).

6 Calculated from data assembled by Elsas, and to be found, among other places, in Riemann (1953: appendix).

7 The English wages and prices are from Rogers (1866–1902:IV, 524f. v, 664f.) and Steffen (1901–5:I, 471; II, 13, 30; III, 14, 25), the Strasbourg figures from Hanauer (1878:11, 417f.), the Vienna figures from Pribram (1938:601, 641f.) and the information on Leipzig from Elsas (1940:11A, 592f.).

Chapter 10   The solution to the problems of inadequate food supply

1 ENGLAND: we have the interesting series compiled by Mitchell and Deane (1962:348ff., 411f., 488ff.). The wage series have been supplemented from the work of Steffen (1901:1, 371; 1904:11, 13, 30; 1905:111, 19, 25) and Abel's notes in the first edition of this book (1935b: 172, 176). The groups were made up as follows:

Grain: wheat, barley, oats (average English prices from the *London Gazette*)

Animal products: beef, mutton, pork, butter, tallow, whale oil, cheese throughout the period; milk up to 1850, and after 1850 bacon and cod liver oil

Industrial products: coal, pig iron, tin, lead, copper, hemp, cotton, flax, tar, tobacco, hides, skins, tallow, silk, building wood; mercury and fleeces up to 1850, olive oil and linen after 1850. Manufactured goods are almost absent from this list, but it should be noted that from 1860 to 1910 the prices of industrial raw material and of manufactured goods developed along practically the same lines (see Maynard, 1962:171)

Wages: farm labourers, typesetters, builders, workers in a cotton factory (weekly wages), carpenters (day-wages)

FRANCE: *Annuaire Statistique* (1928: vol. 44, pp, 103ff., 132):

Grain: wheat, rye

Animal products: beef

Industrial products: cast iron, iron, copper, cotton

Wages: index numbers from the *Annuaire Statistique*

GERMANY: the price series were taken from Jacobs and Richter (1935). An examination of prices as intricate as that undertaken by Jacobs when calculating the indices for industrial products would not be justified here, since it is impossible to establish the fluctuating importance of the various products in relation to each other and during the period. The experiment of giving the big sub-group of cotton a double value within the framework of industrial product indices made very little difference to the percentages (up to 3 per cent) and none at all to the general trend. The wage series are based on the data of Kuczynski (1947:39f., 101f., 178f.; 1961:245f.). Extra material has come from Neumann (1911:330f.) and Buchenberger (1914:478).

Grain: wheat, rye, oats, barley in Berlin, Hamburg, Königsberg and Munich

Animal products: beef, pork, butter

Industrial products: coal, iron, non-ferrous metals (copper, tin, zinc, lead), textiles (wool, cotton, raw silk, flax, linen thread, hemp)

Wages: workers' wages from coal mines (Saar, Aachen and Ruhr districts), iron mines (left and right banks of the Rhine), copper mines (Halle-Mansfeld), and from printing-works (average from eight towns), farming and forestry (average from thirty Prussian administrative areas)

2 Feilen made use of data from Jacobs and Richter (1935). Wool prices cover only 1810 to 1913.

3 According to Warren and Pearson (1933:197) the purchasing power of wages in the United States more-or-less trebled between 1840 and 1914, equalling an annual increase of 1.71 per cent.

4 These figures and the idea of the graph come from the work of Hanau (1962:44f.). The statistics used in the graph were taken from the *FAO Product Yearbook* (1962:246ff.) and the *Yearbook of National Accounts Statistics* (1960).

5 Graphs and figures have been taken from Abel, Riemann and Welling (1954). The subject is also treated in Abel (1967b:244). Most of the source material was drawn from the official regional statistics.

6 Le Roy Ladurie draws attention to this in connection with Jacquart's thesis (1974). Near the big city of Paris a concentration of farms and landed estates took place, similar to that which occurred in the German–Polish east under the influence of long-distance trade. Both phenomena were caused by economic factors, though in Paris the concentration was determined more by capital and in the east more by feudal power.

7 Used by the classic writer of English agricultural history, Lord Ernle, and, following his example, by Chambers and Mingay (1970), who chose it as a heading to their chapter 7, which should be read to supplement my few remarks on the subject.

8 The values in general use include the following: 1dz grain = 1 dz GV, 1 dz oil seeds = 2 GV, 1 dz tobacco = 2.5 GV, 1 dz pigs = 5 GV, 1 dz butter = 10.5 GV (based on Woermann, 1944).

Chapter 11   Agrarian crises during the industrial era

1 This short outline is derived from the reports of the parliamentary Select Committees on Agriculture (2 August 1833, 4 March 1836, 15 April 1836 and 21 July 1836). In the German language, especially notable is the seminal work by Levy (1902). The prices in figure 68 are taken from the collections in the appendix.

2 See the rents recorded for the Netherlands, 1820–70, by Brugmans (1963:137). If 1820 = 100, these rents rose by about 270 per cent in 1870.

3 The farm's rent mostly changed every seven years, but in two cases the period was longer. Altogether ten renewed leases for seven different amounts have been recorded. For calculating the 10-year averages the rents paid for the ten years in question have been used. The information on rents comes from Thompson (1907:587f.), the wheat prices from Tooke and Newmarch (1858:1, 514f.).

4 The data in table 27 are from Weyermann (1910:178f.). The material consists of price and debt figures from one estate out of each of six districts in the administrative areas of Königsberg, Marienwerder, Bromberg, Köslin, Frankfurt and Oppeln.

5 The prices relating to Königsberg, Berlin, Hamburg, Leipzig, Cologne, Munich and London are to be found in the *Viertelj. z. Stat. d. Deutschen Reiches* (1935:44, 296f.). Prices for Budapest, Rome, Belgium (national average), Odessa, Sweden (national average) and New York are from *Handw. d. Staatswiss.* (4th edn: vol. 4, p. 899). Prices for Finland are from Földes (n.d.:467f.), for Lisbon from Godinho (1955:78), for Denmark (Zealand) from Pedersen (1905:788). The figures for Udine come from *Movimento dei Prezzi* (1886:xxxvf.); those for Paris from *Annuaire Statistique* (1905:31). The Amster-

dam, Vienna and Strasburg prices arc taken from the price series in the appendix accurately worked out by Posthumus, Pribram and Hanauer, which have already been quoted on many occasions in this work.

6 Sources for figure 72: English wheat prices 1770–1885 from Tooke and Newmarch (1862:11, 512), after *Statistical Abstract for the United Kingdom* (1856).

French prices 1797–1814: *Archives Statistiques* (1837:14); after 1815: *Annuaire Statistique de la France* (1938:62).

German prices up to 1934: *Viertelj. z. Stat. d. Deutschen Reiches* (1935:44, 273).

All countries after 1934: *FAO Production Yearbook* (1951:199; 1962:292).

7 The data on which figure 73 is based comes from a manuscript which the author was kindly permitted to examine at the Institute for Research in Agricultural Economics, University of Oxford: *The rent of agricultural land in England and Wales 1870–1939.* Introduction by A. W. Ashby, Memorandum by H. A. Rhee.

8 The calculations represented in figure 74 are from Prothero (1912:456, 466), Williams (1960:121f.), and Ministry of Agriculture and Fisheries (1952).

9 Thus, for instance, in the report of a study made by a committee of distinguished representatives of the English economic sciences during the 1920s, it was maintained that 'in the past hundred years the three severe and protracted depressions have in each case been due to falling prices ... and these price movements had their origin primarily in monetary causes' (report of the Committee on the Stabilization of Agricultural Prices, 1925:21). The same views could be found in other lands too, however. Gustav Cassel stated that to attribute the price decline after the First World War to any but monetary factors was plain *stupidité.*

Summary and conclusion

1 The builders' wages are taken from the Phelps-Brown and Hopkins collection (1955:195ff.; 1956:296–314). The population estimates are from Abel (1935:674f.; 1976:37ff.), supplemented by Franz (1943:53). The following are some rough figures for France, England and Germany: in the year 1200 the total population was about 22.2 million (France 12, England 2.2, Germany 8); in 1340 it was 39.5 million (France 21, England 4.5, Germany 14); in 1470, 27 million (France 14, England 3, Germany 10); in 1620, 42 million (France 21, England 5, Germany 16); in 1740, 41 million (France 17, England 6, Germany 18); in 1800, 60 million (France 27, England 9, Germany 24); in 1900, 128 million (France 39, England 33, Germany 56).

2 To make the changes of price structure clearer, various criteria have been used in the graphs. The height ordinate at any given time corresponds to the index of the price group with the greatest increase in the selected period and country in question. It must be re-emphasized that the figure ignores fluctuations. Each line merely connects two points in time. It should be noted that in the 'agricultural period' the lines start in a price 'valley' (fifteenth century) and lead to a price summit (1801–50). The trend of grain prices, however calculated, was directed less steeply upwards. The documentary sources of the above graphs are:

ENGLAND: *iron prices* for 1401–50, Rogers (1866–1902:IV, 400), five prices for different sorts of iron; for 1801–50, Mitchell and Deane (1962:492f.); for 1951–60, *Statistical Yearbooks*

wages and wheat prices: Rogers, Phelps-Brown and Hopkins, Mitchell and Deane and *Statistical Yearbooks*

GERMANY: *iron prices* for 1401–50, Elsas (1940:11A, 257), Frankfurt am Main, 28 price entries for pig-iron; for 1801–50, Jacobs and Richter, Hamburg, various sorts of iron; for 1951–60, *Statist. Jahrbuch f.d. Bundesrepublik*

wages for 1401–50, Hanauer (p. 417f.), Strasburg, carpenters, masons, mortar mixers; Elsas (1936:1; 1940:11A), Frankfurt am Main, Würzburg, Munich, various jobs; for 1801–1850, Kuczynski (1961:1, no. 1, 375), Wurtemburg, carpenter; Neumann (1911:258), Prussia, farm labourer; Aden (appendix) Emden, unskilled labourer; for 1951–60, *Statist. Jahrbuch f.d. Bundesrepublik* (average male earnings in the building industry)

For rye prices see appendix, tables 1–3, page 304f.

References

ABEL, W. 1935. Wachstumsschwankungen mitteleuropäischer Völker seit dem Mittelalter, Ein Bertrag zur Bevölkerungsgeschichte und Lehre, in *Jahrb. f. National-Ökonomie und Statistik*, 142.

ABEL, W. 1935b. *Agrarkrisen und Agrarkonjunktur in Mitteleuropa vom 13. bis zum 19. Jahrhundert.*

ABEL, W. 1936. Wirtschaftliche Wechsellagen, in *Berichte über Landwirtschaft*, N.F. 21.

ABEL, W. 1937. Wandlungen des Fleischverbrauchs und der Fleischversorgung in Deutschland seit dem ausgehenden Mittelalter, in *Berichte über Landwirtschaft*, XXII.

ABEL, W. 1961. Verdorfung und Gutsbildung in Deutschland zu Beginn der Neuzeit, in: *Morphogenesis of the agrarian cultural landscape*, XIe Congres International de Geographie, 1960, *Geografiska Annaler*, XLIII.

ABEL, W. 1961b. Zur Entwicklung des Sozialproduktes in Deutschland im 16. Jahrhundert, in *Jahrb. f. National-Ökonomie und Statistik, 1973.*

ABEL, W. 1962. Geschichte der deutschen Landwirtschaft vom frühen Mittelalter bis zum 19. Jahrhundert, in G. Franz (ed.) *Deutsche Agrargeschichte*, 11.

ABEL, W. 1964. Die Lage in der deutschen Land- und Ernährungswirtschaft um 1800, in F. Lütge (ed.) *Die wirtschaftliche Situation in Deutschland und Österreich um die Wende vom 18. zum 19. Jahrhundert (Forsch. z. Soz.-u. Wirtschaftsgesch.)*, 6, also in *Jahrb. f. National-Okonomie und Statistik*, 175, 1963, 319f.

ABEL, W. 1967 (2nd edn). *Geschichte der deutschen Landwirtschaft vom frühen Mittelalter bis zum 19. Jahrhundert.*

ABEL, W. 1967b (3rd edn). *Lehrbuch der Ágrarpolitik.*

ABEL, W. 1973. *Crises agraires en Europe (XIIe–XXe siècle).*

ABEL, W. 1974. *Massenarmut und Hungerkrisen im vorindustriellen Europa*, Hamburg and Berlin.

ABEL, W. 1976 (3rd edn). *Die Wüstungen des ausgehenden Mittelalters.*

ABEL, W. 1976b. Einige Bemerkungen zum Stadt-Landproblem im Spätmittelalter, in *Nachrichten d. Akad. d. Wiss. in Göttingen*, 1, Philol.-Hist. Klasse, 1.

ABEL, W. 1978 (3rd edn). *Geschichte der deutschen Landwirtschaft vom frühen Mittelalter bis zum 19. Jahrhundert.*

ABEL, W., RIEMANN. and WELLING, F. (eds) 1954 (3rd edn). *Daten zur europäischen Agrarverfassung*, facsimile MS. of *Agrarsozialen Gesellschaft.*

ACHILLES, W. 1957. Getreidepreise und Getreidehandel europäischer Räume im 16, und 17, Jahrhundert, Thesis, *Göttingen*. Also article of same title in *Zeitschr. f. Agrargesch. u. Agrarsoziologie*, 7, 1959.

Acta Borussica, Getreidehandelspolitik, 1901, 11. Berlin.

ADEN, O. 1963. Entwicklung und Wechsellagen ausgewählter Gewerbe in Ostfriesland von der Mitte des 18. bis zum Ausgang des 19. Jahrhunderts. Thesis, Göttingen.

ADEN, O. 1964. Entwicklung und Wechsellagen ausgewählter Gewerbe in Ostfriesland von der Mitte des 18. bis zum Ausgang des 19. Jahrhunderts in *Abhandl. u. Vorträge z. Gesch. Ostfrieslands*, 40, Aurich.

AHVENAINEN, J. 1964. Der Getreidehandel Livlands im Mittelhalter, in *Soc. Scient. Fennica*, XXXIV, 2.

ALLEN, W. 1734. *The landholder's companion*, or *ways and means to raise the value of land*.

ALLEX, A. 1933. L'évolution rurale des Alpes in *Annales*, 5.

ÅMARK, K. 1921. En Svensk prishistorisk studie, *Ekonomisk Tidskrift*, 23, 154.

ANDRE, C. G. 1965. *Studier Kring Funbo*, in *Hist. Tidskrift*, 4, 385–400.

Annalen der Landwirtschaft.

Annalen der Niedersächsisehen Landwirtschaft.

Annuaire Statistique de la France, 25, 1905.

Anonymous 1696. *The regulating of silver coin*.

Anonymous 1750 (2nd edn). *An essay on the causes of the decline of the foreign trade, consequently of the value of the lands of Britain, and on the means to restore both*. London.

Anonymous 1813. Mutmassungen über die Produktenpreise in der Zukunft für Mecklenburg, in *Neue Annalen der Mecklenburger Landwirtschafts-Gesellschaft, 4 January 1813*.

ANTON, K. G. 1799–1802. *Geschichte der teutschen Landwirtschaft*.

ARASKHANIANTZ, A. 1882. *Die französische Getreidehandelspolitik bis zum Jahre 1789*.

Archives Statistiques du Ministère des Travaux Publics de l'Agriculture et du Commerce, ser. I, 1837. Paris.

ARNIM, V. VON 1957. Krisen und Konjunkturen der Landwirtschaft in Schleswig-Holstein vom 16. bis zum 18, Jahrhundert, in *Quellen und Forschungen zur Geschichte Schleswig-Holsteins*, 35.

ASHBY, A. W. Introduction to *The rent of agricultural land in England and Wales 1870–1939*. Institute for Research in Agricultural Economics, University of Oxford.

ASHLEY, W. J. 1896. *English Agricultural History*, 11.

ASHTON, T. S. 1959. *Economic fluctuations in England 1700–1800*.

AUBIN, G. 1911. *Zur Geschichte der gutscherrlich-bäuerlichen Verhältnisse in Ostpreussen*.

D'AVENEL, VICOMTE G. 1894–1926. *Histoire économique de la propriété des salaires, des denrées et de tous les prix en général depuis l'an 1200 jusqu'en l'an 1800*, I–VII. Paris.

BAASCH, E. 1927. *Holländische Wirtschaftsgeschichte*.

BARATIER, E. 1961. La démographie provençale du XIIe au XIVe siècle ..., in *Ecole Pratique des Hautes Etudes, VIe Section*, Centre de Recherches Historiques.

BARTOLINI, D. 1878. Prezzi e salari nel Commune di Portogruaro durante il secolo XVI, in *Annali di Statistica*, 2a, I.

BAUER, S. 1890. Zur Enstehung der Physiokratie in Frankreich, in *Jahrb. f. Nat. u. Stat.*, XXI.

BEAN, J. M. W. 1963. Plague population and economic decline in the Later Middle Ages, in *Economic History Review*, XV.

BECKER, A. 1912. Beiträge zur Siedlungskunde des Hohen Westerwaldes, Thesis, Marburg.

BECKMANN, J. 1788. *Beyträge zur Ökonomie*, XI.

BEHRE, O. 1905. *Geschichte der Statistik in Brandenburg-Preussen.*

BEISSEL, S. 1885. Geldwert und Arbeitslohn in Mittelalter, in *Stimmen aus Maria Laach*, VII, 27.

BELOW, G. VON 1909. Die Frage des Rückgangs der wirtschaftlichen Verhältnisse Deutschlands vor dem Dreissigjährigen Kriege, in *Viertelj. Soz.-u. Wirtschaftsgesch*, VII.

BENINGA, E. 1910. Ostfriesische Chronik aus dem Jahre 1543, mitgeteilt in einem längeren Auszug von F. Swart, Zur friesischen Agrargeschichte.

BERESFORD, M. W. 1954. *The lost villages of England*, London.

BERESFORD, M. W. and ST JOSEPH, J. K. S. 1958. *Medieval England: An aerial survey*, Cambridge.

BESCHORNER, H. 1904 (6th edn). Wüstungsverzeichnisse, in A. Tille (ed.) *Deutsche Geschichtsblätter.*

BEVERIDGE, W. H. 1939. *Prices and wages in England from the twelfth to the nineteenth century*, London.

BEVERIDGE, W. H. 1936–7. Wages in the Winchester Manors, in *The Econ. Hist. Rev.*, VII.

BIANCO, F. J. VON 1855. *Die Universität Köln . . .*, I, 1.

BITTERMANN, E. 1956. *Die landwirtschaftliche Produktion in Deutschland 1800–1950*, in *Kühn Archives*, 70.

BLASCHKE, K. H. 1958. Die landesgeschichte und ihre Probleme in Sachsen, in *Blätter für deutsche Landesgeschichte*, 94.

BLOCH, M. L. B. 1956. *Les Caractères originaux de l'histoire rurale française*, 11.

BLOTENBURG, J. 1960. Der Gnadenfonds zur Beförderung der Leinen-Manufaktur in Bielefeld, in *Jahresbericht des Historischen Vereins für die Grafschaft Ravensberg.*

BODIN, J. 1568. *La Response . . . aux paradoxes de Monsieur de Maletroit, touchant l'enchérissement de toutes choses* (most of this work repeated in his *République* republished by H. Hauser, Paris, 1932).

BOG, I. (ed.) 1971. *Der Aussenhandel Ostmitteleuropas 1450–1650.*

BOIS, G. 1976. *Crise de féodalisme*, Paris.

BOISGUILLEBERT, P. DE. 1843. Détail de la France. 1697, in *Economistes-Financiers du XVIIIe siècle*, Paris.

BOISLISLE, A. M. DE. 1874. *Correspondance des Contrôleurs Génereaux de Finances avec les Intendants des Provinces*, I. Paris.

BOISSONNADE, P. 1927. *Le socialisme d'état, l'industrie et les classes industrielles en France pendant les deux premiers siècles d'ere moderne* (1453–1661).

BOLIN, S. 1942. Die Bevölkerung der drei skandinavischen Länder in Mittelalter zusammenstellte, in *Cambridge Econ. Hist.*, I.

BÖLTS, J. 1966. *Die Rindviehhaltung im oldenburgisch-ostfriesischen Raum . . .*, in F. Lütge, G. Franz and W. Abel (eds) *Quellen und Forsch. z. Agrargeschichte*, XIV.

BOURDE, A. 1967. Agronomie et agronomes en France au XVIIIe siècle. Thesis.

BOURGIN, G. 1911. L'agriculture et la révolution, in *Revue d'Histoire des Doctrines Economiques.*

BOWDEN, P. 1967. Agricultural prices . . ., in *The Agrarian History of England and Wales*, VI: 1500–1640.

BOWLEY, A. L. 1900. *Wages in the United Kingdom in the nineteenth century*, Cambridge.

BRÄKER, U. 1948 edn. *Der arme Mann in Tockenburg.*

BRAUDEL, F. 1949. *La Méditerranée et le Monde Méditerranéen à l'époque de Phillipe*, II.

BRAUDEL, F. 1963. In *Annales*, 18 Jahrg.

BRAEUER, W. 1968. Frankreichs wirtschaftliche und soziale Lage um 1700, in *Marburger Rechts und Staatswiss. Abhandl.*

BRENTANO, L. 1927. *Eine Geschichte der wirtschaftlichen Entwicklung England*, II.

BREWSTER, F. 1695. *Essays on trade and navigation*, I. London.

BREYSIG, K. n.d. Der brandenburgische Staatshaushalt in der Zweiten Hälfte des 17. Jahrhunderts, in *Schmoller's Jahrb.*, XVI.

BRISCOE, J. 1696 (3rd edn). *A discourse on the late funds of the Million Act, Lottery Act and the Bank of England.*

BRODNITZ, G. 1918. *Englische Wirtschaftsgeschichte.*

BRUGGER, H. 1956. *Die schweizerische Landwirtschaft in der ersten Hälfte des 19. Jahrhunderts.*

BRUGMANS, J. J. 1963. *De arbeidende Classe in Nederland in de 19e eeuw*, 1813–1870. Antwerp.

BUCHENBERGER, A. 1858. Über den Wert der ritterschaftlichen Güter in Mecklenburg-Schwerin, in *Beitr. z. Statistik Mechlenb.*

BUCHENBERGER, A. 1897. *Grundzüge der deutschen Agrarpolitik.*

BUCHENBERGER, A. 1914 (2nd edn). *Agrarwesen und Agrarpolitik*, I.

BUCHER, K. 1886. *Die Bevölkerung von Frankfurt am Main im 14. und 15, Jahrhundert*, I.

BUCHER, W. L. 1805. *Uber die jetzige Theurung des Getraides mit besonderer Anwendung auf die preussischen und sachsischen Staaten.* Gotha.

BUCHWALD, G. 1881. Holsteinische Lohnverhältnisse im 15. Jahrhundert, in *Zeitschr. d. Gesellsch f. Schlesw.-Holst. Geschichte XI.*

BUCK, H. 1935. *Das Geld- und Münzwesen der Städte in den Landen Hannover und Braunschweig.*

BUJAK, F. 1928–49. *Badania z dziejów spolecznych i gospodarczych, Poznán.*

BURET, E. 1841. *De la misère des classes laborieuses en Angleterre et en France*, II.

BÜSCH, J. G. 1802. Das papierene Jahrhundert, 10th supplement of his *Sämtlichen Schriften über Bank and Münzwesen*. Hamburg.

CAREY, H. C. 1871. *Principles of Social Science*, I.

CARPENTIER, E. 1962. Autour de la peste noire ..., in *Annales*, 17.

CESSE, R. 1921. La crisis agricola negli Stati Veneti a meta del sec. XVIII, in *Estratto dal Nuovo Archivo Veneto*, n.s., 42.

CHAMBERS, J. D. and MINGAY, G. E. 1970. *The agricultural revolution, 1750–1880.*

CHAPTAL, J. A. 1819. *De l'industrie française.*

CHEVALIER, L. 1959. *Classes laborieuses et classes dangereuses à Paris penθant la première moitié du XIXe siècle.*

CHILD, J. 1964 (2nd edn). *A new discourse of trade.*

CHRISTENSEN, A.E. 1934. Der handelsgeschichtliche Wert der Sundzollregister, in *Hans. Gesch. bl.*

CHRISTENSEN, A. E. 1938. Danmarks befolkning og bebyggelse i middelalderen, in *Nordisk Kultur*, II.

CHRISTENSEN, C. A. 1930–1. Nedgangen in Landgilden i det 14 Aarhundrede, in *Historisk Tidsskrift*, 10, 1.

CHRISTENSEN, C. A. 1960. Krisen på Slesvig domkapitels jordegods 1352–1437, in *Hist. Tidsskrift*, 11, 6, 2.

CHRISTENSEN, C. A. 1964. Aendringerne i landsbyens Økonomiske og sociale struktur i det 14. og 15. århundrede, in *Hist. Tidsskrift*, 12, 1. Copenhagen.

CIBRARIO, L. 1842 (2nd edn). *Della Economia Politica del Medio*, III.

CIPOLLA, C. M. 1950. The trends in Italian economic history in the later Middle Ages, in *Econ. Hist. Rev.*, II.

CIPOLLA, C. M. 1952–3. The decline of Italy, in *Econ. Hist. Rev.*, V

CIPOLLA, C. M. 1955. Le prétendue 'revolution' des prix . . . , in *Annales*, 10.

CIPOLLA, C. M. 1963. Currency depreciation in Medieval Europe, in *Econ. Hist. Rev.*, XV.

CIPOLLA, C. M. 1963a. In *Cambridge Economic History of Europe*, III.

CIRIACY-WANTRUP, S. VON. 1936. Agrarkrisen und Stockungsspannen, in *Berichte über Landw.*, Sonderheft, 122.

COKE, R. 1671. *That the Church and State are in equal danger with the trade.*

COLE, G. D. H. and POSTGATE, R. 1938 (1949 4th edn). *The Common People, 1746–1946.* London.

Committee on the stabilization of agricultural prices, 1925. Report, Ministry of Agriculture and Fisheries, London.

CONRAD, J. 1879. Die Preisentwicklung der gewöhnlichsten Nährung- in Halle a.d. S. von 1731 bis 1878, in *Jahrb. f. Nat. u. Statistist*, 34.

CONRAD, J. 1900 (2nd edn). Art. Domänen, in *Handw. d. Staatswiss*, III.

CONRAD, J. 1909 (3rd edn). Art. Agrarkrisis, in *Handw. d. Staatswiss.*

CONZE, W. 1954. Vom 'Pöbel' zum 'Proletariat', in *Viert. f. Soz.-u. Wirtschaftsgescn*, 41.

CUNNINGHAM, W. 1905. *The growth of English industry and commerce*, I.

CUNO, H. 1929. *Allg. Wirtschaftsgeschichte*, III.

CURSCHMANN, F. 1900. Hungersnöte in Mittelalter. Ein Beitrag zur deutschen Wirtschaftsgeschichte des 8. bis 13. Jahrhunderts, in *Leipziger Studien aus dem Gebiete der Geschichte*, 6, 1.

DAVENANT, C. 1771. *The Political and Commercial Works*, II.

DEBY, P. 1825. *De l'agriculture en Europe et en Amérique.*

Deeds and official documents concerning the history of the Prince Elector Friedrich Wilhelm of Brandenburg (Urkunden und Aktenstücke zur Geschichte des Kurfürsten Friedrich Wilhelm V. Brandenburg), 10, 1880.

DENIFLE, P. 1889. *La désolation des églises, monastères, hôpitaux en France pendant la guerre de Cent Ans* II, 1.

DETLEFSEN, D. 1892. *Geschichte der holsteinische Elbmarschen*, II.

Deutsche Vierteljahresschrift, 1850.

DEVEZE, M. 1961. *La vie de la forêt française au XVIe siècle.*

DIDEROT, D. 1778. Population, in Diderot and d'Alembert's *French Encyclopedia*, 27.

DIEHL, K. 1932. Über die Zusammengehörigkeit wirtschaftstheoretischer und wirtschaftsgeschichtlicher Untersuchungen, in *Schmoller's Jahrb.*, special edition for Sombart.

DIETERICI, C. F. W. 1846. *Der Volkswohlstand im Preussischen Staate.*

DIETERICI, C. F. W. n.d. *Jahrbuck f. d. amtl. Stat. d. preuss, Staates*, 2.

DIETZEL, H. 1901. *Kornzoll und Sozialreform.*

DION, R. 1946. *La part de la géographie et celle de l'historie dans l'explication de l'habitat rural du Bassin parisien*, Lille.

DITZ, H. 1868. Die Landwirtschaftliche Krise in Bayern, in *Jahrb. f. Nat. u. Statist.*, X.

DOLLINGER, P. 1956. Le chiffre de population de Paris au XIVe siècle 210,000 ou 80,000 habitants?, in *Revue historique.*

DOPSCH, A. 1928. *Verfassungs- und Wirtschaftsgeschichte des Mittelalters.*

DOPSCH, A. 1930. *Die ältere Wirtschafts-und Sozialgeschichte der Bauern in den Alpenländern Osterreichs.*

DOUGHTY, R. A. 1975. Industrial prices and inflation in southern England, 1401–1640, in *Explorations in Economic History*, 12.

DOWD, D. F. 1961. The economic expansion of Lombardy, 1300–1500, in *Jnl. Econ. Hist.*, XXI.

DRUMMOND, J. C. and WILBRAHAM, A. 1958 (new edn). *The Englishman's Food.*

DUBY, G. 1954. La révolution agricole médiévale, in *Revue de Géographie de Lyon*, 29.

DUBY, G. 1962. *L'Economie rurale et la vie des campagnes dans l'Occident Mediéval*, 11.

DUNHAM, A. L. 1943. Industrial life and labour in France 1815–1848, in *Jnl. Econ. Hist.*, III.

EIKENBURG, W. 1976. *Das Handelshaus der Runtinger zu Regensburg.*

ELSAS, M. J. 1936. *Umriss einer Geschichte der Preise und Löhne in Deutschland*, I.

ELSAS, M. J. 1940. *Umriss einer Geschichte der Preise und Löhne in Deutschland*, IIA.

ENGEL, F. 1965. In *Schaumberger Studien*, 9.

ENGEL, L. H. H. VON. 1798. *Versuch zur Beantwortung der Frage: Welche Vorteile hat die Landwirtschaft von der Aufklärung im 18. Jahrhundert.* Leipzig.

ENGELS, F. 1845. *The Condition of the Working Class in England.*

ENNEN, E. 1976. *Wechselwirkungen in mittelalterliche Agrarwirtschaft und Stadtwirtschaft*, illustrated by the example of Cologne, in *Cultus et Cognitio.*

ERDMANNSDÖRFER, B. 1892. *Deutsche Geschichte, 1648–1740.*

ERMISCH and WUTTKE (eds). 1910. *Haushaltung in Vorkwerken. Ein landwirtschaftliches Lehrbuch aus der Zeit Kürfurst Augusts von Sachsen.* Leipzig.

ERNLE, LORD. 1961 (6th edn). *English Farming Past and Present.*

ESSLEN, J. B. 1912. *Die Fleischversorgung des Deutschen Reiches.*

FABER, J. A. 1960. The rise of intensive husbandry in the Low Countries, in *Papers in Dutch and English History.*

FABER, J. A. 1972. Drie Eeuwen Friesland, in *A. A. Bijdragen*, 17.

FABER, R. 1888. *Die Entstehung des Agrarschutzes in England.*

FALBE-HANSEN, V. 1904. Kapiteltakster i âeldre og nyere tid, in *Danmarks Stat. Meddelelser*, 4R, 15. Copenhagen; *Stavnsbaands – Løsningen og Landboreformerne set fra Nationalokonomiens Standpunkt*, 1. Copenhagen.

FALKE, J. 1869. Geschichtliche Statistik der Preise im Königreich Sachsen, In *Jahrb. f. Nat. u. Stat.*, XIII.

FARMER, D. L. 1957–58. Some grain price movements in thirteenth century England, in *Econ. Hist. Rev.*, 10.

FEBVRE, L. 1911. *Philippe II et la France-Comté.*

FEILEN, J. 1935–6. Preisstruktur und Preisbewegung, in *Vierteljahresheft z. Konjunktur-forsch.*, 10.

FICHTE, J. G. 1925. H. Schulz (ed.) *Briefwechsel.* Leipzig.

FIERRO, A. 1971. Un cycle démographique: Dauphiné et Faucigny du XIVe au XIXe siècle, in *Annales*, 26.

FINBERG, H. P. R. (ed.) 1952. The local Historian and his Theme. An Introductory Lecture. Department of English Local History, University College, Leicester, Occasional Papers.

FITZHERBERT, A. 1523. *Book of Husbandry.*

FIUMI, E. 1962. La popolazione del territori volterranosangiminagnese ed il problema demografico del' età comunale, in *Studi in Onore di Amintore Fanfani*, 1. Also 1961 *Storia Economica e Sociale di San Gimignano.* Florence.

FOLDES, B. n.d. Die Getreidepreise im 19. Jahrhundert, in *Jarhb. f. u. Stat.*, Series 29, III.

FOURQUIN, G. 1966. *Les débuts du fermage. L'exemple de Saint-Denis*, in *Etudes rurales*.

FRANCK, S. 1538. Deutsche Chronik.

FRANZ, G. 1943 (2nd edn). *Der Dreissigjährige Krieg und das deutsche Volk.*

FRANZ, G. 1961 (3rd edn). *Der Dreissigjährige Krieg und das deutsche Volk.*

FRANZ, G. 1967. *Quellen zur Geschichte des Deutschen Bauernstandes im Mittelalter.*

FRIIS, A. and GLAMANN, K. 1958. *A History of Prices and Wages in Denmark 1600–1800.* London.

FRITZE, K. 1967. Am Wendepunkt der Hanse, in *Veröff. d. Hirt. Inst. d. Ernst Moritz-Arndt. Univers.*, Greifswald, 3.

FUCHS, C. J. 1898. *Die Epochen der deutschen Agrargeschichte und Agrarpolitik.*

FURTAC, T. 1935. Ceny w Gdansku w latach 1701–1815, in *Bujak, Badania . . .*, 22, Lvov.

GABRICI, G. and COLETTA. 1886. Movimento dei Prezzi di Alcuni Generi Alimentari. . . .

GAYER, A. D., ROSTOW, W. W. and SCHWARTZ, A. J. 1953. *The growth and fluctuation of the British economy, 1790–1850*, II.

GENICOT, L. 1943. L'économie rurale Namuroise au Bas Moyen Age (1199–1429) in *Univ. de Louvain, Recueil de Travaux d'Histoire et de Philologie*, sér 3, fasc. 17, Vol. 1.

GENICOT, L. 1962. L'étendue des exploitations agricoles dans le comté de Namur à la fin du XIIIe siècle, in *Etudes rurales*, 5.

GENICOT, L. with colleague. 1970. La crise agricole du Bas Moyen Age dans le Namurois, in: *Univ. de Louvain, Recueil de Travaux d'Histoire et de Philologie*, 4, 44.

GISSEL, S. 1976. Agrarian Decline in Scandinavia, in *Scand. Journ. Hist.*, 1.

GODINHO, V. M. 1955. *Prix et Monnaies au Portugal, 1750–1850.*

GOERTZ-WRISBERG, W. GRAF VON. 1880. *Die Entwicklung der Landwirtschaft auf den B.-W.-gütern.*

GOLTZ, T. VON DER. 1903. *Geschichte der deutschen Landwirtschaft*, II.

GÖRLITZ, W. 1956. *Die Junker.*

GOTHEIN, E. 1892. *Wirtschaftsgeschichte des Schwarzwaldes*, I.

GOUBERT, P. 1960. *Beauvais et le Beauvaisis de 1600 à 1730.*

GRAS, N. S. 1915. *The Evolution of the English Corn Market.*

GRAUS, F. 1963. Autour de la peste noire . . ., in *Annales*.

GRAUS, F. 1969. Das Spätmittelalter als Krisenzeit. Ein Literaturbericht als Zwischenbilanz, in *Mediaevalia Bohemica*, Suppl. 1. Prague Hist. Inst. of the Bohemian Academy of Sciences.

GROSSER, M. 1590. *Kurze Anleitung zu der Landwirtschaft.*

GRÜLL, G. 1963. Bauer, Herr und Landesfürst . . ., in *Forsch. z. Gesch. Oberösterreichs*, 8.

GRUND, A. 1901. Die Veranderungen der Topographie im Wiener Wald und im Wiener Becken, in *Geograph, Abhdlg.*, ed. Penck, XIII, 1.

GÜLICH, G. VON 1830. *Geschichte des Handels*, II.

HAGEDORN, B. 1910. *Ostfrieslands Handel und Schiffahrt im 16. Jahrhundert.*

HAGEDORN, B. 1912. Ostfriesischer Handel und Schiffahrt vom Ausgang des 16. Jahrhunderts bis zum Westfälischen Frieden, in *Abhandl. z. Verkehrs-u. Seegesch.*, VI.

HAGELSTANGE, A. 1898. *Süddeutsches Bauernleben im Mittelalter.*

HALCROW, E. M. 1954–5. The decline of demesne farming on the estates of Durham Cathedral Priory, in *Econ. Hist. Rev.*, VII.

HALLAM, H. E. 1961–2. *Population Density in Medieval Fenland*, XIV.

HAMILTON, E. J. 1929. American treasure and the rise of capitalism, in *Economica*, 27.

HAMILTON, E. J. 1934. *American Treasure and the Price Revolution in Spain, 1501–1650.* Cambridge, Mass.

HAMILTON, E. J. 1947a. *War and Prices in Spain, 1651–1800.* Cambridge, Mass.

HAMILTON, E. J. 1947b. *Money, Prices and Wages in Valencia, Aragon, and Navare (1351–1500).* Cambridge, Mass.

HAMILTON, E. J. 1960. The history of prices before 1750, in *XIe Congrès International des Sciences Historiques,* Stockholm.

HAMMARSTRÖM, I. 1957. The 'price revolution' of the sixteenth century, some Swedish evidence, in *Scandinavian Econ. Hist. Rev.,* V.

HANAU, A. 1962. Entwicklungstendenzen der Ernährung in marktwirtschaftlicher Sicht, in *Entwicklungstendenzen der Ernährung.* Forschungsrat f. Ernähr., Landw. u. Forsten.

HANAUER, A. C. 1876. *Etudes économiques sur l'Alsace ancienne et moderne,* I. Paris.

HANAUER, A. C. 1878. *Etudes économiques sur l'Alsace ancienne et moderne,* II. Paris. *Handw. d. Staatswiss* (4th edn) vol. 4.

HANSEN, J. 1912. *Beiträge zur Geschichte des Getreidehandels der Freien und Hansestadt, Lübeck.*

HANSEN, R. 1897. Zur Topographie und Geschichte Dithmarschens, in *Zeitschr. d. Gesch. f. Schleswig-Holsteinische Gesch.,* XXVIII.

HANSEN, V. 1964. Landskab og bebyggelse i Vendsyssel, in *Kulturgeografiske Skriften,* 7.

HANSSEN, G. 1832. *Historische-statistische Darstellung der Insel Fehmarn.*

HANSSEN, G. 1880. *Agrarhistorische Abhandlungen.*

HANSSEN, G. 1884. *Agrarhistorische Abhandlungen,* II.

HANSSEN, J. with WOLFF, H. 1832. *Chronik des Landes Dithmarschen.*

HARMS, B. 1907. Die Münz und Geldpolitik der Stadt Basel in Mittelalter, in *Zeitschr. f. d. Ges. Staatsw.* supplement 23.

HAROUARD, 1805. In *Annales de l'agriculture française,* XXIV.

HASUND, S. 1933. Korndyrkinga i Noreg i eldre gid, in *Bidrag til Bondesamfundets Historie,* I. Oslo.

HATCHER, J. 1969. A diversified economy: later medieval Cornwall, *Econ. Hist. Rev.*

HAUSCHILD, U. 1973. Studien zu Löhnen und Preisen in Rostock in Spätmittelalter, *Hanseatische Geschichtsverein,* N.F. XIX.

HAUSER, H. 1927 (5th edn). *Ouvriers du temps passé, XVe–XVIe siècle.*

HAUSER, H. 1936. *Recherches et documents sur l'histoire des prix en France de 1500 à 1800.* Paris.

HAUSHERR, H. 1954. *Wirtschaftsgeschichte der Neuzeit.*

HAUSHERR, H. 1963. *Hardenberg, Eine politische Biographie,* I.

HEDEMANN-HEESPEN, P. VON. 1914. In *Zeitschr d. Ges. f. Schlesw.-Holst. Geschichte,* 44.

HEGEL, K. 1862. *Chroniken der deutschen Städte, Nuremberg,* I.

HEIMPEL, C. 1966. Die Entwicklung der Einnahmen und Ausgaben des Heiliggeistspitals zu Biberach an der Riss von 1500 bis 1630, in F. Lütge, G. Franz and W. Abel (eds), *Quellen und Forschungen zur Agrargeschichte,* Vol. XV.

HEINE, H. 1862. *Sämtliche Werke, 8, Französische Zustände,* I. Hamburg.

HEISIG, J. 1884. Die historische Entwicklung der landwirtschaftlichen Verhältnisse auf den reichsgräflich-freistandesherrlich-Schaffgotschischen Güterkomplexen in Preussisch-Schlesien, in *Sammlung nationalökonomischer u. Stat. Abhandl. d. Staatswiss. Seminars zu Halle a.d. S.,* III, 3. Jena.

HEITZ, E. L. 1876. *Übersicht der Literatur der Preise in Deutschland und in der Schweiz aus den letzten 60 Jahren.*

HELBIG, H. 1952–3. *Quellen zu älteren Wirtschaftsgeschichte Mitteldeutschlands.* Weimar.

HELFERICH, J. 1843. *Von den periodischen Schwankungen im Werte der edelen Metalle von der Entdeckung Amerikas bis zum Jahre 1830.* Nuremberg.

HELLEINER, K. F. 1967. The population of Europe from the Black Death to the eve of the vital revolution, in *The Cambridge Economic History of Europe*, IV.

HERBERT, C. J. 1910. Essai sur la police générale des grains, 1775, in *Collection des Economistes*.

HERESBACH, C. 1570. *Rei Rusticae Libri Quattuor*.

HERLIHY, D. 1965. Population, plague and social change in rural Pistoia, 1201–1430, in *Econ. Hist. Rev.*, XVII.

HERMANN, F. 1832. *Staatswirtschaftliche Untersuchungen*.

HERRMANN, P. (ed.). 1932. *Zimmerische Chronik*. IV.

HERTZOG, A. 1911. Eine landwirtschaftliche Enquête aus dem XIV. Jahrhundert, in *Landwirtschaftlich-Historische Blätter* X.

HEUNISCH, A. and BADER, J. 1857. *Das Grossherzogtum Baden*.

HEUSER, A. 1916. Getreidehandelspolitik des ehem. Herzogtums Cleve, vorwiegend im 17. and 18. Jahrhundert, in *Düsseldorfer Jahrb*.

HEYNE, M. 1901. *Das deutsche Nahrungswesen von den Ältesten geschichtlichen Zeiten bis zum 16. Jahrhundert*.

HILDEBRAND, B. 1922. *Die Nationalökonomie der Gegenwart und Zukunft*, in *Waentig Collection*, vol. 22.

HINZE, K. 1927. Die Arbeiterfrage zu Beginn des modernen Kapitalismus in Brandenburg-Preussen, in *Veröff d. Ver. f. Gesch. d. Mark-Brandenburg*.

HOBSBAWM, E. J. 1957. The British standard of living, 1790–1850, in *Econ. Hist. Rev.*, X.

HOBSBAWM, E. J. 1962. En Angleterre: Revolution industrielle et vie materielle des classes populaires, in *Annales*, XVII.

HÖHLBAUM, K. 1887. *Das Buch Weinsbergs, in Publ. d. Ges. f. Rheinische Geschichtskunde*, IV, II.

HOLMES, G. A. 1957. *The estates of the higher nobility in fourteenth-century England*.

HOLMGAARD, J. 1962. *Bol og by*, 3. Copenhagen.

HOLMSEN, A. 1941. *Eidsvoll Bygds Historie*, I, I.

HOLMSEN, A. 1950–61. *Eidsvoll Bygds Historie*, 2 vols. 5 parts. Oslo.

HOLMSEN, A. 1962. Desertion of farms around Oslo in the late Middle Ages in *Scandinavian Econ. His. Rev.*, X.

HOSWZOWSKI, S. 1954. Les prix à Lwow (XVIe–XVIIe siècles), in Ecole Practique des Hautes Etudes, VIe Sect, *Oeuvres Etrangères*, I.

HOSZOWSKI, S. 1960. The Polish Baltic trade in the 15th–18th centuries, in *Poland at the 11th International Congress of Historical Sciences in Stockholm*. Warsaw.

HOSZOWSKI, S. 1961. L'Europe centrale devant la révolution des prix XVIe et XVIIe siècles, in *Annales*, 16.

HOUTTE, H. VAN. 1920. *Histoire Economique de la Belgique à la fin de l'Ancien Régime*.

HURST, J. G. 1974. Wandlungen des mittelaltlichen Dorfes in England, in J. Bog et. al. (eds), *Wirtschaftliche und soziale Strukturen im säkularen Wandel* (volume in honour of W. Abel).

ILZHÖFER, H. 1942. Die Deckung des Vitaminbedarfs in früheren Jahrhunderten, in *Archiv. fur Hygiene und Bakteriologie*, 127.

IMBERT, G. 1959. *Les mouvements de longue durée Kondratieff*.

INAMA-STERNEGG, K. T. VON. 1864. Die volkswirtschaftlichen Folgen des Dreissigjährigen Krieges für Deutschland, in *Raumers Historisches Tagebuch*, 4.

INAMA-STERNEGG, K. T. VON. 1879. *Deutsche Wirtschaftsgeschichte*, I.

INAMA-STERNEGG, K. T. VON. 1891. *Deutsche Wirtschaftsgeschichte*, II.

INAMA-STERNEGG, K. T. VON. n.d. (*a*) (3rd edn). Art. Bevölkerung des Mittelalters und der neueren Zeit bis Ende des 18. Jahrhunderts, in *Hdw. d. Staatswiss*, 11.

INAMA-STERNEGG, K. T. VON. n.d. (*b*) (2nd edn). Art. Bevölkerungsbewegung, Mittelalter, in *Handw. d. Staatswiss*.

INAMA-STERNEGG, K. T. VON, and HÄPKE, R. 1924 (4th edn). Art. Bevölkerungswesen (Geschichte der Bevölkerungsbewegung) in *Handw. d. Staatsw.*, 11.

IRSIGLER, F. 1975. *Kölner Wirtschaft im Spätmittelalter*.

JACOBS. A. and RICHTER, H. 1935. Die Grosshandelspreise in Deutschland von 1792 bis 1934, in *Sonderhefte des Inst. f. Konjunkturforsch.*, 37.

JACQUART, J. 1974. La crise rurale en Ile-de-France, 1550–1670. Thesis, Paris.

JÄGER, H. 1951. Die Entwicklung der Kulturlandschaft im Kreise Hofgeismar, in *Göttinger Geogr. Abh.*, 8.

Jahrbuch für die amtliche Statistik des Preussischen Staates, 11, 1867.

JANSMA, T. S. 1960. De 'Wüstungen' der Late Middeleeuwen, in *Landbouwgeschiedenis*.

JANSSEN, J. 1895. *Geschichte des deutschen Volkes*, 1.

JANSSENS, V. 1959. De goud- en zilverwaarde der geldeenheid, in Verlinden *Dokumenten voor de geschiedenis van prijzen en lonen in Vlaanderen en Brabant*.

JEANNIN, P. 1956. Les relations économiques des villes de la Baltique au XVIe siècle, in *Viertelj. f. Soz. u. Wirtsch. gesch*, 43.

JEANNIN, P. 1964. Les comptes du Sund comme source pour la construction d'indices généraux de l'activité économique en Europe (XVIe–XVIIIe siècle), in *Revue Historique*, 470.

JESSE, W. 1928. Der Wendische Münzverein, in *Quellen u. Darst. z. Hans. Geschichte*, N.F. VI.

JESSE, W. 1952. Münz- und Geldgeschichte Niedersachsens, in *Werkstücke aus Museum, Archiv. und Bibliothek der Stadt. Braunschweig*.

JOLLES, O. n.d. Die Ansichten der nationalökonomischen Schriftsteller des 16. und 17. Jahrhunderts über Bevölkerungswesen, in *Jahrb. f. Nat. u. Stat. N.F.*, XIII.

JONES, E. L. 1967. *Agriculture and economic growth in England 1650–1815*. London.

JÜRGENS. A. Zur Schlesw.- Holst. Handelsgeschichte des 16. und 17. Jahrhunderts, in *Abhdl. z. Verkehrs. u. Seegesch.*, VII.

JUSTI, J. H. G. VON. 1755. *Staatswirthschaft* ..., 1.

JUTIKKALA, E. 1955. The great Finnish famine in 1696–97, in *Scandinavian Econ. Hist. Rev.*, III.

KANTZOW, T. 1817. (2nd edn). *Pomerania*.

KELTER, E. 1953. Das deutsche Wirtschaftsleben des 14. und 15. Jahrhunderts im Schatten des Pestepidemien, in *Jahrb. f. Nationalökonomie und Statistik*, 165.

KERRIDGE, E. 1953–4. The movement of rent, 1540–1640, in *Econ. Hist. Rev.*, 6.

KEYNES, J. M. 1930. *A treatise on money*, 11. London.

KEYSER, E. 1943. *Bevölkerungsgeschichte Deutschlands*.

KLEIN, H. 1968. Das Grosse Sterben von 1348–9 und seine Auswirkung auf die Besiedlung der Ostalpenländer, in *Mitt. d. Ges. f. Salzburger Landeskunde*.

KNAPP, G. F. 1887. *Die Bauernbefreiung und der Ursprung der Landarbeiter in den älteren Teilen Preussens*, 1.

KNAPP, G. F. 1891. Die Erbuntertänigheit und die kapitalistische Wirtschaft, in *Die Landarbeiter in Knechtschaft und Freiheit*.

KONDRATIEFF, N. D. 1928. Die Preisdynamik der industriellen und landswirtschaftlichen Waren. Zum Problem der relativen Dynamik und Konjunktur, in *Archiv. f. Sozialwiss, u. Sozialpol*.

KÖNIG, M. 1958. Die bäuerliche Kulturlandschaft der Hohen Schwaben-Alb und ihr

Gestaltwandel unter dem Einfluss der Industrie, in *Tübinger geogr. Stud.*

KORNER, F. 1958. Die Bevölkerungsverteilung in Thüringen am Ausgang des 16. Jahrhunderts, in *Wiss. Veröff, d. dtsch. Inst. f. Länderkunde*, N.F., 15–16.

KÖRNER, F. 1959. Die Bevölkerungszahl und -dichte in Mitteleuropa zum Beginn der Neuzeit, in *Forsch u. Fortschritte* 33.

KÖTZSCHKE, R. 1908. Deutsche Wirtschaftsgeschichte bis zum 17. Jahrhundert, in *Grundriss der Geschichtswissenschaft*.

KÖTZSCHKE, R. 1924. *Allgemeine Wirtschaftsgeschichte des Mittelalters.*

KOWALEWSKY, M. 1901. *Die ökonomische Entwicklung Europas*, V.

KRAUS, C. J. 1808. *Vermischte Schriften*, I.

KRAUSE, H. 1964. Art. Aufzeichnung des Rechts, in *Handwörterbuch zur deutschen Rechtsgeschichte*, I.

KRIEDTE, P., MEDICK, H. and SCHLUMBOHM, J. 1977. Industrialisierung vor der Industrialisierung, in *Veroff. d. Max. Planck Institut f. Geschichte*, 53.

KRUG, L. 1805. *Betrachtungen über den National-Reichtum des preussischen Staates . . .*, Part 2. Berlin.

KRÜGER, H. 1958. Zur Geschichte der Manufakturen und der Manufakturarbeiter in Preussen, in *Schriftenreihe des Instituts für allgemeine Geschichte an der Humboldt-Universität Berlin*, 3.

KRUSE, E. 1888. Kölnische Geldgeschichte bis 1386 nebst Beiträgen zur kurrheinischen Geldgeschichte bis zum Ende des Mittelalters, in *Westdeutsche Zeitschrift f. Geschichte u. Kunst, Ergänzungsheft*, IV.

KUCZYNSKI, J. 1947 (3rd edn). *Die Geschichte der Lage der Arbeiter in Deutschland von 1800 bis in die Gegenwart*, I.

KUCZYNSKI, J. 1960–3. *Die Geschichte der Lage der Arbeiter unter dem Kapitalismus.*

KUCZYNSKI, J. 1961. *Die Geschichte der Lage der Arbeiter in Deutschland von 1779 bis 1849.*

KUCZYNSKI, J. 1963. Einige Überlegungen über die Rolle der Natur in der Gesellschaft anlässlich der Lektüre von Abels Buch über Wustungen, in *Jahrbuch für Wirtschaftsgeschichte*, III.

KUCZYNSKI, J. 1964. Thomas Mann, in *Jahrb. f. Wirtschaftsgesch.*, 1963, IV. Berlin.

KUHN, W. 1957. *Geschichte der deutschen Ostsiedlung in der Neuzeit*, 2 vols.

KUHN, W. 1964. Die Siedlerzahlen der deutschen Ostsiedlung, in *Studium sociale*.

KULISCHER, J. 1965. *Allemeine Wirtschaftsgeschichte des Mittelalters und der Neuzeit*, I, II.

KULLAK-UBLICK, H. 1953. *Die Wechsellagen und Entwicklung der Landwirtschaft im südlichen Niedersachsen vom 15, bis 18. Jahrhundert, Thesis Göttingen*.

KUSKE, B. 1956. *Köln, der Rhein und das Reich.*

LABROUSSE, C. E. 1933. *Esquisse du mouvement des prix et des revenus en France au XVIIIe siècle*. Paris.

LABROUSSE, C. E. 1944. *La crise de l'économie française à la fin de l' Ancien Régime et au début de la Révolution*. Paris.

LADURIE, E. LE ROY. 1957. Sur Montpellier et sa campagne aux XVIe et XVIIe siècles, in *Annales*, 12.

LADURIE, E. LE ROY. 1959. Histoire et climat, in *Annales*, 14.

LADURIE, E. LE ROY. 1977. *The Peasants of Languedoc*. Urbana, Illinois.

LADURIE, E. LE ROY. 1973. *Times of Feast, Times of Famine*. London.

LAMOND, E. 1954. *A Discourse of the Common Weal of this Realm of England*. Cambridge.

LAMPERT VON HERSFELD. n.d. *Annalen* (trans. A. Schmidt) Berlin.

LAMPRECHT, K. 1885. Die Wirtschaftsgeschichtliche Literatur ..., in *Jahrbuch f. Nat. u. Stat.*, N.F., XI

LAMPRECHT, K. 1885–6. *Deutsches Wirtschaftsleben im Mittelalter*, I–III. Leipzig.

LAMPRECHT, K. 1909. *Deutsche Geschichte*, V, I. Berlin.

LAMPRECHT, K. and BELOW, G. VON n.d. (4th edn). Art. Grundbesitz, in *Handw. d. Staatsw.*

LANDES, S. 1950. The statistical study of French crises, in *Jnl. Econ. Hist.*, X. *Landwirtschaftlich-historiche Blätter*, VI, 1907.

LANGETHAL, C. E. 1854–6. *Geschichte der teutschen Landwirthschaft.*

LARSEN, E. 1961. *Graf Rumford, ein Amerikaner in München.*

LAVERGNE, M. L. DE. 1877, (8th edn). *Economie rurale de la France depuis 1789.*

LAVES, T. 1884. Die bayerische Armenpflege von 1847 bis 1880, in *Jahrb. f. Gesetzg. Verwalt. u. Volkswirtsch. im Deutschen Reich, 8.*

LEINGÄRTNER, G. 1956. Die Wüstungsbewegungen in Landgericht Amberg, in *Münchener Hist. Stud. Abt. Bayerische Geschichte*, III.

LEONARD, E. M. 1900. *The Early History of English Poor Relief.*

LESNIKOW, M. P. 1957–8. Beiträge zur baltisch-niederländischen Handelsgeschichte am Ausgang des 14. und zu Beginn des 15. Jahrhunderts, in *Wiss. Zeitschr. der Karl-Marx-Univ. zu Leipzig, 7.*

LEVASSEUR, E. 1889. *La Population Française*, I.

LEVASSEUR, E. 1892. Rapport sur deux concours pour le prix Rossi, in *Compte Rendu de l'Academie des Sciences Morales et Politiques*, N.S. 38.

LEVASSEUR, E. 1900 (2nd edn). *Histoire des classes ouvrières en France avant 1789.*

LEVY, H. 1902. Die Not der englischen Landwirte zur Zeit der hohen Getreidezölle, in *Münchener Volkswirtschaftliche Studien, 56.*

LIPS, A. 1830. *Deutschlands Nationalokönomie.*

LJUBLINSKAYA, A. D. 1959. Foreword to Russian edition of Marc Bloch's *Caractères originaux de l'histoire rurale française*. (French trans. in *Annales* 14).

LOBE, W. 1845. *Geschichte der Landwirtschaft im altenburgischen Osterlande.*

LOCKE, J. 1727 (3rd edn). *Works*, II.

LOHSE, H. 1957. *Die Wechsellagen der skandinavischen Landwirtschaft in vorindustrieller Zeit (16–18. Jahrhundert).* Thesis, Göttingen.

LOTZ, W. (ed.). 1893. *Drei Flugschriften über den Münzstreit der sächsischen Albertiner und Ernestiner um 1530.*

LUCAS, H. S. 1930. The great European famine of 1315, in *Speculum*, 15.

LÜTGE, F. 1958a. Die wirtschaftliche Lage Deutschlands vor Ausbruch des Dreissigjährigen Krieges, in *Jahrb. f. Nationalökonomie und Statistik, 170.*

LÜTGE, F. 1958b. Strukturelle u. konjunkturelle Wandlungen in der deutschen Wirtschaft vor Ausbruch des Dreissigjährigen Krieges, in *Bayerische Akad. d. Wiss., Phil.-histor. Klasse, Sitzungsberichte, 5.*

LÜTGE, F., FRANZ, G. and ABEL, W. (eds). 1965. *Quellen und Forschungen zur Agrargeschichte.*

MACAULAY, T. B. 1849. *The history of England.*

MCCULLOCH, I. R. 1834 (2nd edn). *A Dictionary, practical, theoretical and historical of commerce.*

MACPHERSON, D. 1805. *Annals of Commerce*, II.

MĄCZAK, A. 1972. Agricultural and livestock production in Poland: internal and foreign markets, in *Jnl. Eur. Econ. Hist.*, I.

MAGALDI, V and FABRIS, R. 1878. Notizie storiche e statistiche sui prezzi e salari in alcune citta d'Italia, in *Annali di Statist.* 2 a, III.

MAITLAND, F. W. 1894. History of a Cambridgeshire Manor, in *Eng. Hist. Rev.*, 9.

MALOTKI, M. VON. 1932a. *Hinterpommersche Landwirtschaft.*

MALOTKI, M. VON. 1932b. *Die Entwicklung der Landwirtschaft Hinterpommerns bis zum Ende des 18. Jahrhunderts.*

MALOWIST, M. 1959. The economic and social development of the Baltic countries from the fifteenth to the seventeenth centuries, in *Econ. Hist. Rev.*, XII.

MALTHUS, T. R. 1905 (Waentig edn). *Eine Abhandlung über das Bevölkerungsgesetz.*

MALTHUS, T. R. 1910. *Grundsätze der politischen Ökonomie.*

MANKOV, A. G. 1957. *Le mouvement des prix dans l'Etat Russe, du XVIe siècle* (Ecole Pratique des Hautes Etudes, VI, III).

MARSHALL, A. 1885. Theories and facts about wages, in *Annals of the Co-operative Wholesale Society*, VII.

MARSHALL, A. 1905. *Handbuch der Volkswirtschaftslehre*, I.

MARSHALL, A. 1925 (8th edn). *Principles of Economics.*

MARTIN, J. M. 1967. The Parliamentary enclosure movement and rural society in Warwickshire, in *Agricultural History Review*, XV.

MARWITZ, L. VON DER. 1909. Von dem Zustande des Vermögens der Grundbesitzer, 1820, in *Forsch. Zur brandenb.-preuss. Geschichte*, XXIL.

MASCHKE, E. 1963. Die inneren Wandlungen des deutschen Ritterordens, in *Geschichte und Gegenwartsbewusstsein, Festschrift für H. Rothfels.*

MATTHIESSEN, C. n.d. Die Käseproduktion in Eiderstedt im 17. Jahrhundert, in *Zeitschr. d. Ges. f. Schleswig-Holstein Gesch.*, 20.

MAUER, H. 1921. *Stock Exchange List from the Literary Remains.*

MAURUSCHAT, H. H. 1975. *Gewürze, Zucker und Salz im vorindustriellen Europa.* Thesis, Göttingen.

MAYNARD, G. 1962. *Economic Development and the Price Level.*

MEITZEN, A. 1871. *Der Boden und die landwirtschaftlichen Verhältnisse des Preussischen Staates*, III.

MELON, J. F. 1843. *Essai politique sur le commerce, 1734* (Economistes-Financiers du XVIIIe siècle de Daire).

MEUVRET, J. *Etudes d'histoire économique.*

MEYN, D. 1966. *Wurde die Wüstung der mittelalterlichen Nygenstad by de Elve gefunden?* in *Zeitschr. d. Ges. f. Schleswig-Holsteinische Gesch.*, 91.

MIANI, G. 1964. L'économie lombarde aux XIVe et XVe siècles Une exception à la règle?, in *Annales*, 19.

MILL, J. S. 1852. *Principles of Political Economy.*

MILL, J. S. 1864 (Soetbeer edn). *Grundsätze der Politischen Ökonomie.*

MINGAY, G. E. 1955–6. The agricultural depression 1730–1750 in *Econ. Hist. Rev.*, 8.

MINGAY, G. E. 1963. 'Agricultural Revolution' in English History: a reconsideration, in *Agricultural History*, 37.

Ministry of Agriculture and Fisheries. 1952. *Agricultural Statistics 1945–49, England and Wales*, I.

MIRABEAU, M. DE. 1756. *L'ami des hommes*, I. Avignon.

MISKIMIN, H. A. 1963. *Money, prices and foreign exchange in fourteenth-century France.*

MITCHELL, B. R., and DEANE, P. 1962. *Abstract of British Historical Statistics.* Cambridge.

Möglinsche Annalen der Landwirtschaft.

MOLESWORTH, R. 1697. *An account of Denmark as it was in the year 1692.* Cologne.

MOLS, R. 1954. *Introduction à la démographie historique des villes d'Europe du XIVe au XVIIIe siècle.*

MOLS, R. 1959. Die Bevölkerungsgeschichte Belgiens im Lichte der heutigen Forschung, in *Vierteljahrschrift für Sozial- und Wirtschaftsgeschichte*, 46.

MOMBERT, P. 1921. Aus der Literatur über die soziale Frage und über die Arbeiterbewegung in Deutschland in der ersten Hälfte des 19. Jahrhunderts, in *Archiv. f. d. Gesch. d. Sozialismus u. d. Arbeiterbewegung*, 9.

MOMBERT, P. 1929. *Bevölkerungslehre*.

MOMBERT, P. 1931. Die Anschauungen des 17. und 18. Jahrhunderts über die Abnahme der Bevölkerung, in *Jahrb. f. Nat.-Ökon. und Statistik*.

MONE, F. J. 1859. *Beiträge zur Geschichte der Volkswirtschaft aus Urkunden*.

MONTESQUIEU, M. DE. 1784 (6th edn). *Lettres Persanes*.

Movimento dei Prezzi di alcuni generi alimentari dal 1862 al 1885. 1886. Veröff d. Ackerbauministeriums des Königreiches Italien, Preise aus Udine.

MÜLLER, K. O. 1959. Quellen zur Verwaltungs -und Wirtschaftsgeschichte der Grafschaft Hohenberg (1381 bis 1454), in *Veröff d. Komm. f. Geschichtliche Landeskunde in Baden-Württemberg*, A. 4, 11.

MÜLLER, M. 1897. Getreidepolitik, Getreideverkehr und die Getreidepreise in *Schlesien während des 18. Jahrhunderts*.

MÜLLER, W. 1833. In *Möglinsche Annalen*, XXX.

MURET. 1888. Mémoire über den Stand der Bevölkerung des Waadtlandes, Bern, 1766, abstract in the *Zeitschr. f. Schweiz, Statistik*. 24.

NABHOLZ, H. 1941. Medieval agrarian society in transition, in *Camb. Econ. Hist. of Europe*, I.

NAUDE, W. 1896. Die Getreidehandelspolitik der europäischen Staaten vom 13. bis zum 18. Jahrhundert, in *Acta Borussica, Getreidehandelspolitik*, I.

NAUDE, W. and SKALWEIG, A. 1910. Die Getreidehandelspolitik und die Kriegsmagazinverwaltung Preussens 1740–1756, in *Acta Borussica, Getreidehandelspolitik*. Berlin.

NEF, J. U. 1937. Prices and industrial capitalism in France and England, 1540–1640, in *Econ. Hist. Rev.*, VII.

NEMNICH, P. 1809. *Tagebuch einer der Kultur und Industrie gewidmeten Reise*, I.

Neue Annalen der Mecklenburger Landwirthschafts-Gesellschaft, n.d.

Neue Staatsbürgerliches Magazin, 1834. II. Schleswig.

NEUMANN, A. 1911. Die Bewegung der Löhne der ländlichen 'freien Arbeiter' ... im *Königreich Preussen gegenwärtigen Umfangs vom Ausgang des 18. Jahrhunderts bis 1850*.

NIELSON, A. 1906. Dänische Preise, 1650–1750, in *Jahrb. f. Nationalök u. Stat.*, 86.

NIELSEN, A. 1933. Dänische Wirtschaftsgeschichte, in *Handb. der Wirtschaftsgeschichte*. Jena.

NIEMANN, F. A. 1830. *Vollständiges Handbuch der Münzen, Masse und Gewichte aller Länder der Erde*.

NOBACK, C. and F. 1858. *Münz-, Mass- und Gewichtsbuch*.

NORBORG, L. A. 1958. Storföretaget Vadstena Kloster, in *Bibliotheca Historica Lundensis*, VIII.

NORBORG, L. A. 1959–60. Agrarkrisen i senmedeltidens Sverige, in *Historiclärarnas Förenings Ånsskrift*.

NORTH, D. 1958. Ocean Freight Rates and Economic Development 1750–1913, in *Jnl. Econ. Hist.*, 18.

Northern Historians' Conference, Bergen, 1964. *Ødegarder og ny bosetning i de Nordiske Land i senmiddelalderen*, Copenhagen.

O'BRIEN, P. K. 1959. British incomes and property in the early nineteenth century, in *Econ. Hist. Rev.*, XII.

OLDEKOP, H. 1906–8. *Topographie der Herzogtümer Schleswig und Holstein*, II.

OPPENHEIMER, F. 1924 (5th edn). *System der Soziologie*, III, 2.

PAASCHE, H. 1881. in *Jahrb. f. Nationalökonomie u. Stat.*, N.F. II.

PACH, Z. P. 1960. Das Entwicklungsniveau der feudalen Agrarverhältnisse in Ungarn in der zweiten Hälfte des XV. Jahrhunderts, in *Studia Historica, Acad. Scient. Hungaricae*, 46.

PARENTI, G. 1939. Prime ricerche sulla rivoluzione dei prezzi a Firenze, in *Pubbl. dell' Univ. degli Studi di Firenze, Facoltà di Econ. e Comm.*, XVI. Florence.

PARENTI, G. 1942. Prezzi e mercato del grano a Siena, in *Pubb. dell' Univ. degli Studi di Firenze, Facoltà di Econ. e. Comm.*, XIX.

PATERNA, E. 1960. *Da stunden die Bergleute auff*, II.

PEDERSEN, E. H. Copenhagen. *Landbrugskrisen 1818–1828. Et forsøg pa en nuancering*, in *Landbohistorik Studier*. Copenhagen.

PEDERSEN, H. 1905. Die Kapitelstaxen in Dänemark, in *Jahrb. f. Nat. u. Stat.* series III, vol. 29.

PELC, J. 1935. Deny w Krakowie w latach 1369–1600, in *Bujak, Badania* ... 14. Lvov.

PELC, J. 1937. Ceny w Gdansku w XVI i XVII wieku, in *Bujak, Badania* ..., 21. Lvov.

PERROY, J. 1955–6. Wage labour in France in the later Middle Ages in *Econ. Hist. Rev.*, 8.

PESEZ, J.-F. and LADURIE, E. LE ROY. 1965. Les villages désertés en France: vue d'ensemble, in *Annales*, 20.

PETERS, I. n.d. *Jahrb. d. Eiderstedter Gesch. von 1100 bis 1620*, in Eiderstedter Propstei-Archiv.

PETERSEN, E. L. 1966. Jordprisforhold i Dansk Senmiddelalder, in A. E. Christensen (ed.) *Middelalderstudier*.

PETERSON, A. G. March, 1929. Historical Study of Prices Received by producers of Farm Products in Virginia, 1801–1927, in *Virginia Polytechnic Institute, Technical Bulletin*.

PETZET, W. 1929. *Der Physiokratismus und die Entdeckung des wirtschaftlichen Kreislaufes.*

PEZ, H. 1721. *Scriptores rerum Austriacarum*, I.

PFEFFER, M. 1640. *Manuale emporeticum. Das ist: Ein Neues sehr nützliches ausgerechnetes Hand-und Kauffmansbüchlein Wolfensbüttel.*

PHELPS-BROWN, E. H. and HOPKINS, S. V. Seven centuries of the prices of consumables, compared with builders' wage rates, in *Economica*, XXIII. 92.

PHILIPPI, F. 1909. *Die erste Industrialisierung Deutschlands.*

PICKL, O. (ed.). 1971. *Die wirtschaftlichen Auswirkungen der Türkenkriege*, in *Grazer Forschung zur Wirtschafts und Sozialgeschichte*, I.

PICKL, O. 1973. Routen, Umfang und Organisation des innereuropäischen Handels mit Schlachtvieh im 16. Jahrhundert, in the *Festschrift. für H. Wiesflecker.*

POHLENDT, H. 1950. Die Verbreitung der mittelalterlichen Wüstungen in Deutschland, in *Göttinger Geogr. Arbeiten*, III.

PONGRATZ, W. 1955–6. Zur Frage der partiellen Ortswüstungen im oberen Waldviertel, in *Jahrb. f. Landeskunde von Niederösterreich*, XXXII.

PORTER, G. R. 1912. *The Progress of the Nation.*

POST, J. D. 1973. In *Jnl. Interdisciplinary History.*

POSTAN, M. M. 1950. Some economic evidence of declining population in the later Middle Ages, in *Econ. Hist. Rev.*, II.

POSTAN, M. M. 1959–60. A note to W. C. Robinson, Money, population and economic change in late medieval Europe, in *Econ. Hist. Rev.*, 12.

POSTAN, M. M. 1967. Investment in medieval agriculture, in *Jnl. Econ. Hist.*, 27.

POSTAN, M. M. and TITOW, J. 1958–9. Heriots and prices on Winchester Manors, in *Econ. Hist. Rev.*, 11.

POSTHUMUS, N. W. 1946 and 1964. *Inquiry into the history of prices in Holland*, I and II. Leiden.

Pragmatische Geschichte der bayerischen Gesetzgebung und Staatsverwaltung seit den Zeiten Maximilians I., I, 1836.

PREUSS, J. 1834. *Frïedrich der Grosse*, IV.

PRIBRAM, A. F. 1938. *Materialien zur Geschichte der Preise und Löhne in Österreich*, I. Vienna.

PROBST, C. 1963. Die Städte im Burgwald, in *Marburger Geogr. Schriften*, 19.

PROTHERO, R. E. 1912. *English Farming Past and Present*.

QUELLET, F. and HAMELIN, J. 1962. La crise agricole dans le Bas-Canada (1802–1837), in *Etudes Rurales*.

QUESNAY, F. 1756. *Art. Fermiers*, in *Oevres de Quesnay*, Oncken edn, 1888.

QUESNAY, F. 1757. *Art. Grains*, in *Oevres de Quesnay*, Oncken edn., 1888. See also Y. Guyot 1896. *François Quesnay et la Physiocratie*.

RAFTIS, J. A. 1957. *The Estates of Ramsey Abbey*.

RAVEAU, P. 1924*a*. L'agriculture et les classes paysannes dans le Bas-Poitou au XVIe siècle, in *Revue d'Histoire Econ. et Soc.*

RAVEAU, P. 1924*b*. L'agriculture et les classes paysannes dans le Haut-Poitou au XVIe siècle, in *Revue d'Histoire Econ. et Soc.*

RAVEAU, P. 1926. L'agriculture et les classes paysannes en Haut-Poitou au XVIe siècle, in *Revue d'Histoire Econ. et Soc.*

REINCKE, H. 1951. Hansische Geschichtsblätter, 70.

REINCKE, H. 1954. Hansische Geschichtsblätter, 72.

REY, M. 1967. Actes du Colloque sur la Forêt, Besançon, 21–22 Octobre, 1966, in *Cahiers d'Etudes Comtoises*, 12.

RHEE, H. A. 1949. Memorandum to *The rent of agricultural land in England and Wales 1870–1939*.

RICARDO, D. 1911. *The Principles of Political Economy and Taxation*.

RICHET, D. 1968. Croissance et Blocage en France du XVe au XVIIIe siècle, in *Annales*, 23.

RICHTENTAL, U. VON. 1882. M. R. Buck (ed.). *Chronik des Constanzer Concils 1414–18*.

RIEHL, W. H. 1850. Der vierte Stand, in *Deutsche Vierteljahrsschrift*, 4.

RIEMANN, F. K. 1953. Ackerbau und Viehhaltung im vorindustriellen Deutschland, in *Beihefte zum Jahrbuch der Albertus – Universitat zu Königsberg/Pr.*, III. Würzburg.

ROBINSON, W. C. 1959. Money, population and economic change in late medieval Europe, in *Econ. Hist. Rev.*, 12.

RODBERTUS-JAGETZOW, C. 1868. *Zur Erklärung und Abhülfe der heutigen Greditnoth des Gutsbesitzes*, I.

ROGERS, J. E. T. 1884. *Six Centuries of Work and Wages; a History of British Labour*.

ROGERS, J. E. T. 1866–1902. *A History of Agriculture and Prices in England*, I–VIII. Oxford.

ROGERS, J. E. T. 1894 (3rd edn). *The Economic Interpretation of History*, I.

ROGERS, J. E. T. 1909. *The Industrial and Commercial History of England*.

ROGERS, T. 1898. *Geschichte der englischen Arbeit*.

ROHR, J. B. VON. 1722. *Hauswirthschaftsbuch.*

ROLFS, C. 1891. *Geschichte der Gemeinde St Annen,* Lunden.

ROMANO, R. 1966. L'Italia nella crisi del XIV secolo, in *Nuova Rivista Storica,* 50, V–VI.

ROMEUF, L. 1902. La crise agricole sous la Restauration. Thesis, Paris.

ROSCHER, W. 1857. Ein Beitrag zur Geschichte der Kornpreise und Bäckertaxen, in *Zeitschr. f. d. ges. Staatswiss.,* XIII.

ROSCHER, W. 1885. *Nationalökonomie des Ackerbaues.*

ROSDOLSKY, R. 1951. The distribution of the agrarian product in feudalism, in *Jnl. Econ. Hist.,* XL.

RUBNER, H. 1964. Die Landwirtschaft der Münchener Ebene und ihre Notlage im 14. Jahrhundert, in *Vierteljahrschrift für Sozial-und Wirtschaftsgeschichte,* 51.

RUDE, G. E. 1953–4. Prices, wages and popular movements in Paris during the French Revolution, in *Econ. Hist. Rev.,* 6.

RUDING, R. 1817–19. *Annals of the Coinage of Britain and its dependencies,* 3 vols. London.

RUNNE, B. 1956. Die rechtliche Lage der Dienstboten im Lande Hadeln vom 16. bis. 19. Jahrhundert, in *Jahrb. der Männer vom Morgenstern,* 37.

RUSSELL, J. C. 1948. *British medieval population.*

RUSSELL, J. C. 1958. Late ancient and mediaeval population, in *Trans. American Philosoph. Soc.,* N.S. 48, 3.

RUWET, J. 1943. *L'agriculture et les Classes rurales au Pays de Herve sous L'Ancien Régime,* Paris.

SAALFELD, D. 1960. Bauernwirtschaft und Gutsbetrieb in der vorindustriellen Zeit, in *Quellen und Forschungen zur Agrargeschichte.*

SAALFELD, D. 1964. Die Bedeutung des Getreides für die Haushaltsausgaben städtischer Verbraucher in der zweiten Hälfte des 18. Jahrhunderts, in *Landwirtschaft und ländliche Gesellschaft, Festschrift Wilhelm Abel. Schriftenreihe für ländliche Sozialfragen.* Hanover.

SAALFELD, D. 1977. Steigerung und Wandlung des Fleischverbrauchs in Deutschland 1800–1913, in *Zeitschr. f. Agrargesch. u. Agrarsoziologie,* 25.

SACHS, C. L. 1922. Metzgergewerbe und Fleischversorgung der Stadt Nürnberg bis zum Ende des Dreissigjährigen Krieges, in *Mitt. d. Ver. f. Gesch. d. Stadt Nürnberg,* 24.

SACHS, P. 1637. *Annales Eiderstadiensium.*

SARS, J. E. n.d. Til oplysining fra det 13. til det 17. aarhundrede, in *Norske Historiske Tidsskrift,* 2, 3.

SANDES, J. 1970. *Ødetid og Gjenreising.*

SATTLER, H. B. 1962. Die Ritterschaft der Ortenau in der spätmittelalterlichen Wirtschaftskrise. Eine Untersuchung ritterschaftlicher Vermögensvershältnisse im 14. Jahrhundert. Thesis, Heidelberg.

SCHARLAU, K. 1933. Beiträge zur geographischen Betrachtung der Wüstungen, in *Badische Geogr. Abhandl.*

SCHARLAU, K. 1954–5. Die hessische Wüstungsforschung vor neuen Aufgaben, in *Zeitschr. d. Ver. f. hess. Gesch. u. Landeskunde.*

SCHILLER, K. 1940. Marktregulierung und Marktordnung in der Weltagrarwirtschaft, in *Probleme der Weltwirtschaft,* 67.

SCHOLZER, C. VON. 1807. *Anfangsgründe der Staatswirthschaft,* II. Riga.

SCHLÜTER, O. 1903. *Die Siedlungen im nördlichen Thüringen.*

SCHMALZ, F. 1808. Über Pachtungen, in *Thaer's Annalen der Landwirtschaft,* VII.

SCHMALZ, F. 1827. In *Jahrbücher der preussischen Landwirtschaft,* III.

SCHMID, C. 1695. *Commentarius in ius provinciale Bavaricum,* I. Supplement to Decree of 20.6.1650.

SCHMITZ, H. J. 1968. Faktoren der Preisbildung für Getreide und Wein in der Zeit von 800–1350, in *Quellen u. Forsch. z. Agrareschichte*, XX.

SCHMOLLER, G. 1870. Über Fleischconsumtion, in *Zeitschr. d. landw. Central-Vereins für die Provinz Sachsen*, 27.

SCHMOLLER, G. 1871. Die historische Entwicklung des Fleischkonsums sowie der Vieh- und Fleischpreise in Deutschland, in *Zeitschr. f. die ges. Staatswissenschaften*, XXVII.

SCHMOLLER, G. 1886. Studien über die wirtschaftliche Politik Friedrichs des Grossen, in *Schmollers Jahrb.*, X.

SCHMOLLER, G. 1896. Die Epochen der deutschen Getreidehandelsverfassung und -politik, in *Schmollers Jahrb.*, XX.

SCHMOLLER, G. 1914. Die Tatsachen der Lohnbewegung in Geschichte und Gegenwart, in *Schmollers Jahrb.*

SCHMOLLER, G. 1919. *Grundriss der allgemeinen Volkswirtschaftslehre* I.

SCHOLLIERS, E. 1959. *Pryzen*....

SCHOLLIERS, E. 1960. *De Levensstandaard in de XVe en XVIe eeuw te Antwerpen*.

SCHÖNFELDT, G. 1903. In *Viertelj. f. Soz. u. Wirtschaftsgesch.*, I.

SCHOPENHAUER, J. 1958 edn. *Jugendleben und Wanderbilder*.

SCHREINER, J. 1948. *Pest og Prisfall i Senmiddelalderen*.

SCHRODER, W. R. VON. 1713. *Fürstliche Schatz- und Rentkammer*, Leipzig.

SCHRÖTTER, F. VON. 1904–13. Das preussische Münzwesen im 18. Jahrhundert, in *Acta Borussica, Münzgeschichtlicher Teil*, 4 vols.

SCHRÖTTER, F. VON. 1922. *Die Münzen Friedrich Wilhelms des Grossen Kürfursten und Friedrichs III. von Brandenburg, Münz- und Geldgeschichte 1640–1700*.

SCHRÖTTER, F. VON. 1926. *Das preussische Münzwesen 1806–1873*.

SCHUBERT, F. W. 1847. Statistische Beurteilung und Vergleichung einiger früheren Zustände und der Gegenwart für die Provinz Preussen, mit besonderer Berücksichtigung des jetzigen Notstandes dieser Provinz, in *Ztschr. d. Ver. f. deutsche Statistik*, I.

SCHULZ, W. 1938. *Die zweite deutsche Ostsiedlung im westlichen Netzegau*.

SCHULZE, E. O. 1896. *Die Kolonisierung und Germanisierung der Gebiete zwischen Saale und Elbe*, Appendix V.

SCHUMPETER, J. 1926. Gustav Schmoller und die Probleme von heute, in *Schmollers Jahrb.*, 50.

SEE, H. 1927a. L'économie rurale de l'Anjou, in *Revue d'Histoire Economique et Sociale*.

SEE, H. 1929. *Esquisse d'une histoire écon. et soc. de la France*.

SEE, H. 1930. *Histoire économique de la France*.

SEETZEN, 1801. Über den Handel mit Landgütern, in Thaer (ed.) *Annalen der Niedersächsischen Landwirtschaft*, III.

Select Committee on the Depressed State of Agriculture of the United Kingdom, Report, 18 June 1821.

Select Committee on Agriculture, Report, House of Commons, 2 August 1833.

Select Committee appointed to inquire into the State of Agriculture.

First report, 4 March 1836.

Second report, 15 April 1836.

Third report, 21 July 1836.

SERING, M. 1887. *Die landwirtschaftliche Konkurrenz Nordamerikas in Gegenwart und Zukunft*.

SERING, M. 1925. *Agrarkrisen und Agrarzöllen*.

SERING, O. DE 1605 (3rd edn). *Le Théâtre d'Agriculture*.

SEUFFERT, G. 1857. *Statistik des Getreide- und Viktualienhandels im Königreiche Bayern mit Berücksichtigung des Auslandes,* Munich.

SILLEM, J. A. 1901. Tabellen van Marktprijzen van Granen te Utrecht in de Jaren 1393 tot 1644, in *Verh. de Koninklijke Akad. van Wetenschappen te Amsterdam, Afd. Letterkunde, N.R.,* III, 4. Amsterdam.

SIROL, J. 1942. *Le rôle de l'agriculture dans les fluctuations économiques,* Paris.

SKALWEIT, A. 1906. Die ostpreussische Domänenverwaltung unter Friedrich Wilhelm I. und das Retablissement Litauens, in *Staats- und Sozialwissenschaftliche Forschungen,* 25, 3.

SKALWEIT, A. 1910. Die Getreidehandelspolitik und Kriegsmagazinverwaltung Preussens 1740–1756, in *Acta Borussica, Getreidehandelspolitik,* III.

SKALWEIT, B. 1915. *Die englische Landwirtschaft.*

SKAPPEL, S. 1937–40. Høstingsbruk og Dyrkingsbruk, in *Historisk Tidsskrift,* 31.

SLICHER VAN BATH, B. H. 1957. *Een samenleving onder spanning.*

SLICHER VAN BATH, B. H. 1958. (with Robert Loder and Rienck Hemmema) in It Beaken, *Tydskrift van de Fryske Akademy,* XX.

SLICHER VAN BATH, B. H. 1963. *The Agrarian History of Western Europe, 500–1850.* London.

SLICHER VAN BATH, B. H. 1964. Studien betreffende de agrarische geschiedenis van de Veluwe in de middeleeuwen, in *A.A.G. Bijdragen,* 11.

SLICHER VAN BATH, B. H. (with colleagues). 1965. Contributions presented to the Third International Conference of Economic History, in *A.A.G. Bijdragen,* 12.

SMITH, Adam. 1776. *The Wealth of Nations.*

SOETBEER, A. 1866. *Forschungen zur deutschen Geschichte,* VI.

SOETBEER, A. 1879. In *Göttingen Gel. Anz.,* 12.

SOMBART, W. 1916–28 (3rd edn). *Der moderne Kapitalismus.* Munich and Leipzig.

SPANGENBERG, C. 1585. *Mänsfeldische Chronik,* I.

STADELMANN, R. 1878. Friedrich Wilhelm I. in *Seiner Tätigkeit für die Landeskultur Preussens,* I.

STAFFORD, W. 1876 edn. *A Compendious Examination of Certayne Complaints* by J. Hales (1549).

STAFFORD, W. 1895. Drei Gespräche über die in der Bevölkerung verbreiteten Klagen, hsg. v. Leser.

STEFFEN, G. F. 1901–5. *Studien zur Geschichte der englischen Lohnarbeiter.*

STEINBORN, H. C. 1973. *Abgaden und Dienste holsteinischer Bauern im 18. Jahrhundert.* Thesis, Göttingen.

STEINBRUCK, C. 1900. Die Entwicklung der Preise des städtischen und ländlichen Immobiliarbesitzes von Halle (Saale) und im Saalkreise, in *Samml. nat. u. statist. Abhandl. d. Staatswiss.,* 10.

STELZNER. 1826. Aufruf an Deutschlands Landwirthe, in *Möglinsche Annalen der Landwirtschaft,* XVIII.

STENZEL, G. 1841. *Geschichte des Preussischen Staates,* III.

STOY, S. 1935. Zur Bevölkerungs- und Sozialstatistik kursächsischer Kleinstädte, in *Viertelj. f. Sozial-und Wirtschaftsgesch.,* IV.

STRAUB, A. 1887. *Die abgegangenen Ortschaften des Elsass.*

SWART, F. 1910. Zur friesischen Agrargeschichte, in *Schmollers Staats- u. Sozialwiss. Forsch.,* 145.

TAINE, H. 1908 (3rd edn). *The Ancient Regime.*

TESSIER. 1819. *Annales de l'Agriculture Francaise,* VI.

TEUTE, O. 1910. *Das alte Ostfalenland Diss.* Erlangen.

THAER, A. 1978a. *Einleitung zur Kenntais der englischen Landwirtschaft*, I.

THAER, A. 1798b. *Vermischte Schriften*, I.

THAER, A. 1844 (English edn). *Principles of Agriculture.*

THIEDE, G. 1955. Verzehrsgewohnheiten wandeln Absatzchancen, in *Die Ernährungs-wirtschaft.*

THIELE, C. G. VON. 1768. *Churmärkische Contributions- und Schosseinrichtung.*

THIELE, O. 1906. François Quesnay und die Agrarkrisis im Ancien Regime, in *Viertelj f. Sozial-und Wirtschaftsgesch.*, IV.

THOMPSON, R. J. 1907. An inquiry into the rent of agricultural land in England and Wales during the nineteenth century, in *Jnl. Royal Statist. Soc.*

THORPE, H. 1965. The Lord and the Landscape, in *Trans. Birmingham Archaeolog. Soc.*, 80.

THÜNEN, J. H. VON. 1875a (3rd edn). *Der isolierter Staat.*

THÜNEN, J. H. VON. 1875b. Reflexionen über die gegenwärtige Zeit in Beziehung auf die Wohlfeilheit des Getreides, in *Der isolierter Staat*, II, 2.

TITOW, J. Z. 1959–60. Evidence of weather in the account rolls of the Bishopric of Winchester, 1209–1350, in *Econ. Hist. Rev.*, XII.

TITOW, J. Z. 1961–2. Some evidence of the thirteenth century population increase, in *Econ. Hist. Rev.*, XIV.

TITOW, J. Z. 1970. Le climat à travers les rôles de compatabilité d l'évêché de Winchester (1350–1450), in *Annales*, 25.

TITS-DIEUAIDE, M.-J. 1975. *La formation des prix céréaliers en Brabant et en Flandre au XVe siècle.*

TOEPPEN, M. *Acten der Ständetage Preussens unter der Herrschaft des Deutschen Ordens.*

TOMASZEWSKI, E. 1934. Ceny w Krakowie w latach 1601–1795, in *Bujak, Badania ...*, 15. Lvov.

TOOKE, T. and NEWMARCH, W. 1838–57. *A History of Prices and of the State of Circulation, from 1793–1857*, II. London.

TOPOLSKI, J. 1958. I. *Gospodarstwo Wiejskie W Dobrach Arcybiskupstwa Gnieznienskiego Od XVIII Wieku*, Poznan.

TOPOLSKI, J. 1962. La regression économique en Pologne du XVIe au XVIIIe siècle, in *Acta Poloniae Historica*, VII.

TORFS, L. 1859. *Fastes des calamités.*

TOUTAIN, J. C. 1961. *Le produit de l'agriculture française de 1700 à 1958*, in *Cahiers de l'Institut de Science Economique Appliquée, Histoire quantitative de l'économie française.*

TROW-SMITH, R. 1957. *A History of British livestock husbandry to 1700.*

TUCKER, G. S. L. 1963. English pre-industrial population trends, in *Econ. Hist. Rev.*, XVI.

TUSSER, T. 1557. *Hundred Good Pointes of Husbandry.*

UCKE, A. 1887. *Die Agrarkrisis in Preussen während der zwanziger Jahre dieses Jahrhunderts.*

UNGER, J. G. 1752. *Von der Ordnung der Fruchtpreise und deren Einflusse in die wichtigsten Angelegenheiten des menschlichen Lebens* I, Göttingen.

URSINI, A. *Thüringische Chronik.*

USHER, A. P. 1930. The general course of wheat prices in France, 1350–1788, in *Review of Economic Statistics.*

VAUGHAN, A. 1675. *A Discourse of Coin and Coinage.*

VERHULST, A. 1964a. Die Binnenkolonisation und die Anfänge der Landgemeinde in Seeflandern, in *Vorträge und Forschungen.*

VERHULST, A. 1964b. Bronnen en problemen betreffende de vlaame landbouw in de late middeleeuwen (XIIIe–XVe eeuw), in *Agronomisch-Historische Bijdragen*, VI.

VERHULST, A. 1964c. l'Economie rurale de la Flandre et la dépression économique du Bas Moyen Age, in *Studia Historica Gandensia*, 7.

VERHULST, A. 1965. *Het landschap in Vlaanderen in historisch perspectief.* Antwerp.

VERLINDEN, C. 1959. *Dokumenten voor de geschiedenis van prijzen en lonen in Vlaanderen en Brabant.*

VIVIER, R. 1920. Une crise économique au milieu du XIVe siècle, in *Revue d'Histoire des Doctrines Economiques*, XIII.

VOLKMAR, W. 1795. *Versuch einer Beschreibung von Eiderstedt in Briefen an einen Freund im Holsteinischen, Garding.*

WÄCHTER, H. H. 1958. Ostpreussische Domänenvorwerke im 16. und 17. Jahrhundert, in *Beihefte z. Jahrb. d. Albertus-Universität*, XIX. Königsberg.

WAGEMANN, E. 1928. *Konjunkturlehre.*

WAGEMANN, E. 1929. *Einführung in die Konjunkturlehre.*

WAILLY, N. DE. 1857. *Sur les variations de la Livre Tournois.*

WARREN, G. F. 1933 (with F. A. Pearson). *Prices*, New York.

WASCHINSKI, E. 1959. Währung, Preisentwicklung und Kaufkraft des Geldes in Schleswig-Holstein von 1226–1864, in *Quellen und Forschungen zur Geschichte Schleswig-Holsteins*, 26.

WATTS, D. G. 1967. A model for the early fourteenth century, in *Econ. Hist. Rev.*, XX.

WEBER, F. B. 1807. *Staatswirthschaftlicher Versuch über die Theuerung und Theuerungspolizey*, Göttingen.

WEBER, F. B. 1810. *Theoretisch-praktische Handbuch der grösseren Viehzucht.*

WEE, H. VAN DER. 1963a. The growth of the Antwerp market and the European economy (fourteenth–sixteenth centuries) 3.

WEE, H. VAN DER. 1963b. Typologie des crises et changements de structures aux Pays-Bas (XVe–XVe siècles), in *Annales*, 18.

WELLSCHMIED, K. 1963. Die Hospitäler der Stadt Göttingen, in *Studien zu Gesch. d. Stadt.*, 4. Göttingen.

WEINSBERG, H. VON 1887. Das Buch Weinsberg, in *Publ. d. Ges. f. Rheinische Geschichtskunde*, IV.

WENTE, G. n.d. *Das Wirtschaftsleben des altmarkischen Klosters Diesdorf im ausgehenden Mittelalter.*

WERNER, W. 1969. Spätmittelalterlicher Strukturwandel in Spiegel neuerer Forschungen: Das Italienische Beispiel, in *Jahrb. f. Wirtschaftsgesch.*

WERVEKE, H. VAN. 1950a. La famine de l'an 1316 en Flandre et dans les regions voisines, in *Revue du Nord*, 41.

WERVEKE, H. VAN. 1950b. De Zwarte Dood in de Zuiderlijke Nederlanden, 1349–1351, in *Mededelingen v. d. Kon. Vlaamse Acad. v. Wetensch ...*

WESTPHAL, H. 1925a. Die Agrarkrisis in Mecklenburg in den zwanziger Jahren des 19. Jahrhunderts, in *Mecklen. Landwirtschaftl.*, 6.

WESTPHAL. H. 1925b. Die Agrarkrisis der Zwanziger Jahre des vorigen Jahrhunderts in Mecklenburg, in *Mecklenb. Landwirtschaftl.*, 6.

WEULERSSE, G. 1931. Le mouvement prephysiocratique en France, in *Revue d'Histoire Econ. et Soc.*, XIX.

WEYERMANN, M. 1910. Zur Geschichte des Immobiliarkreditwesens in Preussen in *Freiburger Volkswirtsch. Abhandl.*, I, 1.

WHITMORE, W. W. 1822. A letter on the present state and future prospects of agriculture addressed to the agriculturalists of the County of Salop. London, in H. Levy. Die Not des englischen Landwirts zur Zeit der hohen Getreidezölle, in *Münchener Volkswirtschaftliche Studien*, LVI, 1902.

WIARDA, D. 1880. *Die geschichtliche Entwicklung der wirtschaftlichen Verhältnisse Ostfrieslands.*

WIDERA, B. 1963. Getreideausfuhr in die vormongolische Rus, in *Jahrb. f. Wirtschaftsgeschichte*, II, Berlin.

WIEBE, G. 1895. *Zur Geschichte der Preisrevolution des 16. und 17. Jahrhunderts.* Leipzig.

WIESE, H. 1963. Der Rinderhandel im nordwesteuropäischen Küstengebiet vom 15. Jahrhundert bis zum Beginn des 19. Jahrhunderts. Thesis, Göttingen.

WIESE, H. 1966. Der Rinderhandel in nordwesteuropäischen Küstengebiet vom 15, bis zum Beginn des 19. Jahrhunderts, in H. Wiese and J. Bölts. Rinderhandel und Rinderhaltung im nordwesteuropäischen Küstengebiet vom 15. bis zum 19 Jahrh., in part 7, *Quellen u. Forsch. Agrargesch.*, edited by F. Lutge, G. Franz and W. Abel.

WIESSNER, H. 1934. *Sachinhalt und Wirtschaftliche Bedeutung der Weistümer im Deutschen Kulturgebeit.*

WILLIAMS, H. T. 1960. *Principles for British Agricultural Policy.*

WOEHLKENS, E. 1954. *Pest und Ruhr im 16 u. 17. Jahrhundert.*

WOERMANN, E. 1944. Ernährungswirtschaftliche Leistungmassstäbe, in *Mitt. f. d. Landw.*, 59.

WOLTERS, F. 1905. *Studien über Agrarzustände.*

WOUDE, A. M. VAN DER. 1963. De consumptie van graan, flees en buter in Holland op het einde van de achttiende eeuw, in *A.A.G. Bijdragen*, 9. Wageningen.

WOUDE, A. M. VAN DER. 1972. Het Noorderkwartier, in *A.A.G. Bijdragen* XII, pt II.

WRIGLEY, E. A. 1966. Family limitation in pre-industrial England, in *Econ. Hist. Rev.*, 19.

WYCZANKI, A. 1963. L'économie du domaine nobilaire moyen (1500–1580), in *Annales.*

Yearbook of National Accounts Statistics, United Nations Statistical Office, New York.

YOUNG, A. 1812. *An Enquiry into the Progressive Value of Money in England.* London.

YVARTS, V. 1807. In *Annales de l'Agriculture Française*, XXIX.

ZIEKURSCH, J. 1915. Hundert Jahre schlesischer Agrargeschichte, in *Darst. u. Quell. z. Schles. Gesch.*, XX, Breslau.

ZOLLA, D. 1893–4. Les variations du revenu et du prix des terres en France au XVIIe et au XVIIIe siècle, in *Annales de l'Ecole Libre des Sciences Politiques.*

A supplementary bibliography
on English agrarian fluctuations

Bibliographies

BREWER, J. G. 1972. *Enclosures and the Open Fields; a Bibliography*, British Agricultural History Society.
CHALONER, W. H. and RICHARDSON, R. C. (compilers) 1976. *British Economic and Social History: a Bibliographical Guide*, Manchester University Press.

Books and articles

The asterisked items contain further substantial bibliographies which should be used to extend this list. The place of publication is London unless otherwise stated.

APPLEBY, ANDREW B. 1978. *Famine in Tudor and Stuart England*, Liverpool University Press.
BAKER, A. R. H. 1966. Evidence in the *Nonarum Inquisitiones* of contracting arable lands in England during the early fourteenth century, *Econ. Hist. Rev.*, 2nd ser., XIX, pp. 518–32.
*BAKER, A. R. H. and BUTLIN, R. A. (eds) 1973. *Studies of Field Systems in the British Isles*, Cambridge University Press.
BAKER, D. 1970. The marketing of corn in the first half of the eighteenth century: north-east Kent, *Agric. Hist. Rev.*, 18. pp. 126–50.
BARNES, D. G. 1930. *A History of the English Corn Laws from 1660–1846*, Routledge.
BELLERBY, J. R. 1956. *Agriculture and Industry: Relative Income*, Macmillan.
BENNETT, M. K. 1935. British wheat-yield per acre for seven centuries, *Econ. hist.* III, pp. 12–29.
*BERESFORD, M. W. 1954. *The Lost Villages of England*, Lutterworth Press.
BERESFORD, M. W. 1961. Habitation versus improvement: the debate on enclosure by agreement, in Fisher, F. J. (ed.) *Essays in the Economic and Social History of Tudor and Stuart England*, Cambridge University Press.
BERESFORD, M. W. and HURST, J. G. 1971. *Deserted Medieval Villages: Studies*, Lutterworth Press.
BLANCHARD, I. 1970. Population change, enclosure, and the early Tudor economy, *Econ. Hist. Rev.*, 2nd ser., XXIII, pp. 427–45.

BRENNER, R. 1976. Agrarian class structure and economic development in pre-industrial Europe, *Past and Present*, no. 70, pp. 30–75.

BRENNER, Y. S. 1961–2. The inflation of prices in early sixteenth-century England, *Econ. Hist. Rev.*, 2nd ser., XIV, pp. 225–39.

BRENNER, Y. S. 1962. The inflation of prices in England, 1551–1650, *Econ. Hist. Rev.*, 2nd ser., XV, pp. 266–84.

CAMPBELL, MILDRED. 1967. *The English Yeoman Under Elizabeth and the Early Stuarts*, Merlin Press.

CANNADINE, D. 1977. Aristocratic indebtedness in the 19th century: the case re-opened, *Econ. Hist. Rev.* 2nd ser., XXX, pp. 624–50.

CHARTRES, J. A. 1977. *Internal Trade in England, 1500–1700*, Macmillan.

*CLARKSON, L. A. 1971. *The Pre-Industrial Economy in England, 1500–1750*, Batsford.

CLAY, C. 1968. Marriage, inheritance, and the rise of large estates in England, 1660–1815, *Econ. Hist. Rev.*, XXI, 3, pp. 503–18.

*COLEMAN, D. C. 1977. *The Economy of England, 1450–1750*, Oxford University Press.

COLLINS, E. J. T. 1969. Harvest technology and labour supply in Britain, 1790–1870, *Econ. Hist. Rev.*, 2nd ser., XXII, pp. 453–73.

COLLINS, E. J. T. 1969. Labour supply and demand in European agriculture, 1800–1880, in Jones, E. L. and Woolf, S. J. (eds) *Agrarian Change and Economic Development: The Historical Problems*, Methuen.

COLLINS, E. J. T. 1978. *The Economy of Upland Britain, 1750–1950*, Centre for Agricultural Strategy, University of Reading.

COLLINS, E. J. T. and JONES, E. L. 1967. Sectoral advance in English agriculture, 1850–80, *Agric. Hist. Rev.*, XV, 2, pp. 65–81.

CRAFTS, N. F. R. 1967. English economic growth in the eighteenth century: an examination of Deane and Cole's estimates, *Econ. Hist. Rev.*, 2nd ser., XXIX, 2, pp. 226–35.

DARBY, H. C. 1940. *The Draining of the Fens*, Cambridge University Press.

DARBY, H. C. 1940. *The Medieval Fenland*, Cambridge University Press.

DARBY, H. C. (ed.) 1973. *A New Historical Geography of England Before A.D. 1800*, Cambridge University Press.

DAVID, P. A. 1970. Labour productivity in English agriculture, 1850–1914: some quantitative evidence on regional differences, *Econ. Hist. Rev.*, XXIII, 4, pp. 504–14.

DEANE, PHYLLIS and COLE, W. A. (2nd edn) 1967. *British Economic Growth, 1688–1959*, Cambridge University Press.

DODGSHON, R. A. 1976. The economics of sheep farming in the southern uplands during the age of improvement, 1750–1833, *Econ. Hist. Rev.*, 2nd ser. XXIX, pp. 551–69.

DONNELLY, JAMES S. JNR. 1976. The Irish agricultural depression of 1859–64, *Irish Econ. & Soc. Hist.*, III, pp. 33–54.

DYER, C. C. 1968. A redistribution of incomes in fifteenth-century England, *Past and Present*, no. 39, pp. 11–33.

EMERY, F. 1976. The mechanics of innovation: clover cultivation in Wales before 1850, *Jnl Hist. Geog.*, II, 1, pp. 35–48.

FAIRLIE, SUSAN. 1969. The Corn Laws and British wheat production, 1829–76, *Econ. Hist. Rev.*, XXII, pp. 88–116.

FAIRLIE, SUSAN. 1976. Contribution to a Discussion on the Standard of Living in the Industrial Revolution, in Büsch, Otto *et al.* (eds) *Industrialisierung und europäische Wirtschaft im 19. Jahrhundert*, Veröffentlichungen der historischen Kommission zu Berlin, vol. 46, pp. 83–95, Berlin and New York, De Gruyter.

FARMER, D. L. 1969. Some livestock price movements in thirteenth-century England, *Econ. Hist. Rev.*, XXII, I, pp. 1–16.

FARMER, D. L. 1977. Grain yields on the Winchester manors in the later Middle Ages, *Econ. Hist. Rev.*, 2nd ser., XXX, 4, pp. 555–66.

FISHER, F. J. 1935. The development of the London food market, 1540–1640, *Econ. Hist. Rev.* V, pp. 46–64.

FLETCHER, T. W. 1968. The great depression of English agriculture, 1873–96, in Minchinton, W. E. (ed.) *Essays in Agrarian History*, vol. 2, pp. 239–58, Newton Abbot, David & Charles.

FLINN, M. W. 1976. Real wage trends in Britain, 1750–1850: a reply, *Econ. Hist. Rev.*, 2nd ser., XXIX, 1, pp. 143–5.

FLINN, M. W. *et al.* 1977. *Scottish Population History from the Seventeenth Century to the 1930s*, Cambridge University Press.

GOTTFRIED, R. S. 1978. *Epidemic Disease in Fifteenth-Century England. The Medical Response and Demographic Consequences*, Leicester University Press.

GOULD, J. D. 1962. Agricultural fluctuations and the English economy in the eighteenth century, *Jnl Econ. Hist.*, XX, pp. 313–33.

GOURVISH, T. R. 1976. Flinn and real wage trends in Britain, 1750–1850: a comment, *Econ. Hist. Rev.*, 2nd ser., XXIX, 1, pp. 136–42.

GRAS, N. S. B. 1915. *The Evolution of the English Corn Market*, Harvard University Press.

GRIGG, D. B. 1966. *The Agricultural Revolution in South Lincolnshire*. Cambridge University Press.

HABAKKUK, H. J. 1954. Economic fortunes of English landowners in the seventeenth and eighteenth centuries, in Carus-Wilson, E. M. (ed.) *Essays in Economic History*, vol. I, pp. 187–201.

HABAKKUK, H. J. 1971. *Population Growth and Economic Development Since 1750*. Leicester University Press.

HARLEY, J. B. 1958. Population trends and agricultural developments from the Warwickshire Hundred Rolls of 1279, *Econ. Hist. Rev.*, 2nd ser., XI, pp. 8–18.

HARRISON, C. J. 1971. Grain price analysis and harvest qualities, 1465–1634, *Agric. Hist. Rev.*, 19. pp. 135–55.

HARVEY, B. F. 1966. The population trend in England between 1300 and 1348, *Trans Roy. Hist. Soc.*, 5th ser., XVI, pp. 23–42.

HARVEY, B. F. 1977. *Westminster Abbey and its Estates in the Middle Ages*, Oxford, Clarendon Press.

HARVEY, P. D. A. 1973. The English inflation of 1180–1220, *Past and Present*, 61, pp. 3–30.

HATCHER, J. 1970. *Rural economy and society in the Duchy of Cornwall, 1300–1500*, Cambridge University Press.

HATCHER, J. 1977. *Plague, Population and the English Economy, 1348–1530*, Macmillan.

HAVINDEN, M. 1966. *Estate Villages; a Study of the Berkshire Villages of Ardington and Lockinge*, Lund Humphries for University of Reading.

HAVINDEN, M. 1967. Agricultural progress in open-field Oxfordshire, in Jones, E. L. (ed.) *Agriculture and Economic Growth in England, 1650–1815*, Methuen.

HILTON, R. H. 1947. *The Economic Development of some Leicestershire Estates in the Fourteenth and Fifteenth Centuries*, Oxford University Press.

HILTON, R. H. 1966. *A Medieval Society: the West Midlands at the End of the Thirteenth Century*, Weidenfeld and Nicolson.

HILTON, R. H. 1969. *The Decline of Serfdom in Medieval England*, Macmillan.

HILTON, R. H. 1975. *The English Peasantry in the Later Middle Ages*, Oxford, Clarendon Press.

HILTON, R. H. 1978. Symposium: agrarian class structure and economic development in pre-industrial Europe, *Past and Present*, no. 80, pp. 3–19.

HOSKINS, W. G. 1964. Harvest fluctuations and English economic life, 1480–1619, *Agric. Hist. Rev.*, XII, pp. 28–46.

HOSKINS, W. G. 1968. Harvest fluctuations and English economic life, 1620–1759, *Agric. Hist. Rev.*, XVI, pp. 15–31.

HOWELL, CICELY. 1975. Stability and change, 1300–1700, *Jnl Peasant Studies*, II, 4, pp. 468–82.

HOWELL, D. W. 1977. *Land and People in Nineteenth-Century Wales*, Routledge.

HUECKEL, G. 1976. English farming profits during the Napoleonic wars, 1793–1815, *Expl. Econ. Hist.*, XIII, 3, pp. 331–45.

HUECKEL, G. 1976. Relative prices and supply response in English agriculture during the Napoleonic wars, *Econ. Hist. Rev.*, 2nd ser., XXIX, 3, pp. 401–14.

HUNT, E. H. 1967. Labour productivity in English agriculture, 1850–1914, *Econ. Hist. Rev.*, 2nd ser., vol. XX no. 2, pp. 280–92.

HUNT, E. H. 1970. Quantitative and other evidence on labour productivity in agriculture, 1850–1914, *Econ. Hist. Rev.*, XXIII, 4, pp. 515–19.

HUNT, E. H. 1973. *Regional Wage Variations in Britain, 1850–1914*, Oxford, Clarendon Press.

JOHN, A. H. 1954. The course of agricultural change, 1660–1760, in Carus-Wilson, E. M., (ed.) *Essays in Economic History*, vol. 1, pp. 221–53.

JOHN, A. H. 1976. English agricultural improvement and grain exports, 1660–1765, in Coleman, D. C. and John, A. H. (eds) *Trade, Government and Economy in Pre-Industrial England: Essays Presented to F. J. Fisher*, Weidenfeld and Nicolson.

JOHNSON, A. H. 1963. *The Disappearance of the Small Landowner*, Merlin Press.

JONES, E. L. 1964. The Agricultural Labour Market in England, 1793–1872, *Econ. Hist. Rev.*, 2nd ser., XVII, pp. 322–38.

JONES, E. L. (ed.) 1967. *Agriculture and Economic Growth in England, 1650–1815*, Methuen.

JONES, E. L. (ed.) 1968. *The Development of English Agriculture, 1815–1873*, Macmillan.

JONES, E. L. and MINGAY, G. E. 1965. Agriculture and economic growth in England, 1660–1750: agricultural change, *Jnl. Econ. Hist.*, XXV, pp. 1–18.

KERRIDGE, E. 1953. The Movement of Rent, 1540–1640, *Econ Hist. Rev.*, 2nd ser., VI, pp. 16–34.

KERRIDGE, E. 1969. *Agrarian Problems in the Sixteenth Century and After*, Allen & Unwin.

KERRIDGE, E. 1967. *The Agricultural Revolution*, Allen & Unwin.

KERRIDGE, E. 1970. The agricultural revolution reconsidered, *Agric. Hist.*, XLIII, 4, pp. 463–75.

KERSHAW, I. 1973. The great famine and agrarian crisis in England, 1315–1322, *Past and Present*, no. 59, pp. 3–50.

LADURIE, E. LE ROY and BOIS, G. 1978. Symposium: Agrarian class structure and economic development in pre-industrial Europe, *Past and Present*, no. 79, pp. 55–69.

LENNARD, R. 1932. English agriculture under Charles II: the evidence of the Royal Society's 'Enquiries', *Econ. Hist. Rev.*, IV, pp. 23–45.

LLOYD, T. H. 1973. *The Movement of Wool Prices in Medieval England*, Cambridge University Press for *Econ. Hist. Soc.*

MATE, MAVIS.   . High prices in early fourteenth-century England: causes and consequences, *Econ. Hist. Rev.*, 2nd ser., XXVIII, I, pp. 1–16.

MILLER, E. 1971. The twelfth and thirteenth centuries: an economic contrast?, *Econ. Hist. Rev.*, 2nd ser., XXIV, pp. 1–14.

MILLER, E. 1975. Farming in Northern England during the twelfth and thirteenth centuries, *Northern Hist.*, XI, pp. 1–16.

*MILLER, E. and HATCHER, J. 1978. *Medieval England: Rural Society and Economic Change, 1086–1348*, Longman.

MINCHINTON, W. E. (ed.) 1971. *Wage Regulation in Pre-Industrial England*, Newton Abbot, David & Charles.

MINGAY, G. E. 1956. The agricultural depression, 1730–50, *Econ. Hist. Rev.*, 2nd ser., VIII, pp. 323–38.

MINGAY, G. E. 1962. The size of farms in the eighteenth century, *Econ. Hist. Rev.*, 2nd ser., XIV, pp. 469–88.

MINGAY, G. E. 1963. The 'agricultural revolution' in English history: a reconsideration, *Agric. Hist.*, XXXVII, pp. 123–33.

MINGAY, G. E. 1969. Dr Kerridge's 'agricultural revolution': a comment, *Agric. Hist.*, XLIII, 4, pp. 477–81.

MINGAY, G. E. 1970. *Enclosure and the Small Farmer in the Age of the Industrial Revolution*, Macmillan.

MITCHISON, R. 1965. The movement of Scottish corn prices in the seventeenth and eighteenth centuries, *Econ. Hist. Rev.*, 2nd ser., XVIII (2), pp. 278–91.

MITCHISON, R. 1978. Local and central agencies in the control of famine in pre-industrial Scotland, *Proceedings of the Seventh International Economic History Congress*, II, pp. 395–405, Edinburgh University Press.

*ORWIN, CHRISTABEL S. and WHETHAM, EDITH H. (2nd edn) 1971. *History of British Agriculture, 1846–1914*, Newton Abbot, David & Charles.

OUTHWAITE, R. B. 1970. *Inflation in Tudor and Early Stuart England, 1470–1630*, Macmillan.

OUTHWAITE, R. B. 1978. Food crises in early modern England: patterns of public response, in Flinn, M. W. (ed.) *Proceedings of the Seventh International Economic History Congress*, II, pp. 367–74, Edinburgh University Press.

PARKER, R. A. C. 1975. *Coke of Norfolk: a Financial and Agricultural Study, 1707–1842*, Oxford, Clarendon Press.

PERREN, R. 1978. *The Meat Trade in Britain, 1840–1914*, Routledge & Kegan Paul.

PERRY, P. J. 1972. Where was the 'Great agricultural depression'?, *Agric. Hist. Rev.*, XX, 1, pp. 61–3.

PERRY, P. J. (ed.) 1973. *British Agriculture, 1875–1914*, Methuen.

PERRY, P. J. 1974. *British Farming in the Great Depression, 1870–1914*, Newton Abbot, David & Charles.

PHILLIPS, A. D. M. 1969. Underdraining and the English claylands, 1850–80: a review, *Agric. Hist. Rev.*, 17, pp. 44–55.

POSTAN, M. M. 1973. *Essays on Medieval Agriculture and General Problems of the Medieval Economy*, Cambridge University Press.

POSTAN, M. M. and HATCHER, J. *et al.* 1978. Symposium: agrarian class structure and economic development in pre-industrial Europe, *Past and Present*, no. 78, pp. 24–55.

RICHARDS, ERIC. 1974. 'Leviathan of Wealth': West Midland agriculture, 1800–50, *Agric. Hist. Rev.*, 22, 2, pp. 97–117.

SKIPP, V. H. T. 1970. Economic and social change in the Forest of Arden, 1530–1649, in Thirsk, Joan (ed.) *Land, Church and People*, pp. 84–111. British Agricultural History Society.

SMOUT, T. C. and FENTON, A. 1965. Scottish agriculture before the improvers – an exploration, *Agric. Hist. Rev.*, XIII, 2, pp. 73–93.

STURGESS, R. W. 1966. The agricultural revolution on the English clays, *Agric. Hist. Rev.*, XIV, 2, pp. 104–21.

STURGESS, R. W. 1967. The agricultural revolution on the English clays: a rejoinder, *Agric. Hist. Rev.*, XV, 2, pp. 82–7.

TATE, W. E. 1967. *The English Village Community and the Enclosure Movements*, Gollancz.

TATE, W. E. 1978. In Turner, M. E. (ed.) *A Domesday of English Enclosure Acts and Awards*, University of Reading Library.

TAWNEY, R. H. 1967. *The Agrarian Problem in the Sixteenth Century*, New York, Harper & Row.

THIRSK, JOAN. 1959. *Tudor Enclosures*, Historical Association, General Series, 41.

THIRSK, JOAN. 1961. Industries in the countryside, in Fisher, F. J. (ed.) *Essays in the Economic and Social History of Tudor and Stuart England*, Cambridge University Press.

THIRSK, JOAN (ed.) 1967. *The Agrarian History of England and Wales, IV, 1500–1640*, Cambridge University Press.

THIRSK, JOAN. 1970. Seventeenth-century agriculture and social change, in Thirsk, Joan (ed.) *Land, Church and People*, British Agricultural History Society.

THOMPSON, F. M. L. 1957. The land market in the 19th century, *Oxford Economic Papers*, new ser., 9, pp. 285–308.

THOMPSON, F. M. L. 1963. *English Landed Society in the Nineteenth Century*, Routledge & Kegan Paul.

THOMPSON, F. M. L. 1968. The second agricultural revolution, 1815–1880, *Econ. Hist. Rev.*, 2nd ser., vol. XXI, pp. 62–77.

THOMPSON, F. M. L. 1969. Landownership and economic growth in England in the eighteenth century, in Jones, E. L. and Woolf, S. J. (eds) *Agrarian Change and Economic Development*, pp. 41–60, Methuen.

THRUPP, SYLVIA. 1965. The problem of replacement rates in late medieval English population, *Econ. Hist. Rev.*, 2nd ser., XVIII, pp. 101–19.

TITOW, J. Z. 1969. *English Rural Society, 1200–1350*, Allen and Unwin.

TITOW, J. Z. 1972. *Winchester Yields: a Study in Medieval Agricultural Productivity*, Cambridge University Press.

TURNER, M. 1976. Parliamentary enclosure and population change in England, 1750–1830, *Expl. Econ. Hist.*, XIII, 4, pp. 463–8.

TURNER, M. 1976. Recent progress in the study of parliamentary enclosure: a review and a bibliography. *Local Historian*, XII, 1, pp. 18–25.

WARD, J. T. and WILSON, R. G. 1971. *Land and Industry: the Landed Estate and the Industrial Revolution*, Newton Abbot, David & Charles.

* WHETHAM, EDITH H. 1978. *The Agrarian History of England and Wales*, vol. VIII, 1914–39, Cambridge University Press.

YELLING, J. A. 1968. Common land and enclosure in East Worcestershire, 1540–1870. *Trans Inst. British Geographers*, XLV, pp. 157–68.

YELLING, J. A. 1977. *Common Fields and Enclosure in England, 1450–1850*, Macmillan Press.

Index